Especially for a Woman

The Lamppost Library

Christ United Methodist Church
Memphis, Tennessee

This Book is Given
by
Mrs. Trudy Simpson
in honor of
Mr. Jane Sharpe

A
JANET
THOMA
BOOK

THOMAS NELSON PUBLISHERS
NASHVILLE

Published in Nashville, Tennessee, by Thomas Nelson, Inc., Publishers, and distributed in Canada by Word Communications, Ltd., Richmond, British Columbia, and in the United Kingdom by Word (UK), Ltd., Milton Keynes, England.

ISBN 0-7852-8201-7

Library of Congress 94-065562

Printed in the United States of America

3 4 5 6 - 99 98 97 96

Contents

Contents

Contents

A Journey to Wholeness

If you are a woman and you picked up this book, you have started on a journey. Perhaps in your journey you are searching for the answer to a specific need or problem. Or perhaps you know you are searching for you, a journey that you will travel a lifetime—a journey to wholeness.

The whole woman is made up of many facets—the physical, the emotional, the spiritual, the relational, the professional. There are so many facets to being a woman that sometimes we feel scattered, separated, pulled apart by our lives. When any one part of us is wounded or unhealthy or incomplete, it affects the other parts—it affects the whole woman. To be all that God has made you to be, you must know each part of you, and heal or complete it on your journey to wholeness. If you truly want to relate to the needs of others, you must first understand and relate to your own needs.

In *Especially for a Woman* we hope to help you gather and heal the pieces of your life as you travel on your journey to becoming a whole woman. We have chosen some of today's most respected inspirational authors and Christian counselors to speak to women about the pertinent issues in your lives. For the part of you that is emotional, you'll read about anger, depression, and stress. You'll learn to reveal and heal wounded emotions to find the courage to dream again.

For the part of you that is physical, you'll learn to deal with the unhealthy—such as obesity, anorexia and bulimia, and sexual shame—to find your way to a healthy, physically fit body. For the part of you that is spiritual, you will learn to use The Power, prayer, and obedience to heal the other parts of you—for they are all connected.

Especially for a Woman addresses the part of you that works on being related to others, from healing families to having a close friend and a spouse. The part of you that is professional will learn how to maximize home life with a working mate and avoid the pitfalls of losing your femininity or becoming addicted to work. And, as there is a part of all of us that is aging, we want to help you through your initiation into the second half of your life and help you anticipate the joys of your children's children.

Throughout the book, you will read articles that Laura Ingalls Wilder wrote in the early 1900s. She speaks for women as much today as she did over seventy years ago. In her first article, "To Stand by Ourselves," which we have chosen to open *Especially for a Woman*, she vocalizes the purpose of this special book for women—to help you grow "well-developed and balanced," "strong and symmetrical," "a thing of beauty and satisfaction." That is our wish for you as you read *Especially for a Woman*.

PART ONE

I Am a Gift from God

To Stand by Ourselves

APRIL 1920

*O*ut in the woods the other day, I saw a tree that had branches on only one side. Evidently, other trees had grown so near it that there had been room for it to grow in only the one way, and now that it was left to stand alone its lack of good development and balance showed plainly.

It was not a beautiful thing. It looked lopsided and freakish and unable to stand by itself, being pulled a little over by the weight of its branches. It reminded me of a person who has grown all in one direction; in his work perhaps, knowing how to do only one thing as those workmen in factories who do a certain thing to one part of a machine day after day and never learn how to complete the whole, depending on others to finish the job.

Or a woman who is interested in nothing but her housework and gossip, leaving her life bare of all the beautiful branches of learning and culture which might have been hers.

Or that person who follows always the same habits of thought, thinking always along the same lines in the same safe, worn grooves, distrusting the new ideas that begin to branch out in other directions leading into new fields of thought where free winds blow.

And so many are dwarfed and crooked because of their ignorance on all subjects except a very few with the branches of their tree of knowledge all on one side!

Lives never were meant to grow that way, lopsided and crippled! They should be well-developed and balanced, strong and symmetrical, like a tree that grows by itself against the storms from whatever direction they may come—a thing of beauty and satisfaction.

The choice lies with us as to which we shall resemble. We may be like the young woman devoted to dress and fancywork who, when asked to join a club for the study of current events, replied, "What! Spend all the afternoon studying and talking about such things as that! Well, I should say not!"

Or, if we prefer, we may be like Mr. and Mrs. A. Mr. A is a good farmer; his crops and livestock are of the best, and besides he is a leader in farm organizations. Mrs. A is a good housekeeper; her garden is the best in the neighborhood, and her poultry is the pride of her heart.

As you see, they are very busy people, but they keep informed on current affairs and, now that the son and daughter are taking charge of part of the farm work, are having more time for reading and study. Their lives are branching out more and more in every direction for good to themselves and other people, for it is a fact that the more we make of our lives the better it is for others as well as ourselves.

You must not understand me to mean that we should selfishly live to ourselves. We are all better for contact and companionship with other people. We need such contact to polish off the rough corners of our minds and our manners, but it is a pitiful thing when anyone cannot, if necessary, stand by himself sufficient to himself and in good company even though alone.

Laura Ingalls Wilder
Little House in the Ozarks

Throwing Away the Pieces

elf-awareness is not vanity. Self-evalua-
tion is not pride. As you read this chap-
ter from my book, "Who Am I?," I hope you will begin to see yourself as
a special gift hand-delivered from God. It is important to Him, to you,
and to the special people in your life that you fully examine, learn to
know, and appreciate this one-of-a-kind being He has created in you.
There is so much more inside this special gift than you have ever
dreamed. He wants you to know yourself as He knows you—in all
your wonderfulness, all your love, all your emotions, all your complexi-
ties, all your giving.

Elizabeth Baker
Who Am I?

It may surprise or even shock you, but I believe Christians in general are not self-centered enough. I know that idea shocked me the first time I was honest enough to admit it. The whole idea sounded so prideful!

But before you judge my attitude as non-biblical, please understand what I mean by "self-centered." When I say Christians need to be more self-centered, I am not talking about being self-indulgent, selfish, preoccupied with self-defense, or giving ourselves permission to engage in self-destructive behaviors.

When I say "self-centered," I am talking of the need to clear enough time and emotional energy to take a long, honest appraisal of reality: Our personal reality. We stand alone in a white spotlight and shut our mouth long enough to quietly, thoughtfully consider what God created when He made us a unique individual with our special history, our feelings, and our thoughts. We look at all we are by birth and circumstance and consider the choices we have made and the effect these have had on who we are now.

This is a true centering on self, and I believe it is a necessary step in the process of spiritual growth, but it is also a scary step. Not many are willing to risk such self-examination.

I know for many years I was not willing to do that examination because I thought that consideration of self was something a Christian must avoid at all cost. If I wanted to be Christlike, I had to run away from any thoughts about self. Self was to be forced so far into the background that it was almost non-existent. Self-forgetfulness was the goal I was to aim for, not self-awareness!

But after years of struggling to achieve peace and ministry through self-avoidance, I found that running away from my reality, refusing to admit my needs, fighting against the nature God gave me, avoiding emotional awareness, and turning my head each time a memory from the past came into consciousness did little to advance true spiritual growth. Time has shown that I was not alone in my misguided project of self-avoidance. Many of God's children work hard at avoiding a knowledge of self and think that what they are doing is being spiritual.

Below is a list of statements that have been taught by various churches and well-intentioned families. Some of the statements about self have likely affected your life. Grade each statement by circling the appropriate response. As you work, remember that if you heard a statement repeated often enough, it probably influences you on an emotional level even though you may fight it on a logical level.

1. People who express personal wants and desires are selfish.

Strongly agree   Agree   No opinion   Disagree   Strongly disagree

2. "I" is the center of "sin" and is a word we should try to eliminate from our conversation.

Strongly agree　　*Agree*　　*No opinion*　　*Disagree*　　*Strongly disagree*

3. It is a prideful act to send someone a picture of yourself.

Strongly agree　　*Agree*　　*No opinion*　　*Disagree*　　*Strongly disagree*

4. When someone gives you a compliment, it is wrong to feel good and/or mentally agree with the statement.

Strongly agree　　*Agree*　　*No opinion*　　*Disagree*　　*Strongly disagree*

5. It is not Christlike to admit you have done a good job or excelled in some way.

Strongly agree　　*Agree*　　*No opinion*　　*Disagree*　　*Strongly disagree*

6. Pride in all forms is always wrong.

Strongly agree　　*Agree*　　*No opinion*　　*Disagree*　　*Strongly disagree*

7. A good motto to live by is: I will always consider God first, others second, and myself last.

Strongly agree　　*Agree*　　*No opinion*　　*Disagree*　　*Strongly disagree*

8. The Bible tells us to "take no thought" about ourselves.

Strongly agree　　*Agree*　　*No opinion*　　*Disagree*　　*Strongly disagree*

9. We should be careful not to compliment children too much, or they may think everything is OK and quit trying.

Strongly agree　　*Agree*　　*No opinion*　　*Disagree*　　*Strongly disagree*

10. If we occasionally daydream about people admiring us or of doing something special and being noticed, we are likely full of ungodly pride.

Strongly agree　　*Agree*　　*No opinion*　　*Disagree*　　*Strongly disagree*

I would encourage you to review your responses when you finish this chapter and see if any of your opinions have changed.

Sometimes the teaching we have received or even passed on to others is misleading. I find this especially true for those who come from a family background of abuse or neglect. They are very prone to use statements like those above to prove to themselves that they really are as worthless as they feel. If taken to extreme, teachings such as these give Christians a "holy" excuse for not examining the past or exposing what they really feel to others, themselves, or even to God.

Christians often try to be compassionate toward others but avoid personal feelings of sorrow. They want to live a life of forgiveness by never admitting to pain. Troubling memories are brushed under their mental rug. Personal needs are never acknowledged until the pressure of unmet needs makes them go off like a volcano spewing lava.

All this activity may look good on the outside and it can give the illusion of progress, but it most often does nothing more than sap spiritual energy. Remember: The wind going past your ears is not always a sign of progress being made. It can be a sign that you are falling.

Self-search is not an ego trip or a source of vanity.

Trying to live a Christian life while avoiding a knowledge of self is like trying to score a home run in baseball while avoiding first base.

Self-search is not an ego trip or a source of vanity because it is only after we have looked inside ourselves and come to some sort of peace about what we have found that we are in a position to minister to those outside. After we have passed this first step of growth, we can serve others without becoming a doormat, and we will be able to hold our dignity even in situations where we are not given respect by others.

The Final Authority

The Bible is our final authority for determining whether any particular thing we do is a sin. It is the measuring stick by which all things are judged. And it will tell us whether or not self-examination is acceptable to God.

The following brief Bible study is designed to walk you through the scriptural principles of pride and self-examination. Look up the

Bible references and mark your answers true or false. Remember, *this is not a test.* Feel free to make qualifying notes by your answers or mark both true and false if that seems right. I have given my responses and a brief explanation in the answer key that follows this exercise.

1. When Jesus' disciples gave Him the compliment of calling him "Teacher" (master) and "Lord" (boss, owner, ruler), Jesus gave them an example of humility by playing down those comments (John 13:13).
   True   False

2. It is always right to boast (feel good about, comment favorably) about the Lord, but a person should never boast (feel good about, comment favorably) about their own ability (Compare Ps. 34:2 and 2 Cor. 10:8).
   True   False

3. The Bible commands us to spend time examining ourselves and looking inward (1 Cor. 11:28).
   True   False

4. It is wrong for a person to feel good about being lifted up, exalted, or honored (Matt. 23:12; James 4:10; 1 Peter 5:6).
   True   False

5. Some of the writers of the Bible spent time thinking to themselves and carrying on a mental dialogue (Ps. 77:4–6).
   True   False

6. It is a waste of time to remember the past or spend effort to put it in the proper perspective (Deut. 5:15; Rev. 2:5).
   True   False

7. It shows a lack of faith to examine our belief system (2 Cor. 13:5).
   True   False

8. It is wrong to take pride in our work for the Lord (Gal. 6:4).
   True   False

9. It is OK to compare ourselves with others because competition spurs us on to greater work for the Lord (2 Cor. 10:12–13). True   False

Answer Key

1. False. Jesus accepted their compliments because they were true.

2. False. Paul rejoiced in the abilities God had given him, and did not avoid talking about his joy.

3. True.

4. False. If God exalts or honors someone, failure to accept or be happy about that honor would be a dishonor to God.

5. True. Asaph (the writer of Psalm 77), David, and Solomon are only a few of those who spent time considering themselves, their past, and their feelings.

6. False. Both Old Testament Jews and Christians are commanded to remember their past.

7. False. Christian faith stands up well to honest scrutiny. There is no question we should be afraid to tackle with faith and honesty.

8. False. We are encouraged to take godly pride without comparison.

9. False.

Home and church are usually the first place we learn what pride is and how much attention can be paid to personal needs and feelings. Hopefully, these teachings were in line with the Word of God, but for some of us they were not, and now as adults we need to go back and examine what we have learned. On a separate piece of paper, write about a specific memory where you were taught by example or word about the subject of self-consideration and pride. Answer these questions as you write:

- How did this teaching make you feel?
- Do you think it affected your feelings later in life?
- Do you believe this teaching was consistent with Bible truth? Why or why not?

Identifying what is and is not pride can be a problem for the Christian who is in rebellion, but it can also be a problem for those with a tender conscience who have either been taught incorrectly or who have received good teaching through the filter of childhood abuse.

Below you will find a list of statements that indicate a sinful form of pride. Some may be a bit confusing until you read the rest of the chapter and understand why I believe they indicate pride. To complete this exercise, check those statements that remind you of yourself even if you have trouble thinking of them as prideful.

1. I frequently use the phrase, "I know what you are thinking . . ." when I am angry at someone.

2. When I walk into a room, I am instantly aware of the men (women) in the room and how they perceive me.

3. I frequently apologize for inconsequential things.

4. I am uncomfortable being seen as one of the crowd.

5. When I listen to a performer or speaker or preacher, I critique them to others around me.

6. I drop names.

7. I exaggerate when I tell personal stories or talk about my feelings.

8. When someone else is telling something positive about themselves, I feel compelled to humble them and bring them back down to earth.

9. When someone tells a personal story, I immediately follow with a bigger story about my life and accomplishments.

10. I depend on external things such as clothes, makeup, or car to make myself acceptable to others.

11. I frequently criticize those in authority.

12. I feel that people have been unfair to me most of my life.

The Trap of Pride

Pride was listed by the ancient church as one of the seven deadly sins. Proverbs 13:10 warns us that ALL struggling among people and fighting is rooted in pride. When pride comes, shame and destruction are not far behind (Prov. 11:2; Prov. 16:18). Jesus listed pride right along with murder, adultery, theft, and lewdness, and God says that He hates pride and arrogance (Prov. 8:13).

If we accept the Word of God, we have no trouble believing that pride is wrong, but we may have a lot of trouble defining exactly what pride is and what it is not.

In our Americanized English when we see someone who does not take care of themselves or their possessions, we say "they have no pride." Is it pride to treat ourselves and our belongings well? Does the word *proud* always indicate sin? Thinking back on my rural heritage, it was common to ask an older person how they were doing and have them respond, "Oh, I am doin' real proud," meaning that they felt healthy and things were going well.

When struggling with the question of pride, it has helped me to differentiate between the good feelings connected with reaching a standard and the wrong use of a split standard when judging. Feeling joy because we reach a goal set for ourselves is godly pride, but using one standard for ourselves and a different standard for others is sinful pride.

When I excuse or rationalize away my errors but hold my neighbor responsible for every minor mistake, I have put myself above him unjustly and I am guilty of sinful pride. That double standard is what most of us normally think of as the sin of pride.

But there is another double standard that is not so quickly recognized, yet it is just as sinful and just as much ungodly pride. Christians sometimes make the mistake of calling this pride "holy." This form of pride is the double standard where I put myself below everyone else. If I hold myself accountable and beat myself without mercy each time I fall short of the standard while I excuse others for the same error, I am still guilty of pride because I am still using a split standard. This false humility is nothing more than the same old pride, only in this case it's running in reverse gear.

This condemning of self is pride because every time I hit myself with an "I should have" statement, I indicate that I believe I "could" have done it if I had only tried harder. Deep down, we think that the ability is in self, or we would not be beating self for failure.

We would never tell a man without legs that he should walk because we recognize the obvious truth that the ability is just not there, but we tell ourselves that we should have been perfect and never blink at the incredulity of that absurd statement.

Godly pride is a rejoicing in the soul over a job well done or a lesson of character learned.

It is one thing to repent and/or accept our responsibility for an issue, but it is quite another to punish ourselves for oversights, honest mistakes, being human, and—that most common but most absurd—failure to make everyone around us happy all the time.

We often criticize and punish ourselves for not meeting these impossible and absurd goals, and unfortunately, we sometimes identify this self-punishment as humility.

Paul talked about those who used a standard of humility that looked good on the outside but did nothing to constrain sinful indulgences (Col. 2:23). This was a false humility of self-effort that made a show of harsh treatment for self, and although it had the appearance of wisdom, it was full of regulations and lacked real value.

Godly pride is a rejoicing in the soul over a job well done or a lesson of character learned. This kind of pride may notice the difference between self and others and may even recognize that the conduct of self is more righteous than the conduct of another, and that creates another problem with pride. How can I know I am better than someone else without being prideful?

Holier Than Thou?

I remember my teenage daughter's shyness when she approached me. She was the firstborn, a gentle soul who would rather give in than fight. Her tender conscience was often causing her unnecessary trouble and this time seemed no different.

"Mama," she tentatively began while looking at the floor, "how do you keep from feeling holier than thou when . . . well . . . you know."

"When you really are more holy than someone else?" I asked, finishing her sentence for her.

The problem had come about at school when others called her names and accused her of pride because she did not engage in the same activities as many of her peers.

The answer to that dilemma is found not in the split standard, but it is a question of who sets the standard. Is it me against them? My standards against their standards? If so, we have become unwise and are close to the sin of pride. But if we are using the standard God set and judging both self and others, then we are on safe ground.

There is no doubt about it. A true believer is more holy than a hypocrite. An honest man is better than a thief. Someone who drinks and curses and fails to support their family is wrong and someone who is temperate, loving, and faithful to work as they can is right.

We do not have to sit in judgment on someone who is caught in a lie; we simply agree with the judgment that God has already passed. Lying is wrong, and we are free to say so without being proud or judgmental.

However, there are two cautions we need to remember when we begin this observational judging. First, we can only see the outside results, not the motive. And second, we must make sure that it is God's standard we are using, not our own personal preferences.

We have limited access to the heart. In fact, it might be more accurate to say that we have none. We can only judge the outside, the behavior. We are almost always on dangerous ground when we say "I know what you think" or "I know why you did that." Only God knows someone's intent and purpose. We can only say, "By your behavior you appear to believe."

Sometimes we attempt to judge where God has made no clear direction in His Word. In a situation like this we often want to insist that others meet our standards, and we refuse to give them the freedom to be themselves. We try to do God's job for Him and set standards where none exist. This is totally off limits for God's child, and besides that, it makes others mad real quick!

God's Gift

In a very practical sense our personal self is the greatest gift God has given us. This gift of self involves all our physical attributes, personal history, and freedom. It is our mind and our body and our spiritual ears that have the capacity to hear and know Him.

Our personal self is the greatest gift God has given us.

One way to visualize this concept is to imagine that God has sent us a big box by special messenger. We hear a knock at the door and answer to find the box sitting on the step. The box has a big tag on it reading, "Fragile, box contains one human. Handle with care and upon completion, return to sender." Signed, "Heaven's Shipping House, Sincerely, God."

It would be an insult to our Creator to turn our eyes away and fail to examine everything He gave us when He sent that box. The Bible says that we will learn about God by studying His creation (Rom. 1:20). There will never be another fragment of creation we can observe as closely as our own heart; there will be no history we will have as much insight to as our own; we will never see grace as close up as we can observe it in action on our own shame. What a pity to let this opportunity for learning go by as we disregard God's gift!

However, we must be aware of certain dangers as we examine our gift, and perhaps it is because of these dangers that so much teaching has discouraged people from opening their box and examining with delight their gift of self. One trap is pride, which we have already discussed and the other is its close cousin: Measurement.

The Trap of Measurement

All measurement is a comparison. We might compare the length of a pencil to a ruler or the heat of the day to how high the mercury rises on a scale; we can only measure one thing as we compare it to another thing.

The Bible gives us a whole bag of measuring devices to be used for various purposes. For instance, the Law is a balance scale we can use to measure what is good and what is bad. The Sermon on the Mount is a yardstick for determining how our daily living measures up to God's expectations. Calvary measures the horror of sin; resurrection measures the power of God.

But there is one measuring stick that we are strongly warned *never* to use. Of course, that is the first one we want to grab. We have a strong inclination to measure ourselves against each other.

As we unwrap our gift box from God and begin a delightful search to find and accept all it contains, we have a tendency to look down the street at all the other people standing on their front porches unwrapping similar boxes from God.

We notice that the man next door got more talent. Sister Sue got more money. Aunt Sophie got a great body. And we heard that a man named John who lives on the next block got a life where God answers all his prayers instantly, and he never was sick a day in his life, and he will appear on TV next week to tell everyone about how they can get a life like that too!

All this observation of others is not sin; the sin only comes when we look back at our own box and start to measure ourselves or God's fairness by how our box stacks up against others'. If we compare and come out with what we believe is less than others, we are embarrassed and we begin to question God. If we compare and come out with what we think is more than others, we view it as His special attention to us or proof of our personal worth, thus setting ourselves slightly above most of our neighbors.

Paul warned us about comparison in Galatians 6:4–5 when he states: "Each one should test his own actions. Then he can take pride in himself, without comparing himself to somebody else, for each one should carry his own load" (NIV).

A few years later in another letter, when Paul's own worth and ability were brought into question, he replied, "For we dare not class ourselves or compare ourselves with those who commend themselves. But they, measuring themselves by themselves, and comparing themselves among themselves, are not wise. We, however, will not boast beyond measure, but within the limits of the sphere which God appointed us" (2 Cor. 10:12–13).

If we want to be wise and happy as we unwrap and examine our heavenly gift, we had best keep our hands off the measuring stick of comparison.

As long as we leave the measurement of others up to God, we will never be in any danger of sinning. When we engage in an honest search for the self we feel we have lost, we will become better and stronger servants, not selfish egotists.

Our Example: Jesus

One of the clearest examples of how knowledge of self-worth and true humility work together for the service of others is given in John 13:3–5.

John begins this story by talking about Jesus' knowledge of Himself: "Jesus knowing that the Father had given all things into his hands, and that He had come from God and was going to God, rose from the supper and laid aside His garments, took a towel and girded Himself . . . and began to wash the disciples' feet."

Knowledge of who He was and an awareness of personal worth was the springboard for service. Jesus did not avoid compliments, run from knowledge of Himself, pretend that He was less than what He knew Himself to be, or apologize for the truth about Himself. Rather, it was this secure knowledge of His personal worth and dignity that made service so noble as others looked at His example. It was this knowledge that made it possible for Him to perform without self-depreciation.

Self-evaluation

Self-evaluation is not pride. Even when that evaluation has an element of rejoicing, it is not sin and is nowhere discouraged by the Lord.

Self-examination was encouraged by Paul. We are to examine everything about ourselves (1 Cor. 11:28) and to pass judgment on what we find (v. 31). We are to check out our actions and feelings and see how these confirm or deny our faith (2 Cor. 13:5). The psalmist Asaph remarked that he meditated and inquired with himself about himself, his history, and his God (Ps. 77:5, 6) and how all these fit together. Both Jews and Christians are told to remember their past and consider it (Deut. 5:15; Rev. 2:5). It is not necessary to avoid knowledge of self and the influences that have molded us into what we are in order to be spiritual. In fact, avoiding such knowledge will make spiritual growth more difficult.

Self-evaluation is not pride.

We are told that we can learn about God by examining the creation God has made (Ps. 19:1), and there is no reason to assume that this consideration should exclude the examination of the creation of self.

The human experience is different than that of animal or vegetable or angel or demon, and if we don't include self in our consideration of creation, we have left out a major part that is unlike all else. We are unique in our ability of conscience to know both good and evil (Gen. 3:22). This is the problem that awakens shame when we know we are less than what we should be. And we are unique as we participate in redemption and Jesus pays the price to take our shame away.

I remember an old hymn that we sang in the church where I grew up. One line was: "But when I sing redemption's story, They shall fold their wings. For angels never knew the joy that my salvation brings."

What a wonderful and mysterious gift God has given when He gave us our self. I hope and pray that you will find this book of self-exploration to be a joyful adventure, not a doubtful experience that we suspect a "good" Christian would never undertake!

It is my prayer and expectation that taking the time for self-examination will make you more like the Master, not less, and that servanthood will become easier and have a new freedom that is not marred by the bondage of false humility that too often marks a Christian's work.

Swimming in Strange Waters

How did we get to be the way we are? Much of our image of ourselves as women is based on our interactions with our own dad. A dad gives us a model for how to relate to boys as we are growing up, how to relate to men when we are grown, how to relate to God the Father—indeed, he helps us define our own femininity. The absence or detachment of a girl's father at any age can make a severe difference in her self-esteem and her relationships with men. Whether you are a woman who grew up without a dad, or you are a woman raising a daughter without a dad, I hope this chapter from Daughters Without Dads *will help you see what a loving, nurturing relationship with our dads should have provided—and the effects on us if that fatherly model has been torn from us, detached itself from our lives, or was abusive when we were children.*

Lois Mowday
Daughters Without Dads

Ray, a good friend of mine, used to delight in telling me about his eleven-month-old son, Grayson. Each morning, after Grayson cried from his crib, Ray would go into Grayson's room, bounce the young child, and lift him enthusiastically in the air. Both father and son enjoyed this early morning ritual, and both would laugh heartily.

Next, Ray would carefully place Grayson on the rail of the crib, holding him tightly with both hands under Grayson's arms. As Grayson steadied himself, Ray would very cautiously let go and hold his hands outstretched a few inches in front of the poised toddler. He would smile and coax Grayson to leap into his arms. Squealing with delight, the trusting child would fling himself into his father's arms.

Grayson was confident that he would be safely caught. Apparently, the young child never worried about landing on his face on the floor. He had total faith that his father would be there and would catch him. And that's the way fathers should be.

A Man Is Someone to Trust

Ideally, a father should be like Grayson's dad—the first male person that a child learns to completely trust. In a healthy, normal situation, a child can count on that.

A little girl's first experience with maleness is with her father. The interaction will affect her attitudes about men. If she can trust him as Grayson trusted Ray, she will have a positive early reference point in relating to men for the rest of her life.

If, on the other hand, a little girl finds she cannot trust her father, she may begin on shaky footing in her relationships with men.

If her parents are divorced, the whole issue of who daddy is gets complicated. If her father isn't there consistently, routines like that enjoyed by Grayson are interrupted. Even if a daughter had a wonderful relationship with her father, and it continues in some way after a divorce, the relationship is strained and unnatural. The role model has already changed from a man who is present to one who is absent.

More complicated still is the father who is physically there but emotionally distant. He might be able to be trusted sometimes, but he can withdraw without notice. Imagine the picture of Grayson with a father who sometimes answers Grayson's morning calls and sometimes does not. Sometimes he comes in and they play the jumping game. Sometimes he comes in and quietly takes Grayson out of bed and puts him down. And sometimes he doesn't come in at all. The male role model for any child who experienced this kind of paternal interaction would be twisted and complex, and it wouldn't be long before the child would distrust what his father would do.

Worse yet is the father who is emotionally, physically, or sexually abusive. Such a father can destroy a young girl's self-esteem and image of males.

If a girl's father is dead, she may not have a negative or frightening image of what a man is, but she may not know what it is like to trust a man. She will have to learn a process of relating that comes more naturally to a little girl with a trusting, loving father.

Men = My Daddy

Daughters aren't born with a preprogrammed mental image of what a loving father looks like. Instead, they learn men are what their fathers are, and through fathers, they learn what men are like. As daughters grow, they learn words and feelings that describe their fathers.

Of course, a little girl doesn't realize that all men are not like her father. That important distinction comes much later. But in her earliest years a girl considers daddy "nice," "kind," or "big"—or perhaps even "mean," "angry," or "scary." A girl whose father has died simply thinks, *My Daddy is . . . gone.*

In the early years, daddy is simply who he is, and a little girl learns to live with that. She may see that she is welcome in his lap when he comes home from work or that he likes to be left alone. She learns in what areas she can trust him and in what areas she cannot. Maybe she can call him in the morning to come in and wake her with a hug and kiss. Maybe he doesn't live in the same house with her and mommy anymore.

If a father isn't a consistent, loving presence in a daughter's life, a lasting impression is formed in her mind as she continues to revise her image of what men are. Even if she has other male role models in her life, she is most closely tied to her father. His projected image to her will influence how she views all males and how she views herself in regard to them.

Other Fathers and Other Men

I remember the never-married woman in her thirties whose father and mother divorced when she was about five years old. Her sense of loss for her absent father was compensated by an overly idealistic view of other men.

She told me, *"I thought that anyone who had a father at home had a perfect father."* She went on to say that the most painful times in her childhood were when she was around her friends who had seemingly happy relationships with their fathers. As she watched bits and pieces of these relationships, she concluded that they were perfect. The feeling made her all the more sad that she didn't have that with her own father.

As this young woman entered her teens, she expected to share some of this bliss in her relationships with boys. But her experiences were less than she hoped for, and her conclusion was that good things happened only to other people. She didn't realize that no relationship is perfect.

Now, as an adult, she knows that her beliefs were wrong. But her ability to change her expectations is greatly limited. As soon as she hits a snag in a relationship with a man, she is certain that the relationship is much less than what it ought to be and that she has—once again—been dealt a bad hand. It seems to her that good men come along for other women, but never for her. The absence of a healthy male role model early in life still creates problems for her in relating to any man.

The Search for the Perfect Father

Unfortunately, many girls define a model father as whatever they do not have. Like the woman mentioned above, they see only that what they lack seems to be given to others. They may observe their friends' fathers and envy what their friends have. Those fathers may become the ideal.

Even the ideal father is less than perfect. Instead of a daughter without a dad looking at other girls' fathers as the source of perfect fatherhood, she needs to look to God as her Father. Other girls' fathers are unavailable to her the way that they are available to their own daughters. And in their imperfection, they are probably not as wonderful as she may imagine. God is the perfect Father, and He is as readily available to the daughter without a dad as He is to the daughter with a human father.

Translating the image of God the Father into human terms is difficult. A man living up to that image is as rare and as wonderful as a woman living up to the image of the wife in Proverbs 31. But the standard set forth is not meant to imply that perfection can be reached. Because we are also finite in our ability to be perfect children, we experience that relationship imperfectly as well most of the time.

We must realize that no earthly man can fulfill the model given us by God the Father, and we must acknowledge that human fathers will fail us in many ways. But certain qualities of relationship between daughter and father should be present. Love, trust, acceptance, care, protection, and guidance should be present, even if imperfectly.

Many women define a model father by listing what he is *not*. He is not to be one who abuses, who shuts out, who neglects his responsibility to provide and care for, who ignores, or who hurts with unkind words and deeds.

An irony I have noticed is that daughters whose fathers have died often have better relationships with men than daughters whose fathers are alive. Part of that is because a deceased father does not hurt or disappoint his daughters. And even if he was less than perfect when alive, such memories may often perish with him.

When a girl or young woman loses her faith in the ideal of a model father, that ideal is often replaced by the model of an irresponsible father. Then she has two things to overcome: first, redefining the image of a healthy male along with the new model of a male-female relationship; and second, discovering how to heal the wounds of the possibly abusive male-female relationship she experienced with her father.

"Boys Are Sooooo Weird!"

If girls aren't born with a preprogrammed image of the ideal father, they are born with even less information to help them figure out boys. Most often, girls think all little boys are a very strange breed.

That's normal enough. But little girls growing up without fathers have to unravel the mystery of boys without the benefit of a male perspective.

And not just any male perspective will do, either. Only a father can give a view of boys that takes into account that his daughter is very special. A divorced father living apart from a daughter can be really helpful here, but he still misses much of his daughter's sexual development and intense questioning by not living at home.

Many women I interviewed said that the hardest thing about being without their fathers was that their fathers just weren't there for significant incidents. By the time dad got there on a weekend, the confusing and troubling incident at school on Tuesday was old news.

One woman in her forties whose father died when she was a toddler compared learning about boys to learning to swim, with some major differences: *"It was like learning to swim in a pool with Mom as the instructor. The only other people in the pool were other little girls and their mothers. After learning to swim, Mom took me out to a big pool she called an ocean.*

"I was a good swimmer, so she let me go in some deep water. She was close by, and I felt pretty confident. But then the strangest thing happened. I was swimming just under the surface of the water and this other 'being' swam up next to me. It didn't have hands or feet but had a tail that swished around and moved through the water. It circled around me as if it wanted to play. But I didn't know what to do with it. It didn't look like I did, it didn't talk like I did, and I didn't know what it wanted.

"Mom explained that it was a 'fish.' It could swim in the ocean, too, and it was not anything that would hurt me. But I thought, How do you talk to a fish, or play with a fish, or just hang around a fish?"

For girls who have no consistent father figure around to interpret the "weirdness" of little boys, little boys might seem as strange as some unusual form of marine life.

Mothers can offer some insights, but they have a serious disadvantage. They don't think like little boys, and they never did. They can only guess about what is going on in those wonderful little boy minds.

I had no way to reasonably explain to my two daughters why little boys who liked them would hit them instead of saying something nice. I could tell them that that was the way it was, but I couldn't help them understand. I still can't.

Lisa and Lara and I have had many a laugh around the kitchen table trying to understand the male creature. I have often thought that their father could have relayed useful information, whereas I could only shake my head and wonder with them at the strangeness of males.

Sometimes when boys hurt my daughters—or when men hurt me—we could only cry as we reflected upon the whys and wherefores of the matter. I remember staying up late one night with my older daughter after a boyfriend had really hurt her feelings. She was trying to decide if she should still go to the prom with him. As a godly mother, I had a loving and mature response to the situation.

"Dump that jerk," I said, mustering all my maternal wisdom and insight. "Call up your friend John in New York and ask him to go to the prom with you."

She was so hurt that she considered my proposal. Thankfully, we made no decision that night.

The next morning in church I was sitting with a married couple who are good friends of our family. I told the wife, in a tearful but controlled way, what had happened. After the service she looked at me and started crying herself.

She said she could not imagine knowing what to say to her own daughters in a similar situation without the perspective of their father. We had a good cry, and I decided to let my daughter decide how to handle the prom. She wound up going with the young man who had hurt her. Meanwhile, I prayed for forgiveness of my anger toward him. They stopped seeing each other after the prom, so I didn't have to waste any more energy trying to figure out what motivated his inscrutable behavior.

When a daughter grows up without a father in the home, even the most normal male endeavors may seem strange. Since my girls became teenagers, we have had a lot of young people in our home. I am always amazed at the way boys—even big boys who otherwise act very grown up—love to wrestle around on the floor. They look to me as if they are going to kill each other. I get anxious and utter embarrassing warnings like, "Oh! Be careful." Meanwhile, they continue to throw each other across the living room.

It is tempting for single mothers to try to cut out all masculine influences and live in an all-feminine world. For such mothers, it might be easier to not allow boys to wrestle in the house, to talk judgmentally about boys when they hurt their daughters, or to categorize all men as "jerks" when there's no logical explanation for why they do what they do.

But such isolationism can be damaging to girls' development into caring young women who will be able to have healthy relationships with men. It is not really necessary for mothers to understand boys to teach their daughters to relate well to them. Principles of godly and loving behavior also apply to the mystifying behavior of boys.

"My Dad Dates"

Teenagers who grow up in traditional families—with a mother and a father married and at home together—don't have models for dating. If they are fortunate, they have a model for a godly relationship between a man and a woman in the context of marriage.

But when a daughter's parents are divorced, she gets an up-close look at how her mother and/or father handle the dating game. If the daughter lives with her mother, she has a bird's-eye view of how mom handles relationships with men.

We will also consider how dating can affect the relationship between fathers and daughters, but for now it's important to realize that the way a father treats the women he dates—not just the way he treated his wife during their marriage—will say something to the daughter about how she is to let men treat her.

One divorced father told me that his daughter's relationship with boys had been largely determined by the way he had treated women he dated. His daughter would overhear him tell a woman he would call her, and then he would deliberately not call. His daughter saw him date several women at once, but she heard him tell each of them that she was *the* special woman in his life. His daughter would hear her father argue with these women and make promises to them that he never kept. His daughter, in turn, allowed boys to mistreat her. He said he lost his credibility with her in advising her to not allow boys to treat her badly because she saw him act the same way.

In short, parents can't expect a daughter to listen to their advice on dating if they do not live it out in front of her.

Models for Marriage

Daughters without dads also develop unique ways of evaluating potential marriage candidates. For many girls, the most sensible place to start taking notes on the subject is their parents' marriage. Daughters weren't there for the process of choosing, but they sure are there for the living out of the results of that choice. And for many girls, this is a powerful training experience.

If the daughter gives her mom a passing grade for her choice of a husband, she may try to choose her husband in the same way. If the results were bad, she may make just the opposite choice. And both could be very poor ways to choose a husband.

In the case of death, often the daughter has an idealistic, and unrealistic, view of her father. Her mother may unintentionally perpetuate that image. Nothing seems wrong while in the process of keeping this positive image alive. It relieves pain, and it creates warm memories of the past.

The damage, however, comes when the daughter tries to follow her mother's example in choosing a spouse. Her evaluation of her father may have become so idealized over time that no *real* man could even meet her lofty demands. The higher the daughter's image of her father, the more unlikely it will be that any man can measure up.

If her parents are divorced, a girl may conclude that her mother made a bad choice in picking her husband. She may not be able to see that her father and mother were different at the time of their marriage than they were at the time of their divorce. She may determine to choose someone just the opposite of her perception of her father.

Without having the opportunity to see how a healthy marriage is lived out, daughters without dads may base their choices on trying to find the security they lack while trying to protect those vulnerable and painful things they do have.

Most of the women I interviewed fell into one of two categories: either they had unrealistic expectations of a man, or they lived with poor self-images, which were reflected in the kind of men they thought they would inevitably marry.

"God Wanted to Punish Kids, So He Put Them in Families"

Children in blended families—that is, children from two previous marriages joined in one new family—often have difficulties adjusting to their new parents and siblings. That was definitely the case of the daughter who told her mother, "God wanted to punish kids, so He put them in families."

Daughters whose parents had an unhealthy relationship can't accurately picture a good marriage.

This daughter did not dislike the man her mother had married the second time. But she could clearly remember the bad times when her father and mother were married, and she didn't want to relive them. The pain of a broken home can make marriage look pretty bleak.

A friend whose parents are divorced recalls the many times when she heard her mother and father having terrible screaming battles. She and her brother would hide in a closet and fearfully wait for each skirmish to end. When her mother decided to remarry, my friend was apprehensive about being in that situation again. Her only model of marriage was a fractured, distressful image. She certainly didn't want to live on a battlefield again.

Daughters whose parents had an unhealthy relationship can't accurately picture a good marriage. Most of them say they want a good marriage, but they don't know how anyone can have that, and they wouldn't know how to tell it if they saw one up close.

"I Want to Marry, but I'm Scared"

Many girls I interviewed were from divorced homes, and they repeatedly echoed one theme: "I want to marry, but I'm scared." Their predominant feeling about marriage was fear that they would have the same kind of marriage that their parents had.

Some adults I interviewed felt that their poor childhood experiences had led them to enter marriage with negative self-fulfilling prophecies.

One woman whose marriage had violently broken apart said, "*I always expected my husband to leave. My father left. And my husband left. I knew he would. Men leave.*"

This fear prevents some women from marrying at all. If they have nothing to lose, they reason, there's no way they can lose it. If they don't marry, they can't have bad marriages.

The lack of a godly role model of marriage can produce protective behavior that robs women of fulfilling partnerships that *can* be different from the unhealthy and destructive relationships they may have seen at home. Or, they can enter marriages with so much fear that they miss how to have good relationships.

The Search for Utopia

The other side of the fear-and-negative thinking coin is utopian thinking—the belief that marriage can save one from bad memories, emotional scars, and self-examination, and that this marriage in particular will be the answer to the pain of life.

This thinking resembles that of the fatherless little girl who assumes that anyone with a father has a perfect one. A child who has grown up without a father and has not seen how marriage works may conclude that a good marriage means a perfect one. Like the girl with unrealistic expectations of a husband, she may have unrealistic expectations of the marriage relationship itself.

Then when the inevitable tough times come, she is disappointed. She wonders what happened. Her frustration mounts as she asks herself, *Why is this marriage not working out as I expected?* She has no frame of reference to fall back on in evaluating what is normal and what is not.

The Mystery of Men

Girls who have had no godly model for marriage certainly have the opportunity to have good marriages themselves. But they have a few discoveries to make about everyday things that daughters raised in traditional homes take for granted.

One woman I interviewed lost her father when she was very young. She had two sisters and no brothers. She married a wonderful man, and she enjoys a fulfilling relationship. She talked of her first year of marriage with amusement: *"Men were a real mystery to me. I had no idea what it would be like to actually live in the same house with one. On our honeymoon, I found that men and women keep different things in the bathroom. It seemed so strange to me to see shaving gear. It just never occurred to me."*

This woman's experience was not negative—just different. She had never seen shaving gear in the bathroom.

After my husband died, I became acutely aware of some of these differences. For example, men don't smell like women do. It's not just the difference between after-shave and perfume. And it's not just the smell of sweat. There is a different scent about men that I never really noticed until it was gone.

I also noticed that men have deep, calm voices. After spending prolonged periods of time in a house full of females, I found that when I was around men, they sounded distinctly male.

How many more normal male traits would seem strange to a girl who has not been around her father and never been married? This lack of experience in living around men may necessitate a period of adjustment—and a sense of humor.

Daughters without dads may also have trouble evaluating how a prospective mate may fulfill the role of father. How will this man act as a father? And how will the fact that her children have two parents, instead of one, affect the way she is a mother?

The daughter is used to seeing her mother serve as both parents. What will marriage be like when the roles of mother and father are divided between the woman and the man? This mysterious person she now lives with will be fulfilling a role she hasn't seen lived out as it was intended.

Fathers and the Image of God

God should inform all our decisions. Ideally, we should base all our actions on a sound knowledge of the nature of God and what He wants for us.

When we define what fathers are, we should start with God and model a godly father after Him. But in reality, we tend to do just the opposite. We look at our earthly fathers and assume that God is like them. This is understandable, but in many cases it's unfortunate.

The older we are when we come to know the Lord, the more baggage and negative father imagery we have to get rid of. If a girl's only experience with a father figure has been the one of her distanced father, it will be hard for her to imagine God as loving and caring.

I spoke with one woman whose father died when she was little. She described God to me in this way:

"God could not be like my real father, because my real father was not there. I had no frame of reference when I thought about God. I thought of Him as a 'Holy Other.' There was just not enough skin on God."

This same woman talked of how she felt her relationship with God was frozen. Her father had died when she was six. She only knew how to relate to a father up to that age. How does a forty-year-old woman relate to a father? And how does an older woman learn to love God the Father after having experienced the painful loss of her own father?

Without a model for a loving father, a lot of translating has to be done to think properly about God as Father.

Redefining Femininity

History shows us that the definition of the perfect woman is ever-changing. The perfect woman used to be Suzy Homemaker who devoted all of her time and attention to her loving husband and children.

Then the perfect woman was the business executive. Dressed for success and determined not to let sexual bias in the workplace stop her from achieving her ambitions, she charged into male-dominated boardrooms to exercise her will.

Next, it seemed that the perfect woman was a combination of the homemaker and the business executive. The magazine covers read, "A Family AND a Career: You Can Have It ALL!"

So, who is today's perfect woman? What we are told about the feminine ideal is, at best, confusing. Women have more options today about how they will live than they ever have before. There is no single socially defined norm. That may be good news in the freedom it brings. But it may also be bad news because of the uncertainty and tension it causes in many women's minds as they struggle to achieve some poorly defined goals.

Some of the college-age women I interviewed expressed this dilemma. They all want to have careers. Most of them also want to marry and have children. They feel freedom to do both—even if there is still conflict in the church on this issue—but realize the enormity of the challenge before them if they are to be successful in both areas. Along with the complexities of living several roles at once is the risk of losing who they really are as women.

Women are at war with themselves. In addition, as soon as they step out into society, they are torn between the conflicting roles of femininity others place on them. Hope Stedman, the character in the TV show "thirtysomething," exhibits these internal and external conflicts in episode after episode.

A woman can now be considered totally feminine while holding down a high-powered executive job. She can carry a briefcase and supervise men at work. She cannot, however, cry at a top-level meeting and still be viewed as completely competent. Is it all right for a woman to cry? Or is it acceptable only in certain situations? Is crying a sign of weakness or strength? Competence or dizziness?

It's a real mixed bag. And daughters without dads—lacking their intended protector, provider, and source of security—are forced to define femininity in isolation from one of the sources God intended in the shaping of feminine character.

Mary and the Modern Dilemma

For me, many of the trials and tribulations of daughters without dads were summarized in my conversations with Mary, who had struggled with the loss of her father as well as what it means to be a woman in today's world.

Mary's father divorced her mother when Mary was thirteen years old. She was the oldest in a family of three children and had to take on many of the household chores when her mother went to work. She gave up some school activities to be home for her younger brother and sister. She became like a parent to them because her mother was gone a lot.

One day at school, her brother got in a fight with a bigger boy and went to Mary for comfort. Mary took matters into her own hands and found the offending bully. She made it clear that she would cause the bully some problems if her brother were bothered again.

Mary developed a reputation of being a tough cookie. She had no father to defend her brother. She didn't go home and tell her mother what happened because Mary considered it settled. It was settled. But the result was that Mary, at a young age, began to be viewed as less than feminine.

Mary knew how she was perceived. She would cry alone in bed at night about it. She hated the way boys teased her about how tough she was. But she never told them she cried. In many ways Mary was a very feminine young woman, but her femininity was never revealed to her friends at school. She didn't know how to express that side of herself and fill the role of protector to her younger siblings at the same time.

Eventually Mary achieved success in a demanding career as a patent lawyer. Many would applaud her as an example of a troubled person achieving triumph over adversity. But she continues to struggle with her self-identity as a woman. She yearns to be soft, loving, and vulnerable, but has no relationships to provide such outlets. She also denies these yearnings as incompatible with her image of someone who "gets the job done."

Your Box Is Too Small

Years ago the Christian scholar J. B. Phillips wrote a book entitled *Your God Is Too Small*. The book described the various incomplete images of God that some of us carry around in our heads, like "the kind old man in the sky." Phillips urged his readers to open their minds and allow themselves to come into contact with the real and living God who confounds some of our confining concepts of who He is.

In a similar vein, we can see that part of the reason for the confusion today about what is feminine and what is not is that we keep putting people into neat little boxes. We label everything, and then we draw conclusions based on those labels.

If a woman never cries, we call her tough and insensitive. If she cries at a business meeting, we call her weak and incompetent. If she wears man-tailored suits, she may project an image of unapproachable professionalism. But if she wears frilly dresses, we may call her flirty as we wonder how she could wear such inappropriate clothing.

It's not only women in the workplace who face such criticism. The woman who sees her calling as a modern-day Suzy Homemaker is ridiculed and belittled, and many ask themselves if the woman has even a portion of a brain. She may be a champion gourmet cook and have a spotless house, but some may call her "domestic," not feminine.

Fathers and Self-Esteem

What's all this have to do with being fatherless? Simply put, fathers can be a solid source of self-esteem for growing and developing women.

Fathers who show love and acceptance for their daughters can help women define their personal identity. A girl who lives for eighteen years with an accepting father has a chance to be herself—which is a large part of being feminine—regardless of what the loud and conflicting voices around her are saying. She may have learned that it is OK to cry and be comforted and still know that she is competent. Her father's input may have given her the confidence to be what she wants to be regardless of the image conveyed.

Fathers can be a solid source of self-esteem for growing and developing women.

Likewise, the absence of her father may have left her uncertain of who she is, placing her in a harsh arena to learn to survive as a woman.

The Church Catches Up

If there is confusion in the world, there is more in the Christian community. Even though the Christian ideal for the role of women has not changed too much, the reality of many women's lives has changed drastically.

There is a high percentage of working women—single, married, with children—in even the most conservative churches. Some of them may be in that situation by choice and some by necessity. But they are there—adrift in an institution that often tends to define femininity in terms befitting Suzy Homemaker—and they do not exemplify the ideal.

Does that mean they are not feminine? Or does the Bible allow for a broader view of femininity than that proclaimed from pulpits across our land? If the woman in Proverbs 31 showed up in your church next Sunday, would she be booted out because she is too industrious, too hard-working, and too contemporary?

This issue has caused many women to become frustrated. One woman told me she overheard some of her Christian brothers discussing her lack of femininity. The men complained that she was always "opening her own doors." She said, "Nobody gives me anything. I either open my own doors, or I get hit in the face with them as they slam shut."

Problems on Parents' Night

The single mother's attempts to get involved at her children's school can be upsetting.

My daughter, Lisa, graduated from a conservative Christian high school where her sister, Lara, is now a senior. Usually, when a parent wants to discuss something with school administrators (who, interestingly enough, are all male), the father goes to do the talking. But if our family wants to discuss something, I'm the one who goes.

Fortunately for me, the administrators at my daughters' school are gracious and receptive to me, although this is not universally true. These men allow me to express myself, yet I'm aware that some in the school view me as being overly aggressive. I'm aware that I'm perceived in this way, but I see my choice as either to speak on behalf of my daughters the same way their father would if he were here or to keep quiet and accept whatever comes our way.

My daughters have watched me be an active participant in several trying areas for over nine years now. It has affected the way they relate to friends and teachers alike. Like me, my daughters can seem very strong willed and even unapproachable at times. But we can't deny who we are, even though we risk being viewed incorrectly.

Sure, we're aggressive when we need to be. In the case of my daughters, they can be very aggressive on the basketball or volleyball court. This doesn't diminish our femininity, but it does challenge our confidence in how that is played out.

Standing as Women Before God

A woman who has grown up without the positive reinforcement of a loving father can realize that a large part of her femininity is defined in who she is before her heavenly Father. No matter what other people think or say, a woman can be completely who she is before God. He accepts her crying or screaming, mild or aggressive. She is always completely feminine with Him because that is how she was created.

Some things about women are distinctly female, such as their biological uniquenesses. Some reactions more commonly associated with women are not necessarily feminine at all, such as crying. But who a woman is as a created female being is always completely accepted before God. God may have allowed her to be in a role that appears less feminine than another role, but that does not make her less feminine.

So, what is femininity? Femininity is an attitude rather than a list of characteristics. It is accepting me as me and not being defensive about who I am. Sometimes I am aggressive. Sometimes I am weak. Sometimes I confront, and sometimes I back down and cry.

It is also accepting men for who they are. I don't think it is as important to define who they are with distinctive labels as it is to accept them—and accept them as different from women. A lot of books discuss the differences between men and women in terms of temperaments, personality, willpower, or genes. Such books are helpful in their way, but the true meaning of who we are doesn't depend on some formula. It depends on who we are as we stand before God. After we realize God has accepted us, then we can accept ourselves and others in a noncritical way.

The overall attitude that best reflects femininity to me is one of softness. Softness is not weakness or apathy. It is the manifestation of a meek and gentle spirit that flavors all of life touched by a woman who possesses it. It is the result of a godly confidence in who she is based on her relationship with God. She is not threatened by what people think or by the role she is called to live. She has a calm assurance that she is accepted by her Creator and therefore has little to prove elsewhere. God is the Author of this soft spirit, and He can create it—or re-create it—in any woman who is willing to stand before Him and ask for it.

*An adequate self-concept
is a precious possession.
It is the premise upon which
a person can devote himself wholeheartedly
to living a useful and productive life.*

—Dr. Maurice E. Wagner

Affirmation

> O ne of the things we must learn as women is balance. As twins, Ann and I have achieved a certain balance between us: in many ways we are different, and in many ways we are alike. We can balance each other's views, perspectives, and ideas as we did in our book Struggling for Wholeness. In these two chapters, we present two sides of one coin: the need to receive affirmation from others to help us truly see ourselves, and the need to be able to affirm ourselves. When you have learned this balance, you can change the world by becoming an affirmer. As Jan says, giving the gift of affirmation is giving a gift to yourself.
>
> *Ann Kiemel Anderson & Jan Kiemel Ream*
> Struggling for Wholeness

Ann

affirmation. we all need it.

the last four years have so affected my confidence. it is so hard for me, today, to know how people feel about me because they do not often verbalize it.

a woman had run from jackson, wyoming, to idaho falls. 57 years old. a tough, well-conditioned athlete, especially at her age. a few women in my neighborhood had a little coffee for her, & invited me.

i was delighted to be included, but with 2 babies, 11 months apart, i did not know how i could get them bathed & dressed . . . & myself ready . . . & to the baby-sitter's . . . back to the neighbor's home by 10:00 A.M.

with much energy, i delivered two clean babies & bottles & diapers to the sitter's . . . & flew into the coffee about 5 minutes late. people asked how the children were. they were warm & gracious. the food was delectable. meeting the runner was most enjoyable. but walking out to the car, i was consumed with a sad feeling. no one had said: "ann, i love what you are wearing . . ." or "ann, you look *so* wonderful . . ." or "oh, you have lovely children." the conversation was friendly & chatty, but not affirming. i had no sense of how I really looked, or what i was as a person.

affirmation can change the worst day into something decent & lovely.

WHY is there so little affirmation in the world? i have some ideas, but i am beginning to believe that unless i help educate those around me, i will just continue to feel more & more unsure & empty.

affirmation can change the worst day into something decent & lovely. everything can go wrong, but i can fly into the grocery store to get a carton of milk, & have someone say, "ann, you're looking wonderful," & suddenly the whole world seems better.

we were eating brunch at a beautiful chalet in sun valley. will & i & some dear friends. i kept watching the table across from ours. a family. they were animated. laughing. their spirit of camaraderie could be felt even where i was sitting. when we left, i slipped over & tapped the mother on the shoulder. they all turned toward me. "i have been enjoying your togetherness over at my table. you exude such warmth & love that those around you can feel it. it seemed important that i stop & just say 'thank you.' " their faces were radiant.

will & i were in the gigantic anaheim stadium at a convention. a beautiful woman was walking toward us, on her way to the next balcony. i tapped her arm. "you are a beautiful lady," i smiled. her whole face lit up. a split second. a passing in the crowd. just a few words. i believe it touched her life.

every chance i get, i try to affirm my little sons & husband. with specifics.

"brock, you have the most beautiful brown eyes."

"taylor, i was so proud of you yesterday, when you did not cry & you played by yourself."

"honey, i like that shirt. you look sharp."

"will, you are a terrific father."

we are too busy in our own little struggles. our own insecurities. too caught up with living to give those around us a moment of praise. you may say i am too dependent & wrapped up in other people's opinions. that it should not matter. that i am narcissistic. maybe so. you can *never* convince me, however, that the world would not have more ego strength & there would be more joy dancing around . . . more confidence . . . more courage . . . if one could learn to verbalize more of the positives that we think & feel about others.

a pretty dress. flawless skin. an impeccably dressed man in the elevator. a little girl with new barrettes. a little boy's idea. someone's beautiful, new home. the neighbor's new car . . . or yard. *everywhere* there are things that deserve praise. verbal celebration.

& all the while, we sit around like hungry beggars. longing for reassurance of our value. waiting. starving.

jan taught 3rd grade once. a long time ago. one bright-eyed boy would stand at her desk. watch her. talk to her. all the while wrapping his finger around a piece of her hair into a little curl. he thought jan was the shining star in the night. over & over, however, he did poorly in his work assignments & daily quizzes.

one day jan stopped, looked at him, & said, "rodney, you are very smart. you could be doing so well in school. in fact, you are one of my finest students . . ." before she could continue to tell him that he should be doing much better in school . . . he looked up at her with sober, large eyes:

"i did not know that!"

from that moment on, rodney began to change. his papers were neater. cleaner. his spelling improved. because he was one of her top students. all because she affirmed him. she told him something no one ever had before. it changed his life.

there are thousands of readers who are fans of my writings, & through the years have written me letters of love & support. without them, i would have evaporated into a nothing state. into a person with little concept of my worth. the people who are often the closest to me never let me know. i spend a lot of time feeling my clothes are defective. feeling i look very below par. knowing i must be rather blah & limited. without jan, & will (who is learning), i would have no happy, healthy concept of my value. if i receive such little affirmation, where does that leave the rest of the world? surely i am not that much more defective than anyone else.

once, after lunch, i confessed these feelings to a friend.

"ann, you always seem so self-assured! probably none of us feel you need anything from us." what a tragic reason to not verbalize something positive . . . that is honest . . . to someone who is human, & thus always will need reassurance & support.

please . . . join me. every time you see a happy child, praise him for his sunshine. every time you think a beautiful thought about someone, express it to them in words. if with every human being we encounter . . . in an elevator, across a store counter, in a restaurant, at a party . . . we could look for & find one lovely, beautiful quality, & VERBALIZE it, there would be a new level of productivity. fresh, creative energy. a joy & confidence that the world has not, as yet, experienced.

i will not become cocky with too much praise. i will never leave you out of my life because i feel more valuable. instead, there will be more love for you because you have given me worth, & freedom to reach beyond myself & my own flaws. all the positive, admiring thoughts in the world will *never* generate a magical, wonderful moment unless they are spoken. shared.

one quiet, honest statement of praise to human beings can change them.

today, running across the street . . . downtown . . . after having my driver's license renewed . . . a lady passed me.

"what a beautiful outfit you are wearing!" she yelled across the wind.

i stopped. overwhelmed. smiled widely.

"what a lovely, kind, wonderful thing to say," i responded.

one simple woman. one beautiful statement. & i was changed.

Jan

After observing at the private school my children formerly attended, Tom and I met with two of their teachers. I had an issue to bring to the table.

"My children have been attending here now for several months, and I've observed your classrooms on different occasions. There is one aspect of your system that is bothering me. I have never heard you express any personal statements of affirmation to my children nor to any of the others. I have listened to hear you say, 'My, Nash— that is a wonderful picture you have drawn,' or 'Tre, I feel you did an exceptional job on your book report.' "

One of the teachers was ready with a quick response, obviously anxious to inform me on the *why* of this. "No, and you never will," she replied firmly. "We find that the most insecure children are those who have received a lot of external affirmation and are always looking to an adult figure to affirm them before they seemingly are able to move on to another project independently. We rather like to make statements like, 'My, Nash, you must be proud of how hard you have worked on that picture,' and 'My, Tre, you really must be pleased with the way your book report turned out.'

"We want these children to learn how to affirm themselves and become more self-directed as opposed to externally directed."

Now this is the other side of the coin of what Ann just spoke to— that of being affirmed by others. I see it over and over again as a therapist—this tremendous need for each of us to learn how to affirm ourselves.

I am reminded of my adviser, one of my major professors, in graduate school. In her closing statements to me she said, "You have some tremendous skills and strengths for being a wonderful therapist. There is just one thing I want to comment on. Therapy can be very lonely, and there may be days and weeks when you won't receive much feedback from your clients about your work. You are a person who underestimates your own value and who is unsure of yourself. You tend to look to and be dependent on external sources to assure you of your strengths. You are going to have to learn to support and reinforce yourself more, or you may end up very discouraged. You must begin to believe that you are good at what you do."

I said to a client today, "Tell me three things about yourself that are positive and strong." She is beautiful, brilliant, charming, and social, but she sat there and said, "I can't." "You *won't*," I retorted. Facing and acknowledging my own strengths is a part of my facing reality. The fact that I am still alive makes a statement to my belief that there is something—even just one thing—I believe to be of merit in myself or I would have died long ago.

However, practicing self-support can never be enough. It will never eliminate nor devalue the great healing power and encouragement I will receive from your verbal affirmation.

I really must have both. Too much self-support and too little need and appreciation for your support will keep me from the love and insights that only you can give me. On the other hand, very little belief in myself leaves me almost totally dependent on you and makes it impossible for me to survive without you. I have to keep remembering that when you affirm me, however, you are simply reporting your individual perspective—not the entire world's nor necessarily the absolute truth. But in that moment in time, your loving words to me, genuinely spoken, can alter my behavior and perhaps my life if I will hear and respond to them.

As children, most of what Ann and I received from our peers was negative. I can tell you that I concluded early in life that those negatives must represent the truth and nothing but the truth. I wasn't mature enough to realize that those negative comments represented only a small fraction of how a poll of a thousand individuals would have responded. A very brilliant, young, male client of mine finishing up his Ph.D. in biochemistry said to me, "I was overwhelmed last week at my farewell party by the loving and kind words of the people I have worked with. I find myself still believing more the feedback I received as an eighth and ninth grader." Someday, if he can keep hearing positive affirmation, maybe he will be able to rebuild his self-concept.

Affirmation that is wrapped up in specifics and not generalities is the most powerful. "I love you." "I'm glad to see you." "We have a lot in common," can apply to many different friends. I remember the day I turned to Tom after we had been married about three months and with deep feelings said, "Honey, I so love you." He looked at me and winked and said, "Why?" *Why?* Well I hadn't really thought about why. But it is in the *whys* I realize now that we are able to influence people's concepts of themselves.

My father, whenever he stood by me in church and could hear me sing, would comment on my "beautiful" voice. I grew up feeling proud of my voice and always am confident joining a church choir. Affirmation that tends to be directed at specific attributes often gives me the confidence I need to develop that part of me further. I have a couple of clients who are models and in the fashion business. They keep telling me I have a creative flair with clothes. With their affirmation I find myself much more confident to tie a sash a unique way or wrap something around my neck that normally goes around a bedspread. I march out of the house with a new internal belief that maybe I am creative.

I don't even need someone standing at the door every moment to reinforce my decision. See, the more you are willing to express your positive response to some part of me you believe to be unique and beautiful, the more I can stand on my own—keep developing and improving that part of me and become more self-directed. The ones of you who are free to affirm me—to point out to me where you see I am strong—are the people who are really responsible for helping me become who I am today. Telling me you love me is important, but not nearly as important as words that point out some beauty in me I cannot see and maybe never will. As a therapist I know that there is a part of me I can *never* see, regardless of how much introspection I pursue, unless you show it to me. I am blinded to parts of myself and desperately need you to reveal them to me—and then to remind me of them *again*. Telling someone once that you admire their ability to be clever must be said again and again. Sometimes it takes a few times before I am able to really hear and believe you. And if we are growing individually and together, we will discover new and different beautiful pieces of each other to affirm. It's endless. Please keep telling me so I can keep growing and become more able to believe in myself.

I will never forget the night not long ago, that Ann said, "If I could look as good as you I would be willing to gain ten pounds." I've had a baby in the last year and for the first time in years and years, I weigh more than Ann. I've struggled with this. To hear Ann, who I have desperately always wanted to be "as good as" share with me that she wants to be like me, was a moment of deep healing for me. I closed my eyes feeling I must be beautiful and worthwhile if Ann wanted to look like I did.

*Tap someone on the arm and remind them
that you believe they have worth and you will
find you are giving a gift to yourself as well.*

Your children, husband, next-door neighbor, mother, father, are waiting to hear some beautiful thing about themselves. People will do a lot of things in a desperate attempt to hear someone say something affirming to them. I had a very attractive, young woman come to see me depressed and unsure of herself. "I need help with my obsession of spending money. I go shopping when I'm depressed and buy hundreds of dollars worth of clothes. I'm desperately trying to gain approval, but nobody tells me I look good anyway, so it doesn't really help."

Look around you today and begin to find the beauty and strength in those you see. Don't keep these thoughts to yourself. Beautiful thoughts—unspoken, unexpressed verbally—are lost treasures. Give them away. Tap someone on the arm and remind them that you believe they have worth and you will find you are giving a gift to yourself as well. The Bible says, "Give and it will be given to you" (Luke 6:38). When we are kind, we give the gift back to ourselves.

And if there is a person in your life you need to hear some affirming words from—*ask*. "John, can you tell me three things you liked about me when you married me?" or "What part of my personality do you enjoy the most?"

Remember:

1. As you observe the people who will pass through your life today, look for the unusual, and use words to give away your thoughts.

2. Give yourself at least one compliment and visualize in your mind a picture of how you would like to look or behave.

3. Be willing to *ask* for what you need. This is a sign of becoming a responsible adult.

Play the words you receive that are affirming over and over again in your thoughts. They can be useful even years after they are heard. Sit and think a moment of some of the positive statements that have come your way.

I remember driving along in the car with Tre on his sixth birthday. I began to tell him about the day he was born. "Tre, I will never forget the day you were born. After hours of great struggle, because delivering a baby is *hard work*, you came into the world. You didn't scream or cry like most newborns. You just lay on my tummy and looked all around. You never closed your eyes. Dr. Adams repeatedly told us what a beautiful baby you were. And when they took you down to the nursery to wash you up and dress you, you were still looking all around—quietly."

Tre was absorbed with my words, and when I was done, he smiled and said, "Mommy, I just loved that story. Tell it to me all over again."

When someone affirms you, don't treat it like a non-important message you read and throw in the trash. Carry it with you. Repeat it over and over again in your mind. When someone sends me a note full of beautiful thoughts they have of me, I carry it in my purse for days. I read and reread it. Those words are great treasures that restore my soul, straighten my shoulders, and put laughter in my life.

Ann, you are absolutely right when you say that "affirmers are world changers." I want to be one!

PART TWO

I Am Emotional

Lesson from an Irish Fable

NOVEMBER 1922

*S*ome time ago I read an Irish fairy story which told how a mortal, on a fairy steed, went hunting with the fairies. He had his choice of whether the fairy horse should become large enough to carry a man-sized man or be small enough to ride the horse as it was.

He chose to become of fairy size and, after the magic was worked, rode gayly with the fairy king until he came to a wall so high he feared his tiny horse could not carry him over; but the fairy king said to him, "Throw your heart over the wall, then follow it!" So he rode fearlessly at the wall, with his heart already bravely past it, and went safely over.

I have forgotten most of the story and do not remember the name of the author, though I wish I did; but often I think of the fairy's advice. Anyone who has ridden horses much understands how the heart of the rider going over fairly lifts the horse up and across an obstacle. And I have been told, by good drivers, that it holds true in taking a motor car up a difficult hill.

But the uplift of a fearless heart will help us over other sorts of barriers. In any undertaking, to falter at a crisis means defeat. No one ever overcomes difficulties by going at them in a hesitant, doubtful way.

If we would win success in anything, when we come to a wall that bars our way, we must throw our hearts over and then follow confidently. It is fairy advice, you know, and savors of magic, so following it we will ride with the fairies of good fortune and go safely over.

Laura Ingalls Wilder
Little House in the Ozarks

I Choose to Put Away My Blue Blanket

D id you have a security blanket as a child? A little blue "banky" that comforted you when things got unsure and insecure? Don't you wish as an adult woman you still could reach over and find the corner of that satiny blanket waiting to make all the discomfort go away?

When we grew up, the need to get away from the turmoil and pain was the same, but our blue blankets changed. In this chapter from my book My Blue Blanket, *I wanted to give you an overview of the security blankets of comfort that we women wrap ourselves in to keep us from the pain of our lives. There is pain in life. We cannot cover it up. It is wise that we don't; and it is courageous when we choose to face it. It is my hope that you will find the wisdom to recognize your own blue blanket and the courage to fold it away high on a closet shelf.*

Joyce Landorf Heatherley
My Blue Blanket

The supermarket was about five blocks away from my home. There was nothing particularly religious or educating about the large building or its busy parking lot, the even busier management people, checkers, or the box boys (except for one box boy, a teenager, my wonderful son Rick). But that particular grocery store served me well for a number of years, not only with nourishment and all those non-food products I always bought but as a resource of a number of very special lessons. As I recall, some of my very best material was acted out right in front of me and my unyielding grocery cart, like some rare new art form of a dramatic play. More often than I can remember, as I observed those one-, two-, or three-act performances unfolding, I was enlightened or encouraged or given some unexpected tutelage on the intricate and fascinating ways of people and their relationships.

This incident at that store, as you may recall from reading *The Richest Lady in Town* (Austin, TX: Balcony, 1991), happened late one Saturday afternoon. Naturally, I had put off the job of grocery shopping for as long as I could. We all know about the time it takes, the expense involved, and the horrible fact that when we get our grocery bags home, our work has only just begun. It never stops.

We still face the long routine of carrying it all in, washing the produce and putting everything away. Then we have to take it all out of the fridge or the cupboards again, prepare and cook it, do something with the left-overs, clean up the kitchen, take out the trash, and then—then, we get to start the whole process all over again. AUUUGH! But back to that Saturday.

There couldn't have been a worse time to shop. Furthermore, I hadn't been able to con anyone into coming with me to push the basket or at least to give me moral support as I spent all that time and money. So there I was, impatiently alone and trying to push my cart through the streaming throng of shoppers.

It was the only cart that was left. One wheel went south and the other due east, and everyone before me had abandoned it. I decided to pull myself together and try to keep in mind that the main priority here was to get the shopping done in the shortest amount of time possible.

I was concentrating so hard, going down each aisle, writing out menus in my head, and trying to race the clock that I almost failed to notice I was making absolutely no headway.

The roadblock was just ahead of me. She was a young woman and I couldn't get around her no matter how hard I tried to outmaneuver her cart. She had her two darling sons with her. One must have been four or five and the other probably not quite two. It required no course in Psychology 101 to ascertain that from the top of her supersized pink rollers in her hair, down to her sandals, this near hysterical mother was just quite possibly going to go "crackers," as the British say.

I imagined her story like this.

All week she'd tried to find time to shampoo her hair and do her nails (preferably alone, without one of the little people asking, "What are you doing?") but as all mothers of young children understand, she'd run out of time. So, earlier today, I was guessing, she decided that she'd clean up the house, and after the kids were in bed tonight, she'd give herself some TLC with bath and shampoo time. Tomorrow, she'd do her grocery shopping.

However, I fantasized, just a few moments ago, her husband phoned and said, "Honey, I know this is short notice but it's important. I've invited the boss and his wife over for dinner tonight."

I could imagine her standing there, staring first at the phone in her hand and then at one of her boys who was gleefully pouring a white trail of milk on the floor for the dog who was joyously lapping it up, and I could hear her mumble, "Are you serious? Tonight?"

At least, that's how I called it because she was about as calm and collected as a volcano getting ready to erupt. Her boys, on the other hand, were having the most delightful time of their lives! You could just tell they had been cooped up all week and this coming to the grocery store with both of them riding in the front seat of the cart was a Big Deal, almost as good as a new ride at Disneyland.

They were tickled pink to be there, thrilled to "help" their mother. They handed her a can here and a box of cookies there. I could tell she was trying not to scream as she put each item back on the first available shelf space she found. (I could see my son Rick stocking shelves later and the puzzled look on his face, wondering how that sack of sugar made it across two aisles and ended up beside the dill pickles.)

The boys climbed in and out of their seat in the cart and once the littlest one started to get into my basket. I handed him back to his mother and said, "I believe this belongs to you?" Nary a word passed her lips as she took him back and rolled her eyes toward the ceiling in the traditional mother's gesture of helplessness.

Both of us had worked our way down several aisles and were almost halfway through the store. By now, I was in more of a hurry than ever, but no matter how hard or how persistent I was in trying to get past her, I just couldn't do it.

As we headed for the wide meat aisle, hope soared within me. "Aha!" I thought. "I'll cut her off at the pass!" So I maneuvered, raced, picked up less meat than I had planned, grabbed a few pieces of fruit in the produce department and sprinted through shoppers in my cross-store marathon, with my head lowered for action and my cart sailing along. (Well, actually with those wheels, the cart didn't *sail* along; it just felt that way.)

Into the final lap, I dashed, right up to the front of the store and made it to the checkout! Instantly, other customers formed a line behind me. The store was jammed with rush-hour shoppers.

I hardly had time to congratulate myself on having made it to the finish line when I looked up, and lo and behold, there in line, right in front of me, was the young mother and her two boys. So much for my great maneuvering!

I figured I shouldn't fight it, so I practiced a few deep-breathing relaxation techniques and resigned myself to waiting my turn. However, someone invisible tapped me on the shoulder, and I heard in my head, "Pay attention." I wasn't too sure if that was a "God-suggestion" or a "Joyce-suggestion," but I paid attention, just in case.

About then, it happened. The youngest boy in the cart ahead of me had apparently run out of inspiring things to do because he was playing a new game. He was tugging on the tall wire rack beside him, which was loaded with candy, gum, and tons of other goodies. I'm not sure what tantalizing thoughts raced through his little mind, but he looked as if he'd decided he needed a little more action in his life. With all his little might, he gave the rack a very healthy yank and pulled the whole thing over, showering him and his brother with a fantastic rainfull of candy.

It was every kid's dream come true. Both boys were delighted!

As the rack began its fall, it hooked itself onto another one filled with a jillion candy bars. The two racks meshed and toppled down together, doubling the treasure and spraying gum, Lifesavers™, cough drops, Rolaids™, and giant Peter Paul Almond Joy™ bars over the area around the cash register. One-sixteenth of a second later, the volcano I mentioned earlier did indeed erupt into a hot molten mass of hysterical screaming. All of which, need I tell you, was directed at the petrified boys.

We were all knee-deep in candy bars, and it caused pandemonium all over the store. The mother went noticeably berserk. She was wild-eyed, crying and frantically yelling, "What am I going to do?

How could this happen to me? I can't believe this whole mess. Do I have to pay for it?"

A deep male voice came over the intercom speakers. "Code four . . . code four . . . code four." Personnel came running from every direction. The manager, meat packers, their assistants, produce people, clerks and box boys all flew toward the front of the store, geared for action. They seemed to know this was no drill! At this same moment (we all know that word of mouth is the best advertisement), kids were telling other kids about this wonderful natural disaster. Soon, gangs of kids were running into the store, stuffing candy in their pockets and racing for the outer doors. Customers were rolling around in Rolaids™ and crushing candy bars to death and my feet were hidden in a sea of Lifesavers™ and Dentyne™ gum.

By now, the volcano was pouring a hot torrid stream of big words, hissing words, bad words, and small threatening words into the four little ears still sitting in the cart below her. Apparently, even after she called them by their first, middle, and last names, she still didn't think she was getting through. So she thundered down at them, grabbing one boy by his sweater collar and the other by one shoulder, and tried to swoop them up to eye level, an arm's length away from her face, where she could verbally let them have it.

I say "tried to lift them up." Have you ever tried to pull a kid out of a grocery cart? Yes? Then, you know that if they think they're "gonna git it," they lock their legs around the basket seat so when you try to bring them out, you lift up the cart with them. Imagine trying to get two legs untangled, much less four! For a second there, I thought she was going to have to break bones, but she finally freed them both and shook those terrified boys until I was sure blood would come spurting out of any convenient opening. After a final violent shake for emphasis, the volcano slammed them down on the floor yelling, "Now, shut up and don't you move!"

They stood frozen, like two little soldiers in ramrod positions, no color in their faces, their eyes peeled open in astonished horror.

Bedlam still reigned in the store. But, I'll give her credit, the mother turned from the boys, and even though she was still hysterical and crying uncontrollably, she pulled herself together and started helping the clean-up crew.

Slowly, I came out of shock and was about to move to help also when, out of the corner of my eye (I couldn't believe it), I saw the littlest boy *move. Oh darling child,* I thought, *don't do that or your mother is going to snap you in two like a fresh green bean.* We are talking total destruction.

Never taking his eyes off his mother's face, the boy began inching backward, and with one hand, he searched the air behind him until he found what he wanted—her large open straw handbag. Warily eyeing his mother, he pulled out a small, faded blue blanket. As he moved back to his mark on the floor, he tucked the tattered remnants of that blanket firmly under his chin, and almost instantly, his tense shoulders relaxed and lowered. He breathed a loud sigh and color returned to his face. Tranquility spread over him, erasing the fear from his eyes, and he began to sway from side to side ever so gently, humming a little tune.

I was enchanted by this peaceful little boy and the way his blanket had brought such pleasure and serenity to his face. I felt as if the Lord whispered down some corridor of my mind, "Did you see that?" When the child's whole world crashed down around him, when everything went wrong, when his very life was in jeopardy, he did not reach for his mother but for the only thing that would make everything all right: his faded blue blanket. He was gentled by its presence.

I thought that Saturday afternoon, and have thought many times since then, that his faded blue blanket had probably never given him a moment of pain, never a teeth-rattling, head-shaking, brain-jarring lecture. In fact, that blue blanket had probably never given him anything but joy and comfort, except perhaps when he lost it to the washing machine and didn't find it until his mother took it out of the dryer.

There in the grocery store, he sought, found, and hugged his blanket, and the broken pieces of his world clicked silently back into place.

Over the years of observing my children and grandchildren and many other children, as well, with their "blue blankets," I've noticed that blue blankets are not necessarily brand new or without holes and tears. Usually, they are neither very clean nor one whit loved because of their beauty or their gorgeous condition. No siree! Mostly, blue blankets are like the bedraggled skin horse of *The Velveteen Rabbit,* whose hide and skin had been dearly loved and hugged off of him. And when blue blankets come up missing, there is great gnashing of teeth and heartrending tears until the prized blanket is found.

Most of us parents fondly and knowingly smile when we remember the noteworthy episodes we have had with our children's blue blankets. And any child who has ever dragged one around á la Linus in the "Peanuts" cartoon—whether it was a blanket, a stuffed teddy bear, a soft toy—knows exactly how valuable this blanket is to his or her own peace of mind and overall security.

We can all feel for children who are distressed and wanting their blue blankets. I can still feel the little boy's relief in the grocery store amidst all the ruckus he'd caused as he reached for and found his blue blanket.

We do not outgrow our need for security, our need for comfort, our need for gentling, our need for someone to please just understand, our need for healing and wholeness. We just trade in our child's small faded blue blanket for a larger adult's blue blanket.

Here are some times I think we grown-ups reach for our blue blankets of comfort.

When we fear what is happening right now.

When we sense we've lost all control in our life because of death, divorce or forced separation from loved ones.

When we suffer major pain, physically or emotionally.

When we lose our job, face bankruptcy or watch finances disappear.

When we are threatened by transition and change which seems to be happening in every single arena of our lives.

When we feel absolutely no emotional support from the loved one closest to us.

When we see that we are all alone, ignored or abandoned by our friends.

When we can't stand *anymore* pain.

When we are convinced that no one on God's green earth understands that pain, or even cares.

When there's no easing or tapering off of our loneliness.

When we feel trapped and can see no hope of things ever changing.

Believe me, any or all of the above combined can send us by the most direct route to our very own blue blanket whether we are two or ninety-two years old.

You could probably write your own list of anxieties which have sent you scurrying to grab your blue blanket, or as Dr. Pannabecker called mine, your "escape hatch."

I can readily see the truth in this catchy little saying (one of hundreds Barb Johnson has sent me over the years), for it spells out our need to have an adult blue blanket:

> Sometimes, just when things look the bleakest,
> You have to look life squarely in the eye and say,
> "Go ahead, life . . . take your best shot . . .
> I can take whatever you dish out."
> Other times, it's best to just go to bed
> With a really good book, a big plate of fudge
> And a box full of donuts!

I think there are very few people living under, or in the midst of, today's stress and pressure who don't have a blue blanket or two. Some may deny it or refuse to admit it, but I suspect most of us, when frightened or hurting, run pell-mell for that particular escape hatch of ours and desperately clutch our favorite blue blanket to our hearts.

Now, our blue blankets may not share exact descriptions, so let me list some of the blue blankets I've heard about, including the name of my own. These are true-to-life blue blankets, common escape hatches. They are what we long to have, tucked under our chin, when the pain of what is happening right now is very scary or growing by the nanoseconds, downright unbearable.

Sometimes a blue blanket is simple to identify and is relatively harmless to you or someone else. Other blue blankets are very dangerous. They are hidden escapes and agendas. They are well-kept secrets of ours, not easily detected by others. These menacing blue blankets can become entrenched in our daily lives until they encroach disastrously on our lives and consume us or others. It is paramount to lay aside these perilous blue blankets. I give you this list so that we can examine and learn not only about our own blue blanket but about the blue blankets of others.

The Blue Blanket of Sleep

The young newly divorced single mother unveiled her secret blue blanket to me in a word: *sleeping.*

Quietly, she confessed that she went to bed whenever she needed to escape the overwhelming pain of the responsibility of financially supporting herself and her children. To escape, she would go to bed. Often for hours at a time, she slept, leaving her two preschool children in front of a TV with a VCR movie running.

She wasn't reaching for her blue blanket out of anger toward her former husband, or society in general, nor was she trying to act in a potentially dangerous or foolhardy way. She was in pure despair. Sleeping was her escape route.

We talked of some of the alternatives and choices open to her. Primarily, in our brief time together, we spoke of ways she could begin to lay aside her potentially harmful blue blanket. One option was that when she felt the financial pressure building and the panic attack closing in, she would choose to sleep only when her little ones were napping. I reminded her that all mothers with little ones were perpetually tired and very much in need of naps themselves.

The mother of Charles and John Wesley had twenty-one children. Each day she reserved one hour alone for prayer, instructing that no one was allowed to disturb her. I have a sneaking suspicion that in between praying for her children, she managed an occasional nap. (At least, with twenty-one children that's how I would have done it.)

Another option the young mother and I talked about was that she try reducing the amount of time she slept a little each day.

I'm not a professional psychologist and my instant sidewalk counseling is certainly not long-term therapy, but I believe we must lay aside our blue blankets that could be destructive to others, even when we ourselves can barely stand the pain.

When the young mother and I parted, I felt she had made up her mind to make good choices and to take her first, shaky and tentative steps toward laying aside her blue blanket of sleeping. She'd begun to realize that she had choices, and her face reflected that her inner attitudes had gone from panicked depression to a small measure of hopefulness.

The Blue Blanket of Reading or Watching TV

I have to admit that I am a passionate and zealous reader. My unquenchable love of books, part of the inheritance my mother gave me, runs deep and fervidly within me. Reading could be my blue blanket, because if I was ever in the enviable position of having nothing to do (not likely in my lifetime on this planet), I'd lie on a beach and read, read, read.

I am not only a reader but a writer as well, and I'm heavily into stories which deal with the truth concerning the vast subject of life and relationships. I'm also into stories wherever I can find them. Books, theatrical plays, operas, sermons, interviews, and (despite my upbringing which forbade me to go to the show) movies, which brings me to another love of mine: television. Television, since its emergence into our homes in the late forties, has continually received bad press from the pulpits of our land (much like radio did in its early days). But the beauty and the pleasure of watching TV lies in the hand holding the remote control unit. So for me, movies and television could also be blue blankets. That these aren't problems to me is no credit to my intelligence or spirituality. Rather, I feel guilty if I read books when I have a deadline and am supposed to be writing books instead of reading them. And I have found with TV that there's only a little time at night to watch, and Francis and I are practically gifted with a remote control unit.

But I can easily understand how both of these activities could control my life if I used them as blue blankets for my escape from reality. I've talked with many of you who see this blue blanket as a monopolizing time stealer and a potentially difficult habit to break, even after the pain has abated and a blue blanket is not as urgently needed.

Again, what I suggest here is laying aside this or any other blue blanket, which is destructive to our souls or a dictator of our life's priorities.

The Blue Blanket of Eating or Not Eating

Often when I talk privately with a person about her blue blanket, she almost immediately blurts out the name of what she eats or how she starves herself when she feels stress closing in on her or when chronic pain or depression knocks the hope out of her and brings her to her knees.

"Chocolates!" from a twenty-seven-year-old high school teacher.

"Junk food, all kinds!" from a business associate.

"Food in general!" from a movie star.

"Donuts," from me.

My mother, brother, and sister all knew that in times of crisis, my dad would head for the refrigerator. But even without a crisis, I noticed that Dad always timed his visits to me during the lunch or dinner hour, and in his later years as he'd walk into my house, his first question after the briefest of hellos was, "Got any cold juice?" Eventually, if I knew he was coming, I'd have cold juice ready and waiting. But we all just accepted that in stressful or nonstressful situations, Dad ate.

Whenever my mother or I was hospitalized, we'd look at each other and ask, "Where's Dad?" We'd smile, and then say together, "In the cafeteria." Naturally.

If we don't abuse this blue blanket, it can serve us well. We are all comforted and sustained by food or by eating together with someone we love. The ancient ceremony of breaking bread is still necessary and wonderful.

My memory is rich with times when I was in kindergarten in Battle Creek, Michigan. My mother and I stayed with Grandma Miller, my father's Irish mother, while he was away in evangelistic meetings with the evangelist C. M. Ward. My grandma firmly believed that 90 percent of the world's ills could be cured by sitting down (me on her lap) and sharing a cup of hot tea laced with milk and sugar.

During another year of my dad's traveling, my mother and I lived in Highland Park, Michigan, with my Hungarian Grandma Uzon. Now she believed that 90 percent of the world's ills could be cured by eating. Period. But what I loved the most was that she'd sit down (me on her lap) and share her cups of coffee, gloriously delicious with cream or canned condensed milk and four teaspoons, at least, of sugar. It was a great and lovely blue blanket.

Lovely that is, unless it were to become a compulsive way of life.

When our weight balloons, our cholesterol rockets skyward, our hearts are endangered by fat and our self-esteem disappears, food becomes a life-threatening blue blanket. And for our health's sake, we must deal with it and choose to lay it aside.

When we eat or when we don't eat (as with a compulsive eater versus an anorexic or bulimic patient), we are physically and mentally in denial about the pain and truth of our lives. This blue blanket helps us to walk away from conflicts or confrontations. It becomes our refusal to see our life as it really is. It could become a life-threatening problem.

I'm not professionally adroit enough to diagnose the seriousness of the problems of over- or undereating, and I can't begin to lay out the steps to help you choose to put down your blue blanket. But others can. And if your blue blanket, no matter how secret or how innocent it looks, is controlling your life, you need help. Go for it. Go to a qualified counselor or to a program, but go. Go to someone you can trust.

The Blue Blanket of Telephoning

I never knew her last name nor did I ever meet her in person, but in the early 1970s a woman called me long distance from a pay phone in a suburb of Los Angeles, California. She called to talk with me every day and eventually several times a day for a solid six months.

Our conversations always ran the same. She told me how bad Christians had treated her. She was unable to hear my remarks so she just repeated her statement about Christians and how they had let her down.

In those daily phone calls, filled with street and traffic noise and sometimes the sound of wind or rainfall, I was never able to get her to tell me anything about herself or her life's circumstances. Even my attempts to set up correspondence with her so I could write to her or send her books failed as she would never give me her address. But I kept answering my phone because I felt I should answer and respond to her calls. She had value as a human being. She was another child of God, and I could almost hear the bleak, cold sound of her loneliness pouring through the phone lines. It was easy to sense that emotionally she was very fragile.

After six months of phoning me, she stepped up the number of calls a day until I became emotionally fragile. My efforts to get her to seek help repeatedly failed and my family life suffered. So I finally made the difficult decision to obtain an unlisted number.

I have always wished it could have been different. She was such a tormented woman, tragically addicted to that blue blanket of phoning me or someone. Why she was the way she was, how she got that way, or what drove her to that particular blue blanket, I'll probably never know. But I do understand that the people who escape their hurts by obsessive phoning are troubled and lonely souls. And sadly, they drive friends and family away precisely when they need all the friends and family they can get.

Since my first encounter with that woman, I have dealt with five or six other people who have repeatedly called me, sometimes at great expense. One woman, who eventually went for counseling about this blue blanket, told me years later: "Joyce, you must have hated to hear the phone ring during my marathon phoning days!" Then she added, "And I hated to pay the five- and six-hundred-dollar-a-month phone bills. But when I was depressed about my divorce and when I felt the world closing in, I'd call you and some other friends. I didn't even know it was an addiction, I just ran for the phone every time I felt overwhelmed by my crisis."

Women at my speaking engagements have often told me of a person in their family, church, or neighborhood who plagues them morning, noon, or night with long involved (and tragic) phone calls. Callers who are on the phone to you daily over long periods of time need professional help, and often, wellness and recovery happens only after long-term therapy.

Phoning is a convenient, larger-than-life blanket for a growing number of people who are hugless and who struggle emotionally in our touchless society. A phone call may very well be the only way a person reaches out or feels any connection with others.

The Blue Blanket of Busy-ness

"My husband is a workaholic but even when he's home, all he does is watch sports on TV."

"My wife is married to her job."

"My wife is never home, and when she is, she's too busy or too tired."

"My husband never talks to me."

"My wife bores me to death with small talk."

"All my husband ever says about his day is 'fine.' "

"All my wife really loves is shopping."

"Our family never eats any meals together."

"My dad is an absentee father."

"Mom never has time to listen to us kids."

"My son or daughter never calls or visits me."

I hear these complaints frequently from everyone—kids, teenagers, young adults, and senior citizens—about their daily lives. Frankly, they are giving us some tough messages to swallow about the roots of isolation and estrangement within many of yesterday's, today's, and tomorrow's families.

. . . there are no easy and quick answers
. . . no "they just ride-off-into-the-sunset-
and-live-happily-ever-after" endings.

It is not my intention here to use these quotes (or some of the others I routinely hear) as if they represent the only problems in the home, nor do I mean ever to imply that this whole matter of family living is just the typical, simplistic, and trivial struggle everyone goes through . . . that it's no big deal or just a matter of adjusting, pacing oneself, or merely thinking great positive thoughts . . . no, not at all!

You'd have to be seriously dead to be unaware of the intricate complexities in today's family relationships. And I know for an absolute fact that there are no easy and quick answers . . . no instant solutions and no "they just ride-off-into-the-sunset-and-live-happily-ever-after" endings.

But perhaps it would help us all to see our relationships and family struggles by some different lights. Small lights, yes, but lights nevertheless.

Intertwined with the need to put food on the table, to provide a roof over the family's head and to produce an emotional safe harbor for our loved ones is the noisy, false countertheme of our problem with busy-ness. I see two kinds of busy-ness.

Most all of us are caught up in a normal busy-ness as it relates to our personal finances and family support systems . . . and rightly so. But if getting or making money becomes our god, "the love of money is the root of all evil" becomes far more than a biblical truism.

When we give this first kind of busy-ness a higher priority than most anything else in our family, our relationships are thwarted and never have the chance to be all God designed them to be. We may live together, but we become as ships passing in the night, vaguely aware of each other's presence but never close enough to talk or communicate. Obviously, this creates and promotes profound neglect in relationships between husbands and wives and between parents and children. Our struggles, questions and differences are left hanging, unresolved or abandoned altogether, and we sum up our family ties with a shrug of the shoulder and with the guilt of the unfinished business. Sometimes as we look back over the years, we realize we've missed the point of family life: to know, love and esteem each other's presence.

Then, in order to compensate for what we know or perceive is a dysfunctional family lifestyle, we begin the search for a blue blanket to soften the onslaught of past memories and present pain. And, guess what? Very often the blue blanket we run to find is more busy-ness to escape the ill effects of the first kind of busy-ness. It is a second kind of busy-ness designed to help us get even busier so we can escape the ill effects of busy-ness in the first place.

Plunging headlong into the blue blanket of busy-ness happens when we see clearly that we have bad relationships at home. We may have serious marital problems, conflicts with our kids or some heavy abuses from our past, but one thing we know for sure is that we can't and won't break up the home. So in an all-out effort to keep the stress levels down and the family together and survive with our sanity intact, we create our own escape route called keep busy at all costs.

Busy-ness is a very effective blue blanket and can be a well-entrenched, even respectable way of life. In fact, it's so effective that we rarely have time to think in depth about what we are doing or to come to terms concerning our struggles. But I believe the most damaging thing busy-ness does to our souls is that it depletes the strength we need that's required to make decisions or to deal with the highly volatile relational conflicts at hand.

We can become workaholics, in or out of the home. Some may even applaud our efforts and point with pride to our accomplishments, labeling us "success oriented" or "self-made millionaires." But the cost of this blue blanket in terms of damage to husband, wife, kids, and other extended family members is exorbitant.

This blue blanket of busy-ness also does something subtle but nonetheless real, for it lets us stay within the framework of our home life. It allows us to keep up our respectable appearances at home, job, and church. Many times busy-ness makes it look as if our vows to protect and cherish our loved ones are all intact, even when they are unraveling. Busy-ness turns the light on above the doorway marked Exit, and whenever we escape beneath the blanket of busy-ness, we are usually walking away . . . not toward our loved ones.

The final tab is usually a dysfunctional family to one degree or another. Husband/wife, mother/father, brother/sister, grandparents end up distanced from one another, feeling unwanted, isolated, abandoned and deeply troubled. They are puzzled by their own feelings of anxiety and some suffer from self-imposed guilt.

It occurs to me that some of you may hold dear this blue blanket of busy-ness not because you don't want to deal with family conflicts but because the dysfunctions of your home were, from the beginning, products of a profoundly basic personality disorder. I know some of you who could not live without this blue blanket because those deep-seated wars of someone's life drove you away from, not toward, home.

I say this as kindly as I can: Busy-ness is never going to be a permanent solution. If you are depending on it to get you through life, it may do that. But you will be accepting a sentence to living death.

Should your busy-ness keep you away from solvable family conflicts, I would urge you to reexamine your priorities and lifestyles. Don't wait for a life-threatening event or accident to jolt your reality awareness. Often I have read or heard of someone who is either in the final stages of cancer or who has walked away from a major airline crash or auto accident. These people make virtually the same comment: "Every day I have now is a gift. This (illness or death or accident) has changed my life. Now I see new beauty in a sunrise and I feel new joy when I kiss my baby's face. Life is precious to me now and I thank God for each new day to live as His child." Their newfound knowledge forever changes their thoughts and attitudes and, thereby, their way of living. If they had the blue blanket of busy-ness *before* their experience, they would choose to do everything they could *afterward* to lay it aside, perhaps in record time.

If we are to have a family or a home at all, some changes in attitudes and behavior patterns have to happen. We have to deliberately decide to lay aside our blue blankets of busy-ness and thoughtfully choose to see each new day as a gift and each relationship at home as very, very precious.

The Blue Blankets of Alcohol, Drugs, and Prescription Pills

I haven't listed the various types of blue blankets in any specific order nor have I attempted to lay a guilt trip on any person for *having* a blue blanket. We all have one sort or another, and I'm well aware that blue blankets are our own built-in system for coping with the pain of our wounds.

But perhaps of the most destructive blue blankets around in our society today, this blue blanket could be placed at the top of the list. Addiction to alcohol, drugs, and prescription pills produces an almost certain death warrant.

Although this is not my particular blue blanket, I've talked with hundreds of people who deal or cope with addiction, either in their own lives or in the lives of loved ones. And these conversations have only underscored the need for me to understand the addict and for the desperate need of getting help to that person so he can lay aside this lethal blue blanket.

If we do not care about the addicted simply because it's not "my problem" or it's not "touching my family," we fail one of the basic tenets of Jesus' teaching—that of loving one another. Left alone to run its course, this blue blanket will continue to wipe out loved ones and families at an increasing rate each year.

Volumes have been and are being written about these venomous blue blankets. Scores of big-screen movies and television shows explore the hazards, the havoc, and the lethal toxicity of these escape routes. I believe these blue blankets are a present-day symptom of what Henri Nouwen calls our feelings of "disconnectedness" and our attempt to escape the pain of "boredom, resentment and depression."

Biblically, it is clear that ingesting alcohol was not wrong, nor did it make the drinker a bad person. Paul makes a point of telling the new Christians at Ephesus not to be drunk with wine (Eph. 5:18). Paul outlined the behavior for the deacons of the early church to Timothy. We read, "Deacons likewise must be serious, not double-tongued, not addicted to much wine" (1 Tim. 3:8 RSV). But later in the fifth chapter Paul admonishes, "No longer drink only water, but use a little wine for the sake of your stomach and your frequent ailments" (1 Tim. 5:23 RSV). The early Christians were neither to use Paul's words as a command never to drink wine nor as an excuse for drinking themselves into a stupor. Being drunk and out of control and allowing a substance to play havoc with our thoughts, actions, and responses was the issue then and is the issue now.

Addiction is the name of the real killer.

This blue blanket can start innocently enough, with small increments of single or combined substances which may provide a few precious moments of relief or give us highs from the tension and stress of the hour. But it also has the unbelievable potential of being lethal to ourselves and stabbing to death the loving vitality out of our most precious relationships with others. It rapes, plunders, and violates the very core of our personhood, ultimately enslaving us and addicting us to an almost unbreakable lifestyle that can only deteriorate down a dark street whose grim sign reads Dead End.

Also, it is truly scary that we never know for sure, or at least right up front, whether we are in that "one out of twelve" (or whatever percentage it is today) who can become addicted. And what's more frightening is that unless the addict recognizes his problem and seeks help, or loved ones choose to use the intervention process, there is little chance or hope of ever being clean and free from the addiction. Sadly, the addiction not only endangers the addict's life and family relationships but the lives of future generations.

Rescuers from God come into our lives in the most dire of times.

By now, I can tell you are sick of all this bad news and are ready for the good news. Naturally, there is good news because God always has His own plans for our safety from our self-destructive blue blankets.

It should come as no surprise that when God designed "rescue and recovery operations," He would also train and provide the rescuers. He can rescue those of His children who hold tightly to this particular blue blanket. And He chooses to work through His people as He has throughout the ages.

Rescuers from God come into our lives in the most dire of times. They come in different genders and with different mission statements. But make no mistake about it, God sends them. They are missionaries such as the great Hudson Taylor, who opened up inland China to the gospel, or Florence Nightingale, who set new standards of nursing and rescued thousands of the sick and the dying.

There was Dr. Sam Shoemaker, the spiritual pioneer and seed-founder of Alcoholics Anonymous, who was one of God's great rescuers for this blue blanket. This man conceived the idea of support groups years before the idea became popular in the 1960s and 1970s. As Bruce Larson noted in the introduction of *Extraordinary Living for Ordinary Men,* "He (Sam Shoemaker) believed that two drunks who found sobriety through the power of surrender to a living Christ could start a fellowship (support group) that could help other drunks."[1] Out of that concept the "Twelve-Step" program blossomed and is still branching out, vibrantly growing, rescuing, saving, and giving people new lives and new purposes.

God commissions His children to the rescue. He works through us to save, to liberate, and to snatch the afflicted away from death's bony hand.

If our blue blanket is alcohol, drugs, or prescription pills, then I believe our first move toward wholeness is, as the greeting goes at A.A.: "Hi, my name is (fill in the blank). I am a (fill in the addiction)."

Then, listen for God's welcoming "Hi" back to us through His children. This is unconditional love in action. The tip-off that it's God who is working through His children comes from the noticeable absence of human judgment, rejection, or criticism. When love like this is practiced, blue blankets can be folded up and put away.

The Blue Blanket of Analyzing and Agonizing over Our Past

Even though it was years ago, I remember the look in the woman's eyes who stood before me after one of my meetings. She had poured out a litany of grievous events from a thirty-year span. It was full of sorrow and heartache. Her mother died when she was eleven; her college scholarship fell through ending her dream of teaching; her first marriage produced two children but ended in divorce; her second marriage left her a widow; she spent years seeking help from one counselor after another; her teenaged son committed suicide. I wept with her and felt helplessly inadequate to offer solutions for such overwhelming pain. The woman had suffered more than an ordinary or normal share of tragedies. Then, suddenly, I was aware that she was looking into my face and asking, "Tell me what to do. Give me something to help me."

Thousands of times I've stood on this scary spot, looking into the tear-stained face of a woman, wondering what possible help or hope I could give. But then just as many times before—I know of no other way to explain it—I recognized the familiar inner quickening of the Holy Spirit in my soul, and I risked saying what I believed needed to be said.

Sensing strongly that the woman had carried and clutched the weighty past for so long, she was drained of all spiritual, physical, and emotional energy and guessing that she was emotionally fragile, I began by simply listening to her. When it was my turn, I talked with her about some basic things I felt might comfort her and give her some hope for recovery. In my three-point list, I gave her (1) several suggestions, (2) a minimal maintenance plan for her sanity, and (3) a long-term option for her future hurts.

Perhaps I was overconfident in my counsel, or maybe I was suffering from a touch of pride. I remember, however, being struck by the woman's response. She listened, or at least I thought she did, and then she said, "But I wish you'd tell me one, two, three, what to do."

"But I did," I replied.

"No," she said, "I want to hear step one, step two, and step three."

"I did. I gave you one, two, three," I said again and then repeated the points.

"No, no. I want one, two, and three." And with that she walked away from me shaking her head and saying, "I wish someone would just tell me what to do."

Certainly my three-point plan or my lack of professional counseling skills may have terminated our conversation. Or maybe she was more seriously ill than I thought, but because of some encounters with other women, I tend to think that she was a person who was avoiding the pain of her life through snugly wrapping up in her blue blanket. And her blue blanket was constantly analyzing and reviewing her past, never doing anything about her painful memories, or taking any action, only examining what went wrong, why it went wrong, who was to blame. She seemed determined to spend life continually agonizing over her regrets and what ifs and if onlys.

Like that woman, we can use our catastrophic childhood or wretched past as a blue blanket to cover our heads and minds. That way, we don't have to get beyond the past and move on to what should be done now. We feel safe and snug hiding under this blue blanket.

It is occasionally and appropriately called "navel gazing." In this great escape hatch for dealing with yesterday's pain, we can endlessly review and reconstruct our past and find someone or something to blame for it all. This blue blanket can isolate us from people, relationships, and the world around us, sequestering us like a jury in deadlock, closing all the doors and windows of our lives and leaving us emotionally alienated and well on our way to living as lonely recluses.

We can take our cue from David to come from beneath this blue blanket. With this incredible past, which went from shepherding and flute playing, to king, adulterer, and murderer, David had every "reason" to hide beneath his blue blanket. Perhaps for a period of time he did, but when we read his words, "I have chosen the way of truth" (Ps. 119:30 KJV), we know that at some time or place David decided on an attitude change. He chose to move up and out of that hideous past and to lay aside the familiar comfort of this blue blanket. He gave himself freedom and permission to deal with the day's opportunities and challenges.

I am in no way suggesting that people with painful pasts can heal emotionally by simply "deciding" to have a positive attitude about it or that they should not talk about and deal with their pasts. However, when the talking becomes a rut instead of a bridge to recovery, the blue blanket of navel gazing takes control. If we are strong enough, we should make the choice to put down that blue blanket, move into the present and on to the future. If we've tried without success until we're practically hopeless, we should find professional help and trust God to use His "doctors" to turn our heart and face forward. Otherwise, the blue blanket of forever analyzing our past will only hold us more tightly in its grip.

Now, for my blue blanket: the one that is most difficult for me to nail down on paper.

The Blue Blanket of Good-bye

Flying fully unfurled, yet held taut in the hurricane winds over the tallest cloud-covered pinnacles of my soul, used to be the flag of my blue blanket.

The flag represented heaven, the country I've always called home: that perpetually exquisite, glorified, and safe place; that wonderful place that is eternally free from death, war, hunger, poverty, brokenness, tears, loneliness, and pain-saturated nights.

I began fantasizing about heaven, this real but unseen country, when I was a little girl listening to my mother read aloud the classic story *The Pilgrim's Progress*. Established early in my mind was this story of Christian, who along with all of us, had begun a rather adventurous journey here on earth and was headed always in the general direction of our ultimate destination: heaven.

From hearing that story, I learned to believe as we walked the road of life it would at times be cold and snow clogged, hot and dusty, or filled with occasional steep inclines to traverse or cliffs to scale or crevices to jump over. I believed that perhaps the street pavement would be rough with potholes and sometimes a path or a bridge would be washed away by a flood. But all in all, nothing seriously harmful or bad could happen to us on our journey here to keep us out of heaven. After all, Christian made it; so will we. Even if death were to speed up the trip, that would only get us home sooner. Wasn't that our supreme goal?

My mother's enthusiasm for life gave me the optimistic courage of hope, and I felt sure that no matter how difficult the path, my journey would be a brief one—over like a flash of light or a snap of a finger and then, like Christian, I'd be home!

Good-bye, Earth!

Hello, Heaven!

However, on my way to heaven a funny thing happened. I grew up.

That nice little path of learning, that quiet tree-lined street of experience, and gently curving highway of life, love, and relationships were more like

no-exit alleys,

costly toll roads and bridges,

detours and alternate routes,

traffic snarled inner-city grid patterns,

fog- or ice-bound interstate highways, and

accidents on neighborhood streets or busy turnpikes which

crippled, maimed, or killed.

This kind of mental growing up and awareness to the heartsick pain of our journey knocks our childhood's naiveté and wonder straight out of us. Depression, situational or chronic, sets in; and given "significant losses," as the psychiatrists call them, we become prime candidates for the blue blanket of the "good-bye syndrome."

As I checked off my significant losses—death indiscriminately carrying off so many of my precious loved ones, the force of physical pain eroding and stripping away the last vestiges of energy and strength from me, and a pulverizing divorce, fragmenting and crushing what was left of my emotions—believe me, I was sick of the road. I was quite ready to trash my suitcase and never set foot outside my doorway again. "I'm not Christian, and this is not *Pilgrim's Progress*," I thought.

I began to visualize, both in my dreams at night and in the clear light of day, the flag of my blue blanket. It grew more tempting by the hour to go home to heaven before something else dark and foreboding took place.

Emotionally and tentatively, I stretched out my hand toward the blue blanket of good-bye and I was amazed. I knew I didn't want to kill myself. There's nothing glamorous or reputable about suicide. Nor did I want to be an unnamed statistic. I just wanted to leave behind all the grief pain. I wanted to *get out!* I wanted God to call me home to Him in heaven, quickly and accidentally, if at all possible.

In the early 1980s, when I touched my blue blanket, a surge of warm soothing anesthetic comfort would run through my whole system. It provided two words: *release* and *escape.* I easily embraced the blanket, and before I knew it, I was addicted. Soon I was like a little child again, never even thinking of going anywhere or spending a day without her blue blanket.

The well-documented statistics say that I'm not alone in clutching my blue blanket of good-bye. It is estimated that one out of ten people (that's 20 million Americans alone) suffer through debilitating episodes of chronic depression each year. And because of their significant losses, more than one million of those twenty million depressed souls will consider and reconsider suicide each year.

Years ago, I wrote of battling my depression and handling my suicidal tendencies. In my immature, gullible state of mind, I thought that depression, once licked stayed licked. Wrong. Unfortunately, unless we are in touch with our emotions and aware of our feelings, it's virtually impossible to assess the havoc that depression ushers into the soul of a person. More recently, I wrote about physical and emotional pain in *Silent September* (Austin, TX: Balcony). My insight about depression has significantly matured.

About the time I wrote *Silent September,* Keith Miller and I were collaborating on composing some songs for me to sing on a vocal album, *For People Who Don't Hear the Music Anymore.* I found understanding Keith's lyrics, especially "Short Cut Home," easy. His words exactly described my deepest heartfelt thoughts, and though the words *Blue Blanket* were not mentioned, Keith was sensitive and clearly heard my inner despair during our phone conversations. Later, he sent me the lyrics to "Short Cut Home." I put them to music and added a chorus. It goes like this:

Short Cut Home

Remember when I was so young
So full of faith and coy,
The world all free from pain and doubt
A kaleidoscope of joy;
And then there came that little pain

The one I hardly knew,
An ache, a knife, and silent screams,
And now my life seems through.
I know I should not stop my days
Leave family and friends,
But something's snapped, the pain has won
So this must be the end;
I'm coming home to be with You
Or should I really try to stay?
Could You have meaning in such pain,
Oh God, I want to fly away.
I'm coming home to be with You.
There's nothing left to give,
Or can I live my pain for You
Dear Lord, I'll try to live;
So I guess I'll stay just one more day
And handle what time will bring,
I'll live my life and give again
But this one song I'll still sing.
Chorus
I wanna come home and be with You
dear Jesus,
I wanna come home and see Your face;
I wanna come home and be with You,
dear Jesus,
For I'm sick and tired of this lonely,
painful place.
I'm sick and tired of this place,
And I'm tired of the race
And I can't stand the pace
And I wanna come home
And be with you.[2]

The emotional pain and depression I was feeling was a few worlds beyond anything I'd experienced. I kept trying to find reasons for staying "one more day," as my daughter Laurie had said in *Silent September,* but my homesick feelings for heaven's shores only increased. There was hardly a moment that I did not frantically clutch my blue blanket and dream of how exquisite it would be to have the psalmist's "wings of a dove" and fly away home to be with God.

I'm afraid when I explained my feeling to family, close friends, or associates, very few could believe, understand, or take me seriously. I do not find fault with or blame them, but say this now because hindsight tells me this truth: Seldom can anyone fathom the mind of a person who actually begs and pleads with God to end their earthly journey. Unless, of course, they themselves have begged and pleaded.

Some people said I was just acting like a spoiled child to get my own way. Another group suggested that my ego wanted attention. Others ordered me to "snap out of it," and one pastor laughed when I told him I was suicidal as if I'd told him an amusing story he could use in the next Sunday morning service. Appallingly, a loved one and a few of my brothers and sisters in the faith suggested to me (and to others) that perhaps suicide was the answer. As they all agreed, "It would certainly settle things quickly and simplify the whole situation . . . and better than divorce."

This blue blanket may sound like today's newspaper. I've written nothing you don't already know. You were the people who, at my speaking engagements whispered in my ear or have written, "My blue blanket is the same as yours." Or maybe you're the woman who came to me after hearing my talk on *My Blue Blanket* and wept as she said, "My husband went out to the car but he asked me to tell you he's got the same blue blanket as you do. Would you remember him in prayer?"

We who are suffering from such depths of depression are not hell-bent on killing ourselves out of insanity or to get revenge or attention, nor do we have some superficial motive designed to make "someone sorry" for what they did to us. No, unfortunately this blue blanket is hugged tightly to our hearts and minds because we sincerely believe we have no more tolerance for life and its painful journey.

We who have been there, and are perhaps there right now, know the incredible and unthinkable truth of this woman's words when she wrote to me not long ago, "Every night I pray and ask the Lord to please not let me wake up *here* in the morning." Homeward to heaven simply becomes the Christian's national anthem, especially when it feels like every bone in our body is broken. Taking one more step feels impossible, and frantically, we long for this earthly journey to end.

"I'm calling Dr. Pannabecker," Francis informed me one morning. He had physically interfered with my attempt to self-destruct the previous night. After he had spent much of the night holding me in his arms as I mentally leaped back and forth over the dark chasm between living and dying, he decided to intervene and get me help.

One moment I'd calmly state, "I want to stay here with you, finish the journey, and carry out our mission statement as I believe God wants." The next instant, I'd plunge into the bottomless pit of depression and be on the edge of hysterics. Frantically, I'd say, "But I can't go on . . . I just can't . . . the pain of everything that has happened and that keeps on happening is too great to bear . . . there's no hope. I've no tolerance for these levels of intense pain." Then, I'd weep and whisper, "Good-bye, darling"—once more vaulting over the great chasm. Heaven was all I could think. If only I could be released . . . heaven.

When he arrived at our house, the tall, lanky doctor walked into our living room having heard only a brief synopsis from Francis about the depression that was oozing out of me. Immediately, he went straight to the heart of the matter. Before he sat down, he abruptly asked, "Joyce, why don't you stop running to your escape hatch?" I hadn't the faintest idea of what he was talking about. "My what?"

Again he was direct. "Your escape hatch. Everyone has one but you can let go of it. So why don't you?"

My escape hatch was my instant desire to say good-bye and my desperate desire to go home to heaven and God. My escape hatch was the place to which I ran when the pain was too excruciating to endure any longer.

I sat down on our couch, stunned. All I could think was, *Stop running to my escape hatch? Give it up? My security blanket? My real source of comfort?* Here I was, teetering on the edge of sheer certifiable madness and quite capable of ending my life and this doctor was asking me to give up the thing that over the years had been my sane and soothing antidote to the insanity of my journey. *Is this man serious?*

He was, and as if he'd read my thoughts, Dr. Pannabecker, with a sense of quiet urgency, began laying out several important concepts for me. Perhaps you will find them important (even appropriate) for you too.

"Joyce, perhaps it feels easier for you to deal with being dead rather than having to deal with the pain of being alive, or the realities of life and what needs to be done in your life." They were stone and steel words, hard to hear, but they were so kindly spoken and rang with such truth I was compelled to listen. He went on.

"If you let go of your escape hatch, it's almost a paradox. For at the point of letting go, your energy is available to deal with the problem rather than always being used to run away from the conflict." He paused. He riveted his attention on me while waiting for my answer. When I remained silent, Dr. Pannabecker probed again, "Why don't you give up your escape hatch?"

"I'll have to think about it," I finally said. "I'll give you an answer when I can."

It was a feeble reply on my part, I'll admit, but I had the feeling that somehow the good doctor had handed me the opportunity to catch a wild tiger by its tail and then, against all odds, tame it. But I wasn't sure I wanted to catch the tiger, much less tame it.

During the two weeks that followed our first session, I began peeling back the layers of my soul. Desperately, I wanted truth to emerge, but I found I didn't want to give up my escape hatch. I didn't want to let go of my special friend, my blue blanket. I spent a good deal of that time prying under the layers of my soul, trying to find out why I couldn't or wouldn't let go of my blanket.

I reasoned that when I held tightly to my blue blanket I didn't have to face any conflicts or take any responsibility for them. That felt good. I didn't have to deal with any ugliness in people, demolished relationships, or failed situations. That felt good. I didn't even have to forgive or pray for any of my enemies. That felt wonderful. I could just disappear into the folds of my blue blanket and fade away. Frankly, when I wrapped my battle-scarred self in such a nurturing and healing blanket, it gave large measures of comfort and relief to my soul. Or was I just deluding myself about the whole thing?

Each time I came close to the decision place of hanging on to or letting go of my blue blanket, the war within me would rage on anew. Then my mind's eye would see Dr. Pannabecker and I'd hear him calmly asking, "Why don't you stop running to it?"

Slowly, I started contemplating what my life might be like if, when pain overwhelmed me and threatened to annihilate my sanity, I let go of my blanket. What if I folded it up out of my mind and heart and set it aside?

Those thoughts frightened me at first. They deeply disturbed and threatened my security. I could scarcely imagine not running to my escape hatch or not hugging my blue blanket of good-bye. But scarier still was the thought that if my journey got any rougher (as I knew it probably would) I could end up wasting a formidable amount of my life's energy forever. I could spend the rest of my time on earth running away from conflicts instead of dealing with them. I could hug the blue blanket until I really did take my life or until God chose to call me home, whichever happened first. But I had to ask myself was that really what, in my heart of hearts, I wanted to do?

Remember, I said earlier that blue blankets are not necessarily harmful in and of themselves but when a blue blanket is abusive and dangerous to one's health, or ruins and destroys other people, then it is very deadly. That is when the blanket, not you, is controlling your life.

I knew my blue blanket was the deadly type, and I decided I didn't want this beloved blue blanket of mine to own me. I had to face the fact that I wasn't an innocent two year old with an equally innocent blue blanket, just wanting the simple security and the warm feelings it gave the little boy in the grocery store. I also understood that I needed a radical attitude change if I was ever going to be in control of my life instead of that blanket.

On the third session we had with Dr. Pannabecker, I told him I was letting go. I was willing to stop running to my escape hatch. I would lay aside my blue blanket. It had to go.

Mentally, I took my tattered, faded, and much-loved blue blanket out of the living room of my life. I folded it up and tucked it away on the top shelf in the closet. I know it's there, but my heart and spirit are a lot healthier now that I have deliberately chosen to put my blue blanket away. I am not a child. I am a responsible adult, dealing, head on, with the pain of reality as I see what needs to be done in my life.

Dr. Pannabecker was right, it was easier to deal with the idea of my being dead and in heaven than with that of my staying alive and trying to work things out. I've always been more comfortable running away from pain than standing bravely in the gap.

Not too long after these painful yet life-giving sessions, an opportunity was presented to me which ordinarily would have sent my panic-stricken heart into a tailspin of depression. Usually, I would have frantically reached for my blue blanket and my bottle of saved-up pills, but I stopped midway to the closet and asked myself if hugging my blanket and retreating to the dark places behind my soul was what I really wanted.

No, I think not. Definitely not.

The journey here on earth seems to get more dangerous with the years and there are no shortcuts home. But in reading and pondering Dr. Viktor Frankl's question to the survivors of Auschwitz concentration camp, "Why *didn't* you take your life in the death camp?" I've taken a different view of these traveling days and my old blue blanket.

Those 1940s death camp survivors who turned away from starving themselves or decided against running into the wall so they'd be shot chose another way. They looked for and found one thread, one slender thread that bound them to keep living rather than giving in to dying. Some chose to stay one more day because there was a child living safely outside of Nazi Germany that they wanted to see once more. One man was a medical doctor and a scholar who had written eleven books of a twelve-book series before his internment and he wanted to live to go home and finish the series. Others had different reasons, but they chose to live, even at Auschwitz. They put away their blue blankets of good-bye because the threads of unfinished business, slim as they might have been, kept their sense of self-preservation alive.

The threads which keep my blue blanket put away in the closet are very real and precious to me, even on the days (like a few weeks ago) when we were at a Christian radio station. I was stunned by the sharp pain of an unexpected encounter with a couple of individuals who did their best to wound me into believing I should leave the field of Christian writing.

Hours later when I was crying into Francis' shoulder, I found myself saying, "It's really okay. I'll be all right, darling, but do you mind if I tell you that I feel like opening the closet door and just looking at my blue blanket for a little bit?" As I said before, I've chosen (and it was not a quick simplistic decision to make) to fold up my blue blanket and put it away in the closet. I've got too many threads to ignore, too many precious reasons for staying, too many hurting people in crisis needing recovery and too many things crying out to be finished before I leave and go home.

If you stood face to face with me right now and you said you were at the end of your rope, and unless something extraordinary happened or some miracle of God took place that you were grabbing your blue blanket of good-bye and leaving, I'd tell you these three things:

1. I believe you. I understand your despair and I don't question your motives nor blame you for your thoughts or your actions. I love you and I wait with you.

2. I'd urge you to look around you to find one thread, no matter how slim or fragile, that calls out begging for you to stay your hand. Look for one thread that provides you with the energy to

continue your journey, to endure and to press on no matter how difficult or insane that may seem.

3. I'd ask you the same question Dr. Pannabecker asked me, "Why don't you stop running to your escape hatch?" Why not choose to fold up your blanket, lay it aside on the top shelf of the closet and shut the door? Why not?

No matter what our blue blanket may be—sleeping, eating, reading, telephoning, watching TV, movies, busy-ness, alcohol, drugs, pills, analyzing the past, saying good-bye, or some private unnamed blanket—no matter how safe or how lethal it is, no matter what intensity of addiction it has for you, and no matter whether it's real or perceived, it's not too late to put away that blue blanket.

I pray that these brief words will help you to choose, as arduous and rough as it may be, to lay aside and let go of your blue blanket, especially the blanket which may set up the standards for your life, which may enslave your heart and mind, and which may deplete your reserves of mental, emotional, and spiritual energy leaving you too exhausted, too hopeless, and too despairing to press on with your journey.

And one last word before I close this chapter: I am choosing to trust God for all of us that He will be our beautiful blanket of comfort for today and for all our tomorrows here on earth before we see Him face to face at journey's end.

In His time, God really does make all things beautiful, especially our decision to lay aside our blue blankets, to get up to hold on to that slender thread, walk the path, to carry the cross, and to continue the journey.

Symptoms of a Lost Self

*M*ore and more women today are realizing we never got to be the
*woman we were intended to be. Somehow we lost ourselves. We cast
off parts of ourself as we grew up to make ourselves more acceptable
or loveable—or maybe we just gave ourselves away to other people.
But lost is lost, and it feels the same—disconnected and drifting.*

In this chapter from Who Am I? *I describe the feeling of the lost self.
It has happened to me. It has happened to millions of women. If you
recognize this person, know that you are not intended to live your life
lost in a fog or lost in others. Know that there is a way out. And the
way out is the journey inward—to reconnect your self to your emotions, to God, and to others.*

Elizabeth Baker
Who Am I?

I remember the first time I became aware of that empty, isolating
fog. I was almost thirty. There had come a rare snow to Texas, and I
was standing by the kitchen window watching my three children play
with their daddy around a newly made snowman. I could hear them

laugh, but it left my heart strangely numb. It was not that my heart was sad, it was just cold.

I stood there and tried to remember the last time I had laughed. I couldn't recall. Oh, there had been times when my throat gave out the sounds called laughter, and times when I could feel my face grin. But it was all surface. Inside, nothing was touched. Nothing was alive. I had lost my sense of identity. Somewhere in the daily rush, self had died.

I wasn't sure when it had happened. The deadness had crept into my life like a mist. Slowly, quietly, it settled over me.

At the time I thought it strange that I could not pinpoint the day the fog rolled in. But now as a professional counselor, I know that most of us who experience this phenomenon are not sure when the mist came or even when we first noticed it. There is just a moment when we wake up and realize a fog has moved in and self has been swallowed up and disappeared.

There are many words in vogue these days used to describe the phenomenon of a lost self. Sometimes we call it an identity crisis, or we may say we feel empty, searching, agitated, or alone. We may feel we don't belong or that deep inside we are not alive anymore.

Some may wonder if they are having a midlife crisis, and others suspect we are just plain going crazy. But a lost sense of self seldom has anything to do with true psychological pathology. There is no pill to cure it. And though feelings such as those described above may be a part of various psychiatric disorders, the feelings themselves do not mean a person is "going crazy." Seeing a counselor or pastor may help if someone is caught in that difficult to describe fog, but most often the hurting individual is both sane and normal.

Below you will find some statements that others have used to describe this separated, lost feeling. Check those boxes that most nearly describe how you currently feel. As you work, remember, THIS IS NOT A TEST. There are no right or wrong answers. You will not receive a grade, and you are not being judged. There is no rule that says you can't change your mind or erase something or make qualifying notes by your check marks. The ONLY purpose for this exercise is that of self-discovery.

1. I often feel like an actor performing my life rather than living it.

2. I know in my head that God forgives me, but I have never felt clean deep inside.

3. I believe that I am very different from other people.

4. When I am in a mall or another public place, I like to study the people around me, but I don't think of myself as one of them.

5. I am very comfortable teaching or giving advice or leading, but I am uncomfortable relating to people as peers.

6. I cry or laugh easily, but it feels shallow and unreal.

7. I feel OK as long as I am serving or complimenting others but find it very difficult when others are serving or complimenting me.

8. I am confused inside and don't know what I want from life anymore.

9. I have continual doubts about my salvation and acceptance by God.

10. I feel distant from God, and He has never comforted me as He has others.

11. I am lonely even in a crowd.

12. The only reason my friends stay around me is for what I can do for them.

13. I believe God will have to do a special job on me because my sins are different from or worse than those of other people.

14. I cry for no reason.

15. I explode for no reason.

The Feelings

I suppose if there is one word to best describe the phenomenon I want to address, it would be "disconnected." A lost sense of self creates a drifting feeling that is instantly identifiable to anyone who has been there. It is a feeling of life going on day after day as it always has, but we don't seem to connect with the flow.

The loss of self can create an isolation that is so intense it is almost palpable. We move through the days like robots performing in a bad play that someone else has written. Cindy Bailey was able to express her feelings about being isolated from others through poetry.

Glass Wall

Surrounded by a glass wall
Seen only by myself
This cool exterior protects me,
Keeps me safe.
Holds the world at a distance
That I might observe it,
Yet not experience the pain
Of its vulnerability.

Surrounded by a glass wall.
Seen only by myself.
Your words I hear plainly, clearly;
The wall does not drown them out.
Inside this wall I'm screaming,
But it is lost and unheard,
Reverberating within my little glass world.

Surrounded by a glass wall
Seen only by myself.
Clenching my fist in desperation,
I reach out to pound on the wall with my fist.
Ask for help, reach out—
But I resist;
Terrified by the sound of breaking glass.

I sometimes use Cindy's poem in therapy sessions. I will ask someone to read it and then ask them to tell me about a time when they felt the wall between themselves and others. On a separate piece of paper write about your own response to the idea of glass walls.

We build walls to protect ourselves from pain. Our basic temperament and family background determine the method we will use in the construction process.

1. Charlene is the life of every party. The attention is always on her as she gives out a steady stream of chatter. Many people think

they know Charlene, but in truth, few if any people know her. Charlene uses the high energy stream of words to turn attention away from her real feelings. She is hiding behind words.

2. Deborah has developed vanishing into a fine art. She smiles pleasantly, but seldom speaks. She is easily overlooked, almost fading into the woodwork if there is a crowd. She is always on the outside looking in and would panic if drawn into the center of attention.

3. Beth has always been large, but she gained an additional fifty pounds about ten years ago when she went through a divorce. She has lost the weight twice since then, but both times her anxiety level got so high she was put on medication to control the panic. Beth can relate well and be somewhat relaxed around others as long as she has her pounds to keep people away and hide her sexuality.

4. Jennifer is a classic workaholic. She is constantly involved in one project after another and has little time for relationships. She avoids her husband. Sex died years ago. She feels inadequate with the children, and although she buys them toys and proudly has their picture made, she seldom really relates to them and prefers to let someone else do the disciplining. Jennifer will give her family anything . . . except her heart.

5. Joan leads a double life. Part of her shows up at work each day and even goes to church a few times each year. But a separate and very large part of her has a cocaine addiction. Her husband has caught on and is threatening to take the kids and leave but even he has no idea of how bad things are. Cocaine is both Joan's master and her hiding place. She can take a hit of coke and check out of life for at least a little while. She can disconnect from painful emotions and the bills and the responsibilities of a family. She can literally make the world go away.

6. Carol has a mouth like acid. She will always find a reason why someone is unworthy or in need of correction. From her bitter, critical viewpoint, every church she has ever been a part of has disappointed her and failed to measure up to God's expectations, every friend has wronged her grievously, every family

member is alienated from her, no one in her life has understood her, everyone has always betrayed her.

These are only a few of the many different methods humans have used to build walls. Charlene with her wall of continual talking, Deborah with her wall of shyness, Beth with her wall of fat, Jennifer with her wall of work, Joan with her wall of addiction, and Carol with her wall of bitter criticism, have all found favored ways to retreat from others, self, and God.

Search for the "New" You

When the walls go up, the fog settles in. We lose ourselves inside that tiny glass world of walls, and the emptiness inside drives us to try and find a way back to life again.

One solution that is often tried is to search for a new person to replace the empty one we have become. It is no wonder that we seek for this "new" person because the news media has been pounding us with the idea for years.

Just take a look at the supermarket tabloids. They continually tantalize us with promises of transforming us into a "new" person. They claim that this diet, that fashion, leaving home to get a job, having a full makeover, having an affair, or going to a spa will solve our problems and make us "new." And, when we are made new we will be in very good company. I have been invited to meet the "new" Liz Taylor a dozen or more times. Even Princess Di has been announced as "new" three times that I can count. But the problem with this tabloid solution is that it doesn't work.

The truth is that we have only one self and no matter how much new we put on the outside, the core of isolation will follow us.

Many women have tried to find themselves by rearranging the present. Some go so far as to change lifestyles completely in a frantic effort to live authentically and achieve a sense of identity: A new diet, changing marriage partners, running away from home, having an affair, switching careers, changing churches, buying a sports car. All have been tried. And all have been unsuccessful.

It is easy to understand why the tabloids are making money with this marketing tool. It hurts to be locked alone in a glass bubble and lost in a fog, and it is logical to assume that a "new" self will fix our problem and set us free.

But the truth is that we have only one self and no matter how much new we put on the outside, the core of isolation will follow us.

Three Areas of Separation

When we lose our sense of self, we lose the connector that would have linked us to at least three vital relationships: Personal emotions, others, and God. If we want to become alive again, we will have to risk the pain of examining and reconnecting life to these three areas.

Go back over the statements in exercise on pages 90–91 and give each a number from 0 to 5 depending on how strongly you feel that statement accurately describes where you are now. Jot those numbers in the margins of that exercise by each check mark before you continue reading.

Statements 1, 6, 8, 14, and 15 correspond to our separateness from self. Statements 3, 4, 5, 7, and 12 correspond to a separateness from others; and statements 2, 9, 10, 11, and 13 correspond to our separateness from God and His cleansing from sin.

Record your scores below, placing the number you gave each statement in the blank spaces next to the numbers and then adding the scores.

Separate from self:	**Separate from others:**	**Separate from God:**
1. ☐	3. ☐	2. ☐
6. ☐	4. ☐	9. ☐
8. ☐	5. ☐	10. ☐
14. ☐	7. ☐	11. ☐
15. ☐	12. ☐	13. ☐
☐Total	☐Total	☐Total

Which area did you score highest in? Do your scores reflect how you feel? If not, in which area do you believe you are the most disconnected and alone?

Separated from Personal Emotions

When we lose our identity, we also strangely become lost from ourselves. A gulf that we cannot bridge separates our emotions from the reality around us. Emotions may pop up and vanish or sit silently for years and smolder without names. We don't know why they come or why they go. We can even become isolated from our own bodies. We look in a mirror and a stranger looks back.

Inside our cold, glass bubbles we vacillate between intently feeling about tiny matters and total numbness. We may completely "lose it" when someone cuts in front of us in traffic and flood the aisle with tears during a movie but feel little or nothing during times of crisis or family joy.

Perhaps you have experienced the strangeness of your head and your heart traveling in two different worlds. Have there been times your emotions didn't seem to match the circumstances in the outside world? Write about it below.

Separated from God

When we lose ourselves, we also lose our connection with God. We still know He is up there. Somewhere. Maybe.

But, whatever the case, we know we can't seem to reach Him anymore. There is no sense of being forgiven and maybe even no sense of needing forgiveness. His presence is lost in the mist. We hear others talk about how they feel Him near or how they get answers to their prayers, but we are different, isolated, alone.

We are also isolated from the Christian family even though we may still attend services each week. We sit in the congregation and we are alone. And although our American culture and many of our church denominations encourage us never to get more intimate with our Christian brothers and sisters than to look at the back of their neck on Sunday morning, something in us tells us there ought to be more. But we know that "more" is not part of our spiritual experience.

When we have lost our identity, we often feel as though we have lost God. We sympathize with David when he cried, "My God, my

God, why have You forsaken me? Why are You so far from helping me, and from the words of my groaning? O my God, I cry in the day time, but You do not hear, and in the night season, and am not silent" (Ps. 22:1–2).

If you have experienced feelings of separation from God, write about it below. He is the Lord God Almighty, and it is not a good idea to either shake our fist at Him or turn our back on Him; yet it is also true that we can't tell Him anything about our hearts that He doesn't already know. Honestly saying what we feel will not surprise or upset Him, and it can be the first step in our healing.

Separated from Others

When we do not know our selves and cannot find our God, how can we expect to connect with others? We feel that something about us is wrong and needs to be hidden. We don't connect on an honest, comfortable level with others because we are frightened of the pain that might occur if we were rejected by them. We can't risk exposure, so we put on a plastic front and the circle of isolation becomes complete as we retreat within our world of glass walls.

Shame

The force that drives us to retreat behind walls is most often shame. We are embarrassed. We don't want to risk exposure to others or God and we don't want to face emotions that we may find unpleasant. We make a judgment on ourselves, and we don't like the verdict. This verdict has been based on two sources of evidence.

The first source of evidence is from the outside. Someone tells us by word or deed that we are bad or lacking or less than adequate. When we believe this external judgment and internalize it, a feeling of shame will result.

The second source of evidence comes entirely from inside. We set up a standard of what "should" and "ought" to be. We hear this internal source in the private conversations that go on in our heads as we talk with ourselves continually through the day. When phrases like "You are so stupid," "They are laughing at you," "You should have known better" continually dance around in our mind, the poison of shame will slowly force us back into an isolated shell and the fog will quickly follow.

The Way Home

Remember the old "Dobie Gillis" show from the 1960s? Its central characters were Dobie—a clean cut, girl crazy adolescent—and his sidekick, Maynard. Maynard was what we called at the time a "beatnik." Complete with beads, sandaled feet, and goatee, he was a comical character who avoided work at all cost and was not noted for his intelligence.

One day Maynard informed Dobie that he would soon be leaving on a long trip. Many real life rock stars of that time were making pilgrimages to the Far East to consult with gurus about the meaning of life. Maynard had decided that he, too, needed to go to a mountain in Tibet to search for himself. There on the mountain he would speak with the ancient wise men and find out who he really was.

Dobie replied with candor, "Maynard, you will never find yourself on a mountain in Tibet." "Why not?" asked his friend. "Because you didn't lose yourself on a mountain in Tibet," the teenage sage replied.

I always get a little uneasy when Hollywood says something profound, but occasionally accidents do happen. It is biblically and psychologically true: We will never find ourselves by searching for a new self out there somewhere. There is no "new" us on a mountain in Tibet.

God does have a solution for the phenomenon of fog and walls and a lost, drifting self, but it will not be found by searching outside ourselves. It is found by searching within. We must know ourselves and accept ourselves, then, once we have a firm hold on who we are, we give ourselves away to Him. When that happens, the fog will lift, the walls will come down, and we will be free.

We shall not cease from exploration
And the end of all our exploring
Will be to arrive where we started
And know the place for the first time.

T. S. Eliot
"Little Gidding" from the Four Quartets

Chapter

6

Why Am I Under All This Stress?

or most of us, stress is something we feel probably every day. Yet we've found that stress can also be a symptom of deeper problems. How stressed out are you? Do you know what causes your stress? In this chapter, you can test your stress level to find out if it is minor, moderate, major, unhealthy, or traumatic. We'll also help you pinpoint the source of your stress and give you some helpful suggestions to correct your stress level if you need to.

In our book, Get a Life Without the Strife, we provide a series of diagnostic tests to help find the root causes of emotional problems that may have your life running a lot like a car in need of a tuneup. To understand this chapter better, it may help for us to define the four personality types we refer to throughout our book. The four descriptive words we use for them will help you decide which one rules your life: Do you need to be perfect, powerful, popular, or peaceful? Check the charts throughout this chapter to see which one (or a healthful combination of two) suits you best.

Fred and Florence Littauer
Get a Life Without the Strife

About the Personality Types

The popular Sanguine wants to have fun.
The powerful Choleric wants to be in control.
The perfect Melancholy wants everything done properly.
The peaceful Phlegmatic seeks serenity and a stress-free life.

Stress became a byword in the eighties and has now firmly settled into the vocabulary of the nineties. Some stress is good. Some is bad. And often we don't know the difference. Picture a large rubberband lying on your desk, limp and useless. It doesn't become functional until it is stretched and put around some loose objects. But if we test it too far the band will break. There's only so much pressure it can handle.

Now look at our lives. To be totally without stress, we would have to lounge in bed all day and have servants wait on us because the minute we arise we put stress on ourselves. If we get up late, we put on more stress. If we run out of gas on the way to work, our patience is really stretched. A certain amount of stress is motivating and some of it is positive, but as with the rubberband, we can never be sure how much stretch we can take before we break. Once the snap comes, it's too late for prevention.

"Stress becomes a problem when it is no longer manageable," wrote Dallas psychiatrist Dr. Doyle Carson. "As problems increase and are not resolved, a person can develop telltale symptoms, including anxiety, irritability, lack of focus, difficulty in sleeping and significant changes in daily routines."[1]

As with all problems the first step is finding the source and being willing to act upon it. The following questions are to help you think about how far you are being stretched. Look at your symptoms now before it's too late. Once you have checked Yes or No on the following questions, we will show you how to evaluate your stress level. We will then divide the areas into categories so you can see what part of your life needs attention first.

Stress Test

Answer each question as to how it applies to your life today. *Leave blank any that do not apply.*

	Yes	No
1. Do you tend to wake up and worry during the night?	____	____
2. Is there someone at work who often makes you feel you're not worth anything?	____	____
3. Do you get nervous when you have to carpool the children home from school?	____	____
4. Do you frequently have headaches?	____	____

5. Are you afraid you may be losing your job or getting laid off soon?   ___ ___

6. Do you tend to get upset with your mate when he or she forgets to do something?   ___ ___

7. Do you tend to feel sexually frustrated in your marriage?   ___ ___

8. Do you tend to pick at your meals or to eat a lot of junk food during the day?   ___ ___

9. Has someone very close to you died within the past year?   ___ ___

10. Do you suffer from PMS?   ___ ___

11. Do you frequently have bad dreams?   ___ ___

12. Do you tend to miss work due to illness more than your coworkers?   ___ ___

13. In high school or college, did you usually "cram" at the last minute for tests or term papers?   ___ ___

14. Are you afraid to ask for a raise even though you know you deserve one?   ___ ___

15. Are you still grieving over someone who died several years ago?   ___ ___

16. Would your children say that you get angry a lot?   ___ ___

17. Do you tend to take on more tasks than you should?   ___ ___

18. Do you find it difficult to forgive people who have been insensitive to your needs?   ___ ___

19. Are you accused of usually being late?   ___ ___

20. Do you have a friend who makes you feel guilty if you don't do what he or she wants you to do?   ___ ___

21. Do you feel that your mate is constantly criticizing you?   ___ ___

22. Do you sometimes feel, *What does it matter, nobody cares about me anyway?*   ___ ___

23. Do you often go to bed exhausted, even though you only finished part of what you needed to do for the day?   ___ ___

24. Do you have an impulse to "get even" when someone cuts you off on the road?   ___ ___

25. Do you complain (or often feel) that your mate doesn't do his or her share of the housework?   ___ ___

26. Are you apt to get panicky or tense when you are in an enclosed or unfamiliar place? _____ _____

27. Would others describe you as a depressed or downcast person? _____ _____

28. Have you gotten violently angry at any time in the past two months? _____ _____

29. Are you presently on any medication for mood elevation or insomnia? _____ _____

30. Have you ever been told you're a workaholic? _____ _____

31. Are you struggling with any compulsions or addictions? _____ _____

32. Are you and your mate apt to have arguments over finances or purchases? _____ _____

33. Do you tend to have dandruff? _____ _____

34. Do you grind your teeth, or have you been told you have TMJ? _____ _____

35. Are you a fingernail biter? _____ _____

36. When the family is going somewhere, are you usually the last one to get in the car? _____ _____

37. Are you apt to use the words "I hate . . . "? _____ _____

38. When you prepare a meal, is it often an emergency, or done in a sense of urgency? _____ _____

39. Are you a "chocoholic"? _____ _____

40. Do you tend to avoid intimate relationships with your mate, and then feel guilty later? _____ _____

41. Are you frequently tired and have less energy than others around you? _____ _____

42. Does any kind of fear tend to control your life? _____ _____

43. Do you have any type of eating disorder? _____ _____

44. Have you been in counseling or therapy, or thought you needed to be? _____ _____

45. Have you ever had dreams of snakes or spiders? _____ _____

46. Do your credit cards tend to be "maxed out"? _____ _____

47. Do you tend to go shopping when you feel depressed? _____ _____

48. Are you a popular Sanguine married to a controlling Melancholy-Choleric? _____ _____

49. Are you afraid your mate may be having an affair? ____ ____

50. Do you often feel defeated when at the end of the month there are still bills to pay but not enough money in the account? ____ ____

Total number of Yes answers checked: ____

Calculating your stress level:

Number of Yes answers you checked ____ multiplied by 2 = ____%

Evaluate your stress level according to the following scores:

0–20 percent, Minor Stress Level

Congratulations! This score indicates your life is probably in balance. You haven't been stretched too far. If you have answered the questions honestly there may not be much to be concerned about. However, by reviewing your Yes answers you may see some areas where you can quickly and easily make some positive changes. Move on to the "Source-of-Stress Analysis." It will help you focus on those specific areas that are contributing to what minimal stress you have.

20–40 percent, Moderate Stress Level

You are above average, but there is probably more stress in your life than you would like to have. Though most stress issues may not be deeply troubling, enough of them warrant digging at the source to bring about some changes and some healing. The "Source-of-Stress Analysis" will enable you to focus on some specific areas.

40–60 percent, Major Stress Level

Your score in this range indicates that significant issues in your life need to be eliminated. Remember, virtually everyone is subject to stress at some time, but your levels indicate you've been stretched too far. Don't be upset, but move on to the "Source-of-Stress Analysis." It will show you some areas where you can begin to improve immediately.

60–80 percent, Unhealthy Stress Level

If your score falls in this range, be very glad you took the time to do this stress test. You already know you've been pulled in too many directions for too long. What you may not have known is that there is hope, and there can be changes in your life, if—and it's a big *if*—you are willing to admit there are problems and if you are willing to put in the effort to bring about changes. The "Source-of-Stress Analysis" will be important for you.

80–100 percent, Traumatic Stress Level

As with the rubberband, you are overstretched, overworked, and overextended. You need relief from your tension. The "Source-of-Stress Analysis" will be important for you.

Your levels of stress are extremely high and you may need the help of an objective and insightful person. Perhaps you should call your pastor, a friend, or a counselor. The sources of some of your present-day stress probably result from unresolved childhood trauma or pain. This possibility is increasingly valid if you have few or limited memories of your childhood years.

If you think your life is in shambles and you often feel depressed, remember that Jesus said, "He has sent Me to heal the broken-hearted, . . . To set at liberty those who are oppressed" (Luke 4:18; see also Isa. 61:1). There is hope for you; help is available. Our Lord can and will heal you . . . if you come to Him! This is not a quick fix but a long-range promise.

Source-of-Stress Analysis

To help you determine the sources of some of your stress, go back to the stress test. For every number that you checked Yes, circle that number wherever it appears below. (For example, if you answered Yes to number 5, put a circle around number 5 wherever it appears on the lines that follow. Some numbers will appear more than once.)

A. Poor Scheduling or Planning: 13, 17, 19, 23, 25, 30, 36, 38

B. Physical Problems: 8, 12, 23, 41

C. Financial Difficulty: 5, 32, 46, 47, 50

D. Marital Stress: 6, 16, 21, 25, 40, 48, 49

E. Low Self-worth: 2, 14, 17, 22, 27, 30, 44

F. Work-Related Stress: 2, 5, 12, 14

G. General Tension: 1, 3, 4, 5, 9, 10, 29, 33, 34, 35, 37

H. Depression: 27, 29, 47

I. Rejection: 7, 16, 20, 22, 39

J. Childhood Victimization: 4, 10, 11, 15, 16, 18, 20, 24, 26, 28, 31, 34, 40, 42, 43, 45

You have now separated the sources of your stress into ten categories. (These sources are often interrelated; that's why they may appear on two or more lines.) It is particularly significant when you have circled *several*, or *most*, of the numbers on any given line.

These ten categories can now be seen as falling into three groups. The first three (A, B, and C), are indications of poor scheduling or planning, physical problems, or financial difficulties; they are sources you may be able to change simply by understanding their nature and determining to do something about them yourself, or by getting someone to help you.

A. Poor Scheduling or Planning

You may be causing much of your stress simply because you don't take time to plan in advance what you can do and what is too much. This is typical of the Popular Sanguine personalities who are impulsive and spontaneous. Their lack of planning will frequently cause unnecessary pressures as they bite off more than they can chew. Some people take on more activity or responsibility than they should to help them overcome feelings of low self-worth and to make sure people like them.

B. Physical Problems

Yes answers in this category also may be relatively easy to deal with. Positive changes in diet, eating habits, nutrition, vitamins, or hormones can be implemented quickly. Checking into the possibilities of hypoglycemia and chronic fatigue syndrome may indicate sources of stress.

C. Financial Difficulties

Financial problems are among the most frequent sources of stress. Ask yourself if you are in trouble because you buy impulsively without thought of how you can pay the bills. Whatever the cause, you cannot afford to sit there and hope the Good-News Bears will arrive tomorrow with bags of money. Constant borrowing with high interest rates is not a long-term solution either. Sit down immediately

Comparison of Strengths and Weaknesses
by Personality Type

STRENGTHS

	Popular- Sanguine	Powerful- Choleric	Perfect- Melancholy	Peaceful- Phlegmatic
E M O T I O N S	Appealing personality Talkative, storyteller Life of the party Good sense of humor Memory for color Physically holds on to listener Emotional and demonstrative Enthusiastic and expressive Cheerful and bubbling over Curious Good on stage Wide-eyed and innocent Lives in the present Changeable disposition Sincere at heart Always a child	Born leader Dynamic and active Compulsive need for change Must correct wrongs Strong-willed and decisive Unemotional Not easily discouraged Independent and self-sufficient Exudes confidence Can run anything	Deep and thoughtful Analytical Serious and purposeful Genius prone Talented and creative Artistic or musical Philosophical and poetic Appreciative of beauty Sensitive to others Self-sacrificing Conscientious Idealistic	Low-key personality Easygoing and relaxed Calm, cool, and collected Patient, well balanced Consistent life Quiet, but witty Sympathetic and kind Keeps emotions hidden Happily reconciled to life All-purpose person

	Popular- Sanguine	Powerful- Choleric	Perfect- Melancholy	Peaceful- Phlegmatic
W O R K	Volunteers for jobs Thinks up new activities Looks great on the surface Creative and colorful Has energy and enthusiasm Starts in a flashy way Inspires others to join Charms others to work	Goal oriented Sees the whole picture Organizes well Seeks practical solutions Moves quickly to action Delegates work Insists on production Makes the goal Stimulates activity Thrives on opposition	Schedule oriented Perfectionist, high standards Detail conscious Persistent and thorough Orderly and organized Neat and tidy Economical Sees the problems Finds creative solutions Needs to finish what he starts Likes charts, graphs, figures, lists	Competent and steady Peaceful and agreeable Has administrative ability Mediates problems Avoids conflicts Good under pressure Finds the easy way
F R I E N D S	Makes friends easily Loves people Thrives on compliments Seems exciting Envied by others Doesn't hold grudges Apologizes quickly Prevents dull moments Likes spontaneous activities	Has little need for friends Will work for group activity Will lead and organize Is usually right Excels in emergencies	Makes friends cautiously Content to stay in background Avoids causing attention Faithful and devoted Will listen to complaints Can solve others' problems Deep concern for other people Moved to tears with compassion Seeks ideal mate	Easy to get along with Pleasant and enjoyable Inoffensive Good listener Dry sense of humor Enjoys watching people Has many friends Has compassion and concern

WEAKNESSES

	Popular- Sanguine	Powerful- Choleric	Perfect- Melancholy	Peaceful- Phlegmatic
E M O T I O N S	Compulsive talker Exaggerates and elaborates Dwells on trivia Can't remember names Scares others off Too happy for some Has restless energy Egotistical Blusters and complains Naive, gets taken in Has loud voice and laugh Controlled by circumstances Gets angry easily Seems phony to some Never grows up	Bossy Impatient Quick-tempered Can't relax Too impetuous Enjoys controversy and arguments Won't give up when losing Comes on too strong Inflexible Is not complimentary Dislikes tears and emotions Is unsympathetic	Remembers the negatives Moody and depressed Enjoys being hurt Has false humility Off in another world Low self-image Has selective hearing Self-centered Too introspective Guilt feelings Persecution complex Tends to hypochondria	Unenthusiastic Fearful and worried Indecisive Avoids responsibility Quiet will of iron Selfish Too shy and reticent Too compromising Self-righteous

	Popular- Sanguine	Powerful- Choleric	Perfect- Melancholy	Peaceful- Phlegmatic

W
O
R
K
	Would rather talk
	Forgets
	  obligations
	Doesn't follow
	  through
	Confidence
	  fades fast
	Undisciplined
	Priorities out of
	  order
	Decides by
	  feelings
	Easily
	  distracted
	Wastes time
	  talking
		Little tolerance
		  for mistakes
		Doesn't
		  analyze details
		Bored by trivia
		May make rash
		  decisions
		May be rude
		  or tactless
		Manipulates
		  people
		Demanding of
		  others
		End justifies
		  the means
		Work may
		  become his
		  god
		Demands
		  loyalty in the
		  ranks
			Not people
			  oriented
			Depressed
			  over
			  imperfections
			Chooses
			  difficult work
			Hesitant to
			  start projects
			Spends too
			  much time
			  planning
			Prefers
			  analysis to
			  work
			Self-
			  deprecating
			Hard to please
			Standards
			  often too high
			Deep need for
			  approval
				Not goal oriented
				Lacks self-
				  motivation
				Hard to get
				  moving
				Resents being
				  pushed
				Lazy and
				  careless
				Discourages
				  others
				Would rather
				  watch

F
R
I
E
N
D
S
	Hates to be
	  alone
	Needs to be
	  center stage
	Wants to be
	  popular
	Looks for
	  credit
	Dominates
	  conversations
	Interrupts and
	  doesn't listen
	Answers for
	  others
	Fickle and
	  forgetful
	Makes excuses
	Repeats
	  stories
		Tends to use
		  people
		Dominates
		  others
		Decides for
		  others
		Knows
		  everything
		Can do
		  everything
		  better
		Is too
		  independent
		Possessive of
		  friends and
		  mate
		Can't say, "I'm
		  sorry"
		May be right,
		  but unpopular
			Lives through
			  others
			Insecure
			  socially
			Withdrawn and
			  remote
			Critical of
			  others
			Holds back
			  affection
			Dislikes those
			  in opposition
			Suspicious of
			  people
			Antagonistic
			  and vengeful
			Unforgiving
			Full of
			  contradictions
			Skeptical of
			  compliments
				Dampens
				  enthusiasm
				Stays
				  uninvolved
				Is not exciting
				Indifferent to
				  plans
				Judges others
				Sarcastic and
				  teasing
				Resists change

Reprinted by permission from Florence Littauer, After Every Wedding Comes a Marriage *(Eugene, Oreg.: Harvest House, 1981). All rights reserved.*

with your checkbook, bank statements, and bills and take an objective look at your situation. If it is too much to face, enlist a Melancholy (perfect) mate or friend to help. Sanguines hate the thought of budgets but they need restraint and responsibility. One Sanguine man who was in severe financial trouble gave the bookkeeper of his company the authority to deposit his paycheck and pay his bills. He didn't even see the money and for two years he lived on a five-dollar weekly allowance. He didn't like it at the time, but he now is out of debt. It's amazing what we can do when we care enough to make changes. The book *When Spending Takes the Place of Feeling,* by Karen O'Connor (Nashville: Thomas Nelson) can help you find the source of your financial problems.

D. Marital Stress

This category begins the second and deeper level of stress sources. These issues are usually the result of long-standing relationships that have gradually gone downhill. Like a huge ocean liner at sea, changing direction requires strong hands on the rudder and plenty of time to swing around. Some root causes, such as personality differences, an overly dominant mate, immature emotions, and unrealistic expectations, can be changed quickly. Deeper issues that will take longer are those born from rejection, sexual frustration, childhood victimization, denial, unwillingness to face real issues, self-righteousness, and rebellious attitudes.

E. Low Self-worth

Many of us do things to compensate for feelings of insecurity, inadequacy, and lack of self-esteem. When these efforts fail or fall short, we are very apt to have financial problems, thereby adding marital stress, and emotional strain. Picture a wife who feels left out socially. Without her husband's agreement she throws a big, expensive party, inviting the people she perceives as keys to social acceptance. After the party, there is no flood of reciprocal invitations, only bills for the party, tension between husband and wife, and added feelings of worthlessness.

Since low self-worth is not a God-given characteristic, it must be the result of something we have learned, something that was put upon us or done to us. The source of much of the stress we bring upon ourselves is the effort made to compensate for our feelings of low self-worth. We need to find the root cause. When the root is removed, or healed, self-esteem is transformed and the stress will be history.

F. Work-Related Stress

Some people bring job-related stress home with them, creating new strains, while others have learned to "leave it at the office." Isn't it interesting that two different people on the job can be subject to the very same stress but handle it in totally opposite ways? Invariably it is because of what is inside them, and because of other issues in their lives. Generally, people who are emotionally healthy have a far higher stress-acceptance factor than those with unresolved deeper issues. Which one are you? If most of your stress is work-related, take steps to cure or change your situation. It may be that easy. If you have high levels of stress in several categories, your difficulties are likely to be related to other sources. Resolving those other issues may go a long way in curing on-the-job stress.

As Christians our gift from the Lord is peace—inner-peace that handles stress, not freedom from strain and tribulation (see John 14:27 and 16:33).

G. General Tension

The eleven questions of the Stress Test that fall within this category will help you identify stress and tension within you. The number of responses you have circled may surprise you, but every single one represents a symptom of inner stress. These are all of a general nature, and the resolution of the roots of the problems may bring surprising changes. You may have wondered about question 33, "Do you tend to have dandruff?" Not long ago, when Fred was telling a young couple in Australia about the changes in his life since his healing from childhood sexual victimization, he added, "Oh, and I used to have bad dandruff, but I don't anymore. It's gone!" The wife, who was a nurse, said to him, "Dandruff is caused by stress. That's a well-known fact."

We had never heard that before, but it does make sense. Since that time numerous other people have confirmed that fact to us.

Find the source or the cause of the tension, deal with it effectively, and you'll be delighted with the changes.

H. Depression

Depression is considered to be the major unsolved mental illness of our time. Even though only three of the questions on the test are directed to depression, many of the others are related to it. Depression often renders a person unable to function normally, and high levels of stress are apt to surface at work or in the home. The growing pile of uncompleted obligations or daily responsibilities adds to the pressure until there seems to be no hope.

Treating depression with medication only deals with the symptom, not with the cause. There are three basic interrelated causes that form a continuing cycle. The first and most prevalent is childhood sexual victimization. The second is rejection, often beginning in childhood. Virtually every victim of sexual abuse, or sexual interference, also suffers from rejection. The third cause is unrelenting stress and a corresponding inability to cope, which brings on depression. This is very common in men and women who have been sexually violated and who therefore suffer feelings of rejection, abandonment, and unworthiness. Each of these feelings is apt to feed the others, and the depression becomes all-consuming. Once again, the attention must be on discovering the roots of the problem.

I. Rejection

No one was reared by perfect parents. The healthier our parents were emotionally the better the chance we had to grow up to be balanced, productive adults. If we had to fight, protect, and hide to survive, we may have missed the nurturing we should have received from childhood. The feelings of rejection are deep and should not be ignored. We cannot leave well enough alone. Others of us were healthy as young adults but entered into a marriage with a person who was deeply hurting inside. In his or her search for self-worth this person unintentionally put expectations on us that we couldn't and shouldn't be expected to fulfill. This spouse pulled us down to his or her level. After a number of years of marriage we feel rejection, unworthiness, and loss of confidence.

Feelings of rejection are so common among Christian adults that unmanageable times of stress inevitably result. Whether the rejection feelings develop during childhood or adulthood, they can be readily healed over time as we learn to replace the inordinate craving to fill the void that we unrealistically expect of others with the certainty of the Savior's love for us.

Emotional Needs and Fears of the Personality Types

	Sexual Desires	Reasons Given for Supposed Need for Drugs or Alcohol	Method of Control	Fear
POPULAR SANGUINE	So desperate for love and excitement, may find it in the wrong place	Looking for fun Needs boost to be life of the party Wants mood elevated	Controls by charm and wit "You'll just love what I have in mind."	Being alone and unpopular Getting old and lonely Running out of money
PERFECT MELANCHOLY	Longs for deep meaningful relationship Likes romance, candles, and music	Tends to be closet drinker Wants to blot out imperfections and failures Wants creativity lifted	Controls by moods "I'll probably get depressed if . . ." "Oh, not that again."	Making a mistake Having to compromise standards Being a failure
POWERFUL CHOLERIC	Likes the chase and conquest more than commitment Needs to be in control of relationship	When control is slipping and he or she needs a boost of nerve When he or she wants to feel strong and in control again	Controls by threat of anger "You remember what happened the last time you did that!"	Losing control Being sick Becoming weak
PEACEFUL PHLEGMATIC	Wants someone who makes him or her feel worthwhile and won't ridicule, one who doesn't demand too much action	Needs to blot out reality and conflict, blur the problems Wants power to tell off bossy people	Controls by procrastination "If I wait long enough, someone else will do it."	Being pressured Being left holding the bag Facing conflict

J. Childhood Victimization

Last and deepest of our ten categories is childhood victimization, which can be either emotional, physical, or sexual. Sixteen of the questions relating to stress are symptoms of this childhood trauma. While all three forms of victimization are highly prevalent, childhood sexual violation has the most significant adult manifestations. It is the cause of much anguish, stress, and dysfunction.

According to a recent comprehensive survey, 75 percent of all women in the church today and 60 percent of all men have either clear knowledge or clear symptoms of childhood sexual victimization. Of those men and women 50 percent have no conscious knowledge of such trauma. Only 25 percent of women and 10 percent of men are aware of what was done to them as children.[2]

Of the men and women who have asked us for help over the past several years, fully 98 percent have shown clear symptoms of sexual violation. Their stress levels are frequently overwhelming. Often they have tried in vain to do everything they can think of to seek relief. Childhood physical sexual violation is pervasive, so common that it is the single most significant cause of stress in adult life. If you suspect this is the root cause of your stress problems, we strongly advise that you seek out the help of a Christian therapist who can help guide you through a healing process with God.

The End of the Chain: The Wall of Depression

Many times the dreams we women dream for our lives are based on unmet childhood needs, and are, therefore, dreams that never can come true. Instead, our dreams set us up for a lifetime of chronic disappointment—disappointment in ourselves, our mates, our parents, or our children. We have begun to build a chain to depression: chronic disappointment leads us to anger and bitterness; when we swallow our anger and turn it on ourselves, we hit the wall of depression. In these two chapters from our book, Saying Goodbye to Disappointments, *we hope you will let us show you how to work through your anger and find the courage to dream dreams that can come true.*

Jan Stoop and Dr. David Stoop
Saying Goodbye to Disappointments

Everyone knew why Cynthia was so depressed, yet no one knew what to do about it. Her husband, Jim, had finally left home and filed for a divorce. Cynthia and her friends knew this was not the first girlfriend he had had, just the one he thought he couldn't live without.

Over the course of eight years Cynthia had overlooked his late nights, his lame excuses, even his quick temper, which led him to "discipline" their children way beyond what was necessary. Instead of acknowledging her problem, she had busied herself taking classes in accounting at the local junior college, she had begun drinking and partying even more herself, and she had increased her chain smoking to four packs a day (the recent articles she read were right: Cigarettes were the perfect drug, a tranquilizer when she needed soothing, a pickup when she needed energy).

Cynthia did not choose disenchantment (to wake up from the fairy tale of her dream world). Instead, she continued to fool herself until Jim broke her reverie. Now she had to face both the reality of Jim's desertion and the fact that his behavior had been going on for years. That made her so angry that she simply shut down. She seldom went outside of the house, and she never got up until lunchtime or later. She stayed up late into the night reading or watching whatever movie seemed halfway interesting.

Eventually, when complex disappointments become overwhelming, women encounter their anger, no matter how much they have tried to numb themselves against the pain. But this anger is rage, not healthy anger that will help them process their losses and grieve. This sort of anger is designed to push people away, which is the type of anger men frequently express.

Disappointed Women: Angry Men

If we were to ask a group of men about their disappointments, the question would probably confuse them. "Who has time for such things?" would be a typical response. Men don't talk about their disappointments as women do.

It isn't that men aren't disappointed; it's just that their response to disappointment is generally quite different from that of a woman. As Tim Allen, the tool man of the popular television program "Home Improvement," says, "Women respond by manipulating; men respond by blowing up bridges." The few men who would admit to being disappointed would see themselves as having a more active role in trying to "fix" the thing that caused their disappointment than women do.

Several years ago, Dave, along with Stephen Arterburn, wrote a book called *The Angry Man.* In doing the research for that book, they found that men generally cover up their disappointments with anger. And anger causes them to take some aggressive action, which may not be productive or wise; they may blow up bridges! Women, on the other hand, turn their anger inward.

This response is not all that surprising, since our culture teaches women to respond differently than men. As Colette Dowling pointed out in *The Cinderella Complex,* little boys are trained to move out of dependency on other people in order to become independent, whereas little girls are trained into dependency.[1] Although men and women are innately different (they are wired differently, you might say, by their genes), many of the differences are the result of cultural influences.

Little Boys Have Permission to Be Angry

When men were little boys, it was more socially acceptable for them to show anger than it was for little girls. And when men become adults, it still is. Anger may be acceptable for little boys, but many other emotions, especially those associated with sadness, are not. "Stop those tears and act like a man," parents or coaches tell little boys when they strike out with the bases loaded in the Little League play-offs.

On the other hand, if a little boy gets angry and kicks the dirt or slams his bat to the ground, his parents or coach may even feel a little proud that he handled the disappointment "like a man." After all, that's probably what Dad would do if he struck out in his softball game.

Over the years we have been taught:
Men can't cry. And women can't be angry.

Over the years boys are taught, both by family and by social pressures, "It's okay to be angry." "It's manly." On the other hand, it is not "manly" to be disappointed—to feel hurt, frustrated, or sad. Of course, some men, as well as some women, were taught that it is unacceptable, or even unsafe, to express any emotion, even anger, so they repressed all their emotions.

Men can't cry. And women can't be angry.

Little Girls Shouldn't Show Anger

The taboo against women displaying anger goes back to ancient times. Some of the first written laws, dating around 2500 B.C., penalized women for being verbally angry with their husbands. In one case, the punishment was to have a woman's name engraved on a brick, which was then used to knock out her teeth!

Over the centuries, our penalties have become a little more civil, but our attitudes haven't changed all that much.

Little girls are usually taught "It isn't ladylike to be angry." One woman was consistently given this message as a little girl: "If something doesn't go the way you want it to go, smile and act like nothing is wrong." She said, "Later I learned that when I was alone, or with a close girlfriend, I could express my anger, but even then, I knew I had to keep it under control."

Little girls are taught "It's not okay to be angry" but "It is okay to cry." The message is loud and clear: "Cover up your anger with disappointment and tears."

And that solution becomes a pattern that follows women into their marriages. One woman told us, "When I'm upset with my husband, I often tell myself, 'I'll wait until a better time to talk to him about this,' and of course there never is a better time. Or I think to myself, 'I don't want to upset things. I just want to keep everyone happy. What I'm feeling doesn't matter that much.'" In both cases, this woman avoids dealing with her anger and, more important, with the issues that caused her feelings.

Basically, women deny their anger because they are afraid: "If I don't hide my anger, I will alienate my husband (or children or friends or coworkers) and lose what little of them I may have." Instead, they express their disappointment by nagging or crying, many times in private, and try to make the best of things. Or by saying, "I'm bothered by . . ." or "I feel upset about. . . ."

Unfortunately, women still feel dependent in their relationships, and the more they think they need the other person, the less they are able to express any negative emotions. Cynthia, the woman whose husband left her after several affairs, told us, "I knew my husband had been unfaithful for several years, but I was afraid. I never worked after college. I don't know how to make a living for myself. I was afraid of what would happen to me and the girls if Jim left home."

A woman in our survey expressed the same fear: "I'm afraid to let my husband know how I really feel. I don't think our relationship could survive such honesty." Does this mean that women are actually less angry than men? Not at all.

But Women Are Angry!

Fatigue, embarrassment, frustration, rejection—all cause women to be angry, according to Dr. James Dobson in *Emotions—Can You Trust Them?* but still women were hesitant to identify their feelings as anger.[2] Yet counselors usually report that once women get in touch with their anger, they are angrier and more willing to honestly express it than men. And when that anger surfaces it is often directed at . . . you guessed it: men and, more precisely, husbands.

According to the survey Dave and Steve Arterburn conducted for the book, *The Angry Man,* men didn't focus their anger on their spouses.[3] They also didn't express as much discontentment with the way their lives were turning out. Perhaps men are so shut off from what they really feel that the anger they do express is simply a defense, designed to keep themselves and others at a distance from their real hurts or feelings of disappointment.

We see this dynamic at work in our relationship. At a certain point in an argument—usually when Dave realizes his reasoning is not well supported—he gets angry and leaves the room. At other times he becomes more insistent and dogmatic, staying with the argument, fiercely protecting his real hurt feelings. After years of hitting each other head-on, Jan has learned to stop talking and recognize his anger as his way to cover his hurt feelings. And Dave says, "I have learned to hear out Jan's disappointments, validate her underlying anger, and not try to fix them. Trying to change them only intensifies the anger I hide deep inside."

Again, women do experience anger, even though they may not be aware of it or call it anger. "We prove we are angry by the fact that we want revenge, much more so than men—we get even when we feel frustrated or helpless," Jan says. "Many times, we are confronted with our helplessness in the situation and the intense frustration we have felt over the years as we have tried to change things. That makes us angry, whether we admit it or not."

The Expression of Anger

When we are hurt, frustrated, or injured in some way emotionally, it is natural to feel angry about what has happened. "The human body is equipped with an automatic defensive system, called the 'flight or fight' mechanism, which prepares the entire organism for action," says Dr. James Dobson. The "fight" part of that mechanism is anger, and "this is an involuntary response which occurs whether or not we will it."[4]

Our emotions are designed by God in such a way that anger results when we are hurt, especially when the hurt reminds us of an emotional injury from the past. It is the kind of anger Paul referred to when he said, "Be angry, and do not sin" (Eph. 4:26). The purpose of anger is to protect us, and it is a natural and healthy emotion— when it is expressed without sin. "Anger is simply a physical state of readiness," says psychologist Neil Clark Warren in his book, *Make Anger Your Ally.* "When we are angry, we are prepared to act. This is all anger is—preparedness."[5]

Unfortunately, both men and women react with defensive anger before they get to this pure, healthy anger.

The Ways We Express Our Anger

We often express our anger defensively, which is the most destructive way. Such anger leads us through a progression of four steps, which can end in bitterness and then lead to depression.

1. Emotional Outbursts   Often we first express our anger as loudly as possible, which is a desperate attempt to get the attention of whoever is blocking our dream. This is pure defensive anger; we're defending ourselves against the hurt we feel so deeply. The women in our survey listed "yelling, raging, pouting, and whining" as common ways they expressed their anger once it came to the surface. Of course, the yelling would often be accompanied by tears. One woman said she did all these things in hopes that "it would shame my husband into caring."

Unfortunately, defensive anger seldom changes another person's attitude for the better. We yell, they yell back, and the war has begun. We know this, but we do it over and over again because a part of us still believes we can coerce this person into acting the way we want him or her to act. Eventually, we become so frustrated that we unconsciously decide to "get even."

2. Getting Even Several women listed their ways of "getting even," especially with their husbands, on their questionnaires: shopping or sabotaging something important to their spouse headed the list. These women said, "I kept score." Looking back, they were able to see that they kept track of their disappointments, and when "the score hit a certain mark," they felt entitled to buy something extravagant for themselves. They found their anger eliminated any immediate feelings of guilt. However, later some of these women couldn't really enjoy what they had bought because it reminded them of the emotional price of their purchases. Other women wore their purchase proudly, feeling they had more than "earned" it.

Women also mentioned forgetting to do something, like "take his suits to the cleaners" or being busy with the children or not feeling well or having car problems as ways they "got even." Still others listed, "Just being late, or making my husband late."

3. Blaming Someone Else Often we may be afraid to direct our anger at the person who has caused our disappointment because doing so would make it even more difficult to get what we desire. Instead, we find ourselves becoming short with our children, snapping at a sales clerk, yelling at someone in another car on the freeway, or in some other way displacing our anger and "kicking the dog."

Sometimes we substitute our original disappointment for a new disappointment with this neutral party. For example, when I am displacing my anger on my children, I actually believe that I am disappointed with their behavior. But the truth is, rather than confront the real disappointment within me, I now displace all this churning anger inside of me at my child, who may deserve my displeasure, but not to that extent.

4. Blaming Ourselves We're back to that same contradictory cycle of blaming others and blaming ourselves. When women first turn their anger inward, they somehow continue to appear to be very "nice" and "ladylike." Eventually, all sense of needing to be "nice" is gone; the disappointment becomes so overwhelming, the woman doesn't care anymore—she shows her anger! Now she doesn't care who sees it.

Carrie described how she started to lash out at her husband because of her disappointment with their lack of emotional closeness. As she lashed out, he simply reacted with his own defensive anger. Their story is all too common—their anger grew as the threats grew, and divorce became a part of the threats. Finally one moved out and the other filed for divorce.

As we talked with her later, Carrie told us how bitter the divorce was. She and her husband fought the whole way through it, but when they met to sign the final papers, they looked at each other with a feeling of longing, coupled with a sense of resignation. "I didn't want to divorce him, and I don't think he wanted to divorce me," she added. "When I said something like that to him, for a fleeting moment I thought he might soften, but then he said, 'We've come this far, I guess we should finish it.' I never really wanted a divorce—I just wanted him to hear me." Her out-of-control, defensive anger led her down a path she didn't want to travel.

Eventually, we turn all our anger and hatred onto ourselves and begin to act out our self-hatred in self-destructive behaviors. One woman said, "I've had affairs. I've had a drinking problem. I've abused credit by spending too much; I owe so much right now that the only way out is to declare bankruptcy. Most of the time I'm just angry with myself."

> *Eventually, we turn all our anger and hatred onto ourselves and begin to act out our self-hatred in self-destructive behaviors.*

As she talked about her struggle, she commented on how often she seemed to create a crisis in her life. "I don't consciously plan to have a crisis, but I've had enough of them that it seems to be a pattern with me," she continued. "I think when I'm in the midst of a crisis I don't have to face my disappointments."

Eventually, self-hatred leads us to bitterness.

Bitterness, the Anger of the Soul

Bitterness is a poison that destroys us, affects our families, and even infects those around us; bitterness leads to depression. The writer of Hebrews warns us to be careful, for "there can spring up.

. . . a bitter spirit which is not only bad in itself, but can poison the lives of many others" (Heb. 12:15, J.B. PHILLIPS).

The Greek root for the word *bitterness* includes the meaning "to cut, to prick." Disappointment punctures our heart and eventually penetrates until it totally infects us and ends up defining who we are. A second definition of bitterness includes the idea of "intense hostility" toward someone. We feel alienated and estranged from people and take on a disagreeable, cynical attitude toward life.

Bitterness also affects our health. The Medical School of Duke University recently identified the number one killer in American culture as unforgiveness, the repressed anger we hold locked within ourselves. Chronic fatigue, hives and other skin disorders, cancer, irritable bowel syndrome, PMS, the common cold, and especially headaches are being identified as having a connection to repressed anger.

After Jim left Cynthia, the bad backaches that had plagued her for years increased; she had been diagnosed with a slightly ruptured disc, but the doctors said the damage shouldn't be producing so much pain. Cynthia spent several months in bed, treating her back with cold compresses and her pain with medication. Then finally she was able to resume her normal activities. She went back to school to get more credits toward an accounting degree . . . until she found the lump in her breast.

The doctors said the lump was malignant, so her breast was removed, and Cynthia tried to overcome her loss—and her fear that no man would ever love her now. Four years later, just when she had decided to have reconstructive surgery on the first breast, a lump was found in the other breast (a mirror image of the first cancer, but apparently not a metastasis). Was the cancer exacerbated by Cynthia's bitterness? No one even raised the question in her case; what would it matter anyway? Bitterness can destroy.

Many of the steps of bitterness are the same as the stages of defensive anger, just on a much deeper level. We continue to play the victim, and we continue to complain about our disappointments and nurse them in our hearts.

The Complaining Stage

Once we become bitter we are often willing to express our feelings of hurt and disappointment to anyone who will listen. Job experienced this when he said, "Therefore I will not restrain my mouth;/I will speak in the anguish of my spirit;/I will complain in the bitterness of my soul" (Job 7:11). As Job talks and talks about his anguish, he experiences what we experience; he ends up feeding the roots of bitterness within himself.

Cynthia told us, "I used to talk for hours about my disappointments and hurt, but I never listened to what others were saying to me. I just needed to talk. Eventually it became a way of life for me."

One of Cynthia's friends finally confronted her about her constant complaining. "When she told me I seemed to always be stuck in the same place, she got my attention. I didn't want to hear what she was saying to me, but she persisted until I did."

When we complain about our pain to someone else, we both become mere observers of the dreadful situation. It was easier for Cynthia to talk about her complaints than to do something about her disappointments.

The Nursing Stage

The next step along the path of bitterness is to pull back within ourselves. This stage is called the nursing stage, or the stage of quiet resentment. Now we say less, except within the privacy of our minds. We experience the truth of the proverb that says: "The heart knows its own bitterness,/And a stranger does not share its joy" (Prov. 14:10).

What an interesting combination of words—joy and bitterness. There is a morbid enjoyment in nursing our hurt and anger, massaging them as we bury them inside ourselves. Eventually bitterness feeds upon bitterness. Cynthia moved into the nursing stage after her friend confronted her with her constant complaining. "At first I wanted to stay in bed and pull the covers over my life. I simply shut up—I quit talking about my problems and most everything else as well.

"Fortunately, my friend knew what I was doing and she kept after me to get help. I found that just talking didn't do anything—neither did not talking. It took a different kind of talking for me to break the cycle."

Cynthia had learned the difference between complaining about her problems and sharing her emotions. When we really talk about how we feel, we are connected to our pain, and we are able to work our way through it to wholeness. Sharing our hurt with someone is always a part of our healing, but bitterness grows out of our complaining.

A spirit of bitterness that is nursed over a period of time eventually leads us into a place of isolation. An example of someone walking this path was Saul, Israel's first king. Soon after we meet Saul, we find him facing a seemingly unresolvable situation. The Philistines, the enemy of Israel, had a giant named Goliath, who paralyzed the Israelite army. The story of how David killed Goliath is well known. The less obvious story is Saul's growing resentment and bitterness at the glory David received for this feat.

> *A spirit of bitterness that is nursed over a period of time eventually leads us into a place of isolation.*

After the miraculous defeat of Goliath (and several others), the crowds sang the following song as Saul and David passed by:

> "Saul has slain his thousands,
> And David his ten thousands."
> (1 Sam. 18:7)

Saul resented the words. His thousands were obviously outdone by David's ten thousands. Would David someday replace him? Saul worried. The possible answer enraged him.

Instead of working through his anger, Saul chose the path of bitterness. Later, "Saul eyed David from that day forward" (1 Sam. 18:9). Or we might say, "Saul nursed his anger in the quietness of his heart."

Over time, David became the close friend of Saul's son, Jonathan. David married Saul's daughter, Michal. Even his family seemed to prefer David, Saul thought. Finally his bitterness became so great, he told his servants and Jonathan to kill David.

Jonathan protested. Why kill someone who has meant you no harm and has even helped you in any way he could? The first time Jonathan protested, Saul listened, but he still nursed his bitterness. The second time Jonathan defended David from Saul's threats to kill him, the king's anger turned against his own son and he almost killed Jonathan. Later, when Saul's daughter, Michal, also tried to protect her husband, Saul gave her to another man specifically to spite David. All of Saul's behaviors were controlled by his irrational passion and bitterness. Eventually, Saul ended up a bitter and lonely man, destroying not only himself, but also those he loved as the walls of bitterness he had built over the years collapsed upon him.

The Dead End of Depression

Just as it was in Saul's case, so it will be in ours—the years of defensive anger and bitterness will lead us into the pit of a paralyzing depression. Once we turn on ourselves with our anger, the path ahead is going to be even more rocky and painful. We've gradually withdrawn from those around us, cutting ourselves off from friends and support systems.

Depression Defined

A simple definition of *depression* is "a condition of general emotional dejection and withdrawal; sadness greater and more prolonged than that warranted by any objective reason."[6] Depression can encompass a wide range of emotions, along with feelings of helplessness, and these emotions do not move along a predictable, continuous path, from the "blues" to a more serious depression and finally to suicide. Instead, our experience of depression can vary.

Counselors use the *Diagnostic and Statistical Manual of Mental Disorders* (commonly referred to as the DSM-III-R) as our guide to diagnosis. The DSM-III-R lists fifteen different types of depression, most of them under the heading of mood disorders. Some are organically or biochemically based, but most result from unresolved issues and conflicts in our lives, both past and present.

One woman described her depression to us in this way. "The despair I'd been feeling over my life and all its disappointments became depression. My energy level was lower, my ability to concentrate was diminished, and my self-hate grew stronger as I saw myself as worthless. . . . I ate out of boredom and my weight shot up. I ended up feeling an extraordinary amount of guilt, and my ability to sleep was changed, adding to the feelings of fatigue I was already struggling with." Her description could be typical of a major depression, depending on how long she had been experiencing these symptoms and how severely they affected her ability to function on a daily basis.

Barbara Minar described these feelings as "The Depression Vulture [who] flapped so close I could feel the wind from his wings." Later, when he landed, she said, "A putrid smell hit my senses as I felt the Depression Vulture land in my emotions."[7] At any given time, more than seven million women in our country experience a major depression. This does not include those who are plagued by milder forms of depressive mood disorders, which are estimated to affect 20 to 25 percent of women. Studies have shown that women are twice as likely to be depressed as men are.

A study published by the American Psychological Association explained why. The higher proportion of women suffering from depression is, in many cases, directly related to women's tendency toward "certain cognitive and personality styles—avoidant, passive, dependent behavior patterns; pessimistic, negative cognitive styles; and focusing too much on depressed feelings instead of action and mastery strategies."[8]

Another study by M. Notman, in 1986, and quoted by Ellen Mc-Grath, pointed out other factors that make women more vulnerable to depression than men.[9] These included differences in the attachment and separation process between boys and girls during early development (those old cultural myths that boys are to be independent, girls dependent), social stereotypes that devalue women in general, and the relatively fewer avenues available to women for activities and the mastery of those activities. Cynthia realized this when she told us she didn't feel equipped to support her girls and herself. "It will be different for my girls," she said. "Women now are supposed to develop their own potential; they often expect to have careers, rather than seeing themselves only as wives and mothers. I think my girls will stand up for themselves more than I did."

Additional factors include the fact that marriage provides a greater advantage for men than for women—that is, they are more easily satisfied and seldom refer to their marriages in negative terms. Women are more vulnerable. "In unhappy marriages, women are three times as likely as men to be depressed than married men and single women."[10]

Women today suffer from depression ten times more than their grandmothers did. Part of this increase is due to their higher expectations and the resulting long-term disappointments that haven't been processed.

The symptoms of depression identified in the DSM-III-R include a loss of interest in pleasurable activities most of the day and nearly every day; significant changes in weight (either losing weight or gaining weight); problems sleeping (either sleeping too much, too little, or awakening in the middle of the night and not being able to go back to sleep); either a slowing of movements or an observable agitation; a loss of energy; feelings of worthlessness; and difficulty concentrating.

Depression appears to be a very inactive state but, in fact, is a very active one. To an observer, depressed people appear immobilized. In reality, their minds are in a frenzy. They cannot function, but internally, they are despising themselves for it.[11]

Other symptoms expressed by women caught in the depressive cycle of their disappointments included experiences of anxiety and panic; sexual difficulties, including frigidity; the inability to trust anyone; a sense of depersonalization, which is experienced as a feeling of detachment from oneself; and emotional deadness.

(If you identify with five or more of these symptoms, talk to your doctor about what you are feeling. There is help for depression, even though you may feel as though everything is hopeless.)

Unfortunately, most depressed women do not seek treatment for their depression, since they feel depression is a sign of weakness. Thoughts like "If only I were stronger, I wouldn't feel like this" or "I just need to discipline myself more to get things done" or "All I need is some rest or a break from the kids" keep them from seeking professional help. Yet a lack of treatment usually leads to a progressive worsening of the problem.

Several women reported that in their despair, they attempted to take their own lives. When we are emotionally dead, our self-hatred grows. We can see no way out of the deepening despair and depression. And our thinking becomes distorted as we isolate ourselves from others, so we often look for a quick way out of the pain. One woman told us, "I learned how to handle the smaller disappointments in my life and move on. But I couldn't see any way I could deal with the pain of my dad's sexual abuse. I've tried to kill myself several times."

Another woman said that she had been forced to slow down the pace of her life because of losing her job. "I overdosed on pills three times last year." When we are spiraling downward in depression, suicide may seem a logical next step.

Depression Caused by Disappointment

A series of experiments done during the nineteenth century by Paul Moebius, a German neuropathologist, illustrates how the frustration of our unfulfilled dreams, and subsequent disappointments, become depression. Moebius would often use experiments involving a pike fish that was swimming in a huge tank with glass walls to introduce the study of psychology to his medical students. The professor would throw a sturgeon fish into the tank, and the pike would immediately eat it.

Eventually, Moebius would put a strong glass partition in the tank, dividing it into two sections. Now he would throw in the sturgeon on the opposite side of the tank from where the pike was swimming. Following its natural bent, the pike would rush toward the small fish, only to slam into the glass and fall to the bottom stunned. As soon as the pike "got his senses back" it would dive toward the sturgeon again, only to hit the glass again.

Finally the professor would remove the glass plate, and the pike would swim around the sturgeon without any attempt to devour it. Sometimes the pike would get hungry enough to try again, and this time successfully enjoy a meal, while other times, the pike would never touch the sturgeon and "give up" on life.[12]

This pike experienced the same disillusionment that we experience when we have "butted our heads against the wall" in our expectations of husbands, family members, parents, or even life itself. Eventually we give up trying to get what we've dreamed of having, and in doing so, we give up on the people in our lives and lose any sense of joy in living—we are depressed.

This hopeless cycle looks something like the chart on page 132.

You'll notice that wall at the end of the spiral, the dead end of depression. This experience of depression is often described as being stuck or as being caught in a box canyon. There is no place to go when we get there! We either keep hitting our head against the wall or we simply lie down and give up.

No one wants to experience emotional pain. It is not a feeling we welcome or embrace. But when we fail to deal with emotional hurts and losses, either by pushing them away with our anger (as men tend to do) or by trying to bury them and becoming overwhelmed by disappointments and depression (as women generally do), the resulting emotional experiences will become more painful than dealing with the original issues.

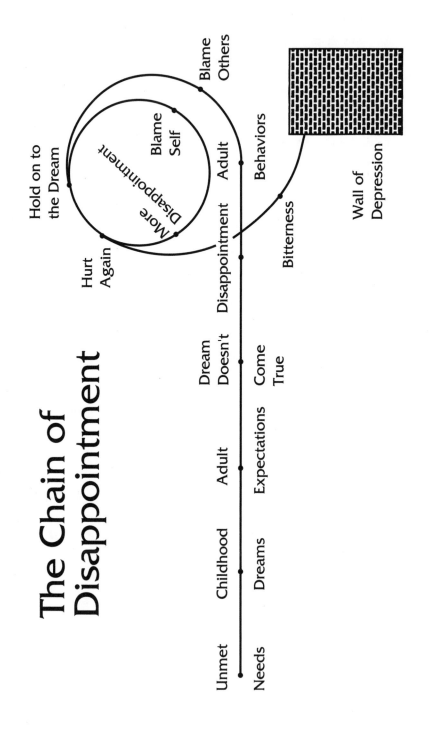

The Chain of Disappointment

Hold on to the Dream

Hurt Again

More Disappointment

Blame Self

Blame Others

Adult — Behaviors

Bitterness

Disappointment

Dream Doesn't Come True

Adult — Expectations

Childhood — Dreams

Unmet Needs

Wall of Depression

Yes, we will find a lot of healthy anger underneath the surface. This can be frightening for us, but it can frighten the men in our lives even more. A colleague of ours commented some years ago, "One day women are going to find out how angry they really are, and then we men are going to be in real trouble!"

Perhaps there will be some temporary trouble for men as women get in touch with their anger, but the ultimate goal in looking at the anger hidden beneath our disappointments is to develop a greater capacity for love. With that as our goal, both men and women will win—it's worth the journey.

What lies behind us
and what lies before us
are tiny matters compared to
what lies within us.

—William Morrow

Finding the Courage to Dream Again

*I*n this chapter we will look at our dreams and adjust them to reality.* Then we will look at how we can dream new dreams in the future. This process is as new as the twentieth century and as old as 1100 B.C., when a godly woman named Hannah lived in ancient Israel. We can adjust our old dreams to reality by following Hannah's example.

Hannah Found Courage to Look at Her Dreams Realistically

The High Holy Days of Judaism take place in the late fall of each year. Sometimes called the "days of Awe," the ten days of Rosh Hashanah mark the beginning of the new year in the Jewish calendar. On the first day of Rosh Hashanah, Jews gather together to chant the *Haftarah,* the portion of scripture that tells the story of Hannah, for it is a story closely tied to one of the basic themes of Rosh Hashanah: "God remembers."

Although the account of Hannah as recorded in 1 Samuel 1:1–

* This chapter was taken from *Saying Goodbye to Disappointments,* by Jan Stoop and Dr. David Stoop (Nashville: Thomas Nelson, 1993).

2:10 is brief and sketchy, it doesn't take much imagination to fill in some of the gaps in the story and to identify with Hannah's hurts. Her disappointments built year after year after year, until finally the pain was more than she could bear.

Hannah, married to a man who had two wives, lived in a culture where a wife's value in the eyes of her husband depended upon her ability to have children, especially sons. Peninnah, the other wife, had given birth to both sons and daughters, but Hannah was childless. According to the customs of the day, Peninnah should have been her husband's favorite and Hannah should have been ignored. But Hannah was the favored one. Elkanah loved her deeply and generously gave her anything she needed. You can imagine how Peninnah felt. Filled with resentment toward Hannah, Peninnah taunted her constantly about her inability to have children. Peninnah made Hannah's life miserable.

Hannah's disappointment at having no child of her own, already great, was multiplied by Peninnah's jeering and the humiliation Hannah felt for letting her husband down. So Hannah did what many of us do: She turned to God for help. But year after year after year passed, and nothing changed.

Elkanah could not understand why Hannah was so devastated by this disappointment. "Am I not better to you than ten sons?" he asked her.

In considering the responses we got to our survey, Elkanah's question was not unreasonable. Many women said they could bear just about anything if their husbands would genuinely stand beside them. One woman spoke for many when she said, "If it was him and me against the world, I would be satisfied." Yet, for Hannah, her husband's openness and affection were not enough. She pushed him away and couldn't accept his love, for she was convinced, "He has to be as disappointed in me as I am in myself."

Isn't that a lot like us? Some really good and important parts of our dreams may have been fulfilled, yet because of our need for one essential part, something that is still lacking, we languish in pain and tears.

During the family's yearly trip to Shiloh to worship the Lord, during their meal one evening, Peninnah provoked and teased Hannah until she wept bitterly. When that miserable dinner was finally over, Hannah went to the temple to pray.

Now, Hannah's was not just an everyday prayer. The Bible tells us she "was in bitterness of soul, and prayed to the Lord and wept in anguish." We don't know what she prayed, but it's easy to imagine: "Would it be so hard to give me just *one* son?" Oh, the pain and sadness that must have been poured out in that prayer! Oh, the envy that consumed her when she looked at Peninnah's children. She must have lashed out at the injustice of it all.

Even though Hannah's prayer was silent, her anguish was so evident that Eli, the priest, who was watching, was certain she was drunk. When he reprimanded her, she assured him, "I have not had so much as a drop of wine to drink." Then she poured out the hurt that flooded her soul.

Hannah "Gave Back" Her Dream

In the midst of your disappointments, have you ever tried to make a deal with God? We certainly have. "God, if you will give me what I ask, I will. . . ."

Hannah didn't bargain with God. She didn't say, "God, if You will give me a son, I'll be the best wife and mother in all of Israel." No, what Hannah did was make a vow to God: "If You will give me a son, I will give him to the Lord all the days of his life."

Sounds paradoxical, doesn't it? "If You give me what I want, I will give it back to You." Something had changed in Hannah's heart. She was giving up what she so desperately desired even before she had it. And God responded by giving her what she wanted.

Hannah did not break her vow. When her son, Samuel, was born, Hannah kept him until he was weaned, then she took him to Shiloh and left him there with Eli. And so she was separated from the son she had longed for so desperately.

And so it is with us. We must come to the place where we are willing to let go of what we so desperately desire, for often in the letting go, we can finally begin to dream again.

"But how can I let go when my expectation is that my husband will be emotionally available to me?" you might be saying. Or "How can I let go of my expectation that my wayward child will turn out okay?" Carole asked us. "How can I let go of my dream that my husband will again be like he was? I picture him back at work. I imagine him helping our son restore his MG. I see him walking straight and tall, reading the newspaper, paying the bills. I imagine him having a real, caring conversation with me, and holding me and loving me like he used to do. How can I let go of all that?"

How do we let go when we have done everything right, yet everything still is turning out so bad? Certainly we must wrestle with such questions before we can even dare to hope again. Let's begin by reviewing the healing process in terms of Hannah's experience.

Hannah Let Go of the Past

Actually, Hannah acted like many of us. Carole, too, clung persistently to her dream that, in spite of the evidence, Rich's illness would just go away. Like Hannah, in order to hold on, Carole had to either deny her pain or to repress it, and this just heaped disappointment on top of disappointment.

But before Hannah's last anguished trip to the tabernacle, an important change took place. She stopped demanding that God fit into her plans and heal her disappointment *her* way. This change made such a profound difference in her life that Hannah went to Shiloh a different woman.

As the story progresses, Hannah's dream also changes. Before Shiloh, she may have dreamed of having her own child so she could show off to Peninnah, or at least so she could shut her up. She may have dreamed of both her and her husband's enjoyment as they played with the little one. But in making her vow with the Lord, she gave up a large part of her dream.

Saying goodbye to our disappointment means releasing our solution and, by faith, opening our hands to receive God's solution.

When Eli told her, "Go in peace, and the God of Israel grant your petition which you have asked of Him," Hannah believed him. She not only let go of certain aspects of her dream about the child, she also let go of the struggle to make the dream come true. She heard the words of the priest, and she accepted them as fact. Now, that's faith.

As we begin to mend our dreams, we, too, need to move over into the arena of faith. Our solution just may not be God's solution. Saying goodbye to our disappointment means releasing our solution and, by faith, opening our hands to receive God's solution.

But that's not all. Hannah also found her fulfillment somewhere else.

God's Plan for Fulfillment

When we look up the opposite of the word *disappointment*, we find the word *fulfillment*. "Fulfillment has to be one of life's choicest gifts," says Charles Swindoll. "A major building block toward authentic happiness. Solomon must have had it in mind when he wrote in Proverbs 13:19, 'Desire realized is sweet to the soul. . . .'" (NASV).

Once we have broken our cycle of disappointment, we can walk a new path toward fulfillment. For Hannah, fulfillment came from obedience to the Lord and the knowledge that He truly had remembered her, not from having her own children around her. Many of us will also find our fulfillment in a totally different place than where we had expected it to be. Be willing to look beyond your own narrow limits and ask God to show you the fulfillment He has for you.

One woman said that a very important dream in her life was to become a teacher. "All my life I have enjoyed children, and I thought the best way to be around them was to teach in elementary school," she said.

When her college career was repeatedly interrupted, her disappointment grew as her goal of teaching seemed to fade away. "But then I realized that the *real* need behind my desire to teach was to be with children, and I am finding all kinds of ways to be involved with them." Yes, she did finish her degree. "But I don't feel such an urgent need to teach anymore. Who knows? I may do something totally different, but whatever it is, I know it will involve me with children."

As we seek other ways to fulfill the need that is the root of our disappointment, we will often struggle with tension between building healthy dreams for our future and falling back into the old patterns of behavior that led to our disappointment in the first place. Obviously, life is still going to have its disappointing experiences. We can never totally say goodbye to disappointment. But we can say goodbye to the destructive pattern of dealing with our disappointments in the same old way. And we can move into the future with dreams, goals, and expectations that are based on the truths about ourselves and those around us. We can learn to dream again! But this time our dreams will be touched by reality.

The secret for you lies in how you hold on to your dreams about the future and in how you perceive your life as it exists right now. It's important to come to the place where you can see yourself, and others in your life, more accurately. When your viewpoint about life is rooted in an accurate understanding, you can experience dreams and hopes that can come true.

Do you want to dream new dreams that can come true? Here are nine important guidelines that will help you do just that.

Paul Learned How to Dream New Dreams

The Apostle Paul experienced many disappointments. He set out to convert the people around the Mediterranean, yet all too often he was run out of town or shipwrecked or almost killed (Imagine yourself hiding from your enemies in a basket and being lowered from the top of the enormous town walls so you can escape!). As he tried to dream new, realistic dreams, he developed principles that we can also use to learn to dream again in spite of the circumstances.

1. Be Honest About Yourself and Others.

When Paul wrote to the church at Rome, he urged them to "be honest in your estimate of yourselves" (Rom. 12:3 TLB). This is where every one of us must begin. It's a difficult thing to do. We usually err on both sides: We think too little of ourselves when it comes to valuing who we are, and we think too much of ourselves when we consider what we can do in any given situation. So how do we arrive at the place where we can "think soberly" about ourselves?

"From the beginning, I was convinced I could make Rick fight against the ravages of Huntington's Disease," Carole said, "and if he would fight, then he would get better—or at least wouldn't get worse."

To think soberly requires that we recognize our own limitations and the limitations of those upon whom we are depending. In other words, we become honest about what we *can* do as well as what we *cannot* do. And we honestly face what the other person involved can and cannot do. In each case, it may not be a question of willingness, but of ability.

Many women, after reflecting on what they had written on their survey sheets, added something like this: "My husband probably doesn't even know how to be the kind of person I've wanted him to be all these years." This kind of honesty is painful, for it forces us to *see what is rather than what we wish it were.*

We will also find ourselves becoming more honest with God about our feelings. The respect many of us have been taught to have for authority figures spills over into the way we talk with God, but if we can't honestly pour out our hearts to God about everything inside us, whom can we talk to? He is the only one who truly knows every part of us and accepts us anyway.

God is not threatened by our emotions, nor is He put off by our anger.

How freeing it is to become comfortable talking to God this way! He is not threatened by our emotions, nor is He put off by our anger. He already knows what is in our hearts—He is just waiting for us to share it with Him.

2. Learn to Be Content.

One of Paul's most profound statements is in the letter he wrote near the end of his life while he was imprisoned in Rome. It was a time of great sadness and disappointment for him. Paul had planned to go to Rome as a free man and to continue on to Spain, but before he even started, he was arrested and put into chains. Yet in prison he wrote these incredible words, which we read so often and wish were true for us: "I have learned in whatever state I am, to be content." He continues, "I know how to be abased, and I know how to abound. Everywhere and in all things I have learned both to be full and to be hungry, both to abound and to suffer need" (Phil. 4:11–12).

We can only be content in the present when we have resolved the issues of the past. When Paul says, "One thing I do, forgetting those things which are behind and reaching forward to those things which are ahead" (Phil. 3:13), he is not using denial as the means of dealing with the past. He is recognizing that until the issues of our past are resolved, they will continue to express themselves in some way. No amount of denial will keep them buried. There has to be resolution. That resolution allowed Paul to be content within his circumstances.

Are you still struggling with contentment in your circumstances? Is the work still unfinished? If so, you may just need time to feel settled about them. Or perhaps God is pointing to something else that needs attention in your life. Ask Him to show you what it is.

3. Speak the Truth in Love.

This step is about confrontation—not confronting the people in your past, but learning how to confront the people in your life now. And it has nothing to do with an angry scene.

Let's look again at Paul and a letter he wrote from a different prison. In Ephesians 4:15 he says that we grow in Christ, partially through "speaking the truth in love." A little later on in the same chapter, he adds, "Putting away lying, 'Let each one of you speak truth with his neighbor'" (Eph. 4:25). Now, here, *lying* does not refer only to obvious dishonesty, but also to more subtle forms. Do you ever hedge the truth with your husband because you don't want to make him angry? Have you skirted around subjects with your mother because you didn't see any reason to "upset her"? Do you sometimes tell a caller that "the check is in the mail" because you don't want to discuss your financial struggles? Most of us have. Yet these forms of lying rob us of our integrity and of the contentment we seek.

Here is the pattern Paul gives us: We are to speak truth, but we are to speak it in love. Sound hard? Here are some guidelines on how to confront in love:

Speak in Love, Not in Anger.   Usually we either speak in love or we speak the truth, but we have a hard time doing both at the same time. Yet that's exactly what we are to do.

Here is an example: A wife is always protecting her husband and letting him off the hook. If he fails to understand her emotional needs or concerns, she says something like, "Honey, I know you're tired. We don't have to talk about this now," or "I'm sorry, it was all my fault. I know I'm pressuring you, so let's just change the subject."

When you fall back into your old patterns like this, you will probably think you have blown the whole process. But understand that at any point in a conversation, you can correct your focus and "speak the truth with love." As soon as you become aware of what you are doing, stop and say something like, "No, that's not what I wanted to say. I'm not going to let this just go by—it's too important to me. I want you to not only hear what I am saying, but also to pay attention to what I am feeling."

The same is true when you err on the side of anger, although this is much harder to correct on the spot, since the other person's anger has probably also been triggered. Still, you can stop yourself and say something like, "I'm sorry I've gotten so angry. I'm afraid you'll only hear my anger and miss what is really important to me. Let's talk about this later when I've cooled down."

These examples are not suggestions of how to "say it right." As we have seen, saying it right is no guarantee that it will come true. We are simply trying to show how important it is to stop those old patterns and bring our communication back into balance by speaking the truth with love. We need to act responsibly with ourselves and to express more clearly what we need from that other person. In doing this, we will also be allowing him or her to enjoy the privilege of being responsible as well.

Describe Exactly What You Need. When you get caught up in a cycle of disappointment, do you tend to complain to everyone except the person directly involved? Sometimes we have been so hurt and have so neglected what we want and need that we don't know how to express it directly. Here is a technique that has helped other women: Choose three things that are of primary importance to you in a given situation and concentrate only on them.

Carole was disappointed in the responses of her family and her husband's family. "They didn't talk much about what was happening, they weren't there to listen to my frustrations and fears, and they weren't offering to help me carry the load that was wearing me out." We suggested that Carole make a list of all the things she wanted from the family, then that she go back over it and pick out the three most important things. Carole listed: (1) Don't criticize what I am doing unless you have suggestions to offer, (2) Be willing to talk to me and let me talk to you, (3) Offer to watch him now and then so I can get out of the house.

"What about all the other things on my list?" she asked us.

"Let them go," we told her.

Over the years, other people learn that if they can get us to talk about all the things that bother us, they are off the hook. Since they can't possibly do everything we expect, the important things get lost in the crowd. But if you focus on three important things, the message will gradually get through. Then it's up to the others to decide what they are going to do.

Don't Explain or Defend What You Need. "I tried to tell them why I needed time off," Carole said. "Time for a dentist appointment or grocery shopping was easy, but when I tried to explain why I wanted to go to lunch with friends or to a movie once in a while, I started to feel selfish and guilty."

Trying to explain why you want or need what you are asking for is another sure way to get off track. Because most of us have been trained to explain, it is very easy to fall into this trap. But the more we explain, the more reasons the other person will find for not doing anything.

As soon as you become aware that you are explaining, stop! You do not have to defend what you desire. If you don't explain, you may get what you want, or you may not. But if you do explain, you will be guaranteeing that you *won't* get it.

Repeat Your Request Until You Are Heard. "I asked my sister-in-law for a Thursday afternoon, then a Friday morning, then some time on Saturday," Carole said. "When none of those times would work for her, I said, 'I know you're busy, too, but I need some time off.' Then I asked *her* to set a time. We were finally able to work out a schedule of three hours every Tuesday."

The purpose of our old patterns of communicating our needs was to change either the other people involved, or to change the situations. Now, because we are emotionally letting go of what we held on to in our dreams, we simply desire to be heard. This is an important part of speaking the truth in love.

When we begin to be more direct in our communication, the others involved will often keep on responding to us as if we were still communicating in our old pattern. They will try to push our buttons and sidetrack the conversation, or to bring up old issues, or to ask for specifics—whatever worked in the past to get us off center. Now, with the pattern broken, they will probably step up these efforts. A simple way to sidestep the problem is to respond by saying, "I understand what you are saying, *but.* . . ." Then repeat what you said in the first place. You can keep on doing this over and over until the other person tells you he or she has finally heard you.

4. Become More Flexible.

The Apostle Paul was a driven man. Part of his greatness came from his tremendous drive to establish and stabilize churches in as many places as he could. At least two times, though, when all his plans were thrown aside, he found he needed to go in a different direction. One was when the Spirit told him to go to Macedonia, including Philippi; the other was when he went to Rome in chains instead of as a free man. His spirit of contentment meant he was not only driven, but he was also flexible.

In Romans 8:28, Paul writes, "We know that all things work together for good to those who love God." Perhaps you've read this promise and wondered how your husband's emotional coldness could possibly work for your good. Perhaps you have questioned how your child's rejection of you and everything you value could work together for good. "What about my husband?" Carole asked. "When he was healthy, he was serving God! How can his illness be for good?"

These are hard questions. In his letter to the Philippians, Paul writes from prison, "I want you to know, brethren, that the things which happened to me have actually turned out for the furtherance of the gospel" (Phil. 1:12). Imagine that! Here is Paul, the victim of a gross injustice, choosing to "swim with the current." In no way is he passive about what is happening, for he protests the injustice every time he gets the opportunity. The ability to actively swim with the current requires that we develop a sense of flexibility that will allow us to effectively handle whatever develops.

In the second chapter of his letter, Paul urges us to "let this mind be in you, which was also in Christ Jesus." Then he points out how Jesus willingly "let go" of His status as God, and willingly "humbled Himself."

Is Paul suggesting we go back to quietly suffering the pain and hopelessness of our situations? Absolutely not! Never was Jesus a passive victim of His circumstances. Even when He was faced with the greatest injustice of all—death on the cross—He moved ahead with a purpose, making choices at every step. People who are victims believe they have no choices. People who know they have choices, whether they choose to act on them or not, are never victims.

All too often, when we are pushed to the wall, we can only think of our choices in terms of extremes. Remember Sarah, the woman whose childhood need for emotional closeness continued to affect her relationship with her husband? She said, "Over the years I've tried everything to reach my husband on an emotional level. Now

I'm finally facing facts. I can either give in and accept my lot in life, or I can leave him."

Because our frustration and hurt have blinded us to the options available to us, we may need objective input from others to help us find our flexibility again.

Once Sarah has identified the unmet needs represented by her disappointment in her husband, she can find other ways to find fulfillment in her life. For example, she might develop abilities that can put her into a job that has a lot of meaningful people-to-people contact. Or she may find that there are things she can do in her church that will be meaningful to her. Or she can volunteer to do things that matter to her. In order to do this, Sarah will not only learn how to say "yes" to helpful situations, she will also need to learn to say "no" to those that don't fit her needs.

Sarah can develop friendships that are meaningful to her. Her husband may not like her friends, but in finding options, she is not going to limit her activities simply to fit his plans. In becoming more flexible, she may even say "no" to her husband's plans.

Any actions we take to bring flexibility into our lives must be done with a caring, loving attitude, never with a desire for revenge or with spiteful anger.

5. Examine Your Thoughts.

Which things are we responsible for and which are outside our responsibility? One way to differentiate between the two is to examine our thoughts. Paul tells us we are to be transformed by the renewing of our minds (Rom. 12:2). How? By "bringing every thought into captivity to the obedience of Christ," he writes (2 Cor. 10:5). This is the only way to monitor our thoughts. Bringing every thought into captivity means listening carefully to the things we are telling ourselves in the privacy of our own minds, especially when we are experiencing disappointments.

It may help to write out the kinds of things you are saying to yourself. Carole told us, "Whenever I become aware of the heaviness of my disappointments, I look back at the things I was thinking about just before, and jot them down in a small notebook I carry around in my purse." Over time, Carole was able to look back through her notes and identify some thought patterns that were related to her feelings of hopelessness and disappointment.

Bringing every thought into captivity means listening carefully to the things we are telling ourselves in the privacy of our own minds, especially when we are experiencing disappointments.

So often we simply let our minds go wherever they want to go without ever realizing the impact our thoughts have on our emotions. Part of changing the way we feel means capturing our thoughts and seeing where they are taking us. As you monitor your thoughts, look for repetitive themes and beliefs that set you up for additional disappointments and frustrations. Here's what Carole found: "The thoughts that came up over and over again were that the troubles were somehow my fault."

Now examine the thoughts you have written and ask yourself such questions as these: How much do I really believe what I am telling myself? Is it accurate? Is it biblical? Then take some time to share your thinking with your supportive friends. Ask them for feedback on how accurate your thoughts are. After that, check your thoughts against your feelings.

"My supportive friends all said the same thing: 'How could this possibly be your fault? Rick has a genetic condition!'" Carole told us. "When I checked my thoughts against my feelings, I came back again and again to the same conclusion—I was consumed with guilt for something that couldn't possibly be my fault!"

Do certain feelings typically follow the thought patterns you are experiencing? Challenge the thoughts you take for granted.

How about the things you are saying about yourself? If a friend said those things about you, would you be hurt or insulted? Then why are you telling such things to yourself? It's important that we be careful about the way we talk to ourselves, for eventually we will end up believing what we hear. Make certain that what you believe squares with what God thinks about you. (If you want a picture of how God thinks about you, read through Romans 5–8 in one sitting. Read it several times, focusing especially on what Paul says in chapter 8 about God's unconditional acceptance and His endless love.)

6. Search Out Alternatives.

You've probably spent a lot of time thinking about what would happen if your dream were to actually come true. Now imagine what would happen if your dream *never* came true. What paths would be open to you that you could take?

"I can't do this," Carole told us, "because I don't have any options."

There are always options. Take time now to think of as many as you can. Don't evaluate any of the ideas that come into your mind. Concentrate on stirring up all the possible paths you can take to either change your life circumstances or to change your reactions and responses to the people who are the focus of your disappointment. Write down every alternative you can think of, then discuss the ramifications and consequences of each one with your supportive friends.

When we finally convinced Carole to try this exercise, she was amazed at how long her list was. "From that list has come an amazingly successful alternative," she told us. "Rich is working a couple of hours a day in a sheltered workshop with other handicapped people. He stays busy, he feels better about himself, he earns a little money, and I get a break each day."

You may be surprised at some of the new ideas you have overlooked!

7. Anticipate the Good.

As we live with disappointments year after year, we train ourselves to anticipate the hurt. If you are going to say goodbye to your disappointments, you are going to have to retrain yourself to see and anticipate the good. We aren't suggesting you set yourself up by thinking your dreams really will come true after all. We are simply saying you can begin to think that something nice just might be about to happen.

When Sarah worked through this step, she started noticing that her husband—in his own way—really was trying to please her. "Sure, he is way short of what I had hoped he would do," she said. "But because of my disappointment, I hadn't even seen the things he *was* doing."

As Sarah started to anticipate good things in their relationship, she was more open to seeing the small things she had missed before. "It didn't make everything wonderful," she told us, "but it did reduce the tension between us. And I do think he tried even harder as a result of my noticing what he was doing."

Sarah also noticed that she was feeling less internal tension. As she changed her focus, she started to relax. "I could actually feel some of the heaviness in me lessen," she said.

This was a more difficult exercise for Carole, but she, too, benefited. "It is so sad and depressing to see Rich deteriorate. What really helped me was when I started doing a Bible study on heaven. It really helps to understand that this life is just a transitory stage of our existence and that the time will come when he and I will be reunited, healthy and whole, to live forever in the presence of God."

8. Review Your Day.

Would you like to challenge and change some of the depressive patterns of your thinking? Then try this: At the end of each day, take about ten minutes to review the events of that day in terms of the changes that are taking place within you. Consider some of the positive things that are happening and some of the good things you are experiencing.

This exercise is especially helpful if you actually write the events down in a notebook. Carole records hers in a pink-flowered journal she calls her blessing book. Over time, she has accumulated a record of the good things in her life as well as the growth she has been experiencing. "When I feel discouraged and disappointed, I read through my blessing book," she says. "It gives me a more balanced perspective than I've ever before had in my life."

9. Move Toward Your Goal.

"I press toward the goal for the prize of the upward call of God in Christ Jesus," Paul writes in Philippians 3:14. He had a goal, and he was committed to reach it. Having a goal means deciding what is important to us. No longer will we live by someone else's agenda. With God's help, we will set the agendas for ourselves.

This is a tough step, for it requires that you take responsibility for yourself. It also means giving up responsibility for those things that are beyond your control. While these two actions are difficult in different ways, both can become excuses for not getting on with your own life.

The Serenity Prayer of Alcoholics Anonymous puts it this way: "God grant us serenity to accept the things we cannot change, courage to change the things we can, and wisdom to know the difference." Carole has a stained-glass lightcatcher with this prayer on the windowsill above her kitchen sink. Every time she is tempted to take responsibility for something beyond her control, she looks at the lightcatcher and prays the prayer.

Getting the responsibility question sorted out will free you to move forward. That can be exciting, but it can also be frightening. Often we get a weird type of comfort with that old disappointment pattern. And our tendency is to stay with the comfortable rather than launch into the new and untested future. But you have worked through the steps of the process, and you are ready to take on that responsibility.

"Imitate me, just as I also imitate Christ," Paul writes (1 Cor. 11:1). This imitation is an attitude, one that is willing "To let go and let God" so He can fill your every need just as He promised He would. If you are willing to take the risk to test His promises, you will find that He really is a God who never disappoints.

Letting Go

"Where did I go?" Jan's mother asked after she came into the room and turned around. We smiled at some of the funny things she said, even though we knew it was not funny at all. Jan's mother was in the beginning stages of Alzheimer's Disease.

"You are *not my daughter!*" she would tell Jan.

As Jan's mother went through each new stage, Jan's heart broke in a new spot. "I watched her make the last stitches as she finished a quilt for my little granddaughter," Jan recalls. "I hovered over her as she hugged the stuffed bear a neighbor brought her. I cried as she looked at me with blank eyes and saw a tear roll down her cheek."

Day after day, then year after year, we struggled with all the "why" questions.

"Mom didn't have an easy childhood," Jan recalls. "When her father wanted something at the table, he grunted. He never used words with the children, he just expected them to jump and figure out what he wanted. And her stepmother demanded that she do all the chores, take care of the younger children, and never, ever wear out her shoes."

And now this.

"So many times in those last few years, as I left Mom's bedside where she lay curled up in a fetal position, all I could think was, *It's not supposed to end this way!* I prayed over her and prayed over her, but the bedsores just got worse. We tried different nursing homes, but they were all awful. And we watched helplessly as my dad wore down with the burden of it all."

Jan had always expected that her parents would spend their final hours lying in their own bed, peacefully listening as all the kids said their last goodbyes. "Nothing could have been further from what was going on," she said. "And I couldn't do a thing."

Jan remembers her dad's oft-repeated words: "There's always something you can do about it." It's a wonderful attitude. An "I can" attitude is a great motivator that encourages us to take responsibility for what can be done. But there is a fallacy in that philosophy. The fact is, there are many things in life about which nothing, *absolutely nothing,* can be done.

Imagine a beautiful butterfly dipping down and landing on your hand. You could grab it and hold it tight, but what good would that be? How much better to open your hand and let it soar off. When we say goodbye to our disappointments, we are opening our hands and letting the disappointments go. We are letting God do His will in our lives.

PART THREE

I Am Physical

It

*T*oday is the day after Christmas. There's not much happening, so I'd like to show you around my office. Like many pastor's offices, mine is peppered with memorabilia and artifacts—things that have been given to me by family and friends. They serve as reminders of people I love and of fond experiences in my life.

If you were here, I'd show you pictures of my kids when they were still young and growing up. I have pictures of all three of them at various stages of their development. I'd show you Simeon's picture, the one I took when he was about three, wearing his "I was custom-made in Heaven" t-shirt. I'd show you the picture of Marcus the artist, sitting at a desk with two pencils, working on a masterpiece. You'd see a photo of Nate holding a fishing rod, wearing that old, red felt hat and his green jacket. Those pictures are special to me.

I save love notes from my wife, Randee, too. Some of them are in my desk drawer, some on my shelves, so that when I'm having a particularly *interesting* day (I like to use the word *interesting* instead of *rotten*), I can walk over and read one of her notes. Great therapy for *interesting* days.

I have a wooden map of Belize, Central America, that my best friend, a missionary, gave me. There are candles I never light (my wife thought they would look good in my office) and a few things mounted on boards, like my degree and my certificate of ordination.

My shelves hold lots of books on all kinds of subjects, a couple of stuffed animals my wife gave me, and Grandpa's old watch encased in glass to protect it from dust. A couple of plastic plants (I kill the other kind) add color. A little cardboard placard sits on my bookshelf. It reads: *Any guy with hair on his head is over-dressed as far as I'm concerned.* Everything in my office, or almost everything, was given to me by a person I love and want to remember. Especially **IT.**

IT sits high and well-protected on the second shelf of my tallest bookcase, next to one of my Bibles. Two hand-carved wooden letters—**IT**—alone, stoic, and stolid as a two-inch wooden Indian. **IT** was a gift from my good friend, Lisa.

I had only been in my present pastorate for a few days when I met Lisa. She was a regular part of our weekly ministry to single adults. She loved music and brought her guitar to share songs she had written. Hers was a sad story, but Christ had restored her life, and she relished her walk with Him.

She was a good parent to two beautiful, bright daughters. She had many friends, and of course, there was Jesus. He was the theme of her song, the anchor that secured her life. She'd been through a lot and knew from experience that any other way was meaningless.

Within weeks of our first meeting, I noticed Lisa limping a bit. She thought she had twisted her knee, and we laughed about getting old.

She was 27.

Doctors eventually told Lisa she had a mysterious degenerative nerve disease that was very difficult to treat. Over the next few years, I watched Lisa go from walking on two legs to being confined to a wheelchair. She was in constant, excruciating pain. As her pastor and friend, I watched her frustration and listened to her story.

IT was one word that always came up.

IT made her mad. **IT** wasn't fair. **IT** was scary, lonely, and very difficult. At times, she would call me and say she thought she was "losing **IT.**" After awhile, she said **IT** didn't matter anymore. Yet the longer I worked with Lisa, the more certain I was that **IT** did matter.

Frustrated doctors tried to relieve her pain. They eventually implanted an electronic device deep into Lisa's brain which they hoped would scramble the signal of pain from her legs.

My wife and I went to see her in the hospital the night before the surgery. They had shaved her head. Lisa told us the surgery was dangerous, and could leave her without the ability to speak, or sing, or even move. Some paralysis was almost certain.

We prayed.

We said good-bye, and the next day, Lisa went in to face **IT.** When she came out of surgery, she had lost the use of her right arm.

After a lengthy convalescence, doctors moved Lisa to a rehabilitation hospital for therapy: long hours of anguish interspersed with brief moments of total boredom. We talked during our visits about feelings and failures and the future. But **IT** came up most often.

IT hurt.

IT seemed like she had been in the hospital forever.

IT made her daughters cry when they had to leave their mother and stay with friends because Lisa was in the hospital for months.

For my fortieth birthday, a group of my friends got together to congratulate me on my passing "the half-way point." Several folks roasted me on the pitfalls of being forty. Before the evening was finished, Lisa made her way to the front, and presented me with one of my most cherished mementos: **IT.** Two letters, painfully carved by Lisa in beautiful wood as part of her physical therapy.

Lisa's condition continued to worsen, and she eventually had to give up caring for her children. **IT** made her feel guilty. She was virtually house-bound, and although she had many visitors, **IT** made her feel lonely. She tried to write, listen to tapes, and read. But **IT** became increasingly difficult. She would ask God why and wonder if today would be the day He would give her an answer. **IT** never came.

Friends brought Lisa to our candlelight communion service on Christmas Eve. She sat in her wheelchair, hands folded. I walked up to her and knelt to greet her. Pain said hello as she looked into my eyes.

"I had to come," she said. "I couldn't miss Christmas Eve."

A kind friend stopped by to see Lisa the next day and take her sick cat to the vet. She found Lisa lying in her bed asleep. But she was not asleep. She had *gone home.*

That was two years ago.

Real life isn't like a television program. In real life, innocent people suffer incredible things, and the things they suffer aren't wrapped in neat packages that get resolved by the end of the show. In real life, there are days when **IT** seems to be a long, long word, with complex meanings and implications. In life, there may be weeks and months and, yes, even years of enduring **IT** without a clue as to why **IT** has happened. Things such as:

- Why did my child's marriage fail?
- Why did my spouse have a nervous breakdown?
- Why does my child have this mental or physical handicap?
- Why did my baby die?

As difficult as those questions are, there are others even more debilitating and insidious. Was **IT** my fault? Was **IT** something I did? Could I have prevented **IT?**

So much of life is pockmarked with questions without answers. And I certainly don't have the inside track on life's deepest mysteries. But if you were here today, I'd show you a reminder Lisa left me—**IT**—a two-inch monument of faith sitting on the second shelf of my tallest bookcase.

IT may come to pass, and **IT** may be difficult, awful and filled with pain. But Christ has not forgotten.

The Man of Sorrows promised never to leave us, never to forsake us.

The One acquainted with grief has sent a Comforter, the Holy Spirit, to encourage us. And as if that were not enough, He left us three last words. Thank God, He left three triumphant words that we must never forget, the last words uttered this side of the tomb. One final blast in the face of life . . . and death . . . and **IT:**

"It is finished!" (John 19:30)

Ken Jones
When You're All Out of Noodles

Chapter

9

Sexuality and Shame

If we are to love others, we must first learn to love ourselves—and that includes our bodies. Do you love your body? Many times sexual abuse or misuse is the reason we first came to hate our bodies and our femininity. And many times the memories of the abuse are buried so deep they are not connected to the way we abuse our bodies by becoming anorexic, bulemic, or obese. If you recognize any of the scenarios in this chapter, we urge you to take the steps outlined, and we recommend both individual and group therapy as discussed here. There is help and healing for you.

Pam Vredevelt, Dr. Deborah Newman,
Harry Beverly, & Dr. Frank Minirth
The Thin Disguise

When Harry Beverly first asked Cindy about possible incidences of sexual abuse in her past, she repeatedly denied any. Even when Harry described the different levels of sexual abuse, Cindy continued in her denial. She had been in therapy for some time before she made a statement on the subject that caught Harry's attention, a statement that began to shed some light on her past experiences.

Harry and Cindy had been discussing her progression from young childhood into adolescence. Cindy described how she had been raised in church, and that she had felt loved and secure in her younger years. But things had changed as she approached her teens. She remembered a lot of friction between her parents. She also remembered how her mother vented anger on her while her father withdrew from Cindy emotionally.

"Things were never the same after that," she said. "I guess maybe that's why I started spending so much time with the Boltons."

"The Boltons?" Harry asked. "I don't remember your mentioning them before. Were they friends of your family?"

Cindy bit her lip for a moment as if she regretted having mentioned the name. She began to twist her hair around her finger. "Um, not exactly," she said, looking away from Harry. "Well, in a way, yes. I mean, Jonathan—Mr. Bolton—he was my piano teacher. He'd been coming to the house to give me lessons since I was about seven, so I guess we'd known him for a long time . . . sort of."

Knowing that the vast majority of persons with eating disorders have, at some time in their lives, been sexually abused, Harry felt they might have stumbled onto something.

"You said you spent a lot of time with the Boltons," Harry commented. "Does that mean you knew the whole family?"

Cindy nodded, turning her eyes back toward Harry. "Yes. Sarah, Jonathan's wife, was really nice. I loved going over to visit her. We used to make cookies together, and I loved to watch her paint. She was really good. Sometimes she let me help with the baby."

"They had a baby," Harry commented. "Did they have any other children?"

"No," answered Cindy, smiling slightly. "Just Mikey. He was really cute."

"So you liked spending time at their place," said Harry.

Cindy nodded again. "Mostly," she said. "I mean, yeah, I did. Except . . ." She dropped her eyes.

"Except what?" Harry asked gently.

Cindy shrugged her thin shoulders. She spoke so softly Harry had to strain to hear her answer.

"Except when . . . when he looked at me or . . . said stuff."

Harry paused a moment, knowing how difficult this discussion was for her. "What kind of stuff, Cindy?" he asked.

There were tears in her huge dark eyes as she looked up at Harry. "Stuff like . . . like how beautiful I was, what a nice body I had, how . . . how sexy I was." Her jawline twitched as she gritted her teeth. "Sometimes he'd put his arm around me or try to hold my hand. I hated it," she said, tears spilling down onto her cheeks. "I really hated it."

What Is Sexual Abuse?

Although Cindy's piano teacher never had sexual relations with her, he was guilty of sexual abuse. At a time when Cindy was feeling rejected and unloved at home, Jonathan Bolton took advantage of her neediness by inviting her into his home and encouraging her to feel like a part of his family. Even as she soaked up this much-needed love and attention, his suggestive actions made her feel dirty and ashamed. She was torn between her need for a surrogate family and her desire to escape Jonathan's abuse. But at thirteen, she was too young and immature to understand how to deal with it. And so, since she saw her maturing body as the cause of all her problems, she began to starve herself in an effort to stave off approaching womanhood.

How common is Cindy's story? More common than most people would like to believe. It is uncommon to find an anorexic or a bulimic who has not, in some way, experienced sexual abuse. Most people with eating disorders deny they have been sexually abused because they are not aware of what constitutes sexual abuse.

Several terms can be used to describe sexual abuse, but we will concentrate on three: *incest, sexual molestation,* and *sexual misuse.* In *Surviving the Secret: Healing the Hurts of Sexual Abuse,* authors Pamela Vredevelt and Kathryn Rodriguez explain these terms this way:

Incest describes any sexual approach, including exposure, genital fondling, oral-genital contact, and vaginal or anal intercourse between relatives by blood, marriage or adoption.

Sexual molestation refers to the inappropriate sexual stimulation of a child, when no family relationship exists.

The *sexual misuse* of a child refers to situations in which a child is exposed to any type of sexual stimulation considered inappropriate for his or her age, level of development, or role in the family. Showing a child a pornographic magazine, touching a child's body inappropriately, or allowing a child to view an X-rated movie can be considered sexual misuse. Encouraging a child to be in bed with the opposite-sex parent, when the parent is naked, can also be considered sexual misuse if the child is old enough to understand that this is wrong.[1]

As you can see, sexual abuse covers a wide range of actions and includes both touching and nontouching offenses. Without a doubt, Cindy's experiences with her piano teacher qualify as sexual abuse.

Eva was sexually abused. From the time she was a little girl, whenever she went anywhere with her parents, her father would stare at other women, making remarks like, "Now that's what a woman's supposed to look like," and "I sure wish your mother looked half as good as that." When Eva witnessed lust in her father, she experienced a form of sexual abuse.

Sexuality and Femininity

A young girl who has been sexually abused is bound to be confused about her sexuality and femininity as she grows older. In addition to Cindy's abuse by her piano teacher, she was confused by her parents' treatment of her compared to their treatment of her brothers. As often happens when girls reach adolescence, Cindy's father was uncomfortable with her emerging womanhood. Afraid of responding inappropriately to his maturing daughter, he withdrew his affection at a time she needed it most. Cindy read his reaction as a rejection of her because she was female. She also believed that being female was the reason her mother treated her with such hostility. Cindy began to hate her femininity, wishing with all her heart that she had been born a boy.

This belief is fairly prevalent among anorexics. The anorexic feels that if she can just look as unfeminine as possible, if she can shrink —even disappear—she won't be hurt anymore. All of her feelings of low self-esteem and unworthiness are tied up with her femininity; therefore, she wants no part of it. Of course, her feelings about sex in general are affected. Sex becomes disgusting and repulsive to her, and she wants to avoid it at all costs.

The bulimic, on the other hand, craves as much love and attention as she can get. She believes that the sexier she is, the more attention she will get from men, and the more easily she will be able to control them. Her self-worth is tied up in the amount of attention men give her. She is often promiscuous from an early age and uses sex to get what she wants. Deep down, she feels she has nothing else to offer.

One way we encourage patients to get in touch with their femininity is to send them out on a pass to shop for a lacy blouse, makeup, or perfume. These young ladies must identify with their femininity in a positive way without feeling the need to act out their sexuality through promiscuity.

Whether male or female, children should learn to validate their sexuality as early in life as possible. A young girl may sense rejection from her parents because they wanted a boy, or a boy may feel rejection because his parents wanted a girl. If that feeling is reinforced through the growing-up years, the child is going to feel uncomfortable with his or her sexuality.

God created us as sexual beings. Understanding that assists us in accepting our sexuality as well as the sexual dynamics in relationships. It also establishes acceptable borders and limits for acting out our sexuality. Without this understanding, a maturing child can easily get these messages: "Sex is evil"; "Being female is being second class"; "Sex is all anybody wants from me, so I might as well use it to my advantage"; "Sex is the only way I can feel loved and accepted."

As a teenager, Constance became promiscuous in an attempt to find love. When she was hurt and rejected by someone she deeply cared for, she decided she would never allow anyone to hurt her again. Not only did she choose not to be involved in any more sexual relationships, she chose not to be sexual at all. In writing a detailed description of herself during therapy, she told about every aspect of her life—her job, her friendships, her hobbies—but she never talked about herself as a woman. When her therapist pointed out this omission to her, Constance was surprised. She had not realized that she was denying her sexuality. By recognizing what had happened, she was able to rediscover her femininity and sexuality and to establish healthy relationships with both men and women.

When a girl is sexually abused, she often turns her rage inward and finds self-destructive ways to abuse her body.

Joanie was the baby in her family. She had one older sister, no brothers. While her mother was carrying Joanie, she and her husband hoped for a boy. Their disappointment upon having another daughter was compounded when the doctors told them that, because of the difficult delivery, they would probably not be able to have more children.

In Joanie's younger years, her father tried to mask his disappointment at not having a son by taking Joanie on fishing trips and to sporting events. She did her best to please her father. She became an active tomboy who tried very hard not to exhibit any feminine traits. When she began to develop in her early teens, however, neither she nor her father could deny her sexuality any longer. Their relationship became strained, and Joanie tried to numb her pain through a growing obsession with food.

Although eating disorders are much less common among males, young boys can lack sexual identity. Martin, for instance, was an only child. His father abandoned him and his mother before Martin was old enough to remember him. He grew up hearing his mother berate men, describing them as "the scum of the earth." She assured Martin that he was the exception to that rule, yet he was never able to believe her. He hated his masculinity and wished he had been born a girl. Food became his escape from himself.

Angie's older brother sexually abused her during her early adolescence. As she grew into womanhood, she carried the message that sex is dirty and that being a woman is disgusting and undesirable. She totally denied her sexuality and refused to see that there could be anything positive in being feminine.

In so many cases, it has been found that eating disorders start soon after the first incident of sexual abuse. That was true for Angie. Almost immediately after her brother first abused her, she began to starve herself. In the mind of the victim, sexual abuse and bodily abuse go hand in hand. When a girl is sexually abused, she often turns her rage inward and finds self-destructive ways to abuse her body. These bodily abuses can range from eating disorders to self-mutilation to excessive exercise to suicide. If you have experienced sexual abuse and find yourself trapped in self-destructive behaviors, particularly an eating disorder, the following sections can help you along in the healing process and assist you in forming a healthy view of your sexuality.

Breaking Out of the Cycle

Eating disorders usually start with a trauma, often a form of sexual abuse. This trauma leads to faulty beliefs, for example, "If I weren't like I am, this wouldn't have happened; therefore, this is my fault." These beliefs lead to illegitimate shame and self-hate, which can be acted out in self-destructive ways.

The first step in breaking out of this self-destructive cycle is for the victim to face and work through past traumas; individual and/or group therapy is essential. Although the person will resist taking this first step on the pathway to recovery for obvious reasons, it must be done if healing is to come.

As the victim acknowledges past traumas, her therapist can help her understand that she is not at fault, that the perpetrator was to blame, and that any guilt she might feel over what happened to her is false guilt. Although she may experience an extreme amount of shame over having been sexually abused, that shame and its accompanying pain can be reduced, possibly even eliminated entirely.

Three Stages of Healing

Many persons with eating disorders choose to limit their therapy to individual sessions, but most therapists strongly recommend combining individual counseling with group therapy. Three stages of healing for sexual abuse victims can occur in therapy.

Kathleen had been in individual therapy for several months before she consented to begin group therapy. Because of her shame at having been sexually molested as a child, she resisted group interaction; she was sure no one would accept her or understand what she had been through. The *first stage* of healing came for Kathleen when she realized the group members did accept her, and they did understand what she had been through because their experiences were similar. She was then able to feel safe with the group. She knew she was among people who would not judge or criticize her. An alliance, based on mutual support and understanding, quickly formed between Kathleen and the other members of the group.

The *second stage* of healing came for Kathleen when she was able to face the need to revisit the memory of the trauma for the purpose of connecting feelings with facts. Most girls who have been sexually abused tend to block out all feelings related to the incident. Revisiting the memory forces them to get back in touch with those feelings, so they can deal with them honestly. One reason stated most often for not wanting to revisit the memory is that it is as if the incident is happening again. In group therapy, Kathleen learned that reenacting the incident did not mean it was happening again; it was simply getting back in touch with the feelings she had repressed since it happened.

The *third stage* of healing can occur when "men" issues are addressed. Those who have been sexually abused, particularly bulimics like Kathleen, hate men, yet exhibit a tendency to act seductively toward them. It becomes a game: they lead men on, then cut them off in a sort of power play, an attempt to allay their own anger and rage. This behavior can be dangerous if the woman encounters a man who is violent or aggressive. Fortunately for Kathleen, group therapy gave her an opportunity to work through her feelings toward men openly and honestly, and to move beyond her hatred to forgiveness, opening the door for healthy relationships in the future.

Overcoming

Although, at first, revisiting the memory of her trauma seemed like the worst thing Kathleen had ever been asked to do, once she did it, she found she had taken a step toward overcoming the aftereffects of her abuse—namely, her eating disorder. But not everyone who has been sexually abused can remember the incident. Sometimes the pain is so great that the memories are repressed and no amount of trying to remember can dredge them back up.

If you believe this might be true in your case, don't despair. Even if you can't recall a specific instance of sexual abuse, you can experience healing from your eating disorder. Try praying this simple prayer: "God, show me what I need to know to overcome my eating disorder." If, over a period of time, you recall an incident, consider discussing it with a therapist. If you never remember anything, assume that you know all you need to know for now to move on in the healing process.

The first emotions Kathleen felt as she recalled her trauma were guilt and shame, mixed with moments of numbness. But as she talked it out with her therapist and in group, she connected her anger and rage to the perpetrator of her abuse. When a victim begins to make that connection, it may be appropriate to get that anger and rage out through an exercise such as writing a letter or talking to an empty chair. For Kathleen, pouring her feelings out in a letter proved beneficial.

After a sexual abuse victim has acknowledged her emotions, she must allow herself to grieve and to express her feelings. Some victims may feel the need to confront the offender; others may feel more comfortable expressing their emotions to the members of their group, as Kathleen did. If a woman does want to confront her offender, we suggest that she do this after she is well on her way to recovery, and that she proceed with great caution. We have seen too many victims revictimized who hastily confronted their offenders before reaching a point of stability and health.

After a sexual abuse victim has acknowledged her emotions, she must allow herself to grieve and to express her feelings.

The next step for Kathleen was to confront the false ideas she had come to believe about herself: "I am worthless"; "My body is ugly and repulsive"; "I would never have had these problems if I had been a different kind of person."

The final and possibly the most challenging step for Kathleen in overcoming the effects of her sexual abuse was that of forgiveness. Even mentioning this step to a sexual abuse victim is difficult, especially if she has revisited the memory of her trauma and is in touch with the anger and rage that were buried for so long.

The Process of Forgiveness and Reconciliation

"Will it ever be possible for me to forgive my father for what he did to me? Can our relationship ever be reconciled?" Kathleen asked as tears filled her eyes.

"My friends at church tell me I have to forgive him. But I can't! He was wrong! All those years he offended me over and over and over again! He knew better. . . . He doesn't deserve to be forgiven!"

Many who were abused as children experience feelings similar to Kathleen's. Forgiveness and reconciliation seem impossible. And humanly speaking, we would agree that it is next to impossible. It requires supernatural help from God. And it doesn't happen overnight. It is a process. As therapists, we see the process happening in three phases.

Phase 1: Choosing to Forgive

Webster's New World Dictionary gives this definition for the word *forgiveness:* "to give up resentment against or the desire to punish." The first step toward forgiveness is honesty. You take a good hard look at your losses and allow yourself to feel the emotions attached to those losses. You fully acknowledge the offenses that require forgiveness. You vent your anger in constructive ways such as writing letters, talking, exercising, and crying. All the secrets come out of the closet, and feelings are fully expressed within safe limits.

You can make the intellectual decision to forgive anytime in life, but during this period of ventilation and grieving, you experientially give up, release, or let go of the bitterness in your heart. Feeling your pain and expressing it in constructive ways eventually lead to the release of your pain. When effective grief work is done in recovery, forgiveness moves beyond a choice of the intellect to an experience of the heart where you emotionally let go of your pain.

When Kathleen chose to forgive her offender, she did not say that what he did was right or condone his offenses. Neither did she have warm, tender feelings toward her father.

One night in her support group she talked about forgiving: "I've worked hard at getting the rage out of my heart. This group has helped me talk about my feelings. You have heard my anger toward my family and God. Prayer and journaling have helped too. When I started therapy, I never thought I'd be able to forgive. I knew God wanted me to forgive so that I might heal, and I wanted to obey Him, but I felt stuck. I just couldn't let my father off the hook. My therapist said that it would take time and that forgiveness was a process. After the first session I remember asking God to help me become willing to forgive. Many months later I see that He answered that prayer.

"A couple of months ago I knelt by my bed and began talking to God. I told Him that I forgave my father, myself, and Him because I refused to be chained to my pain and resentment any longer. I had been stuck in feelings of hatred and anger for twenty-three years, and it was time to move on. Forgiveness had nothing to do with whether or not my father deserved it. Of course he didn't deserve it! I forgave him because I deserved to get past my pain. The bitterness I was packing around wasn't hurting him in the slightest, but it was killing me. Forgiveness was a gift I gave myself. I believe God wants to heal me, and this is part of His prescription. And I think I finally understand that God and the manifestation of sin in this world are not the same thing."

For Kathleen, and for most victims of childhood abuse, forgiveness is a choice that involves a process. It begins with honesty. It continues through grief. And eventually feelings of the heart catch up with the intellectual decision. It takes time. It takes God's supernatural help.

If you are feeling stuck and unable to forgive, perhaps you can start where Kathleen started. Ask God to help you become willing to be willing. He will answer this prayer and make His power available to you. The God who forgave all humankind for all sin can help you forgive those who have sinned against you. May we encourage you to begin the process today? It can start with a simple prayer.

Phase 2: Choosing to Confront

After the forgiveness phase, some women desire to reconcile with their offenders. This is possible if the offender is still living, if his whereabouts are known, and if the risk of being reoffended is minimal.

After a year in therapy Kathleen chose to arrange a face-to-face confrontation with her offender to express her thoughts and feelings about his offenses. The purpose of the confrontation was strictly to inform her offender of his wrongs and to make him aware of how his behavior affected the victim. Before the confrontation Kathleen knew there were no guarantees that the confrontation would automatically lead to reconciliation.

Her father denied his offenses and chose not to right his wrongs. Reconciliation couldn't proceed due to his hardness of heart. The confrontation was very painful for Kathleen since he offered no validation for the losses she suffered. At the end of that meeting she chose to detach herself from further interactions with her father. She told him that whenever he was willing to admit his wrongs and work toward reconciliation, she would meet with him. She prays consistently for God's help to let go of trying to make the relationship work and to leave her father in God's hands.

Unfortunately, in many cases offenders do not responsibly admit their wrongs, and the relationship is never restored. However, in a small percentage of cases, confrontation does prove to be a positive step toward reconciliation. Terri was able to see the reconciliation process through to completion.

Phase 3: Choosing to Reconcile

Terri's father, Mark, responded differently from Kathleen's father when confronted. After two years of separation Terri scheduled a time to meet with her father. She told him that she had been counseling with a therapist for the past year and that she wanted him to come to a session with her. Although he was hesitant, he did agree to attend the session. During the hour, Terri confronted her father about sexually abusing her when she was in junior high school. She explained the pain that his offenses had created in her life.

Rather than deny his wrongs, Mark broke down with tears of repentance and admitted to hurting Terri. He acknowledged that he remembered the offenses she mentioned and wanted to know what he could do to make things right between them.

Terri told her father that one tangible way he could demonstrate his sincerity was to pay for her counseling expenses for the past year. She also requested that he commit to several months of counseling with her for the purpose of rebuilding their relationship. He agreed and followed through on both.

Reconciliation is possible only when both the offender and the victim are involved in an ongoing dialogue and are committed to rebuilding the relationship. The old dysfunctional family rules need to be broken and replaced with healthy ways of interacting. Former victims must risk setting new limits with their offenders. This is often scary and is best accomplished with professional support.

One final caution. When forgiveness occurs and reconciliation begins, we encourage victims to move ahead slowly and not to feel as if they need to give their former offenders carte blanche to their lives and children. Some offenders try to impose guilt by saying, "If you've truly forgiven me and put the past behind you, then why won't you let my grandchildren spend the night?"

Victims must trust their own judgment. There is nothing wrong with not providing what may cause the offenders to sin. In fact, Scripture tells us that we are to guard against making others stumble. Not allowing their children to spend the night may be best for both their children and their offenders. Victims who desire reconciliation must learn to firmly hold to their new boundaries. If offenders are not willing or able to honor these new limits, perhaps the option of reconciliation needs to be reevaluated.[2]

Many with eating disorders were sexually abused as children. Some were not. But whether or not sexual abuse was a part of your experience, sexuality confusion is usually tied in with an eating disorder.

For those on the pathway to recovery, the trek can seem long and hard. But healing is possible. Being pleased with who you are sexually is an option. Be patient. Trust that God is at work in you. With His help you'll see changes happen, and like Kathleen, you'll come to a point where you're able to say good-bye to the tyranny of the past once and for all.

Feeding the Hungry Heart

There is a reason for overeating. Perhaps you are trying to "stuff down" anger and unpleasant emotions, or maybe you are trying to "fill up" an empty heart. If overeating is your addiction, this chapter from Love Hunger *can help you pinpoint the possible causes of compulsive eating. It all has to do with relationships—relationships between you and others, between you and food, between your heart and your stomach. We hope you will take the time to work through this survey of your relationships. It may lead you to the reason for your overeating. We would also like to recommend that you write out all your answers, thoughts, and feelings in a journal. We have found in our counseling that it is extremely therapeutic and many times revealing.*

Dr. Frank Minirth, Dr. Paul Meier,
Dr. Robert Hemfelt, & Dr. Sharon Sneed
Love Hunger

"Do you think you could treat yourself to one of the clinic's group therapy sessions tonight?" Dr. Hemfelt asked Barbara Jamison.

Barbara sighed. She'd been coming for counseling for three weeks now, and every time the question was the same. And every time her response had been the same: "No, I just don't really think I could do that."

That afternoon her answer changed. We had helped Barbara to understand the numerous causes of her compulsive overeating, some of which began in her childhood. She was able to say, "I've got a serious problem" rather than, "Yeah, I eat a little too much because I've been depressed lately."

"Oh, all right," she answered. "What time does this fat fanciers' fellowship meet?"

Even though we told Barbara the exact time of the meeting, she arrived ten minutes late. She quickly took a seat near an attractive, sandy-haired young woman who gave her a smile of genuine warmth. But there was no chance for them to speak because a tall, blond woman named Adrian was just being introduced as an "alumnus" of the group who had agreed to return to share her story. Adrian was tall, nearly six feet, Barbara guessed, with broad shoulders and a large frame, but not at all fat. She looked great in her gray-and-red dress and her sleek page-boy hair style.

Adrian plunged right into her story without preliminaries: "My father was passively abusive. That means he never abused me physically, he never abused me verbally; he abused me passively by doing nothing. In all of my growing-up years, my father never once hugged me, held me, played with me, or spent any time with me. To the very best of my memory, my father never even spoke my first name.

"And Mother just sort of ignored the whole thing—whatever it was. To this day I don't know if my father had been an abused child or if he wanted a son and so rejected his daughter. I can only make guesses. I kept on desperately wondering, *What's so defective with me that my own father won't say my name?* I remember lying awake at night, staring at the black void of my ceiling, trying and trying to figure out what I'd done wrong. Wondering if it was possible to be a monster and not know it.

"I worked harder and harder to please: I became Mother's helper, took over the cooking. I took care of my little brother. I got good grades in school. When I grew up I became a teacher and began writing children's stories. And all the time my weight problem was getting worse and worse.

"When I got more than 250 pounds overweight I turned to medical procedures. First I had an intestinal bypass where they removed a large part of my intestine. I dropped about 50 to 75 pounds with that, then just sort of stuck, so I had my stomach stapled. I got down to being only about 80 pounds overweight, so I thought I had my weight problem under control. After all, I was the slimmest I'd been in years. But you know what? Losing all that weight didn't make me feel a bit better inside. Oh, it was easier to move around, I slept better, and it was nice to be able to sit in a normal chair, but those were just externals. Inside I wasn't any happier.

"Actually a lot of old angers that I had been keeping down with overeating began to erupt. Physically, I just couldn't stuff my anger down with food because my stomach had been stapled to a size that couldn't accept it. So the rage surfaced, and I would have these terrible temper explosions at my husband. . . ."

Here Adrian was interrupted by an expression of surprise from her audience. She grinned. "Oh, yes, I was married. Hard to believe, isn't it? Of course, I wasn't 250 pounds overweight when Dick and I were married, but I was on my way. Dick always has been a very mellow, accepting sort of person. And even when I was erupting with these terrible tantrums, I don't think it upset him as much as it did me. I mean, here I was, a woman who wrote gentle children's stories, my husband was my best friend and a nice guy, and my behavior was totally baffling and unacceptable.

"In therapy later, I learned that deep inside me was this great quantity of hurt, and below that hurt was an even greater quantity of anger. But I'd never allowed myself to deal with the hurt or the anger because I had literally stuffed those feelings with food—pushed them down until I had no idea they were there. But then I couldn't stuff enough food in to keep the rage down, and it all boiled out. I would be fine for days or maybe weeks, and then one day Dick would walk into the room, and I'd have this look on my face, and I would literally attack him and scratch him and hit him. Once the anger was out, I was as baffled as Dick, and I'd apologize to him. I'd be better for a while, but then it would happen again.

> *I'd never allowed myself to deal with the hurt or the anger because I had literally stuffed those feelings with food—pushed them down until I had no idea they were there.*

169

"We were beginning to think maybe I was demon possessed. And that's when I came in for therapy, with a group very much like this, only we were all hospital patients, people whose conditions were so serious they were immediately life-threatening to themselves or to others, or people who needed to be taken out of a bad situation for therapeutic reasons. There were several bulimics, anorexics, and drug abusers in our group.

"Well, anyway, a part of me wanted to be in the hospital and realized I was getting help. But as my therapy made me dig into these pockets of pain, a part of me wanted to run away—to get out of there. So one morning I simply ran out of the hospital and down the highway. For my own protection, the hospital staff called the local police to help find me.

"Now, you've got to get this picture: My hair was long then, and fuzzy-curly, I weighed well over two hundred pounds, and I was wearing this nightie with blue and purple flowers and fuzzy pink slippers. Well, this nice young policeman—he couldn't have been more than twenty-two, and about two-thirds my size—was the one who found me. I turned all my rage on him. I gave this sort of snorting yell and charged right at him. Fortunately he sidestepped or I'd have flattened him. He had the courage to chase me, and at one point he got hold of my wrists. I kicked him in the shins and broke free. The next time he came for me I stampeded right under his arm with my head down like a mad bull rushing a toreador. This was right by Highway 75 during rush-hour traffic, and people were honking their horns at me. Then I think I had some idea of hiding behind a tree—but of course, no tree could hide me. Finally, his partner arrived to help him, and they got me back to the hospital."

Adrian and her listeners all stopped to laugh at the images her story had conjured up. After a few moments she added, still chuckling, "So I guess the moral of that is, if you want to run away, have the sense to put on slacks and running shoes first. But really, I was just so angry. I can still feel the intensity of all that boiling up in me. And I was so afraid to face it that the only thing I knew to do was to run.

"When I saw this policeman, it was like an ultimate authority figure that had to be resisted. Once I calmed down, I worked through that crisis and realized that I needed and wanted to stay in the hospital. Working with the doctors here—Dr. Minirth and Dr. Meier and Dr. Hemfelt—I finally learned that I could trust men. They weren't all like my father, and I learned that people really do care about me— that I'm worth caring about.

"This all happened a year ago. So today is an anniversary for me."

She was interrupted here by applause and cries of, "Congratulations!" "Happy anniversary!"

"Thank you. Only maybe I should call it a birthday because I truly feel like a new woman. You see, for the first time in my life I really dealt with the foundation of my problem, not just the symptoms."

The group applauded again. Then, in the general discussion that followed Adrian's speech, Barbara's neighbor turned to her. "Hi, I'm Ginger. She had a great story, huh?"

Barbara nodded. "Yeah, she sure did. And she looks fabulous— so pulled together—can't imagine her doing that wild scene with the policeman." Barbara paused and probably would have remained silent if Ginger's smile hadn't been so encouraging. "But you know, to be honest, I don't really get this relationship stuff they talk about around here. I mean, I'm fat because I overeat. Every book I ever read said it's a simple matter of mathematics: if you take in more calories than you burn, you'll store it as fat. So what's the big deal about whether my father ever spoke my name or not?"

"Yeah, I felt like that at first too. I mean, when Dr. Meier gave me this relationship survey to work through, I said, 'Hey, that doesn't have anything to do with food!' and he just gave me that slow grin of his and said, 'Yeah, I know. But I want to get to know you a little better. So tell me a little about Mom and Dad and what it was like growing up. . . .' "

Surely this woman couldn't have had a messed up life like Adrian's, Barbara thought as she wondered what Ginger's story was.

As if Ginger had read Barbara's thoughts, she continued, "I guess my story isn't as dramatic as the one we just heard—I never did a bullfight scene with a policeman. But all my weight problems and my marriage problems came from junk in my childhood.

"The whole thing was, my parents never gave me permission to leave home emotionally. There was a lot of codependency in our family . . ." She interrupted herself with a laugh. "Spend enough time around psychologists and you start talking like one. But my father is very authoritarian, and Mama has a big-time weight problem. Real big-time. So my father had me on a rigid diet and exercise program all my childhood, and Mama told me all her marital problems, and I was the scapegoat for everybody's problems. Dr. Meier said that, emotionally, I was functioning like a surrogate spouse to both of them.

"My brother married and left home—no problem. But I never could manage to leave for very long. I made two really bad marriages and never moved more than a couple of miles from home."

Barbara blinked. She truly appreciated Ginger's openness and friendliness, but her story just added to the confusion. "I can see that was very difficult for you, but I still don't see what it had to do with your eating problem."

"Well, I ate to defy my father—what the doctors call a control issue—and I ate to keep Mama happy, and I ate to protect myself from men. And then, just before school started every year—I'm a history teacher—I'd go to Weight Watchers and lose a bunch, which I'd gain back by the end of the year. Then I'd start all over again. But all the time I was—am—aware of my biological clock ticking. I want a good marriage. I want a home. I want children. Here I am thirty-five years old, and I'm having trouble leaving home."

The meeting was breaking up. Barbara nodded as if she understood; but she wasn't at all sure she did.

"Here, it's time to go, but let me show you this. It's really helping me." Ginger pulled a 3×5 card from her purse. "I carry this with me all the time to remind myself that eating can't solve my emotional problems. No matter how much food I stuff into my stomach when I'm feeling angry at my parents or longing for a husband and children, food will never reach my heart and satisfy its hunger."

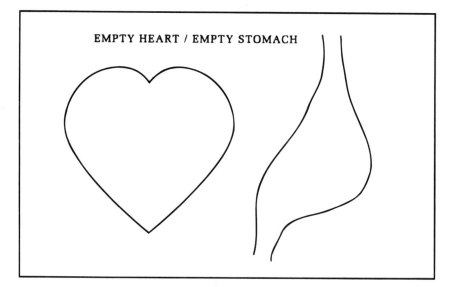

EMPTY HEART / EMPTY STOMACH

Love Hunger

If your problem, as with approximately 90 percent of our patients, is rooted in a multigenerational dysfunction, then you may be walking around with a vacuum in your heart, which is illustrated by our empty heart/empty stomach model, the illustration on the 3 × 5 card that Ginger showed to Barbara. Every human infant is born with a need to be loved. Children with emotionally available parents, will, throughout their growing-up years, have their hearts filled, and then as adults they can fill others' hearts.

But children like Ginger, who are deprived of a heart-filling childhood, will walk around with empty hearts (emotional vacuums waiting to be filled, waiting to suck, pull, shove something into them) by the time they reach late childhood or adolescence. If food is chosen as the agent of addiction, these people begin feeding their gullets, just like an animal feeding its gullet with no consideration of the aesthetic pleasures of taste.

People with heart hunger will stuff their stomachs, either constantly or periodically, in an attempt to fill their hearts, but no matter what they put into or force out of their stomachs, (in the case of the anorexic or bulimic), none of it touches the heart. In fact, the more effort and energy they direct toward their stomachs, the less emotional and psychic energy they can invest in those things that could legitimately fill their hearts.

> *People with heart hunger will stuff their stomachs, either constantly or periodically, in an attempt to fill their hearts.*

So if either of two things have happened to you: If you have come from a dysfunctional family (where, for example, one parent was an alcoholic or rigidly authoritarian), you may have entered adulthood with an empty heart. Or if you came from a normal family, but in adulthood encountered enormous setbacks, such as a disappointing marriage, a job failure, a death in the family, or a serious illness, you may now have an emotional deficit. This deficit can even be caused by the exhaustion and constant giving required by good things in your life: nurturing an active, growing family; career success that demands more and more of you; volunteer work that swells to take so much of your energy that you have no time left to recharge your own batteries.

Often the simple empty heart/empty stomach model causes our patients like Ginger to say, "Now I see it! All the time the real hunger is over here in the heart. I see now that no matter how much I binge or purge the stomach, it's never going to touch my heart issues." Many of the patients put the diagram on a card and carry it around with them, as Ginger did. We suggest they look at it when they feel a desire to overeat and then ask themselves: *Is my stomach hungry, or is my heart hungry?* And they often look at this diagram in counseling to help them remember: *When I'm addressing my heart issues, I'm also addressing my eating disorder issues.*

Our empty heart/empty stomach model is the core of most eating disorders, while a small percentage is primarily caused by physical, chemical, or metabolic problems. Only your physician can determine if you are one of this minority. We recommend you have a physical examination and discuss this possibility with your doctor.

Surveying Your Relationships

Now that Barbara has come to understand the delicate interweaving between food and relationships, she, just like you, our reader, is ready to take a close, detailed look at all areas of her life, past and present. The list we gave her to work through looked something like the one on pages 204 and 205 and, after talking about it for a while, we asked her to take the survey home, think about it, and answer the questions, as deeply and as truthfully as possible in a journal.

"Don't try to edit or map out your answers," we told her. "Just ask yourself a question—tell your subconscious mind you want to get at the truth. Then write nonstop for as long as you can on each question. Don't worry whether or not you're making sense; just keep your pencil moving. If the only thing that comes to your mind is a shopping list, write it down—get it out of the way; then the deeper answer hiding behind it will emerge. You should probably be able to write without stopping for about ten minutes at a stretch. Remember, no editing. If your pencil is moving, you're doing it right."

Relationships with Family of Origin

The first area of your relationships to survey is your family of origin—the family you grew up in, whether your biological parents raised you or you were adopted, either legally or informally. Or did you live in the same house with your biological parents or one parent, but were really raised by a grandparent, babysitter, or older sibling? Or were you the parent in your home, even to your own biological parents, as Ginger was?

Besides recalling who performed these roles, how did you feel about them? Do you have happy memories? Or are you filled with rage or despair when you remember how you were treated?

Although unpleasant, it's particularly important to explore your unhappy memories. There are three types of abuse you need to understand in order to evaluate whether or not your family of origin was dysfunctional.

Active abuse is the easiest to identify because it is violent and often leaves physical marks. Active abuse includes beatings, sexual violation, verbal or emotional violence, or rigid overcontrol.

Passive abuse is harder to identify because it consists of acts of omission rather than acts of commission. You need to look for what was missing. To develop into healthy adults, children must receive time, attention, and affection from their parents. If any of these qualities was missing or compromised in your family of origin, then there was passive abuse.

The *tyranny of the "isms"* in a home creates its own abusive situation which may have elements of both active and passive abuse. The "isms" we refer to include alcoholism, rageaholism, workaholism, perfectionism—any all-consuming behavior of the parents that denied the children time, attention, and affection or that led to beatings or overcontrol.

Relationships with Members of the Opposite Sex

Being able to see repetitious patterns in your relationships with the opposite sex is one of the most valuable discoveries you can make. One of the most devastating patterns is codependency, in which one seeks to gain identity and worth through the approval of a partner. For many of our patients recognizing codependency with the opposite sex is a life-changing experience, which provides insight into their codependent relationship with food. One woman in her forties told us as she smiled her first real smile of excitement since she had entered therapy, "I can see it! For the first time in my life, I see it on paper. I've never—never picked a man that gave to me. I never realized that before. I mean, I knew there was pain, but I didn't understand it. Now I see the pattern that time after time I picked men who needed to be taken care of—who were caught up in their own worlds—and I tried to win their approval, but they never gave love or approval to me."

Being able to see repetitious patterns in your relationships with the opposite sex is one of the most valuable discoveries you can make.

Think about your relations with members of the opposite sex. Think as far back as you can. It's especially important to focus on your first dating experiences, probably about junior high age. These first experiences likely were your first venture in intimacy outside the family of origin. Your choice of dating companions might have seemed to be a matter of accident or luck, but really subtle influences were at work. Early dating experiences are an attempt to transplant intimacy from the family of origin to a larger circle, and one will subconsciously choose situations similar to those in the home. Did you choose fun, caring companions who could give to you and share freely, or did you choose codependent or abusive companions? Simply list all the names that come to mind as you think back through these relationships from adolescence through young adulthood, up to the present. Then, in journal form, sketch out what you remember about each particular relationship. What was enjoyable? What was painful? Are there repeating factors?

Relationships with Family Members and Friends

Now take a close look at your current family relationships. In your mind's eye, put your hand on the doorknob of your home. How do you feel about walking through that door? Are you walking into a warm, fun, safe place? Or does your stomach knot up?

If you are married, focus on your relationship with your spouse. One patient of ours who is married to an alcoholic found this to be a particularly revealing exercise. "I pushed the garage door opener," she said, "and I realized that I relax if Ed's car is gone. If it's there, my stomach tightens up."

When discussing with patients this part of their relationships, we often ask, "To whom are you married?" This always evokes a double take, especially if the spouse is sitting in the office.

Yet the question is not simply one of identification. We are asking, "Where is the greatest intensity of your emotional commitment?" Is your greatest emotional commitment to your spouse? To a parent or a child? To your job? Or to food? Love hunger can be used to build a warm, secure marriage, and that's good. Too often, however, we see cases in which it has led to overbonding with a parent or a child or something outside the marriage relationship or even something nonhuman, like food.

The tightest love bond needs to be between spouses. This, then, creates a secure atmosphere for the children. In any home where the spouses are not truly married to each other, there will be dysfunction. This is an especially important area for compulsive overeaters because there is always some degree to which the food-obsessive person is married to food.

Besides looking at your relationships with those living in your home such as spouse, children, roommate, or elderly parents, look at your friendships. Who are your close friends? What do you do for them? What do they do for you? It's very common for patients to respond to this question with blank stares and astonished silences. A great many compulsive eaters have allowed food to consume their lives so fully that they have no room for normal friendships. It's important, also, to understand that even in the best of marriages, each partner needs healthy outside friendships. It's great to consider your spouse your best friend, but the wife also needs a good female friend she can share with, and the husband needs a male friend to enjoy activities with.

Relationships with Authority Figures

When we asked Ralph, the roller-coaster overeater, to inventory his relationship with his boss, he found a repetitive pattern.

"Every time I got a promotion," he told us, "I'd go on an eating binge. You see, I'd tell myself, deep down inside, *I'm not worth it. If they really knew who I was, they wouldn't give me this job.* And so it would set me off—I'd go into deep depression over guilt feelings that

I'm not who they really think I am, and then I'd start acting out all my diseases, and the weight would spiral back up.

"Then I'd go out the back door and go in for treatment. Go out and stay gone for six or eight weeks. And then I'd come back, and they'd say, 'Where have you been?' And I wouldn't answer, and they'd say, 'Everything OK?' and I'd say, "Yeah, thanks.' And usually it was too late to pull back the promotion. I thought they should, and I offered to step down, but they said no.

"But every time they talk promotion, I think, 'They're setting me up. They want to promote me so they can fire me.' And I go out and binge eat—especially in the last three years since I've been drug- and alcohol-free. Food's the only one of my addictions I can act out in. Around the office they didn't really know what was going on, but the fluctuations in my weight were obvious. Some of the fellows started calling me Yo-yo—I guess that sort of fits anyway, since my last name is Yoland."

Look back through the relationships in your life, and survey the authority figures. Some of this will be repetitious of the first point we surveyed, but this time think of these people as authority figures, rather than in parental, nurturing roles. How was control maintained in your home or classroom or on your teams? Were you disciplined in a loving way? Or were you punished harshly in anger?

To evaluate the authority in your home, you need to understand that authority can be abused in two ways. Undercontrol by parents who ignore a child is as abusive as overcontrol from tyrannical parents. We offer our patients four guidelines to determine whether or not they received abusive discipline.

1. Was there any tissue damage? Were you spanked hard enough to leave bruises or to raise welts?

2. Did the discipline come out of a power struggle arising from the parent's insecurity?

3. Was there any humiliation involved in the punishment? Forcing a child to pull down his pants to receive a spanking in a shopping mall is abusive.

4. Was the punishment disproportionate? An anorexic patient told us, "The punishment never fit the crime. Once I was grounded for two weeks for refusing to eat the crust on a piece of cream pie."

Other aspects of your family of origin besides discipline may affect your relationships with authority figures. An example is a compulsive-eating patient of ours who is an airline executive. He does very well initially in a new position, but "then all the backbiting and power-jockeying start to get to me until I just can't take it anymore," he said. In doing his relationship survey he discovered that these paranoid feelings came from growing up with siblings who were continually tattling to gain their parents' favor.

Relationship with Yourself

Now we come to the hardest part of the survey. Take a look at your relationship with yourself. How do you see you? What kind of a friend are you to yourself? As an old music hall line asks, "Would you want to join a club that would accept you as a member?"

This part of the survey is critical because elements of low self-esteem will begin to show up. When Ralph recalled how the taunting of his classmates made him feel like a withered bean plant, he immediately saw how his relationship with himself and his low self-esteem had started him out on the addiction cycle.

I've got to have a good relationship with myself before I can have a good relationship with people. I've got to have a good relationship with people before I can have a good relationship with food.

One of the major reasons patients come to us for counseling is that they want better relationships with other people. The building block is: I've got to have a good relationship with myself before I can have a good relationship with people. I've got to have a good relationship with people before I can have a good relationship with food.

Often a food addict will come to us and say, "Just break my addiction. Let me make peace with food." We can't do that. We've got to identify the food problems and then go down through all the layers to get to the core issues. To help our patients do this, we often assign two exercises. First, take a clean sheet of paper and complete this sentence as fully as you can: "I don't like me because . . ." An honest assessment of the answer will be helpful in two ways. It may bring up valid areas where self-improvement is needed, but more importantly, it will show areas of unnecessary self-blame.

Now, on another sheet of paper, write a letter of introduction for yourself, commending yourself to a new person you will be meeting. Generously list all of your positive qualities. In this exercise give yourself full permission to lay aside all self-criticism. If possible read out loud this list of attributes to a trusted friend or recovery companion. This sharing may seem awkward, but it is a powerful means of reinforcing your new self-perceptions.

This part of the survey is crucial to your recovery. For at least one patient, it was life and death. Dr. Upton was a fine pediatrician who had saved the lives of many children, but his overweight was so extreme that it was medically defined as morbid obesity. In surveying his relationship with himself, Dr. Upton saw that because his parents never seemed to like him, he never learned to like himself. "I suddenly realized that it was OK for me to save others—to help them live—but that I disliked myself so intensely that I didn't believe I had a right to live. I've been committing suicide with obesity." This insight was the turning point in the doctor's recovery.

Popular recovery writer and speaker John Bradshaw says, "You are the only person you will never leave or lose," so you must have a good relationship with yourself.

Relationships with Food

This brings us to relationships with food. Has food been a friend to you? Most food addicts will talk about food the way drug addicts talk about drugs: "I hate it. I hate what it's done to me. But it's also my best friend. I can't live without it." In your journal, note how food has been a friend and/or an enemy.

It is often important for patients to approach this part of the survey as they did their relationships with the opposite sex, by beginning with their earliest memories.

Look for the progression of your eating addiction. Our patient Sally is a patterncard example of progressive addiction. During Sally's childhood, her mother had a mild tendency to use food as a nurturer, but overall Sally had a healthy relationship with food. As an adolescent, Sally began using food as a form of recreation, but she was active and had a high metabolism, so she remained slim. In college she began using food as a coping mechanism for the stress of grades and boys. Long hours of sitting while studying also contributed to the beginnings of her overweight problem. In early marriage Sally turned to food as a partner to compensate for the absence of a traveling-salesman husband. Now in middle age, Sally finds herself eating out of anger. Self-hatred has led her into a full-blown eating addiction.

Remember that your feelings about (and your activities with) food form a relationship as real as any relationship with another person. Your relationship with food affects all your people relationships—including your relationship with yourself. What are the recurring patterns of your relationship with food? When patients frame their eating history in terms of a relationship and chart it out like the course of a friendship or a marriage, they suddenly see patterns, and footpaths to recovery can be built on recognized patterns.

Relationship with Your Body

Seventh, you need to inventory your relationship with your own body. Again, go back in time and ask yourself, how did I see my body as a child? How did people around me view my body? It is interesting to think about how people respond to a toddler's self-discovery. When the three-month-old, sitting in his infant seat, discovers his toes, Daddy runs for the movie camera, and Mama applauds as Junior kicks his feet in delight. When Junior discovers his own ear and goos and gurgles, the family responds with corresponding oohs and aahs. But when Junior walks in without his diaper on to show what he's discovered, there is dismay. So what were the body messages you received as you grew up?

Then in adolescence and puberty, what did you hear about your body? What were you told about sexuality and body shape and body size? Were you told that if you're not large here or small here, you're not a real man or a real woman? We see many women in our hospital unit—beautiful women physically and emotionally—who had one body part that wasn't the way their parent thought it should be. They were told, "You're not a woman. You're not sexual. No man could want you." To a child or teenager, such messages come with the weight of gospel truth.

Then in your college or post-high-school years, when perhaps you were dating more seriously and in the working world, what kind of messages did you get about whether or not you measured up physically? And, most importantly, in marriage, ask yourself: *Do I feel my body is OK? Have I made peace with my body? Does my spouse affirm my physical appearance?*

We tell our patients to ask themselves, *Am I disembodied?* Obesity and anorexia are ways to leave your body, to abandon control and ownership. Most patients have to give this concept considerable thought, but then they will tell us, "I feel like I've been walking around in shoes that are too big for me. When I turn a corner, my body doesn't really turn with me. I don't fit." On the other hand, something we frequently hear from recovered patients is, "I feel as if I'm back in my body again."

Do you have a sense of being at war with your body? Only when peace is declared can the healing begin.

Relationship with God

Finally, inventory your relationship with God—with the One who is so central to many successful recovery programs for addictions.

Ralph admitted to us, "I have a lot of trouble with all the spirituality stuff in the twelve-step programs. I say the twelve steps every day, but you know, that third step, about making a decision to turn our will and our lives over to the care of God—well, I'd never prayed before in my life.

"Now I do every morning, but it's hard to understand how this applies to my whole life. It was easy enough to apply it to my drugs and alcohol, but I'm just starting to apply it to my food issues. I know it's something I've got to work on, but it's so new to me. And I know there's a whole lot of power that I can tap into—I've proven it by getting off drugs. Now I've got to prove it with controlling food—then apply it to my work—that would be progress. But it's a big change to allow God into my life in any form."

Working The Twelve Steps of the Overeaters Anonymous (OA) program requires inventorying your relationship with God in several areas: Do you believe there is a Power greater than yourself who can restore you to sanity? Have you made a decision to turn your will over to God? Have you admitted to God the wrongs you have done? Are you ready to have God remove your shortcomings? Have you sought through prayer, Bible reading, and meditation to improve your conscious contact with God?

As you work through this relationship survey, you will see many points where relationships dovetail in your life, such as, "Oh, I see— my relationships with my family of origin affected my relationships with authority figures, which now affect my relationships with my spouse. . . ." This was how it worked for Barbara.

For once, the papers surrounding Barbara on her bed were not discarded food wrappers. Long yellow sheets of her relationship inventories filled rapidly with unearthed memories as her pencil moved across the page: Little Timmy in the third grade. Except for his occasional bouts of calling her names on the playground, they ignored each other at school. But because his back yard joined hers with only a scraggly hedge between, it was natural to run to him whenever her father locked her in her room, or later, when she used that exit route to escape his drunken rages. And it seemed she never went out the window without fifteen cents in her hand—Mother always gave her money when she couldn't give her anything else—and Barbara and Timmy would scamper up the street to the drive-in. They could get a large order of fries for fifteen cents in those days. Barbara paused in her writing to lick her fingers, as if the salt still clung.

And then the pencil flew again as she remembered a hurt that must have lain buried for more than twenty-five years. Timmy took off as soon as the fries were gone. He was captain of his Mighty Mites team, and he'd go to practice, requiring her to scramble her way back through the window alone, now feeling abandoned by Timmy as well as by her parents.

Dating as a teenager? She paused and tried to remember. She couldn't think of one boy's name to list. There must have been boys in her classes, but she couldn't name one. Oh, their class president—was he Fred? Yeah, Fred, but she couldn't put a last name with it. All she could remember was turning away every time she came near him in the school corridor. She hadn't thought for years of how terrified she had been at that age of members of the opposite sex. She just remembered being shy and working very, very hard in her classes, especially art classes.

And then college. She left home, and for the first time in her life could live free of physical fear of her father. Maybe that was what had made her feel free to become friends with Calvin. Besides, he was going to be a preacher, so he would be safe. A preacher couldn't be an alcoholic. Yes, if she went back far enough—to the early days with Calvin when she thought she'd found a man who could fill the place her father never had—she remembered there had been some good times. She had felt so fulfilled she hadn't even binged. Not until the pressures of exam week when Calvin caught her coming out of Kampus Korner with a triple order of fries. It was probably the guilty look on her face that ruined her attempt to pass them off as being for a whole study group.

That was her first encounter with the legalistic approach to eating control. Calvin told her, "Now I want you to throw those fries in the garbage and pray for forgiveness right now." Barbara couldn't believe that she could still recall his words. She could even still see his long finger pointing at the garbage can and his bony wrist sticking out beyond the sleeve of his sweater.

From then on, she never left Kampus Korner without looking both ways, and she began purging meals even when she didn't overeat. Because the sermons continued: "God requires good stewardship. Wasting food when millions are starving is sin. Besides, a preacher's wife must look good. It's a good witness, and it helps His image." Did he really *say* that? Or was it just the message she perceived? Either way, she became very adept at sneaking, and the only time he suspected her of purging, she successfully invented a case of flu.

Her hand tired of writing. Barbara looked back over her last paragraph. So was that why she hadn't darkened the door of a church since she left college? What the doctor said about relationships' dovetailing was true. Now she wondered, *Had everyone at that school been as coldly legalistic as Calvin?* Was God really like that? Would God have abandoned her as Calvin did, or did she just assume she was unacceptable after . . . ? She began to write again.

Now she looked at the word that jumped out at her from the page. *Abandoned.* She'd said that about Timmy too. And her father. Her father *abandoned* her for alcohol. Timmy *abandoned* her for baseball. Calvin *abandoned* her for God—after she tutored him through six credits of English literature and he didn't need her anymore.

And then Tom. She thought she really had her life together when she met Tom. She had her bachelor of arts degree and a dream job decorating windows in a big department store. Next stop, a special course in interior decorating, and who could tell—maybe her own shop someday? And she wasn't even overeating much. Weight Watchers worked well when she stayed with it, and she loved her job so much she had other things to think about besides food. But Tom said she couldn't work after they were married. He was rising rapidly as a pharmaceutical salesman, and in his company the wives were expected to attend all the medical conventions with their husbands, to help entertain the doctors, and to be free to travel to frequent sales conferences. He'd never get where he wanted in the company if she didn't play the game with him. Tom was everything her father and Timmy and Calvin hadn't been. She'd willingly give up more than her career for him. Two weeks after the wedding he suggested she lose ten pounds and get three new dresses before the next medical convention.

But that would be all right. She could still paint and sketch at home. And as soon as they had children, she would have a wonderful time doing craft projects with her children. Only Tom didn't want children because he worked so hard and was tired when he came home at night. He wanted it quiet, and he wanted Barbara to be free for him. And she had been a good wife and done her job and seen him through three major promotions before the eating compulsion got out of control again. When she was twenty-five pounds overweight, she couldn't help his career anymore, so he moved out. Abandoned her.

Barbara's pencil quit writing and started sketching—the first "artwork" she'd done in years. She drew a rainbow with clouds at either end and a few last drops of rain falling on a flower bed below. This was her rainbow experience. All the men she'd ever known had used her and abandoned her, and she'd turned to food for comfort. Every time! She was sure she had some watercolors at the back of her cupboard. She wanted to paint her rainbow.

There's No Single Thread

As you have seen, the twelve causes of compulsive eating are intertwined and overlapping. It's a rare overeater who could point to just one item on the list, like cultural pressures, and say, "That's me; that's my problem. There's nothing else to it."

In group therapy we often use the example of a beach ball with its slashes of bright colors. We hold up the beach ball to a group sitting in a circle and ask, "What color is it?" People on one side will say, "It's red," while people on the other side will say, "It's yellow." Those to the left will shout, "Blue," and those across from them declare, "Green." Each answer is legitimate; each group is accurately reporting what it sees. But people need to see all sides of the beach ball in order to answer the question accurately.

Eating disorders are like that beach ball. Paul Meier says, "There are many different aspects to my compulsion. Part of my reason for gaining weight when I got older was the fact that my metabolism slowed down, and part of it was selfishness, a desire to gratify myself when I was feeling sorry for myself for having to study so much in medical school. And part of it was my subconscious desire to please my mother."

Doing your relationship survey should have helped you, like Barbara, to understand why you have a void inside you that you have been trying to fill with compulsive eating.

MY RELATIONSHIP SURVEY

1. *Family of Origin.* During my growing-up years, what were my relationships with my biological parents? Adoptive parents? Grandparents? Surrogate parents such as teachers or coaches? Other extended family members? Siblings? Was there active or passive abuse in my home? Was there an "ism" like alcoholism or rageaholism that rampaged through my home?

2. *Members of the Opposite Sex.* Beginning with junior high or earlier, who were my close friends of the opposite sex? What do I remember about each relationship? What was enjoyable? What was painful? What situations repeat?

3. *Current Family.* What are my relationships with my spouse? My children? Anyone else living in the home? My close friends? Is my current home a warm, safe, nurturing place?

4. *Authority Figures.* What were my relationships with authority figures in the past? In the present? Parents? Teachers? Coaches? Military officers? Doctors? Employers? Do I have a constant feeling that authority figures are just waiting for me to make a mistake? Are people out to get me? How do I respond to criticism, real or imagined? Have I served in an authority capacity myself? How did I feel about it? Was my church atmosphere a loving one or rigidly authoritarian? How do I feel about God as an authority figure?

5. *Myself.* How do I feel about myself? What kind of friend am I to myself? Would I pick me as a best friend? Have I acknowledged that I must have a good relationship with myself before I can build a good relationship with others?

6. *Food.* How do I feel about food? Has it been a friend? An enemy? What was food like in childhood? What was my relationship with food as a teenager? How did I get along with food in college? How did that relationship change when I got married? Am I punishing myself with food? What different roles has food played in my life from childhood to the present? In recent years has food come to assume an increasingly important role in my life? Am I addicted to food?

7. *My Body.* How did I feel about my body as a child? What was I told about my body as a child? Was it OK to be the gender I am? Or did Dad want a boy and I turned out to be a girl, or vice versa? What kind of sex education did I receive in adolescence and puberty? How do I feel about my body now? Am I living comfortably inside my own body? Am I using food to wrap a protective layer of insulation around my body, especially to insulate my sexual features?

8. *God.* What was I taught about God as a child? How do I feel about a Higher Power now? Do I see God as a source of unconditional love, or do I view God as a source of judgment and criticism? Have I formed a personal relationship with God to permit Him to live and move intimately in my daily life?

All It Takes Is a Little Willpower

A re you ready to kick the word, diet *right out of your vocabulary? It's done with self-love and self-acceptance!*

Thousands of women around the country helped me with input about their weight, their weight losses, their diets, and their thoughts about diets. Out of it came twelve fat fables that we queen-sized women have had to endure, like—"You're Just Big-boned;" or "There's a Thin Person Trapped Inside You." I put them all in a book, One Size Fits All (another fable); meet Fable #2, "All It Takes Is a Little Willpower." It's about dieting and, believe me, the word diet is not just used by big women. All across the country you'll find medium-sized, even thin women dieting all their lives—thinking that if they can just lose that five or ten or fifty pounds they'll finally be happy. Believe me —"thin" does not guarantee health, happiness, or a husband! Here are some of my thoughts (along with a nurse's thoughts) about how you too can learn to get happy, get healthy, and get on with your life!

Liz Curtis Higgs
One Size Fits All

This is the fable that cuts to the quick: All it takes to lose weight, stop eating junk food, and stick to a diet is "a little willpower." The late comedienne Totie Fields said it best: "I've been on a diet for two weeks, and all I've lost is two weeks."

We repeat to ourselves over and over: "If I just had more discipline." Never mind that we went to night school while working full time, which took discipline. So what if we get our kids on the school bus every day right on time (well, almost), which takes incredible planning and execution. Forget that we saved hundreds of dollars to buy a house, said "no" to drugs, said "yes" to daily vitamins. As soon as we see that number on the scale, that flesh under our chin, we say, "I have NO willpower!" And so we begin a diet. Oh, do we feel in control of things now! Look out world; I am following this thing to the letter. Four ounces of chicken, no skin, no gravy. No flavor, either, but look at all this willpower!

Why Diets Are Disastrous

The weight loss industry smacks its corporate lips when we get a shot of willpower coursing through our veins. We're talking about those folks who give us lo-cal products, diet books and videos, fitness clubs and weight loss centers. People who benefit when our willpower weakens. It's big business in more ways than one.

In 1990, the diet industry rang up $30.2 billion in sales revenue. We bought more than $13 billion worth of diet soda alone! We spent another $3.5 billion on weight loss centers and hospital-based programs.[1] If we ever figured out how much money we've spent in our lifetime in the name of losing weight, it would probably add up to a few thousand dollars an ounce.

Today, or any day, thirty million American women are on diets of one kind or another.[2] One woman's response to just the word "diet" is telling:

High level of effort—low payoff. Dangerous marketing ploy— abusive to women!

Donna from Kentucky

I remember two of the early diet potions from my childhood. First there was Ayds, a chewy candy-like product that was supposed to control your appetite. It was big in the early 50's, but persisted for years. Remember the full-page ads and before and after photos? I was hypnotized by them.

Then there was Metrecal, which showed up on grocery store

shelves in 1959. As is usually the case, this fad was all the rage for about two years, then faded into obscurity.[3] Even so, I can still see the television commercials featuring the Metrecal for Lunch Bunch dancing before my eyes. I was six.

"Go Where?"

Well-meaning friends and family often say, "You should go to such-and-such diet group!" There are plenty to choose from. Many of the weight-loss support groups we know today got their start around the same time. TOPS was first in 1948,[4] then Overeaters Anonymous in 1960, Weight Watchers in 1963, Diet Control Center in 1968 and so on.[5] No wonder we grew up thinking that dieting was the American way of life. According to a poll published in *USA Today,* 65% of Americans go on a diet each year. More than half of those diets only last thirty days. (Can you say "yo-yo?")

I remember my first trip to a diet organization, in 1976. (Just for the record, I weighed 150, but was still shooting for that elusive 128.)

They gave us a sheet of paper with a brick wall drawn on it. The idea was simple: for each hour that you were "legal" (don't you love that one?), you could fill in one of the bricks. Twenty-four bricks for each day, 168 bricks for each week. A brick wall between you and no willpower.

For those of us striving for perfection in our dieting, this brick wall was the ideal way to measure just how well our willpower was holding up. One tiny crumb of chocolate cake and—horrors!—an empty brick.

Even if 167 hours of my week were brimming with willpower, there was always that one empty brick staring me in the face, shouting out the terrible truth: "You just don't have enough self-control!"

No one else ever sees the brick walls we run into trying to lose weight, but it humiliates us just the same. We suffer defeat in silence, alone. We wouldn't dare tell someone else that we think this dieting thing is impossible, because we know what would be written all over their faces: "She has no willpower." So we conclude that everyone else has willpower except us.

Tuesday Night Meetings

For many of us, our mainstay was Weight Watchers. The food plans were fairly healthy, the classes upbeat, the cost was decidedly less than other options. Just one little problem . . .

I can learn to eat and lose weight successfully with Weight Watchers and I have lost 45–50 pounds several times. I've always gained it back, though.

Phyllis from Tennessee

Interesting how we define "losing weight successfully." Even the most "sensible" diet isn't much like our normal eating pattern. When we return to that pattern, the weight returns too. We sign up again, thinking, "this will be the time . . ."

In her book *Breaking All the Rules,* Nancy Roberts explains that the reason she kept going back to Weight Watchers again and again was because "it allows people already obsessed with food to develop, enhance and perfect that obsession." It was in fact a "winning combination of group dynamics and sanctioned obsession."[6]

How well I remember those weekly weigh-ins. Women lined up by the dozens to pay someone nine dollars for the worst news of their week. We could have found this out for free in our own bathrooms. But no, we wanted a public flogging. We wanted to be shamed into success, or have the chance to gloat if we'd had a good week.

If you've never been to such a meeting, let me give you the ground rules. At least 99 percent of the attendees are women. Weigh-in came right after pay-in, and was preceded by one last trip to the potty (and a "pray-in!"). Night meetings were hard for most of us because they meant an entire day of not eating. No wonder we headed for the nearest restaurant when the meeting was over!

Some people wore the same dress week after week, the flimsiest thing they owned, even in the dead of winter. Shoes always came off first—it helped to wear slip-on flats. I watched women linger at the back of the line while they unhooked belts, slipped off jackets, pulled off sweaters, the works.

One night, I stood behind a woman who had obviously had a bad week. As she got closer to the scale, sweat started popping out in little beads on her forehead. She slipped off her earrings, then her watch, then a little skinny gold necklace, two bracelets and her wedding band. (Her wedding band? How much could that weigh?) She dropped them all in her blouse pocket and got on the scale.

Poor dear. I didn't have the heart to tell her why this didn't help, especially when she gained four and a half pounds. The least I could have done was offered to hold her jewelry.

We'd Rather Die Than Diet

I asked women to tell me on the surveys "What thoughts or experiences come to mind when you think of the word 'diet'?" I was amazed to read over and over, in other women's handwriting, the exact same things I have often felt.

I just get a very tired feeling. A sad, frustrated, and sort of rebellious feeling. I've been on diets that took the weight off, then it came back and brought along "friends."
Pat from Wisconsin

Like the old saying goes, sometimes we get "sick and tired" of being "thick and tired." The word "frustrated" showed up on lots of surveys too.

Agony, futility, frustration, hunger, depression, loss of self-esteem.
Ada from California

Dieting also brings to mind a very specific menu. Barbara from Kentucky admits, "I hate tuna fish and I'm tired to tears of salad." Mary from Pennsylvania has an even more narrow food plan. "Dieting means you're not allowed to eat anything good."

When it comes to willpower, it seems that some people need it and others don't. Now that's not fair!

Our two sons, ages twenty-two and twenty-five, have moved back home after college graduation. They're slim and trim and can eat anything. So I catch myself thinking how fortunate they are to be able to do that.
Dorothy from Kentucky

Dorothy has hit on something there. Her sons "eat anything." In other words, they have no willpower. But it doesn't matter, because they are slim. They are the fortunate ones.

But the Dorothys of the world are expected to come up with loads of willpower simply because they are *not* "slim and trim." H-m-m.

Here's a similar story:

Dieting is a lifetime commitment I just can't handle. I wish I could control my eating like my sixteen-year-old daughter who's 5'7" and size 3.

Janet from Kentucky

Again, here's a comparison of our own bodies at age forty-plus to those of our children who have faster metabolic rates and often higher activity levels. They seldom have to worry about groceries, cooking or clean-up, and they've yet to experience the effects of aging and gravity, not to mention childbirth or decades of diet attempts.

"Won't" Power

Willpower concerning food can lead to serious problems. For many of us, exerting power over our eating habits can produce an obsessive need to control food intake which can lead to eating disorders such as anorexia nervosa and bulimia. In other words, willpower is not always a good thing.

Susan Kano, in her outstanding book, *Making Peace with Food,* lists some of the symptoms of anorexia nervosa, bulimia and chronic dieting. They include:

1. Preoccupation with dietary control; chronic attempts to eat less

2. Preoccupation with eating

3. Preoccupation with thinness/fatness and distorted body image[7]

As you can see, the common word is "preoccupation." Many women have dieted, have thought about the next meal, have wanted to lose 10 pounds. The key here is realizing how *much* those things occupy your mind, time, and activities. Willpower taken to the extreme is no power at all.

The truth is, nobody I've ever met (and liked) had endless willpower. Ugh! Who wants to hang around somebody who never bends her will to meet another's need, who never changes her mind, who never gives in to the desire of her heart? Boring!

A funny fellow named Steve Burns has the perfect solution: "Eat as much as you like—just don't swallow it." Of course, we're awfully hard on ourselves when we do swallow it.

I have no willpower. My "magic number" is 140, and I weigh 148. I have never been able to lose more than two pounds and it lasts a couple days!

Barbara from Ohio

Many of us identify with the "magic number" problem. We think only perfect counts, and perfect is always unattainable. Otherwise it wouldn't be perfect!

The Dreaded Treadmill

Which brings up another word that often surfaces when women talk about dieting. It's a word we repeat like a mantra, the most negative, defeating, discouraging word in American English: failure. It comes from a Latin word meaning, "to disappoint." And when we fail, the person we disappoint most is ourselves.

Pain, punishment, failure, deprived. You are on a merry-go-round of failure and you can't get off!

Martha from Ohio

There's that diet treadmill that just keeps going round and round.

Here we go again! Defeat. "Why couldn't I have kept it off?" I wonder how I could be so stupid to fall off the wagon so many times!

Peg from Kentucky

We can all identify with her frustration, even though we know "stupidity" has nothing to do with it. The problem isn't us, it's the "wagon!"

The embarrassment of gaining back lost weight cannot be understood except by someone who has been there. (I have been there!) People do a double-take when they see you and say things like, "I didn't recognize you. Have you cut your hair?" Or they just stutter, speechless. It's easy to beat yourself up when that happens.

For many of us "yo-yo's," we are aware even at the start of Diet #84 that there will be a Diet #85 someday.

Kind of like planned obsolescence—failure is programmed in at the start. When I hear about someone on or starting a diet I feel sorry for the pain and failure they are in for.

Mary Jane from Kentucky

I feel sorry for them, too, although what most just-starting dieters want us to feel is happy for them.

I've been on and off diets—hoping each one would be "IT." It is my biggest problem.

Monica from Ohio

This breaks my heart, maybe because it sounds like the old me talking. Have you ever felt like your weight was your "biggest problem?" When I think of the energy and angst we have spent on this single, narrow area of our lives it truly makes my heart ache.

Medically Supervised Failure

The diets we are willing to endure are endless in their variety, and in their ability to inflict pain.

I once was put on Dexedrine by my doctor. I went fishing with my son. He wanted to go in and get some lunch. I kept saying "just one more worm." I didn't know then that this was what we call "speed" now.

Nora from Ohio

Many of us have used pots of strong black coffee, to try and accomplish the same thing. The following story describes an experience common to many of us "diet warriors" who have tried everything.

They charged an arm and a leg for required blood work ($160), you had to pay an initial fee of $99 for registration, and after my second visit they said I needed to purchase the "maintenance *package" in advance for $159. They were unprofessional, I never saw a doctor, and the nurse told me she was only part-time. They also weighed me on a different scale each of the four times I went before I became totally disgusted. I began to feel like a piece of meat being inspected and scolded or praised depending on how my week went.*

Vicky Lynn from Ohio

There are plenty more tales where those came from:

I've tried Weight Watchers several times, Take Off Pounds Sensibly, Overeaters Anonymous, American Weight Loss (developed fissures), acupuncture, shots of hormone from the urine of a pregnant cow, Dr. Stillman's Diet (by the seventh day, I was ready to shoot him too!). In recent years, I have learned to be comfortable with myself—no more diets.

Joyce from Virginia

Facing the Bathroom Scale

Those of us who diet at home can be just as ritualistic as "professional dieters." Some women weigh themselves three, four, five times a day. Only one time counts, though, and that's the weigh-in that takes place first thing in the morning.

And, I mean *first* thing: right after a trip to the bathroom, and right before coffee. It's that little "window of opportunity," the thinnest moment in a woman's day.

Fanatics take a shower first to wash off all that heavy dirt. The next step, by necessity, is blow-drying your hair to get out all those pounds of water. Now you approach the scale, totally nude, completely empty, your most svelte self. You check the "0" setting. If the needle is directly over the "0," that's good. If it's ever so slightly to the left, that's even better. Next, you step on the scale, and start moving around. Where is that light spot? Ah. Finally, the last two steps that women of all sizes take: we exhale (air must weigh something), and then we pull in our tummies, the theory being that if you can't see it, it won't weigh anything. (Or, for some of us, so we can see the numbers!)

If we've lost a pound, we celebrate and eat something. If we've had a gain, we console ourselves and eat something. That's dieting the American weigh.

Some of My Best Friends Are Yo-Yo's

When someone tells me they've lost such-and-such pounds on a diet, my next question is always, "How long have you kept it off?" The effectiveness of any weight loss program should be determined by longevity, not how much we can lose or how fast we can lose it. By that measure, the liquid diets would fare pretty well.

Oprah Winfrey showed us on national television how easy it is to lose 67 pounds, and how even easier it is to gain it back.

Read my lips: *She* did not fail! The *diet* failed her!

The effectiveness of any weight loss program should be determined by longevity, not how much we can lose or how fast we can lose it.

Oprah has been, and continues to be, a wonderful role model for all women, but especially for the plus-size woman. She dealt a crushing blow to the liquid diet craze, not just for OptiFast, but for all the hospital and physician-based programs, as well as the across-the-counter versions. According to the *Wall Street Journal,* by September 1992, Ultra Slim-Fast sales were down 45 percent from the year earlier. DynaTrim sales were down 65 percent. People were discovering what Oprah already knew: Very low calorie diets don't work.

Naturally, any weight loss organization will tell you about their success stories. There are always a few people willing to forgo health and self-acceptance in the name of thinness. But the research statistics released in April 1992 by the National Institute of Health are not pretty: 90–95 percent of those who lose weight through a low calorie diet *will* gain back most of their weight within two years, and *all* of it within five years.[8] That puts the success rate at about 7 percent. One five-year study in Denmark logged only a 3 percent success rate.[9]

The insurance world would call that a poor risk. At the track, it would be a long shot. In medicine, it might be called malpractice.

When I dropped three dress sizes through strict dieting in 1982, I landed at a nice size 10–12, 160 pounds. Was I happy with that? Naturally not, it still sounded fat. It looked mighty slim, but it sounded fat. By then, I had raised my goal weight to a more "reasonable" 135. Forget the elusive 128; now, I was shooting for 135. At 5'9". Sure.

The scale never budged. A pound or two, but mostly 160, 161, 159, 162, 160, for two full years of dieting. I still have the weigh-in cards to prove it. If I was down a half-pound, I drew a smiley face. Good girl. When the scale crept up ¾ of a pound, I made a firm red line, like I used to make in league bowling when I wasn't doing well and wanted to tell myself, "I'm starting over as of right here."

I kept that weight off very simply: I ate almost nothing. One meal a day, maybe two. Constant weigh-ins. I had a red patent leather belt from my "fat" days that I would try on as a reminder of where my waist would return to if I wasn't careful.

Two solid years of being legal, good, and righteous. Make that self-righteous. I was convinced if I could do this, anyone could. Weight was all a matter of willpower, I thought, and women who were fat ate too much. Period.

Oh, Lizzie. I was only delaying the inevitable. In the spring of 1984 I finally wearied of toting my plastic scale with me everywhere, of visualizing a pack of playing cards to measure a chicken breast, of eating everything with artificial sweetener and imitation butter. I tired of trying to get to 135. Heck, I'd even raised my goal to 145 by then, the weight I'd weighed all through high school, when 145 seemed fat to me.

Dr. Kathy Johnson, a New York psychiatrist, believes that some women "need a number, an outside source, to validate that they're doing okay."[10] I was not doing okay, because my scale was not telling me what I wanted to hear.

When I went back to normal eating—and I do mean normal, not pigging out, not stuffing my face, not three junk food meals a day—I gained back my weight at a steady one pound per week. That train chugged down the track way past the point where I had started my diet two years earlier.

Was my diet a success? I think not. Most research on yo-yo dieting now concludes that I would have been better off if I had never dieted at all. As Dr. Adriane Fugh-Berman of the National Women's Health Network says, "Yo-yo dieting is for yo-yos."[11]

Diet Defined

To be truly successful, a diet would:

1. Contain easily available, naturally healthy foods.

2. Be served in quantities sufficient for your body's needs and your appetite's satisfaction

3. Produce a high level of pleasure, good for a lifetime of eating

If you have shared anything remotely like my own experiences, chances are good that you did not fail your diet, your diet failed you. Especially if it:

1. Consisted of expensive, chemical-laden substitute foods

2. Was served in tiny quantities sufficient for the body and appetite of a field mouse

3. Produced no level of pleasure whatsoever (Art Buchwald said of liquid diets, "The powder is mixed with water and tastes exactly like powder mixed with water.")

That's not a diet, that's purgatory. Or worse. Dolores hit the nail on the head when she defined the word "diet":

Deprivation, denial, punishment, sentencing, lack of trust, lack of freedom, lack of choice, embarrassment, explaining why I'm not eating, people saying "Oh, good . . ."
Dolores from New York

My hat is off to women who have successfully removed the word D-I-E-T from their vocabularies:

That is a four-letter word and we don't talk like that in our house.
Gwyn from Ohio

How exciting that she may also have a family who is learning about the ill effects of dieting. Many young girls are getting interested in dieting as early as age eight. They need a mom with compassionate concern to teach them that young girls should never diet.

[Dieting] doesn't work and it is not a major religion! Nor does it make you superior if you succeed.

Diana from Kentucky

I was the queen of self-righteousness when I lost weight. It was disgusting really, very us versus them in nature. I honestly thought that anyone who put their mind to it could do it. It was so simple, I reasoned. Just eat less and exercise more. Anybody who wasn't successful with this easy plan was . . . was . . . was . . . uh . . . normal. (Finally, I figured that out!)

A diet is something you do to war criminals while you keep them in bamboo cells.

Janet from Virginia

Sounds like the bread-and-water diet, one of civilization's oldest. We all know the word "diet" just means the food you eat, but in the last century it has come to carry a much more definitive, and more negative, connotation.

The word "diet" is like the word "problem." It doesn't belong in the English language. I consider myself to have "challenges and opportunities" only!

Vicki from Wisconsin

Getting Off the Diet Treadmill

When I talk about doing away with dieting, some women get almost fearful looks on their faces. If you've dieted off and on much of your life, the thought of never doing it again *is* scary.

I have retrained myself not to diet, but to make conscious decisions about what I put in my mouth. Diets don't work!

Lisa from Illinois

Note that this was a deliberate move away from the dreaded "D" word. Decisions, yes; dieting, no.

*I have finally reached a point of being good to my body, nutrition-
ally, emotionally and physically.*

LaDonna from Oregon

This is a woman who has learned to properly care about and for
herself. Here are some specific suggestions for doing that:

*Eat nutritionally and keep fats to a minimum. Balance proteins
and carbohydrates and give your body enough water to allow
natural body function.*

Lauren from Pennsylvania

Then, there's my favorite way to reduce:

Just "diet" from negative people, and you'll be happy!

Maria from Arizona

I heard from an eighteen-year-old reader of *Big Beautiful Woman*
magazine who shared her journey to self-acceptance:

*To me, size isn't everything. Three years ago I wouldn't say that.
Now some of my friends tell me that they wish they were as
comfortable with their bodies as I am with mine.*

Carly from Missouri

How wonderful that she learned that lesson at such a young age.
Some of us take a little longer, but we can get there. Elaine was
released out of diet purgatory by (surprise! surprise!) her doctor:

*One day he said to me, "When are you going to realize you're
always going to be like this and quit worrying about it? You're
healthy and your husband loves you—so quit worrying!" That
freed me, and I don't diet and I'm still healthy!*

Elaine from Ohio

The key words are: "happy" and "healthy." We must focus the
power of our will toward achieving those two important goals—genuine health, genuine happiness—and sell those food scales and bathroom scales at our next yard sale.

Many women are not willing to take such steps because they see
it as "giving up." This is not giving up! It is getting off the diet tread-

202

mill and "getting on" with a healthier approach to eating, to movement, to life. It is also doing away with denial, and embracing reality with a grateful heart.

Just think: we might find out what it's like to live that "normal" life we've often longed for, without worrying about what we'll be having (or *not* having) for lunch!

Begin Building Body Confidence Today

1. Banish the word "diet" from your vocabulary. Get rid of "reducing," "weight loss" and "willpower" while you're at it. (If it's any consolation, these terms are *not* in the Bible!)

2. Throw out your bathroom scale, calorie counting guides, and fad diet books. Instead buy one good "healthy eating" cookbook. No food plans allowed!

3. If your friends start talking about diets, change the subject. If they start criticizing you or anyone else for gaining weight, change friends!

A Nurse Speaks . . .

Anne Khol, N.D., R.N., has a bachelor's degree in psychology from Michigan State University and a doctorate of nursing from Case Western Reserve University in Cleveland. She is currently director of community health education for Sparrow Hospital in Lansing, Michigan.

Liz: Weight gain among women is on the way up. Why?

Anne: *Two reasons: Women are less active. The day-to-day work that we do requires much less physical activity than, say, a hundred years ago. We used to beat our rugs; now we have a high-powered vacuum. We used to knead bread; now we use bread machines (or we buy it at the store). We are not working our large muscle groups all day long, and we lead far more sedentary lives.*

The second reason is: The fashion industry has chosen to use very tall, thin models. This keeps American women constantly dieting to try and fit those clothes. We lose weight, we buy new clothes. We gain the weight back, we buy new clothes. By the time we lose again, the old clothes are out of style, so we buy new clothes. Madison Avenue loves yo-yos!

Liz: What's the problem with dieting?

Anne: *Research keeps telling us that dieting makes you fatter. Dieting itself is the problem. When you think diet, you think about calorie restriction, unfortunately. Not healthy eating, just less eating. Such dieting means you lose lean body weight, you lose muscle, and so your metabolic rate slows down. If you are an educated person in this regard, you will never "diet."*

Liz: You mean it takes more than "willpower?"

Anne: *[Laughs] All the "will" in the world can't fight your body's natural tendencies! Our bodies are designed to protect us from starvation, so calorie reduction will make the body store fat, not burn it. Eating less food tampers with the body's natural regulator, and we are depriving ourselves of what we really want and need to eat.*

Liz: How can we attune ourselves to our bodies' needs?

Anne: *We have to make a conscious effort to re-educate our- selves. The truth is, when we crave chocolates or sweets, our body is asking for more complex carbohydrates—bread, pasta, potatoes. By paying attention to hunger cravings, giving your body real food packed with vitamins, minerals and complex carbohydrates, over time you can become more discerning, as well as genuinely satisfied. It's also important to drink enough fluids. Your body needs at least 64 ounces (8 glasses) of liquids a day to replenish what your body uses—more if you exercise. If we don't provide liquid nourishment, our bodies will signal for more food to meet that need. We are reaching for food when what our body wants is water!*

Liz: Is food the real issue?

Anne: *No. Exercise is the real issue. Not only does it raise the metabolic rate, it improves your mood and cognitive processes, helps you handle stress and enhances how you feel about your- self. It improves muscle tone and skin tone too! Understand that basic changes in metabolic rate through exercise take more than a year. But the benefits begin immediately.*

Liz: You are certainly a well-educated, successful woman who also happens to be big and beautiful. What are your tips for success?

Anne: *Recognize your unique skills and abilities, and make them known. Don't settle for less. And, dress the part! Put on makeup, spend some time on your appearance. Thin women have to do this, too, so good grooming isn't limited to large women.*

Liz: As a Christian, do you think size is a spiritual issue?

Anne: *To me, it's a question of stewardship. I think it is wrong to diet, and to do so harms our bodies. When the Bible talks about the body being God's temple, I don't think it means, "Watch your weight!" I believe it means watch what you are putting into your body—is it healthy or not? And, do you exercise it? God commanded Adam to work by the sweat of his brow. [Laughing] Maybe we need to sweat more!*

Chapter

12

Some Words Should Be Whispered

I chose to include this chapter from my book, Love, Laughter, and a High Disregard for Statistics because I want to share two things with all women. One, life hands almost every one of us some very serious issue to deal with at some time or another. And, two, one of our choice weapons is humor—that special combination of love and laughter cleansed by tears. It is my hope that, whatever the serious issue you must face, you will be able to work through the tears with someone who loves you and find your way to the laughter waiting for you.

Sue Buchanan
Love, Laughter, and a High Disregard for Statistics

My name is Edna Puckett. You don't know me. I'm just one of the little people." She pouts. Then she leans toward someone in the front row and in her most abrasive old lady voice asks, "You can't see my underwear, can you?" The word *underwear* is spoken in a loud whisper, and her eyes dart as though someone might come out of the woodwork to arrest her for saying it. Aunt Edna has opinions about anything and everything.

"Don't get me started," she challenges. But it's too late; she's off and running, waxing eloquent about whatever comes to her mind. Those know-it-alls with tongue depressors in their pockets and stethoscopes dangling around their necks or those *deee*-mon rock-and-rollers who travel in buses with darkened windows. She'll even take on the telephone company. She's had it with those television ads: "I've had about all of this *reach out and touch* stuff I can stomach!"

Every family has a "character" person (mine was Aunt Annie, Wayne's Aunt Naomi). These individuals are the perpetuators of the family name and the preservers and translators of family history. Though they usually lack training, they are at once psychologist, physician, parent, pastor, and philosopher, freely dispensing unsolicited advice in large doses, accompanied by the vigorous shaking of an index finger.

Aunt Edna isn't a real character anymore than Mrs. Vandertweezers, my childhood friend. My friend Joy created her for a church skit and insisted I was the one to play the part.

Aunt Edna didn't go away after the play. Every so often someone calls to ask if she's available for a birthday party, and I pull her out of the bag—knotty little gray wig, sensible old-lady shoes, knee-high stockings, navy polyester skirt, red blouse, and ratty white sweater with a pin that says, "Over the hill, not under it!" Her rouge is uneven, and her lipstick is smeared almost to her nose.

*Aunt Edna believes words such as **cancer**, **underwear**, **breasts**, and **sex** should be spoken in a whisper.*

Her spiritual "gift," she says, is the gift of criticism, and she's quick to tell the minister, whom she calls "preacher," she likes the *beginning* of his sermon and she likes the *end* of his sermon. Then, with a laugh, she suggests, "How 'bout getting the two closer together!" She wants to know all the church gossip, so she can "pray more intelligently."

Edna gets a little more wound up at a party than she does in the church's fellowship hall. She confides, "When I was young, I was a hot little number . . . I once set a young man's tie on fire!" or "In my day, I was kissed more times than the pope's ring."

Aunt Edna believes words such as *cancer, underwear, breasts,* and *sex* should be spoken in a whisper. Her generation wouldn't think of saying such words aloud!

My generation wasn't quite so conservative. As teenagers we spoke the word *sex* aloud and were curious about it, but most of us wouldn't have risked sex outside of marriage, mainly for fear of pregnancy. We also had our parents' wrath to contend with. In those days, it wasn't a case of your parents' grounding you—they would *kill* you!

We didn't have the privilege of attending a class to discuss sex or finding a counselor to help us through it; we simply didn't do it. In fact, it wasn't something we even thought about much because the opportunities weren't there. For one thing, our parents stayed up until our dates left. My mother sometimes even walked my boyfriend to the door! "Bye, Ray! Don't let the cat in when you leave. Drive carefully, and thank your mom for the yellow tomatoes."

About the only hugging and kissing we did was in cars. In the fifties, cars were our drugs! All we thought and talked about. Who had one? What color was it? How fast would it go, and how many people could it hold? Some guys (rarely girls) were lucky enough to borrow the family car occasionally, and a few actually owned one. In those days, a teenager's car was always packed like a jar of olives.

I still love to get into a car that's been closed up overnight and take that first deep breath. If it were possible to have bottled the car smells of my youth, you could blindfold me and I'd pass the sniffing test—tell you which bottle held the smell of the interior of Ray's pink and black Ford, identify that of Gary's yellow convertible, and, without a doubt, know the distinctive smell of Harold's Jeep. I have good memories of cars packed full of laughing teenagers. I also have memories of long, lingering kisses in the backseat of someone's car, interrupted by teeth crashing together because of those bumpy West Virginia roads.

When I became a college freshman, my high school naivete faded rapidly. One of my first college dates was a tall, dark, handsome trumpet major who gave me the impression that I should feel fortunate to be his choice for the evening. He didn't even kiss me; he went straight for the breasts!

My exit line was, "Okay Columbus, you've discovered enough!" I made the mistake of telling my daughters about this experience once when we were discussing sex and they never forgot it. We still say those words and laugh.

That experience awakened an uneasy feeling in me. Having someone touch my breasts was worse than having seventh-grade boys look at them.

As a married woman, I learned that breasts were for admiring and caressing, a satisfying part of the lovemaking process. Just when I'd begun to accept and enjoy my breasts, one was cut off.

How could I not worry that my husband would reject me, think of me as not being whole or sexy? In the hospital I could pull the robes and bedjackets tightly around me, but coming home was a different story.

The first night I went into the dark closet to put on my gown. I pulled out a beautiful floor-length one with a lacy built-in bra and quickly stuffed the left side with socks. I looked in the mirror as I stepped from the closet. *Not bad,* I thought, *Not bad at all.* With a flair I got into my side of the bed. Wayne smiled.

With no hesitation at all he took me in his arms and made love to me, cautiously but passionately. That night an unspoken agreement went into effect between the two of us; for the next year, the nightgown stayed on during lovemaking. I chose to be private about my body, and he respected my decision. Not long before my reconstructive surgery I showed him my scar. He reached out and touched it and looked into my eyes.

"I'll bet you'll be glad to get that fixed," he said and turned back to his book. I can honestly say, my mastectomy didn't threaten the intimacy of our marriage. If anything, it made us closer.

Every case is not like mine. I know of several men who physically walked away from their wives after a mastectomy. I know some who walked away emotionally. Women ask, "How can this surgery *not* affect our love making? How can I go along as though nothing is wrong?" Men ask, "How can I show her it's okay, that I don't want it to affect our sex lives?" Men sometimes ask more questions than women: "Shall I pretend it never happened? Should we laugh? Should we cry?"

I can honestly say, my mastectomy didn't threaten the intimacy of our marriage. If anything, it make us closer.

A very good place to get answers to questions like these is the American Cancer Society's A New Beginning program, which meets regularly to give the breast cancer patient information and emotional support.

Husbands, daughters, and friends are invited and often come. There is usually a program or speaker, but the real purpose of the group is to meet the woman where she is, at whatever stage of emotion, and be there for her.

Because of my busy schedule, I've attended only a couple of times. Both times I intended to duck in and out, simply to hear the speaker, but both times I was pulled into the camaraderie and spirit of the group.

The first time I attended, the meeting was led by a woman named Josie, young, with beautiful, black, almost iridescent skin. I thought to myself, *This woman's never had a bad day in her life. She's being paid to do this; she's a staff member.*

Josie opened the meeting by suggesting we get acquainted. "We'll go around the room, tell our names and where we are right now in our cancer journey. First of all, I'm Josie, and it's been almost seven years since I had a modified radical mastectomy. I had fourteen bad lymph nodes. I was twenty-four when it happened and didn't know a thing about cancer 'til it hit home. I thought I was going to die. Then I said, 'No, I've always thought positively. You're half way there if you can think positively—I can lick it. I have the best doctors in the world, and my belief in God is strong.' I just kept saying, 'You can lick it!' It wasn't easy.

"At the same time I was taking chemotherapy, I was taking radiation—upstairs for chemo, downstairs for radiation—day after day! I had a year of chemo and thirty radiation treatments. Five years later I had reconstruction and now I'm well and healthy." She glowed!

Each woman in the first row stood and told her name and the status of her battle with cancer. Some had been cancer-free for years, some were in treatment and hanging on to the hope that they, like Josie, would lick it! In the second row a woman stood, spoke her name, and burst into tears. We waited for her to regain her composure.

"I thought I was well. I did everything they told me to do, but I've just had a recurrence. It's back. My cancer's back!" We waited in uncomfortable silence, punctuated only by an occasional loud, gut-wrenching sob. Without a moment's hesitation, Josie walked across the room and stood by her side. With her beautiful hands she stroked the woman's face, wiping her tears. The meeting came to a dead halt. The most important thing at that moment was not to hear a speaker, see a film, or listen to a tape, but to comfort. As long as the tears fell—and it seemed an eternity—Josie's glistening hands wiped them away. I'll never forget that moment. It is a strong mental image that appears every time I'm asked, "Just what *does* The American Cancer Society do?"

The question of intimacy after breast cancer often comes up at these meetings, and the volunteers are equipped to help. I asked Donna, another American Cancer Society volunteer, "You've talked to a lot of women, and men too. What gets couples through this mastectomy ordeal with their sexual relationships intact?"

"I think if you start out with a close, intimate relationship you have a better chance, but on the other hand, I've heard of it working the other way; couples having a tenuous relationship can be brought together by the trauma of a mastectomy. I guess there's no pat answer."

As for me and my husband, we found that humor greatly helped ease the intimacy problem. Often what we couldn't talk about, we could laugh about. After my first program of chemotherapy—which began in the hospital—Wayne surprised me with a trip to Puerto Rico, one of the most wonderful, intimate times we ever spent together.

We stayed in an elegant hotel and every day got up late, ate a leisurely breakfast, sunned by the ocean, walked, talked, took naps, dressed for dinner, and strolled the hotel, "people watching," one of our favorite things to do.

My husband made two comments that week that many people would think strange, but for me, they were a turning point in our postoperative relationship, which assured me that things hadn't changed between us at all. One night he bought tickets to what was described as a "Las Vegas Show" in the hotel where we were staying.

Although we weren't warned ahead of time, the dance extravaganza finale featured bare-breasted women. At first, Wayne was all eyes. Then suddenly, aware of the strangeness of the circumstances, he leaned close, took my hand and without missing a beat, said; "I was just counting . . . they all have two! Let's go."

On another day, I teasingly asked him, "Do you think you can love me now for my *mind* instead of my body?" Without flinching, he answered, "Honey, if I'd seen as much of your mind as I have your body, I'd be able to tell you!"

To some, those responses may seem unkind or even cruel. To me, they ensured our sense of humor was intact.

Recently, I was reacquainted with a distant relative at a funeral. Other than playing together once or twice—she lived in Columbus, Ohio, and I lived in Charleston—the thing I remembered most vividly about Janice was that I, as a child, wore her hand-me-down clothes. Every year or so a box came and there would be five or six beautiful, almost new dresses.

After the funeral we went back to my uncle's home for dinner. In the course of the afternoon, Janice shared with me the fact she too had had breast cancer. With a twinkle in her eye she told me she wore a homemade prosthesis—her experience with store-bought ones was unsatisfactory. She explained how she had come up with the ingenious idea of filling a piece of nylon stocking with birdseed, and stuffing it in the pocket she had sewn in her bra.

"Works great," she said. Then with a slight blush, she added, "Tom says you can look in the sky and tell when I'm comin' by the great trail of birds following me!" I knew by the humor that Tom, like Wayne, had helped his wife feel comfortable about a very touchy subject.

Many women have shared with me their first sexual experience after a mastectomy. Some tell of renewed romantic interest; others tell stories best described as nightmares. I went to visit Marlene, at the request of a mutual friend. Marlene, who was unmarried, was belligerent about the subject of reconstructive surgery.

"Why should I have my breasts rebuilt just to make some man happy?" she said. "When I meet someone, he'll just have to get used to it!"

One day she called to tell me she'd gone away on a singles weekend, and after getting chummy with one of the male attendees —and drunk in the process—she ended up in his bed. The man, reaching for a breast and finding instead a thick scar, literally jumped from the bed in horror, practically throwing her to the floor in the process. Marlene didn't learn her lesson; she repeated the experience several times over. The last time I spoke with her she said, "I've had some real bad experiences with sex." It didn't occur to her that a one-night stand isn't the place to find a sympathetic mate.

Kitty came to visit me right after my mastectomy and was appalled that I would consider "putting myself under the knife" again to have reconstructive surgery. "I had a double mastectomy years ago and my husband loves me just like I am. We've had no problems at all, no problems at all." She brought the subject up several times during her visit. Years later I hired a decorator who had worked with Kitty. I explained I'd had a bad year—having had a mastectomy, chemo, and reconstructive surgery—and wanted to spruce up the living room a bit.

"Be glad you had reconstructive surgery," he said, "I work with this woman named Kitty who decided against it. She and her husband had trouble from day one, and it hasn't ended yet!"

Both Marlene and Kitty were unrealistic and had adopted an almost combative attitude toward their circumstances. I'm glad that's not the norm. Donna, my friend from the American Cancer Society, tells me the "unofficial" survey at A New Beginning says most relationships tend to improve during this life-shattering experience, and my own unofficial survey seems to agree.

A young teacher told me she'd had small breasts to begin with so it hardly made a difference. Later her husband repeated the same story. Both told of a new, deeper intimacy than they'd had before, and their eyes told me this was true.

Last week a thirty-seven-year-old woman called from California. We'd never met, but I've discovered sometimes it's much easier to talk to a stranger, miles away, than it is to talk to a friend or family member. After a mastectomy Beverly is in the process of finishing up her chemotherapy. She has two small children and her husband is out of work. She confided that her relationship with her husband, which was tenuous before the mastectomy, was now quite strong. She has no plans for reconstructive surgery.

Joanie did as I did—chose not to let her mate see her naked body after her mastectomy. She told me she kept her body covered, wore teddies or gowns, and locked the bathroom door when she bathed. One day she forgot to lock the door and Will walked in. Quickly she tried to cover herself with the washcloth as she begged him to get out! Undeterred, he moved to the edge of the tub, knelt, took her in his arms, and said, "I love *you,* not your breasts. When will you understand?"

"He cried and I cried and it all ran together . . . *my* tears, *his* tears, and the bath water!" she told me. What a wonderful way to wash away the fear and uncertainty!

PART FOUR

I Am Spiritual

The Light We Throw

FEBRUARY 1922

A wonderful way has been invented to transform a scene on the stage, completely changing the apparent surroundings of the actors and their costumes without moving an article. The change is made in an instant. By an arrangement of light and colors, the scenes are so painted that with a red light thrown upon them, certain parts come into view while other parts remain invisible. By changing a switch and throwing a blue light upon the scene, what has been visible disappears and things unseen before appear, completely changing the appearance of the stage.

This late achievement of science is a good illustration of a fact we all know but so easily forget or overlook—that things and persons appear to us according to the light we throw upon them from our own minds.

When we are down-hearted and discouraged, we

speak of looking at the world through blue glasses; nothing looks the same to us; our family and friends do not appear the same; our home and work show in the darkest colors. But when we are happy, we see things in a brighter light and everything is transformed.

How unconsciously we judge others by the light that is within ourselves, condemning or approving them by our own conception of right and wrong, honor and dishonor! We show by our judgment just what the light within us is.

What we see is always affected by the light in which we look at it so that no two persons see people and things alike. What we see and how we see depends upon the nature of our light.

A quotation, the origin of which I have forgotten, lingers in my mind: "You cannot believe in honor until you have achieved it. Better keep yourself clean and bright; you are the window through which you must see the world."

Laura Ingalls Wilder
Little House in the Ozarks

Chapter

13

How Can I Plug In to the Power?

*Y*ou've looked at the emotional, the physical, the hereditary . . . and you wonder . . . Do I have what it takes to heal all the parts of me to make them a whole? It's just a matter of plugging into the Power! As a Christian you have access to the Ultimate Power of the Ultimate Healer. In this chapter from *Get a Life Without the Strife*, we've provided a spiritual inventory to help you assess the amount of Power you are plugged into and the best way to up the wattage.

Fred and Florence Littauer
Get a Life Without the Strife

P.S. We'll refer again to the personality types so we'll review them here for you.
The popular Sanguine wants to have fun.
The powerful Choleric wants to be in control.
The perfect Melancholy wants everything done properly.
The peaceful Phlegmatic seeks serenity and a stress-free life.

There isn't the money and there isn't the manpower to reach all the people who need help." So writes psychiatrist Christ Zois in his insightful book, *Think Like a Shrink,* in which he suggests that people should try to solve some of their own problems. The reason many of us are not successful in this is that we have no confidence in our own ability and we don't want to go through the hurtful process of uncovering our buried emotions. Instead we build defenses, excuses, and rationalizations to prevent the pain. He suggests that until we are willing to tolerate some degrees of anxiety we won't get to the heart of our problems.

A Christian psychiatrist told us he takes into his clinic sixty new sex-abuse cases a week. Using all the skill and techniques available plus loving concern, he confesses very limited results. In reviewing the last five years of his practice, he feels only ten people made significant progress and three of them are himself, his wife, and her therapist. "Try as we may, we just don't have the answers," he said.

How to Plug In to the Power

From our experience of twenty-five years in Christian ministry, we have found that many of us *can* solve our own problems if we have tools that are simple enough for us to understand—and if we are willing to pick up those tools and get to work. With the tools must come the belief that Jesus Christ is our Ultimate Healer and with Him we can achieve not only the possible but the impossible (see Luke 18:27).

There are no simple answers to our complex life problems, but we do have Power available to give us hope. Before we go any further in our search for an abundant life, let's make sure we know how to plug in to the real Power. Check Yes or No to the following questions and then read the explanations.

SPIRITUAL INVENTORY

	Yes	No
1. Would you consider yourself to be a relatively religious person?	___	___
2. Have you ever felt a real pull toward spiritual matters?	___	___
3. As a child did you attend church activities?	___	___

4. Can you remember when you first asked the Lord Jesus into your life?   ____ ____

5. Did this commitment make a difference in your behavior and lifestyle?   ____ ____

6. Do you attend a church or Bible study regularly?   ____ ____

7. Do you accept that God is the Creator of heaven and earth and is the Father of all true believers?   ____ ____

8. Do you believe that Jesus Christ paid a sacrificial price for your sins, arose from the dead, and is still alive today, making intercession for you and me?   ____ ____

9. Do you believe the Holy Spirit gives power to your life and can bring recall of forgotten events?   ____ ____

10. Do you know that when Jesus is in us we can have a transformed life and that when Jesus sets us free we are free indeed?   ____ ____

If you have answered Yes to all of these questions and you know you are a believing Christian who accepts the Bible as God's Word for the human race, then you are ready to move on to your goal of emotional health and stability.

If you could not say Yes to most of these questions, let's find out why. Do any of the descriptions below apply to you? Check the ones that do.

____ The Pharisee

Being religious doesn't prove anything if you are just obeying a set of rules. The Lord Jesus said those who were outwardly religious but also judgmental and unloving were hypocrites, whitewashed sepulchres, religious on the outside but spiritually dead inside. Does this description fit you or anyone you know? Jesus wants us to be vibrant on the inside and on the outside. He desires truth in our innermost parts. He asks us to practice what we preach.

____ The Nominal Christian

If you grew up in the church and attended regular children's activities as we did, you should understand spiritual matters as an adult, but not necessarily so. Sometimes youthful church attendance causes us to be blasé about the Lord and to never seek a genuine personal relationship. "I'm a good person, go to church, and live by the Golden Rule. Isn't that enough?" you might ask. Sometimes we get too close to some of the people in the church and see their weaknesses. Then we brand them as phonies and never want to be like them. This attitude gives us reason to stay away from the church. Sometimes, if we were required to attend church as children, we rebel when we grow up and determine we will not force our children to go. We say we'll give them—and ourselves—a free choice.

_____ The De Facto Christian

Many people feel they have always been Christians because they weren't raised to be Jews or Muslims. But the Bible tells us we must make a personal commitment to the Lord Jesus, give over our wills to His control, and ask Him to come into our lives and change us. John 1:12 tells us that "as many as received Him, to them He gave the right to become children of God, to those who believe in His name." He didn't say he would give an abundant life to those who have perfect-attendance buttons or who have never missed a church potluck supper, but to those who believe and receive.

If you are not sure whether you have ever received the Lord Jesus, you don't have to get up and go find a cathedral; you can pray right where you are. You can be creative in your words to Jesus or you can read the following prayer with personal feeling and heartfelt dedication:

Lord Jesus, I come into Your presence as I am and where I am at this moment. I don't really know You in a personal way and yet I have this hunger for spiritual things. You say that if I believe in You as a real person and reach out to receive You, You will come in and live in me from here on. I ask You to come into my heart right now, make Yourself real in my life, and change me into what You want me to be. I thank You ahead of time for what You will do with me and I pledge to share what You teach me with others who also need help. I pray, believing that You are true to Your word and that You are already at work in my life. In Jesus' precious name, amen.

_____ The Lukewarm Christian

If you made this commitment in the past, has there been a change in your life? If you prayed just now, do you have a new wave of peace washing over you? The Lord is only as active in our lives as we allow Him to be. He is not pushy; He is always gentle. He gives us a new nature and He changes our desires. He does not send a man dressed like Moses to our doorsteps carrying a big tablet saying, "Thou shalt not have fun ever again." He just quietly goes about rebuilding the parts of our lives that have been torn down. Oswald Chambers wrote, "Our Lord never patches up our natural virtues, He remakes the whole man on the in-side."[1]

_____ The Christian Who Lacks the Power of the Holy Spirit

As children we may have known no more of the Holy Spirit than the line at the end of formal prayers: "in the name of the Father, the Son, and the Holy Ghost." Was He someone spooky who hovered over us or was He someone who peeked at us through the venetian blinds?

As we began to study God's Word we found that the Holy Ghost, also known as the Holy Spirit, was the third member of the Trinity, and He is the One who gives us the power to change. What a blessing for those of us who flunked charm school and who feel we can't win friends or influence people! The Holy Spirit can do what we have failed at doing. For some, transformation comes quickly, but for most of us the changes are gradual. One day, out of the blue, we notice that we no longer think or behave as we used to. Our temper hasn't flared up, our anger has diminished, and we're no longer procrastinating. The power of the Spirit has changed us. Chambers said, "When we are born again the Holy Spirit begins to work His new creation in us and there will come a time when there's not a bit of the old order left."[2]

For some, transformation comes quickly, but for most of us the changes are gradual.

Look again at the story in John 5 about the man, paralyzed for thirty-eight years, who waited beside Bethesda Pool to be healed. When Jesus came along He told the man to pick up his bed—his place of confinement—and walk. When the man did what Jesus told him he was able to walk.

Jesus didn't stay around to take credit for the miracle; He just slipped away through the crowd. Later, the Lord found him in the temple and said, "You have been made well. Sin no more" (John 5:14). The man went away and told the people it was Jesus who had made him well.

In this simple story are some basic principles we need to accept before we will get any healing.

1. **Realize we have a problem.** The man knew he was lame. Many of us have needs that we deny, hurts that we refuse to look at. Until we are willing to admit we have a problem we won't get well. Some people suffer from headaches, stomach problems, and other illnesses their doctors can't heal because the suffering people won't admit they have a problem that is not physiological.
2. **Go where there is help.** The lame man knew that people got healed at the pool, so he went there every day. He waited thirty-eight years in faith, believing that if he went to the place of healing, ultimately he'd be made well. Let's hope we don't have to wait thirty-eight years for healing!
3. **Do what Jesus says.** Once Jesus knows we want help and we

have made a move to receive it, He is willing to give instructions. He told the man to get up and walk. The man didn't argue or say it's impossible; he took the first step. Do we want healing enough to move on it today?

Some of us don't think our problems are big enough for Jesus to notice or to heal. We don't think there's any hope so we don't go to find help. The lame man didn't give up; he went every day for thirty-eight years.

For some of us the "place" of help is a church, a counselor, a friend, or a book. As we listen or read we have to be tuned in to the voice of Jesus so that we will hear Him when He speaks.

SPIRITUAL VARIATIONS IN THE PERSONALITIES

		Barrier to becoming a Christian	Spiritual hangups	Favorite type of church	Favorite hymn and verse
POPULAR	SANGUINE	It doesn't sound like fun and those people are too serious	Trouble with idea of holiness and purity. Too many strict rules and commandments.	One with fun, action, lively choir, dancing in the aisles with tambourines. Likes short, humorous sermons full of stories.	"Oh for a thousand tongues" "A merry heart does good, like medicine" (Prov. 17:22)
PERFECT	MELANCHOLY	I could never be perfect enough to please God	Trouble with forgiveness for those who don't deserve it. Too much unconditional love.	One with serious liturgy and dignified presentation. Likes detailed bulletins. Admires intellectual, spiritual, deep sermons with reference to Greek derivatives.	"When the Roll Is Called Up Yonder I'll Be There" "Therefore you shall be perfect" (Matt. 5:48)

	Barrier to becoming a Christian	Spiritual hangups	Favorite type of church	Favorite hymn and verse
POWERFUL CHOLERIC	I couldn't give up control to someone I can't even see.	Trouble with authority of God. Too little control of one's own destiny.	One with obvious order and organization. Wants service to move right along and be practical. Likes brief sermons that apply to others.	"Onward Christian Soldiers" "Let all things be done decently and in order" (1 Cor. 14:40)
PEACEFUL PHLEGMATIC	Would it mean I'd have to change?	Trouble with truth and responsibility before God. Too much emphasis on good works.	One with a relaxed atmosphere—not too dressy or demanding. Likes pleasant, brief sermons with no mention of hellfire and brimstone.	"Leaning on the Everlasting Arms" "Blessed are the peacemakers" (Matt. 5:9)

The Spiritual Variations in the Personalities table may help you achieve healing by giving you insight into additional spiritual variations that occur in the various personalities. Knowing which traits can become problems for you may help you overcome them; knowing which traits make certain components more appealing may help you find them more easily.

If you do not already attend a church and/or Bible study, you will now want to find a place where God's inspired Word is taught and honored and where you see the love of the Lord reflected in the eyes of the people. Be wary of a situation where the pastor or teacher is being worshiped instead of where the Lord is being lifted up and watch out for groups who try to take control of you, your finances, or your family. Pray for discernment from the Lord as to where you should attend and how involved you should become. Remember that the church is full of imperfect people; don't get disillusioned when one of them behaves in a totally unspiritual way.

For some of us the voice of the Lord will be clear and the instructions life-changing, but others of us will turn away and say it all sounds too much like work. For many people healing is a difficult process, but Jesus is faithful when we are willing to pick up our bed and walk.

We must remember what the lame man said when his friends asked him about his healing. He stood publicly and stated, "Jesus made me well."

No matter what our difficulties are, ranging from personality problems, troubled relationships, poor communication, rejection, or childhood trauma, Jesus can make us well. We must first be plugged in to the Power before we can shine. To help you make the connection, picture for a moment an elegant living room. Perhaps it's your own or one you visited recently. There is a long, plush sofa against the wall with an ornate table at each end. On each table is an expensive lamp with a handsome base and a pleated silk shade.

As the sun sets you reach over and turn on one of these lamps and nothing happens. You check to see if it has a bulb and it does. What could be wrong? The lamp looks perfect but it doesn't work. You follow the cord down the back of the table and you find the problem. The lamp wasn't plugged in; it has no power. Once it's plugged in to the source, it shines brightly as it was created to do.

How about you? Do you have a handsome base and a silk shade? Do you have a bulb that would allow you to shine as a light in the world, but you're not plugged in to the source? Today is the turning point for you. You now have the Power to use in rebuilding a life without the strife.

Our real idea of God may lie buried under the rubbish of conventional religious notions and may require an intelligent and vigorous search before it is finally unearthed and exposed for what it is. Only after an ordeal of painful self-probing are we likely to discover what we actually believe about God.

A. W. Tozer
The Knowledge of the Holy

But God Meant It for Good: Knowing God as Father

Trust. Can a woman (or a man) who has been abused by a father ever be able to totally put her trust in God the Father? How do you gain back trust that was so badly broken it shattered your trust in God? Is it possible to see how God meant it all for good?

My father was an alcoholic who wreaked havoc on our family. Dinnertime was a battleground. My father's hurtful and hateful words were his weapons of choice, shooting down a mother and her children night after night.

This special chapter from No Longer the Hero *shows how particularly difficult it is for a woman to truly trust God the Father after a childhood at the hands of an abusive father or family. It is a difficult, complex job to repair the shattered trust. It isn't simple; it isn't quick— but it is possible and it is powerful. Read with me the way to restore your trust in God the Father.*

Nancy LeSourd
No Longer the Hero

Early in my counseling, Bob challenged me to consider letting God have control of my relationship with Him. I also heard in the Twelve-Step programs that I should, "Let go and let God." That sounded reasonable until I tried it.

"You know, Bob," I explained, "I became a Christian when I was fourteen because someone who knew my family situation said God could help. That sounded wonderful, and I worked very hard to develop faith in a God who could do this kind of a miracle. But nothing happened. I think I'm afraid it is all a great hoax. So, if I give myself up to God like you suggest, and find out He isn't there, then I have really lost out." I shifted in my seat and looked at Bob directly, hoping for an answer to a predicament that had shadowed me for years.

"Nancy, you exude a great deal of energy to win over God's favor. You strive to be faithful. You struggle to trust God in the midst of your circumstances. You work extremely hard to be good. You think that by operating in this way, you can win God's action on your behalf. The end result is that you are in control of your relationship with God," Bob responded. "God wants to take you on a deeper walk with Him. He wants to give you the hope and the faith and the love you so desire, Nancy, but He wants it to be a natural expression of your relationship with Him. God wants you to understand what He is really like. You can't know that until you are no longer dependent on your own beliefs about who God is and how He will work in your life."

"But, Bob," I asked, "what if I give myself up to God and He is not there?"

"That's the risk you'll have to take. Either He is there for you or not. But you can't discover that while you continue to be in control."

Bob challenged me to face this very difficult question head-on. He knew it was the key to faith and to knowing God loved me. But I was too afraid at this point to find out if God was really there or not. I was too comfortable with my ineffective, but predictable, God and too secure in my independence.

Several years later, this issue arose again. In order to complete my financial-aid application for Georgetown law school, I needed a sworn statement from my father that he had not claimed me as a deduction for the last three years. I argued for weeks with the financial-aid office. Why did I need him to sign anything? "I have been on my own now since I was eighteen," I said. But despite the ten years of emancipated financial status, Georgetown held firm. No signed statement from my father meant no financial aid from Georgetown.

I knew that one rarely got anything from my father without paying a price, but when I called him to ask if he would complete the financial-aid form, he surprisingly agreed. Over the next few weeks, however, I suffered through a series of increasingly abusive phone calls, which harped on the same thing over and over again—how much we children had cost him. Finally, he changed his mind about completing the form and said I would have to get along without any more financial help from him. I tried to explain that I didn't need his money, just a signed and notarized statement. No matter, he was on a roll now. He had something I needed and he knew it. He relished the cat-and-mouse game we were playing. I was furious and my anger spilled out in the next counseling session.

"I hate having to depend on my father for anything. I'm twenty-eight years old, and I am at his mercy, just like when I was a child. This has been so frustrating." I paused for a moment and continued, "Bob, I feel like there's got to be more to my anger than just this. Every time my father called to toy with me about whether or not he would provide the form, I would hang up from talking with him and cry for a long period of time. I was furious at being so beholden to him and yet I felt so lonely at the same time."

"Why do you think you felt lonely, Nancy?" Bob asked.

"There's a part of me deep, deep down that wants desperately to trust key people to be dependable. But there is a part of me that is cynical, guarded, and cautious. It is as if I am constantly preparing to be let down again. I know this carries over into my relationship with God. I want to trust myself to God and leave the most important aspects of my life, particularly marriage, up to Him. Yet, each time something like this happens, it just steels my resolve to never be in the position of depending on anyone for anything. Besides, although depending on God is a nice idea, I'm not so sure He's dependable."

"Of course you don't think God is dependable," Bob explained. "You have been let down by so many people in your life that you have closed yourself off, determined that no one, God or man included, will hurt you like that again. Yet you desire to be married. Nancy, do you realize that to be in a relationship with a man, you will have to learn how to be vulnerable and how to be dependent? If you can learn to depend on God, you will find it easier to make yourself vulnerable to a man. God can teach you that He is dependable, if you are willing to let Him."

"How can He do that?" I asked.

"To build dependency, God will have to strip away your independence. He has started to do this already by bringing up these situations in your everyday circumstances that seem larger than life to you. He does this to help you remember all the other hurts, betrayals, and disappointments that occurred in your life. As these memories resurface, you feel deeply that sense of mistrust, loss, and betrayal that you felt before. At this point you have a choice. You can shore yourself up again, garnering your own resources and tackling the job yourself, saying once again, 'I knew I shouldn't have depended on Him.' Or you can enter into this fresh experience, embrace the pain, and ask God to heal the deep hurt. Only as you begin to see how God faithfully heals you, memory by memory, will you begin to understand that He is dependable even when others are not."

I needed a new history with my God.

Bob had a special insight here. He was not asking me to uproot this independent spirit of mine overnight and cast myself unflinchingly into the arms of God. He knew I didn't trust God enough for that yet. He was suggesting that I choose to trust my past pain, which had now attached itself to a present disappointment, to God for healing. If I would be willing to forgo my natural response of shutting down this memory and, instead, embrace the pain of it, I might discover God was faithful to heal that memory. Then I would have a foundation from which to go forward the next time. Slowly, I would build up a storehouse of experiences where God was operating in my life for good. Then when painful times occurred, I would have some place in my history to go and to select a reminder or two that confirmed His love and His care.

I needed a new history with my God. He was willing to rebuild my understanding of Him, bit by bit. Letting go and letting God was not an overnight occurrence but a determined effort of almost a decade to replace my wrong conceptions of Him and to build a new history. It would involve learning to be honest with God, exploring surprising feelings of anger and fears that I had toward Him, and practicing ongoing choices about what I would believe about Him. I would discover, however, that God would return again to this basic question at the root of any authentic relationship with Him: Was I willing to let go of my control and let Him be God?

Relating to God as Father

When Jesus prayed to God, He used the very familiar form of the word *father*. In essence, Jesus called God His daddy. Yet adults from dysfunctional homes find it difficult to know God in this way. This deeply personal relationship with God suffers from the same problems as our relationships with our parents and others. Our ability to make ourselves vulnerable to another is crippled by past rejections. We build stone walls around our hearts, closing others out and keeping ourselves safe. Or so we think.

The fear of rejection or abandonment is so strong that it causes us to throw up barriers that make it impossible for intimacy to occur. There may be moments of self-revelation, but sustained intimacy is impossible without trusting that the risk of revealing oneself is outweighed by the benefits of a deeper relationship. We know this, but we are not sure that this risk is worth it.

We learn to cordon off our innermost self from God in many ways. We may reject God completely before we can be rejected by Him, or we may cloak Him in so many commandments that we spend a lifetime trying to measure up to an impossible standard. Or we may busy ourselves with service for Him to the exclusion of being with Him. Or as in my case, we may fill that aching void for intimacy with a consuming intensity for human love that devours every man that comes along.

My father broke his promises, destroyed my trust, ruined my childhood, and discounted my worth. This caused me to hang back in the shadows, skeptical and unsure about the intentions of this heavenly Father toward me. I wanted to believe that "God meant it for good," but nagging doubts plagued me. I was as skittish about my relationship with my heavenly Father as I was with my earthly father.

Our Distorted View of God

The parent/child relationship has a natural imbalance of power and authority. How our parents handled that power imbalance shapes how we respond to God. If they used their power and authority to hurt and abuse, we respond to God with fear and distrust.

Sandra Wilson, Ph.D., observed six major distortions of the character of God that were common to Christian adult children of alcoholics.[2]

1. The Cruel and Capricious God

This view is most commonly held by adult children who suffered severe abuse, especially if the abuser was the father. Adults most often respond to this God with terror and fear.

If we have become Christians as children growing up in the dysfunctional home, we may turn to God to change our family situation, as I did. Maybe the child even asks God for protection from the abusive parent. If God is really a caring God, a loving Father, He'll help, won't He?

Not only does this make sense theologically, but it is what we are taught in Sunday school, church, or Bible study. God knows your every need. God cares individually for you. If you were the only one left on earth, He still would have sent His Son to die for you. Not a sparrow falls to the ground without the Lord knowing. He has numbered the hairs on our heads. Surely He will help now.

I used to love to read the Psalms. Here I had assurance over and over again that God was powerful enough to protect me and to help me, no matter how difficult the circumstances. Psalm 91 promised He would be my refuge and fortress. Important word pictures for one on the front lines of daily battle in the home.

> You will not be afraid of the terror by night,
> Or of the arrow that flies by day; . . .
> A thousand may fall at your side,
> And ten thousand at your right hand;
> But it shall not approach you. . . .
> "Because he has loved Me, therefore I will deliver him;
> I will set him securely on high, because he has known
>   My name.
> He will call upon Me, and I will answer him;
> I will be with him in trouble;
> I will rescue him, and honor him" (v. 5, 7, 14–15 NASV).

Yeah, Lord. Do it! I just knew God could help . . . if He wanted to.

Sometimes, it does appear that God is helping, that the family is getting better. There may be up times in the cycle of family life where you begin to believe long-hoped-for changes are occurring. These lulls in the storm cause us to begin to trust that God really does care about us and is at work in our deepest concerns. Then, inevitably, the stormy times reappear. Where is God in the thunderclouds? He appears capricious—willing to help in some moments and distant and silent in others. Who is this God? Is He dependable? Does He care? I feared this capricious God.

2. The Demanding and Unforgiving God

This view is most commonly held by adult children who experienced neglect or emotional and verbal abuse, frequently the family Heroes who perceive God as requiring much and forgiving little.

Since the time I became a Christian in the ninth grade, service to God became a venue for earning God's favor. Choir, leadership positions in youth and young adult church groups, involvement in an inner-city children's ministry, and Young Life became places to demonstrate my faithfulness and commitment to God. Why? So He could deem me worthy of His attention and help.

Service to God should be the outward expression of faith in a loving God. It is responsive, not manipulative. When God is viewed as demanding, however, Christian activities can be an attempt to meet the perceived high standards necessary to be acceptable to God.

As a child, I used my achievements to demonstrate to my parents and to outsiders that I was okay. As a Christian, my activities were aimed to prove to God I was worthy of His love and help. When things didn't change in my family, I presumed it was my fault and redoubled my efforts to win over this demanding God.

3. The Selective and Unfair God

This view is most commonly held by those adult children who believe that God is not cruel, capricious, demanding, or unforgiving with all His children, but only with them.

Andrea, a network broadcaster ignored as a child, viewed God like this. Because of her sense of her own unworthiness, she could understand a God who withheld His blessings from her while He dispensed them to others. She didn't even challenge this perspective as unfair. Of course, God singled her out for His disfavor; she was so obviously deficient as His child. Whereas others might rail out at God and challenge this seeming inconsistency and unfairness, Andrea accepted God's perceived actions toward her as logical and justifiable. This demanding, unforgiving God had specially chosen her for His displeasure.

4. The Distant and Unavailable God

The last two views of God are also common to children who had parents who were inaccessible, too busy, or unable for whatever reason, to love and nurture their children. Adult children view this God, like their parents, as inaccessible. Chronic parental unavailability reinforces this distorted view of God.

When Jim became a Christian, he discovered that he rarely brought many concerns to God in prayer. Why bother God? His troubles were his own, and surely God was too busy to care, anyway. So he learned to bottle things in. When his business began to fail, he carried his pain inside. He was competent. He could manage. He didn't think that God would help if asked. In fact, Jim didn't even think to ask. Years of cool parental interactions had taught him otherwise.

5. The Kind but Confused God

This God remains aloof and distant. He is perceived as weak and ineffectual, unable to help with the world's problems or those of the adult child. Dan didn't begrudge God His powerlessness. He accepted it. For years Dan had tried to help his family change, and yet they remained the same. Dan was aware of how hopeless it was, so why should God have any more success?

Dr. Wilson found four statistically significant differences in the spiritual perceptions of evangelical adult children of alcoholics, compared with evangelical adults from nonalcoholic homes. Adult children of alcoholics had significantly more difficulty in experiencing God's love and forgiveness, trusting God's will, believing biblical promises, and forgiving others. For example, 44.8 percent of adult children of alcoholics had trouble experiencing God's love and forgiveness compared to only 4.8 percent of those adults from nonalcoholic homes.[3]

I also saw God in one other distorted image—that of a fairy godmother.

6. The Fairy Godmother God

The amount of fantasizing we did as children affects our relationship to God, so we become stuck in fairy-tale thinking. We begin to view God as the fairy godmother who waves His magic wand, makes good conquer evil, and delivers the happy ending.

One of the underlying assumptions of fairy-tale thinking is the juxtaposition of good and evil. Rarely are the fairy-tale characters a complex enigma of good and bad traits. Rather, there typically is an evil protagonist: a witch, an evil king or queen, or a wicked step-mother. There is also a good hero or heroine, often portrayed by children or adolescents. When we carry that thinking into adulthood, however, and into our relationship with God, we see ourselves as victims of some wicked agent and often do not take responsibility for ourselves. We view the dysfunctional parent as someone from whom we must escape. But have you ever noticed how that person reap-pears in others' clothing? That parent is surprisingly similar to a boss, a coworker, or perhaps a spouse.

With fairy-tale thinking, we learn to wait for the fairy godmother to arrive and change our circumstances. In fairy tales, people are rescued from their circumstances. Dragons are slain. Wicked people killed, banished, or at least put in their place. We often view God in the same way. However, when we wait on God to intervene and change our lives so that they are bearable, we lose the opportunity to experience His faithfulness in the darkest situation.

A third aspect of fairy-tale thinking is how we view ourselves. Not only do we tend to focus on the wicked or evil agent that is ruining our lives—seeing that person as someone from whom we must es-cape—not only do we wait for the fairy godmother's intervention, but we also begin to believe that we must be good enough to deserve this intervention. Cinderella was the good but mistreated stepdaugh-ter. Snow White was the purest, fairest of them all. Perhaps to get this fairy godmother to act on our behalf, we must be good enough to deserve this special dispensation of grace.

This misdirected belief about God puts the burden on us to be worthy enough of His help and His merciful dispensations. Yet this aspect of our relationship with God is not foreign to us either. We feel comfortable trying to be pleasing enough to earn acceptance, love, and favor. It is how we have operated for years. But, ah, there is the dilemma. We must be the good person who deserves the action of an omnipotent being, but at the very depths of our souls we are con-vinced of our unworthiness.

It is easy for us to believe we are unworthy of God's favor and assistance. At the core of our being is self-rejection and lack of self-worth. We accept without question that we are unworthy sinners. The shame that surrounds our souls since early childhood condemns us daily: who would want to love you? You are not worthy. It is tough for us to accept that God loves us, not because of who we are, not because of what we do, but because God has decided to love us. Even so, we do not jettison fairy-tale thinking. It is the basis of our hope.

A child from a dysfunctional home can wait a lifetime for the fairy godmother to intervene and change the little cinder-covered girl to a princess. When she becomes a Christian, she transfers that type of belief into her relationship with God. No one has a greater capacity for hope and endurance in spite of difficult circumstances than our Hero.

What are her hopes and dreams? For me it was first for my family to be restored to health and wholeness. When it became apparent that that would not be happening, I asked God to give me an extraordinary husband. For others, it may be changing a spouse or providing that long-awaited breakthrough in a job situation. The dreams may differ, but the technique is the same. We live in the future anticipation of what God could do. If He would just act and change this or that, we would be happy. Then we apply all of our efforts to convince God how He should act to bring about this dream. It becomes more and more perplexing when the circumstances do not change. We question over and over whether God really cares about us. We equate His love with His action, and without evidence of it in our circumstances, we begin to doubt.

But we must not doubt. We must have faith! So we buck up and call from deep within our own incredible reservoir of endurance, yet one more day of belief in this reluctant God. After all, you never know when He might appear and grant our heart's desire. And so the merry-go-round goes on and on.

A Genuine View of God

Did my relationship with my heavenly Father have to be doomed by my experiences with my earthly father? No, but I would have to work harder at it than others. Much of the hard work I did to correct faulty thinking and poor choices in my earthly relationships had to occur in my relationship with God too. I would have to learn to trust God, to get in touch with my feelings toward God, to relinquish control, and to give up my performance-based understanding of His acceptance of me.

Identify What We Think about God

We need to confront our view of God. To renew our minds, we must first take stock of our basic beliefs about God no matter how counter to standard Christian thought they might appear. For example, I saw God as capricious. He would get me to trust Him and then just when I had, He would pull the rug out from under me with great pleasure. It wasn't until I was in counseling that I had the courage to share this perspective, because as a good, strong Christian I wouldn't malign God like that.

Once I identified a conflict about the way I thought about God and the way God is presented in the Bible, I would search my personal experiences for those events that gave me support for this view of God. I remembered praying to God over and over to help Daddy not yell at Mom so much, for instance. But nothing changed.

How Do You Feel?

As this personal experience came to mind, I would ask myself how I felt about it. Did I feel abandoned? Let down? Angry? I asked myself why I felt that way. "Because God shouldn't be like this; He should be like that," I'd respond. We need to trust our intuitions about what the character of God should be like. Those thoughts may be more accurate than we realize. Many of us will learn of God as Father, not by example, but by contrast. As J. I. Packer explained in *Knowing God:*

> To those who are Christ's, the holy God is a loving Father; they belong to His family; they may approach Him without fear, and always be sure of His fatherly concern and care. This is the heart of the New Testament message.
> Who can grasp this? I have heard it seriously argued that the thought of divine fatherhood can mean nothing to those whose human father was inadequate, lacking wisdom, affection, or both. . . . The thought of our Maker becoming our perfect parent—faithful in love and care, generous and thoughtful, interested in all we do, respecting our individuality, skillful in training us, wise in guidance, always available, helping us to find ourselves in maturity, integrity, and uprightness—is a thought which can have meaning for everybody, whether we come to it by saying, "I had a wonderful father, and I see that God is like that, only more so," or by saying, "My father disappointed me here, and here, and here, but God, praise His name,

will be very different". . . . The truth is that all of us have a positive ideal of fatherhood by which we judge our own and others' fathers.[4]

When I took an honest look at what I thought about God and how I felt toward Him, I was shocked to uncover deep anger and rage. I was angry at Him for letting me be born into my family. I was mad at Him for not changing my father. I hated Him for not caring enough for my mother to give her hope to live. I was furious with Him for not taking care of my brothers when I begged Him to all these years. I buried all these feelings, however, because Christians don't get mad at God.

When I took an honest look at what I thought about God and how I felt toward Him, I was shocked to uncover deep anger and rage.

Bob helped me understand that my rage, at work in my other relationships, was also operative in my relationship with God. As with my love for my mom, I couldn't acknowledge that anything was wrong in my relationship with God. Somehow I needed His love too much. If I acknowledged my true feelings about God—these dark emotions of anger and rage—I might lose His love.

I was trapped in a vicious cycle, however. Something would happen to cause my anger at God to rise up within me. I would be afraid to acknowledge my feelings to myself or to God. That anger, boiling within, would whisper over and over, "I told you God is not to be trusted." Then I would steel myself further to rely only on myself.

I learned from my family to tiptoe gingerly around the house, trying to make everything appear fine, stuffing my feelings about my pain. Now God wanted me to be honest with my feelings, but I had had few natural experiences that told me it was safe to share them. I was comfortable locked in my pain, playing out my role as a strong Christian, but God was not. He jealously yearned for me to know Him as Father, to trust His work in my life, and to enjoy my relationship with Him. He would work in my individual circumstances to bring me to the place where I would speak honestly with Him.

Be Honest with God about These Feelings

Knowing God is relational. He deliberately made it that way from the beginning. When Adam and Eve hid from Him out of fear as a result of their sin, God called out to them, "Where are you?" He does the same thing for us today. He understands the damage that has occurred to us as a result of our families. He understands that our fears cause us to want to retreat into repression or denial and distance ourselves from Him. He calls out to each of us, "Where are you?"

This invitation to honesty is often turned down because we are afraid God can't take it. Or that we will offend Him and catch even more of His wrath. Or we will lose whatever minimal interest He had in us in the first place. The same honesty that is required of us in our personal recovery to break through our denial systems, however, is also required with God. It takes great courage to answer Him honestly. Once I did that, I could begin to have a genuine relationship with Him.

A Genuine Relationship with God

To have a genuine relationship with God, I had to trust in the person of God. In Hebrews, the great epistle on faith in God, it states: "Without faith it is impossible to please Him, for he who comes to God must believe that He is, and that He is a rewarder of those who diligently seek Him" (Heb. 11:6). Coming to know God as Father crystallized for me into two distinct phases: (1) learning that He loved me and (2) learning that He intended good for me.

When people learn of all that I have faced in my life, they invariably respond, "You're such a strong person to have gone through all that." I received a lot of feedback over the years that I had value because I was strong and because I could go through anything. Yet as a little girl, the one thing I wanted more than anything else was the love of my father. I observed that my father valued someone who succeeded in school. Therefore, I applied myself diligently in school to succeed, hoping to secure his love.

My relationship with God was no different. For some reason, I understood and accepted the fact that God had paid the penalty for my sins in the death and resurrection of Jesus and that His act enabled me to have a relationship with Him. But once I was in that relationship, I did the same thing I had with every other man in my life. I placed the burden on myself to stay in His good graces. Then, in the summer of 1983 in three distressing events in the space of four months, my ability to rebound and rise above my difficulties as usual was shattered.

All three situations had to do with relationships with men. These were not the three most important relationships I ever had with men. Nor were these the three most devastating blows I ever had in my life. But there was no time to recover from one disappointment before the next hit. At the end of my second year in law school, I met and dated David, an attorney, for several months. As the summer drew near, however, he told me he didn't know where I got the idea he was interested in a long-term relationship. He was not; he was simply being nice. I was hurt by this but shrugged off the pain.

After all, Steve, a man from law school whom I had been close friends with for two years, had recently written and called and said he wondered if there was more to our relationship than just a good friendship. He thought we should date when he returned to Washington that summer. So I thought, "Well, maybe this relationship will finally take off." The day after he arrived in Washington, at a party, I introduced him to a very good friend of mine and they talked for a moment. The next day Steve called me for her phone number so he could ask her out. I was shocked and hurt and confused.

Years before, I had dated Rob during my graduate school years, a guy that I loved very deeply. Despite his intensive efforts to shape me into the woman of his dreams, an acceptable politician's wife, he had broken off our relationship. I always thought we would get back together, however, someday. We stayed in touch off and on over the years and shortly after the summer began, we talked again. He told me that he had never stopped loving me and that he, too, had always thought we would get married. Since he was about to move from the east to the west coast to begin a new job, he asked if we could get together in a month to talk about where we would go from here. Encouraged, I wrote him that week, but I did not hear back from him.

Six weeks later, I received a letter from his best friend. I raced upstairs to my room, tearing open the envelope, my heart beating fast. I scanned the letter quickly until I got to these words, "Rob married earlier this summer." The wind knocked out of me, I sank onto my bed and held the letter tightly as my eyes filled with tears. Married! "God, why are You doing this to me? I don't understand." I felt numb and empty and so very lonely.

By this time I had nothing left in me to regroup. This was the KO punch. I couldn't recover from it. I couldn't just get up off the mat and stagger on to the next round. This time, I was left with nothing. I felt abandoned.

Bob was out of the country when I received this letter. On his return, he found a letter from me waiting for him:

I tried to think what you would tell me if I could have called you. Remember last time? I remember you telling me this is bigger than David, bigger than Steve. So, I said to myself: "This is bigger than Rob." But I felt so empty. So what if it is part of God's plan and He wants to use it to heal me? I can't take God's methods anymore. Bob, I am scared. I can't seem to hang on to my faith this time. I feel so very alone . . . betrayed even. Why get up and try again in this trusting God stuff? All it gets me is one more crisis, one more disappointment, over and over again. No wonder my mother killed herself. How many times can one person get knocked down and still believe God cares? I feel so afraid; like a pawn in some cosmic game. I know I will see you on Friday. I am so frightened, please help me.

When I saw Bob that week, he explained, "Nancy, I know that there is a lot of pain. This deep-rooted fear of being alone and of being abandoned has been a part of you for so long, but you have covered it up for years by being a good Christian. Be still now for a while and let God nurture you. The pain is necessary so your heart can be open to God the Father's love. Let Him love you as His daughter."

I couldn't respond to Bob. I was so despondent, I left his office quietly. That night I wrote in my journal:

I am afraid
of being alone
rejected
abandoned
I am afraid God will leave me too
that when I most need Him, He won't be there
I am afraid I will never be married
that there is no good man for me.

I want so much to know deep love
to have the longing of my heart satisfied by God
yet I do not know how to make that happen.

So all this pain is Your love,
Your mercy?
I can't see that now.
I am afraid of You.
What if You are not there?

My despair was so deep that for several counseling sessions, I couldn't get past expressing my pain to Bob. I recorded in my journal, "Jesus must have known how hard it is for some of us who have never known this kind of intimate, unconditional love to really accept God's love for them. In His last prayer for us, Jesus defined eternal life as knowing God and pleaded with the Father that the love with which He loved the Son might be ours as well" (John 17:13, 26). That thought began to break through my darkness with a glimmer of light. Jesus was interceding for me to know the Father's love as He had experienced it.

The next counseling session, as I was expressing the agony in my heart once again, Bob said, "Nancy, I want you to trust me. I have some very important things to tell you and I want you to hear me. You are experiencing God pulling up out of you all the loneliness, fear, and abuse you have ever experienced. That's why you feel so shaky now. Listen to me very carefully, Nancy. I know with the depths of my being—now this is not psychology or intellectualism or spirituality; this is the conviction of God—I know that God is preparing you for His love, that all of this loneliness and pain you are going through now is His love too. You cannot see it; I don't expect you to, but I will go through this with you as much as I can. God has stripped you of every resource of your independence to get you alone with Him. Because you've been hurt so often, you have built up quite a reserve of resilience and stubborn persistence. It is that reserve that God has had to empty. You will never know that you can really trust God until He is all that is left."

I know that God is preparing you for His love, that all of this loneliness and pain you are going through now is His love too.

243

"Bob, in Romans 8 it says that nothing, absolutely nothing is capable of separating us from the love of God. I want so much to believe that is true for me. Yet I see God right now as a tall, strong man with arms folded across his chest, looking disdainfully down at a child who is pulling at his pant's leg, clinging to him, saying, 'Please love me.' I guess I need to know God won't just respond to me with tolerance. I wish my mental picture was of Him hugging me and laughing and being excited to see me. I have so many fearful thoughts about God. But right now, all I can trust is you. And if you tell me that all this loneliness and pain is God's love at work in me so that I can know His love, then I will trust that."

Over the next several months, almost imperceptibly, a peace began to fill my heart, an assurance of God's love that I had never known before. As I went about the ordinary activities of my final year in law school, work, and time with friends, I began to believe that God was there, loving me without any action on my part. Now I was coming to believe in Him in the midst of disappointments and to accept the fact that God loved me because He chose to do so, not because I had proven myself worthy. God's Holy Spirit was at work patiently during these months. I could finally understand why Paul said that as Christians we don't have to be "like cringing, fearful slaves, but we should behave like God's very own children, adopted into the bosom of his family, and calling to him, 'Father, Father.' For his Holy Spirit speaks to us deep in our hearts, and tells us that we really are God's children" (Rom. 8:15–16 LB).

In a counseling session at the close of 1983, Bob reflected on what had happened over the last five months and said, "Remember, several years ago I told you that when you could relinquish your independent nature to God and let Him love you, you would be in a position to receive the gift of marriage? I want to encourage you to begin to pray for this now. You are more ready for marriage now than you have ever been in your entire life. All that is missing is the gift of a husband from God. There's nothing else you have to do except wait for this free gift of God. Go ahead now and pray for being married."

"But Bob," I complained, "I am afraid to do that. I'd almost rather live with an unfulfilled desire than to express it to God and not have it be fulfilled."

"Nancy, this may sound strange to you now, but I think God wants to begin to demonstrate His provision for you. He is a Father who gives good gifts. I think that one of the ways God will demonstrate His love for you is through a man. For so long you have desired marriage and wanted God to create for you that new family. That desire goes hand in hand with your desire for God, but you need to come to this desire of your heart fully. God's love is going to come to you in even a deeper way, and I believe it is going to come to you through another person."

The Real God Asks You to Choose

God designed us so that we have the privilege of participating in our own recovery: He gave us the ability to choose. When God created the earth and mankind, He purposefully limited Himself and His control over His creation by giving us free will and the privilege of making choices. We often view ourselves as determined by our home life. Our fate seems sealed from the beginning. We can resort to the "if onlys" of regret. "If only I hadn't been born into this family, I wouldn't be so anxious and fearful now." "If only I had another father, I wouldn't be so driven." "If only I had a loving family, I could relate easily now to God." These are excuses for staying stuck in self-destructive patterns.

But we do have choices. We can choose to blame our pasts for our present problems, or we can choose to examine our pasts for connections to present problems and change as a result. The good news is that we can become transformed people. We do not have to repeat our families. At any point, we can begin to choose to live according to new patterns of relating to ourselves, to others, and to our God.

Choices Have Consequences

We not only have the privilege of making choices but also the responsibility of making choices. Our choices have consequences. "Do not be deceived, God is not mocked; for whatever a man sows, that he will also reap" (Gal. 6:7). We reap the consequences of poor choices as well as the benefits of good choices. Over time our choices measure our lives. Each choice we make becomes foundational for the future as we develop patterns based on our choices.

Sometimes the negative effects of our choices are felt generations later. This is especially true in family life. Those families that are nurturing tend to produce men and women capable of nurturing their own children. Dysfunctional families tend to reproduce their own kind.

Central to breaking the cycle of dysfunction in my family was to learn how to make choices that would result in life and health to me. Bob explained to me the principle of choice making that God laid out in Deuteronomy 30:19–20:

> I have set before you life and death, blessing and cursing; therefore choose life, that both you and your descendants may live; that you may love the Lord your God, that you may obey His voice, and that you may cling to Him.

Life and blessing or death and curses. These were the two distinct paths I could choose. Bob explained that my family had conditioned me to choose those things which were death to me. Each one of my family members had chosen death—a physical, moral, or spiritual death. Three of them had either threatened, attempted, or committed suicide. I had grown up with these people and incorporated these tendencies toward choosing death into my personality. It would take conscious choice making on my part for my life to go counter to these natural tendencies. In counseling, I learned that I had a responsibility to participate with God in determining my future paths. I was not at the mercy of my past. I could make choices that would give me hope for a different future and leave a legacy of life for my children.

When Faced with a Choice, Make the One That Leads to Life

I learned, with Bob's help, not to respond so impulsively to decisions but to step back, examine the choices, trace the consequences that might flow from each of those choices, and then choose the path that led to life, blessing, and health. Nowhere was this more problematic for me than in relationships with men. I was naturally drawn to men who were unable to commit or who were untrustworthy. Stable men who were able to express their feelings and make long-lasting commitments did not interest me. Learning to choose life in this area would be the greatest challenge in my recovery.

I also needed to learn how to choose life in my relationship with God. I had to learn that it was possible to begin to choose to believe what was true about God despite my natural proclivity to believe otherwise. As I uncovered what I believed about God—distorted or not—I could then decide whether to affirm or refute these beliefs.

Take Your New Beliefs about God to Another for Validation or Correction

I took these discoveries to either Bob or to my good friend and running partner, Elaine Griffith, to help me evaluate the truth of my beliefs. This next step was very important. Otherwise, I could stay stuck in my anger, disappointment, or fears about God by mulling over those experiences that gave credence to my distorted view of God. Without validation or correction of my distortions by someone who had already worked through a biblical understanding of God as Father, I would only distance myself further from God, convinced He was just as untrustworthy as I originally thought.

Elaine and I often ran together along the W & OD Railroad bike path in Virginia. One brilliant June day a few weeks after I had graduated from law school in 1984, I explained, "Elaine, I am so confused. I feel like God has stripped me of everything I have depended on these last few years. Last fall, I lost my long-held hope that Rob and I would get back together and be married. I don't see how God could bring anyone into my life that would measure up to him. I leave tomorrow for San Francisco to study for the bar exam. After that I move to San Francisco and start all over. I leave my church and all my close friends here. It doesn't feel right. I don't have any peace at all about this decision I made six months ago to join a San Francisco law firm. But God did not provide an opportunity to stay here in Washington." We kept running, but my pace slowed as I labored to breathe steadily; I felt a tightening in my chest from my fears about the future.

"Nancy," Elaine said, "God knows exactly where you are at this point. He knows your fears and He can help. It's all right to be confused now. You don't have to push so hard to understand."

I suddenly stopped running and turned to Elaine and said, "But I can't seem to trust Him with this. I want so much to stay in D.C., but I don't see any way to do that. My school loans come due in six months. I'm scheduled to take the California bar exam in seven weeks. It's impossible to get a D.C. job at this late date."

Elaine put her hand on my shoulder and said, "So don't trust Him with it. Say instead, 'God, I trust You to give me what I need to know to trust You. You show me the next step.' He'll do that for you, Nancy. Ask Him to show you the next step.''

I cried gently now, brushing the tears away from my cheeks with the back of my hand.

Elaine continued, "Nancy, you are very capable. I think God wants to show Himself to you in a way you have never seen before. I think He wants to show you His power and His ability to work on your behalf. But He's getting you to the place where you can't see how to work it all out. Remember, God is not devastated because He has all the power and all the solutions. He wants to demonstrate this to you, if you'll let Him. Nancy, remember what it says in Ephesians 3:20: God 'is able to do exceedingly abundantly above all that we ask or think, according to the power that works in us.' Ask for this; watch for this. God knows you can't uphold the burden of this. He says He will do something marvelous for you on the basis of His power at work in your behalf. Can you believe this?"

I looked off into the field of wildflowers by the bike path and blinked hard, fighting back the tears. "It's okay," Elaine gently said. "Just ask Him to show you how to trust Him. Tell God, 'Okay, You've brought me this far; I know You love me. It's new territory, however, to believe You want to act on my behalf. Just open the door a little and help me receive.' "

Replace Old Thinking with Truth

As I flew off to San Francisco, I had the verses Elaine shared with me on an index card. Over the next several months, I would look at them over and over, reminding myself what the Bible said was true about God. He was a rewarder of people like me who sought Him. He would make it clear what He wanted for me. He wanted to accomplish it based on His love for me and His desire to act on my behalf.

I discovered that the key to knowing God was to replace distorted beliefs with the truth. This did not happen overnight. I had spent many years in contrary belief patterns, and these perspectives were ingrained in my thinking and my response to God. It took me quite some time to sort through my wrong thinking about God and replace it with the truth. I found I didn't have to plan out an academic journey to do this. God used my present circumstances to help me learn the truth about His character.

Shortly after I arrived in San Francisco, I received a phone call from a Georgetown law professor who wondered if I might be interested in a job with a Washington firm. The firm had called him, and he had called the law review office to ask for some names. It so happened that a friend of mine answered the phone and suggested he call me in California. I was thrilled. Here it was! God was about to act on my behalf. Hallelujah! I hurriedly got off a resume in the mail and waited anxiously for his reply.

I struggled with the waiting. As I wrote to Elaine, "It is difficult to wait. I get so anxious when nothing is happening. This firm has my resume and I haven't heard anything for three weeks now. I can feel that old habit creeping up. I have a tendency to say, 'See, I knew God wouldn't do it.' Oh, Elaine, please pray for me. I want so much to believe that God is at work on my behalf. It's as if God is trying to build into my experience things for which I have no reference point. I knew neither a father's love nor a father's provision. Is this how faith is born—pushing through the familiar, but wrong, concepts to trust the unfamiliar but true? I stand at the threshold of faith and my past, my common-sense logic, my experiences tell me I am a fool. Where I stand now, there is no turning back—it's just hard to leap over. Will a small step do? For me, today, that step is just admitting to you and to God that this is where I am. Please pray with me that Isaiah 64:4 becomes real in my life: 'For since the world began no one has seen or heard of such a God as ours, who works for those who wait for him!' "

A few weeks later, the professor called. The firm was not interested in interviewing me. I was devastated. My emotions swirled around me and I clutched the telephone receiver tightly. Now I had a choice. I could let this experience confirm that God loved to toy with me, getting my hopes up and making me trust Him and then pulling the rug out from under me. Or I could choose to believe what was true about Him despite my circumstances.

I grabbed the index card, went out the door to run, and in cadence with every step, repeated the verses. I told God I chose to believe those verses were true even though my feelings were screaming otherwise. I asked God to make His faithfulness, love, care, and mercy real to me.

The day after the bar exam, I went to San Diego—my three-day reward for the last six weeks of intensive study. I still desired to stay in the Washington area, but it was now three weeks before my scheduled move to California. I took long walks on the island of Coronado and shared my thoughts with God. Over the next three days, as I walked and talked with God, I discovered He had much to teach me, too, about my original decision process to move to San Francisco.

I realized that I had sought my own success. Like many others on law review, I bought into the theory that I should go to a big firm in a big city. These plum jobs were usually reserved for law review graduates. The wisdom around the law school was to go to the big firm, big city first, and then work your way down to a smaller firm, if you wanted. To do the reverse would keep you stuck at a small firm. That sounded reasonable to me, and I had only sent my resumes out to large firms in five major cities. As I prayed, God revealed these words: "Moses, Joseph, Paul, and Jesus." I continued to wait on Him in prayer asking what He meant. After a long silence, He spoke again: "Forty years in the wilderness first, a slave in Egypt first, fourteen years of preparation first, a carpenter's son first." I was deeply humbled. I had sought my own success, and so often God's way is the opposite of how I would accomplish my goals.

I also prayed about marriage. I was thirty-one years old and still unmarried. I seemed to get into one unfulfilling or destructive relationship after another, and yet I yearned to have a marriage of deep, committed love. What was wrong here?

As I prayed about these things, I received assurance from God that these desires—to return to Washington and to be married—were from Him. I received a clear word to trust Him and *to wait on Him.* Yet when I returned to Washington, I spent the first week running around, researching law firms, reworking my resume, printing up 150 copies, arranging to borrow a memory typewriter for cover letters, and other such frenetic activities. After all, God had said I could trust that my desire to stay in Washington was from Him, hadn't He?

As I was rushing out of the house to mail the letters, God brought me up short. "Where are you going?" He asked.

"God, You know where I am going; I'm going to get a job."

"Nancy, you're seeking your own success again. I want you to go back inside and wait for Me to act."

"So, God," I retorted, "I suppose You just want me to wait for the phone to ring?"

"That's exactly right. Do not take any initiative; only wait for Me to bring you the contacts."

"Right," I said halfheartedly and turned out of sheer obedience to climb the stairs to the house. "Sure, with just a few weeks to go before I am supposed to move to California, You want me to just hang out and wait."

And wait I did, even though it struck at the very core of my nature. My emotions were running high. Bob shared with me at the close of a counseling session that I should watch my feelings and not fall back in the trap of letting them take me off the track of trusting God. "The Father wants to do good to you, Nancy. The Father wants to give you good gifts. He knows the future and He wants what's best for you. Don't give in to your feelings of anxiety and become operational once again. Let Him be your Father."

Two weeks before I was to move, the phone rang. Kim Colby, an attorney with the Christian Legal Society who knew of my desire to stay in Washington, said, "Nancy, I don't think this firm is looking for an attorney, but the managing partner, Chip Grange, is on our board and has a lot of wisdom. Why don't you call him and see if you can meet with him?"

Four days later, I was in the law offices of Gammon & Grange, sharing with Chip my spiritual journey this last year and how it had brought me to waiting on the Lord. Within one week after that, I had met all the partners and they had extended me an offer to join their firm. I would be working in a small firm with other attorneys, learning the ropes of nonprofit law to serve the needs of tax-exempt organizations, including Christian ministries. As I left their offices after accepting the offer, I asked, "When did you know you needed an associate?"

Chip responded, "I began praying for God to bring the right person three months ago in June." God had begun to put into place all the circumstances necessary for me to stay in Washington early in the summer. It was the process of trusting God's love for me in His provision of my needs, however, that was His ultimate goal.

All of these principles from counseling—facing self-destructive patterns, choosing life, and believing the truth about God—were soon to coalesce in my greatest desire—to be married. It is one thing to learn principles in the abstract; it is another to apply them in the areas that have always been your greatest struggles. I knew that my understanding of God's love for me had gotten all wrapped up in whether or not He would provide me a loving family of my own. I had unraveled much of this in counseling, but it was not until I was faced with choosing His plan for me over my own natural desires that I would be able to understand God really had intended it all for good.

Fear Can Block God's Power

believe in the power of prayer for individuals, for families, for the church, and for the country. In this chapter from my book, Prayer, *I want to talk about fear. Fear is a powerful, dictating, debilitating, undermining emotion. And it is a sin. If fear is making the decisions for you, it is blocking the power of God in your life. It is through prayer that you can begin to walk again in faith not fear. Any rebuilding by the Holy Spirit is done step-by-step—but it is you who must do the walking and the talking in prayer.*

Beverly LaHaye
Prayer

In the early days of Tim's and my ministry, I was terribly fear-prone. Unfortunately, many of my early decisions were based on the emotion of fear.

One day my husband announced he wanted to take flying lessons. In horror I said, "You mean you want to fly an airplane with only *one engine?*"

"Yes," he said, "that's what I'd be starting off with. What do you think?"

Well, I already had my mind made up. I said, "I think you're foolish! Why would you want to get into a plane with only one engine? What if something goes wrong? You won't have a spare!"

Tim asked me to pray about it. He wouldn't take the lessons, he assured me, unless I agreed, because I would have to make some sacrifices. First there would be a sacrifice of time—Tim would have to be gone a lot more for cross-country flights, ground school training and just logging the necessary hours for a license. Second—and even worse—the day would come when he would want me to fly with him.

"Of course I'll pray about it," I told Tim.

Well, I did pray. Over and over I begged, "Lord, you know how foolish this flying thing is. It's just too dangerous for Tim. Please change his heart. Take the desire to fly away from him."

I'm sure by now you've recognized that I was firmly stuck on that third level of prayer—giving our opinions to God. Fear does that to us. And so I started right off giving God my opinions and drawing my own conclusions. My fear and anxiety was controlling me.

Tim's desire to fly turned out to be one of the major turning points of my life. One day my dear husband, who knows me well, said to me, "Honey, I know you've been praying about the flying lessons. But, I wonder, have you asked God to perhaps change *your* attitude?"

That took me aback. I thought, *What does he mean? I'm not the one who needs to change! I'm praying for him to change.*

"Be open with the Lord," Tim told me. "Share your heart and fears with Him. Let Him know you're afraid of flying, but that you're willing to be changed if that's what He would have."

And that's just what I did. I prayed, "Lord, I still think I'm right about Tim's flying, but if I'm the one who needs to be changed, then I'm ready for You to change my attitude and my fears."

All along, my own conclusion had steadfastly been that God needed to change Tim's heart. But my dread of Tim's being hurt—or even killed—in an accident didn't abate until I got to the point where I was willing to say, "Lord, if it's *my* heart that needs to be changed, then change me."

Over my obstinate resistance, God did just that. He changed me!

Tim took those flying lessons. Every time he went up for a lesson, I prayed and prayed, and over and over I committed him to the Lord.

During the following months I developed a very warm prayer life with God on my husband's behalf!

Then came the day when Tim walked into the house and said, "Okay, Honey, I've got enough hours logged up now that you can fly with me. I'd like to take you up this afternoon."

Suddenly there was a whole different picture on my prayers. Now it wasn't just a matter of committing Tim to the Lord. I had to commit *Beverly* into God's hands, too. It was time to say, "I'll get into that plane with only one engine, Lord, and I'll fly in it because I know I'm in Your care." But I didn't come easily to that point. Again, my fear got in the way.

I thought of every possible reason why I couldn't go in the plane with Tim that day. "I'm right in the middle of doing the laundry and I have to finish it," I said.

But Tim was persistent. "All that will wait," he said. "Come and get in the car. I want to take you up right now while the weather's good."

In the end, I went. But all the way out to the airport, I thought, *Please, oh please, couldn't we delay this?* I finally prayed, *Please, God, help me to have the same peace to get in that plane as you gave me for Tim to fly.*

Well, we got to the airport and everything was fine. The mechanics had thoroughly checked out that single engine and fueled the gas tank. The sky was as clear and blue as could be—not a single cloud in sight. Together Tim and I walked toward the little plane. Tim showed me how to climb aboard and strap myself in. But every step of the way I kept on pleading, *Oh, Lord, is this what You really want?*

Tim turned the engine over and carefully checked off his checklists. Everything went perfectly. We taxied out to the end of the runway, and as Tim was revving up the engine, before he got the clearance to move on down the runway and take off, in desperation I reminded the Lord, *This is Your last chance! Is this what You want? If You do, You are really going to have to come through and carry me in Your arms because this is too frightening for me!*

Well, the Lord didn't stop the plane. We went on down the runway and took off—a beautiful take off, by the way. It was as if the Lord reached out and put His arms underneath the plane and carried us along.

As we went upward, I remember feeling so very close to the Lord. All of a sudden it became a spiritual experience. Just my husband

and me in that little craft high up in the air, supported by God's loving arms underneath.

And you know what? After all my doubting and pleading and begging, I found myself actually enjoying the flight. There truly is an exhilaration in flying, more so in a small plane with all the gusts of wind and the characteristic sounds of the engine than in a big commercial plane.

When a few little gusts of wind came and blew us around a bit, I anxiously asked, "What was that?" My first thought was that the engine might be having problems.

"It's nothing," Tim said. "Just a little wind." Comforted, I went right back to the realization that God's everlasting arms were under me.

I must admit that I didn't exactly jump into the plane with great excitement to make the second flight. Or the third or the fourth. But even when I was nervous to fly, I forced myself to go. And every time I flew, it got a little easier.

You know what? Flying turned out to be a wonderful experience for me. Forced to face my fears, I learned to trust God to lift me above them. I had to ask myself, "Okay, Beverly, is God able to take care of you or not?" I knew He was, since He'd already helped me to overcome the crippling effects of my arthritis. The next logical question was, "So, then, can you totally commit yourself to His care, or can't you?" Of course, I knew I could. The witness of His walking beside me during those hard months when I prepared myself to spend the rest of my life as an invalid proved that He could carry me through any fearful experience.

The Witness of Past Memories

Often when I'm fearful, I practice the art of reviewing the past, something taught to us by the patriarchs of the Bible. It is, in fact, a practice still employed by Jews throughout the world. I think about what has happened before in my life and review the ways God has helped me through other situations. I always try to remember one or two specific events in my life, such as my struggle with arthritis, and to recall the singular feeling of peace and joy I experienced as my fingers straightened out enough that I could once again comb my hair or sign my name.

Moses' last instructions to the Israelite people were to remember. "Remember how God led you out of Egypt." "Remember the way He parted the Red Sea." "Remember how He provided manna for you in the dry desert wilderness." "Remember . . ."

. . . and once a year, he told them, "Celebrate!" Celebrate God's blessing at the feast of the Passover. Spend a whole evening reviewing God's provision for you in the past and enjoying that memory together. "For by strength of hand the Lord has brought you out of this place" (Ex. 13:3). Moses reminded the Israelites, who often forgot—as we all seem to do—God's past blessing whenever they were faced with new hardships (Ex. 13:3).

Likewise, Christians need to remember and to celebrate. Throughout the year, when we are tempted to fall into the sin of fearfulness, we need to remember God's blessings of the past. No other testimony can be greater to us because those experiences are sure evidence of God's hand at work in our lives.

And once a year, why not have a celebration of your own? New Year's Eve has always been an uncomfortable holiday for me. There's an awful lot of false happiness in those scenes of dancing and drinking and wearing silly hats and blowing noisemakers and hugging and kissing people you barely know. What about a feast of New Year's Eve instead? Together your family can remember the ways in which God has provided for them in the past. Or, if the children have other activities, perhaps it might just be Mom and Dad. Certainly the two of you know what a miracle it is that God has brought you through a certain number of years of providing food and shelter and some amount of comfort for you and your children. You also know how miraculous it is that God has managed to protect you from your own weaknesses—fear or worry or anger or lust. Maybe this is a good time to look at family photo albums or films or videos and remember the past year—or years—this way.

God used Tim's desire to fly an airplane as a blessing in my life. Today, I celebrate that blessing. For it was in that experience more than any other that God taught me to lay my fears before Him and move forward in faith and power. "For God has not given us a spirit of fear, but of power and of love and of a sound mind." Fear will limit our experiencing the power of prayer (2 Timothy 1:7).

God doesn't need my counsel. He doesn't depend on me to tell Him whose heart to change or which action is wise and which is foolish. What He does desire is for me to look to Him and be open to His direction. And He wishes me to be willing to change the way He is leading me to change.

I've always battled fear of one sort or another—fear of failure, fear of opposition, fear that I wouldn't be accepted, fear of new situations. I was naturally a fearful person.

My battle with fear began years before that airplane ride. I've always battled fear of one sort or another—fear of failure, fear of opposition, fear that I wouldn't be accepted, fear of new situations. I was naturally a fearful person. And little did I realize that the victory over fear of flying was a stepping stone to prepare me for greater service for Him in the future.

Fear of Failure

My husband and I started our life together involved in the local church. Because Tim was a pastor, I was immediately thrown into leadership. There I was, a young, fearful woman with a very poor self-image, pushed into playing the part of a skillful and capable pastor's wife.

The women looked to me to be a leader. I was expected to teach Bible classes, to play the organ, lead the choir, to stand up and pray eloquently in public, to bake the very best cakes—all this was, I thought, part of my new job description. Suddenly, I found myself thrust into an area in which I felt I was totally inadequate.

Instead of trying to sharpen up and meet these challenges and expectations, I retreated. Where I started out lacking confidence, I became downright fearful. And the more fearful I became, the more intimidated I felt.

During the early years of our ministry, I remember agreeing to give a devotional even though I was scared to death. A few weeks later one of the ladies shared with me that I had not done a very good job and I needed to work on a few things before ever doing it again. This was more than my already poor self-image could handle, so after that when I was asked, I responded, "My husband is the speaker in the family. I'm just his helpmeet." At the time I thought this was an adequate answer. But when I look back on it now, I'm really ashamed of myself. I was hiding behind Tim's ministerial coat and trying to excuse myself for fear of failing again.

One day I was abruptly brought face-to-face with what I was doing. We had been in the ministry fifteen or sixteen years. Throughout that time I had limited myself to teaching young children in Sunday school; only with them did I feel comfortable. Then one day Dr. Henry Brandt took me aside and pointed out 2 Timothy 1:7: "For God has not given us a spirit of fear, but of power and of love and of a sound mind." Then, without trying to spare my feelings, he told me, "Beverly, your fear is based on selfishness and that is a sin. You need to deal with it."

A sin! I was staggered.

Dr. Brandt didn't stop there. "Beverly," he told me, "You're all wrapped up with fear and a poor self-image, and that is caused by selfishness."

Believe me, this was not easy to hear! But it was the best thing in the world for me. And when Dr. Brandt started repeating my own words back to me, just as I'd said them to him, I could see it all. It was obvious even to me.

Fear Is a Sin

Few of us think of fear as a sin. Yet in the next days as I thought about Dr. Brandt's words and read the Scriptures, I realized he was right. I might not be committing murder or stealing or cheating on my husband, but I *was* committing a sin.

In Romans 14:23, the apostle Paul tells us, "for whatever is not from faith is sin." God wants us to walk by faith. But fear is not from faith, therefore fear is sin.

To see the contrast between faith and fear, let's take a look at Daniel. Coerced by governors jealous of Daniel, King Darius signed his name to a royal decree that anyone caught praying to any god or man for the next thirty days would be cast into a den of hungry lions.

Daniel knew all about the law, and he knew the penalty for breaking it. Now, I don't know about you, but if I were faced with a den of hungry lions, I think I would pray in my closet for the next month. God could hear me just as well from there, I'd reason. Besides, what good would I be to God as a lion's main course?

Well, that's not the way Daniel saw it. He went straight up to his room, and in front of his window open toward Jerusalem, he knelt down and prayed to God—out loud. He had done this three times every day of his life, and he wasn't about to change his worship habits now.

Well, you know the story. Daniel was caught in the trap laid by the jealous governors, and there was nothing King Darius could do to help him. But he knew all about Daniel and his faith in God, so even as Daniel was cast into the lion's den, the king said to him, "Your God, whom you serve continually, He will deliver you." I'm not sure the king actually believed it, but Daniel certainly did.

Very early the next morning, the king jumped from his bed and ran to the den of lions. "Daniel, servant of the living God," he called out, "has your God been able to deliver you from the lions?"

From the depths of the den came Daniel's voice, strong and fearless. "O king," he called, "my God sent His angel and shut the lions' mouths. They have not hurt me because I am innocent."

How could Daniel be so fearless? Because of his faith. Faith and fear don't mix. And whatever is not of faith is sin.

All those years God knew my heart. He knew I really wanted to be a godly woman. It was just that I didn't know how to pull myself out of that fearful crippling self-doubt.

The day that Dr. Brandt spoke with me, I began a long struggle to rebuild my life. Actually it was more a matter of allowing the Holy Spirit to do the rebuilding. I began to pray for a way to overcome the fear that was destroying me. I needed to stop controlling my own life with the fearful emotions and allow the Holy Spirit to take control. In answer to that prayer, He immediately began to show me the way— not all at once, but step by step.

As I look back in retrospect, I think I was actually pulling my husband down as well because I was always kind of a wet blanket for him. If he offered, "Should we do this?" or "Do you think we should try that?" I always had a reason why we shouldn't or why it would never work.

I dealt with my fear of failure, but other fears still cowered inside me. I didn't know that, but God did, and in the years that followed He helped me to see those other lurking fears.

Fear of Opposition

At Concerned Women for America, I came to the place where I had to be very honest with the Lord. I had to tell Him how really afraid I was to do what I was convinced He was calling me to do. I'd see Eleanor Smeal and Betty Friedan on television, raising their clenched fists high, screaming out in shrill voices, and I was convinced that God meant for someone else to do this job instead of me.

Now, I am a peaceful woman. I don't like conflict. It's important to me that people like me. It is not my nature to enter such a combative, militant arena. As I watched and listened to the women I knew we had to oppose, I questioned God's leading, and yet God had led me to take a stand for righteousness.

Very quickly I learned that it's not possible to remain fearful and still take a firm stand for righteousness. You can pray for God to protect your family and other families in our land, but you can't take that next step—you can't pray and then *act*—if you are bound by the sin of fear.

Standing for righteousness carries a price tag. In that position one doesn't have the luxury of carefully looking at each situation and weighing it, then asking, "Should I or shouldn't I?" If I were truly going to take a stand for righteousness, I had no choice but to march right in and say, "By God's grace, I *will* do this!" "I can do all things through Christ who strengthens me" (Phil. 4:13).

And so, praying a prayer expressing my fears became a very personal experience. Of course, God already knew my fears. I realized He didn't have to be apprised of them. But for me to learn to express them to Him was a necessary step; as I talked them over with God and asked Him for help in overcoming, I began to recognize and verbalize each fear.

Many times I prayed back to God that Scripture that Dr. Brandt had given me: "For God has not given us a spirit of fear, but of power and of love and of a sound mind." Many times as I spoke out against the deception taught by Eleanor Smeal or Molly Yard or some other feminist leader, my mind clung tightly to that scriptural promise.

Today, at this phase of my work with CWA, I am sometimes criticized. Again and again I am confronted by people who don't like me, and occasionally I get "hate" letters in the mail. Sometimes I even get threats. Without God, my natural fearfulness would rise up and shout, "Enough of this! I'm getting out of here. I'm going back home where I'm loved and secure and comfortable!"

Yet God built a protective shield around me. I'm convinced it is because my prayer has been that, more than anything else, God would enable me to do what He wants me to do—even if it means getting hate letters and having people not like me. In the end, you see, what people think of me isn't really important. What *is* important is that I be obedient to the Lord Jesus Christ—even when I dislike opposition and even when I'm afraid of not being in control. This, you see, is yet another kind of fear God has helped me to overcome.

Fear of Not Being in Control

Sometimes the worst fear of all is the fear of not being in control. In 1987 I was asked to appear in a panel of six people on a segment of Oprah Winfrey's talk show. The subject was advertising condoms on television. Three panelists were in favor of such advertising and three, including me, were against it.

Now, I can tell you, the subject of condoms is one I'd prefer not to discuss at all. Ten years ago I never dreamed I'd be talking about such a thing in mixed company, let alone on national television! Yet the time may come when we have to take on subjects we'd just as soon ignore. This was one of those times. I felt so strongly about my position that I knew I should be there to represent and support it.

Before I agreed to appear on the show, I specifically asked if any condoms would be shown. (Since I was opposed to condoms on television, to have them displayed right there would, I felt, be working against me.) When the production personnel assured me there wouldn't be any, I said, "Okay, then I'll participate on the panel."

As the show started, each panelist had a turn to speak and make specific points. All was going fine when Oprah paused for a commercial break, then left to take a break herself.

We didn't know it, but the two front rows in the studio were filled with homosexuals who had flown in to Chicago from San Francisco. During the commercial break they went out and brought back a big box. Then they proceeded to hand out bags to everyone in the audience as well as to us on the platform. When they handed one to me, I refused to take it. It was as if the Lord whispered to me, "Don't take that. If you do, you're going to get caught with the goods in your hands!" Things happened so fast that I didn't even have time to pray. Still, I sensed the Lord guiding my actions and reactions.

The bags were marked "Safe Sex Kits."

The young woman on the other end of the panel proudly admitted that she had "starred" in a pornographic film that displayed "safe sex" techniques. During a commercial break, she opened her little bag and pulled out a condom and some rubber gloves. She thought it was hilarious. She put on the gloves, making jokes the whole time.

We brought the kits to Oprah's attention and she tried to explain their appearance on the show. Those of us against condom advertising protested loudly. After the program began again, I told Oprah with the cameras rolling, "We came on this show to talk about why we objected to condoms being advertised on television and you've already done it. It's been on television now. I'm really offended by this."

"There aren't any condoms here," Oprah said.

"Look around," I told her. "Everyone here has a bag with several condoms in it."

Oprah was astounded. She had no idea what was going on.

"I want you to know I am offended and terribly disappointed that this show has deteriorated to such a low level," I told her.

The Lord gave me the push to say those words at just that moment. It was something I would never have had the courage to say myself.

But from that point on, the show got more and more out of hand. Oprah totally lost control. I really believe in my heart that if she could have pulled the plug on that show that day, she would have done it in a minute.

One by one the homosexuals spoke into the mike and preached about how we "fundamentalist Christians" are so narrow and insist that everyone else live by our rules.

I don't blame Oprah for what happened. The homosexual contingent were well organized. They knew exactly what they were doing. They were in favor of advertising condoms on television, and they accomplished their goal. Without a doubt, condoms were being advertised loudly and clearly right there that day.

A situation that would have produced great fear in the past was instead, a position of strength and courage. God was faithful and provided the power and sound mind that was promised.

When we walk with God, when we pray first and then act, we will move in God's strength and become all He wants us to be. Way back there in California, so many years ago, God saw Beverly LaHaye a lot differently than I saw myself. Day by day, step by step, He's moved me toward His own vision of the person I am and am to become.

The Wonderful Consequence of Confronting Your Fear

When God confronted me with my fear of flying in a one-engine airplane, I had no idea He would later take Tim and me into areas of the world where we would have to fly in just such a plane. From deep in the jungles of Mexico where Wycliffe trains missionaries, to a little isolated mission village in New Guinea, we ministered to missionaries and their families. Later, I began to make frequent trips into the jungles of Costa Rica to work among the Nicaraguan refugees, and now recently into the interior of Nicaragua, even though I was well aware that the danger of an emergency landing in those remote areas is far greater than in California.

When Tim decided to take those long-ago flying lessons, I never dreamed what was to come. But God knew. And He was preparing me. Had He said way back then, "Okay Beverly, today you've got to pass this test because in twenty years I'm going to have you flying into the jungle right up to the Nicaraguan border in a little plane with just one engine," I couldn't have done it.

None of what God has opened the doors for me to do today would have been possible if I had failed that test back then. But God didn't tell me that. He led me along one step at a time.

Three years ago, Tim and I were flying in a little eighteen passenger commuter plane with one of our attorneys when a turbulent storm blew up. As the sky outside grew darker and more ominous, that little plane bounced and tossed around in the air. Our attorney is not a fearful man, but he was terrified that day. He told me he bowed his head and began confessing every sin he ever committed. Then he begged God to take care of his family after he was gone.

When he opened his eyes, he says, he looked over at Tim and me. Tim was writing away, not at all concerned about the storm. I was sound asleep.

"I don't get it," he told me later. "How could you sleep so peacefully with that terrible storm going on outside?"

"It has to be God," I told him. "Only He could have brought me from that crippling fearfulness I once had to a place where I could fly through such a storm and still be at peace."

How about you? Is there fear or anxiety in your life that is limiting what God can do? Have you admitted that fear to the Lord? Have you asked Him to help you overcome it? Prayer is your weapon against fear. Prayer is the key that opens a reservoir of power for you.

God is moving you one step at a time toward becoming all you can be. I doubt that you can begin to imagine all He has in store for you. I know I couldn't!

Chapter 16

Live in Obedience

In my autobiography, Stormie, I un-folded my long journey to healing and wholeness from a childhood of emotional torture by a mentally ill mother. After publication, I was deluged by people who were suffering the same torment from an abusive childhood. They wanted to know the steps they could take to experience the same healing I had.

In my book, A Step in the Right Direction, *I offer seven steps to emotional health. Step One: Acknowledge God; Step Two: Lay a Foundation in God's Word, Prayer, Praise, Confession, and Ongoing Forgiveness; Step Three: Live in Obedience; Step Four: Find Deliverance; Step Five: Receive God's Gifts; Step Six: Reject the Pitfalls; and Step Seven: Stand Strong. What I would like to share with you are a few of the steps to live in obedience—which I feel is the key to God's healing in your life.*

Stormie Omartian
A Step in the Right Direction

"When will I ever get to the point where I no longer hurt inside?" I asked God one day in prayer a few months after my counseling session with Mary Anne. Even though I had been set free from depression and my life was far more stable than it had ever been, I still lived on an emotional roller coaster. My questions to God during that time went on and on:

- "When will I stop feeling like a failure?"
- "When will I not be devastated by what other people say to me?"
- "When will I not view every hint of misfortune as the end of the world?"
- "When will I be able to go through the normal occurrences of life without being traumatized by them?"

There were no answers from God at that moment, but as I read the Bible the next morning, my eyes fell on the words, "Why do you call Me 'Lord, Lord,' and do not do the things which I say?" (Luke 6:46). The passage went on to explain that anyone who hears the words of the Lord and does *not* put them into practice is building a house with no foundation. When the storm comes, it will collapse and be completely destroyed.

Could it be that I'm getting blown over and destroyed by every wind of circumstance that comes my way because I'm not doing what the Lord says to do in some area? I wondered. I knew I was building on solid rock (Jesus), and I had been laying a strong foundation (in the Word, prayer, praise, confession, and ongoing forgiveness), but it appeared that this foundation could only be stabilized and protected through my obedience.

I searched the Bible for more information, and every place I turned I read more about the rewards of obeying God:

- "Blessed are those who hear the word of God and keep it!" (Luke 11:28)
- "No good thing will He withhold
From those who walk uprightly." (Ps. 84:11)
- "Behold, I set before you today a blessing and a curse: the blessing, if you obey the commandments of the LORD your God which I command you today." (Deut. 11:26–27)

The more I read, the more I saw the link between *obedience* and the *presence of God*. "If anyone loves Me, he will keep My word; and My Father will love him, and We will come to him and make Our home with him" (John 14:23). I was already convinced by this time that I could only find wholeness and restoration in His presence, so this promise that my obedience would open the door to God's dwelling with me was particularly impressive.

I also saw a definite connection between *obedience* and the *love of God*. "If anyone obeys his Word, God's love is truly made complete in him" (1 John 2:5 NIV). According to the Bible, God doesn't stop loving us if we *don't* obey. Even if He doesn't love the way we live, He still loves *us*. But we are unable to feel or enjoy that love fully if we're not living as God intended us to live. Just as surely as living God's way leads to experiencing His love and life, doing things that are *opposed* to His ways will lead to separation from God's love, which is death to us. The Bible clearly says,

> As righteousness leads to life,
> So he who pursues evil pursues it to his own death.
>   (Prov. 11:19)

The more I read about obedience, the more I realized that my disobedience of God's directives could explain why nothing happened when I prayed the same prayers over and over. The Bible says,

> One who turns away his ear from hearing the law,
> Even his prayer is an abomination. (Prov. 28:9)

If I'm not obeying, I shouldn't expect to get my prayers answered, I thought to myself.

Benefits of Obedience

How many times do we ask God to give us what we want, but we don't want to give God what *He* wants? We lack what we desire most —wholeness, peace, fulfillment, and joy—because we are not obedient to God.

Often we are not obedient because we don't understand that God has set up certain rules to *protect us* and work for *our benefit*. He designed us and knows what will fulfill us most. Even the Ten Commandments were not given to instill guilt, but as an umbrella of blessing and protection from the rain of evil. If we choose to live outside the arena of blessing, we suffer the consequences. Spiritual darkness and confusion then have access to our lives, and we are drained of God's best. When we obey, life has simplicity and clarity and unlimited blessing. We *need* God's laws because we don't know how to make life work without them. The Bible says, "If anyone competes in athletics, he is not crowned unless he competes according to the rules" (2 Tim. 2:5). If restoration is the name of the game, then obedience is one of the rules. The more I've searched the Scriptures, the more I've found that the Bible is full of promises for those who obey God:

- *There is the promise of healing.* Make straight paths for your feet, so that what is lame may not be dislocated, but rather be healed. (Heb. 12:13)
- *There is the promise of answered prayer.* If I had cherished sin in my heart, the Lord would not have listened. (Ps. 66:18 NIV)
- *There is the promise of God fighting our battles for us.*
  Oh, that My people would listen to Me,
  That Israel would walk in My ways!
  I would soon subdue their enemies,
  And turn My hand against their adversaries. (Ps. 81:13–14)
- *There is the promise of living a long life in peace.*
  Let your heart keep my commands;
  For length of days and long life
  And peace they will add to you. (Prov. 3:1–2)

There are many more promises like these, and just as many warnings of what will *not* happen in our lives if we *don't* obey. After reading them, I felt inspired to ask God to show me exactly what I needed to be doing. He was quick to answer that prayer.

The Choice Is Ours—The Power Is His

I've learned that God doesn't enforce obedience. We often wish He would because it would be easier, but He gives us the choice. I had to ask Him to teach me to be obedient out of love for Him and desire to serve the One who has done so much for me. If you want the same benefits, you have to do the same thing. It helps to understand that the Lord is on your side and the call to obedience is *not* to make you feel like a hopeless failure if you don't do everything right. Knowing that God asks you to live a certain way for your own benefit because He knows life only works out right for you when it is lived on His terms will help you to desire to know His ways and live in them.

The law was given in the Old Testament to show us that we can't possibly fulfill it in terms of *human* energy, but must depend on God. We need His power to escape the death syndrome that surrounds us. The Bible says that Noah was given new life because he did *all* that God asked him to do (Gen. 6:22). That word *all* seems frightening when it comes to obedience because we know ourselves well enough to doubt we can do it all. And the truth is we can't. But we *can* take steps in the right direction and watch *God* do it.

The minute we take one step of obedience, God opens up opportunities for new life. The minute we start to think it's not necessary to obey, we have opened the door for evil. Oswald Chambers says, "If [a person] wants insight into what Jesus Christ teaches, he can only get it by obedience. . . . spiritual darkness comes because of something I do not intend to obey" (*My Utmost for His Highest*, Westwood, NJ: Barbour & Co., 1984, 151).

> *The minute we take one step of obedience,*
> *God opens up opportunities for new life.*

For anyone who has been emotionally wounded in any way, a certain amount of deliverance and healing will happen in your life just by being obedient to God. The Bible says, "He who obeys instructions guards his soul" (Prov. 19:16 NIV). The more obedient you are, the more bondage will be stripped away from your life. There is also a certain healthy confidence that comes from knowing you've obeyed God. This confidence builds self-worth and nourishes a broken personality. You start the process by being willing to say, "God, I don't want to be a person who collapses every time something shakes me. I don't want anything to separate me from Your presence and love. And I really do have a heart that wants to obey. Please show me where I am not living in obedience, and help me to do what I need to do."

Live in Obedience by Saying Yes to God

When you buy a house, you first make a large down payment. Then, to keep the house, you must make a smaller payment every time it comes due. You can't change your mind and say, "I don't feel like making payments!" without serious consequences.

The same is true for your relationship with God. To make Him your permanent dwelling place, your initial down payment consists of making Him Lord over your life. After that, ongoing payments must be made, which means saying yes whenever God directs you to do something. They are all a part of the purchase, but one happens initially and the other is eternally ongoing. (Just like house payments!) The difference is that the Lord will only take as much from me as I am willing to give Him. And I can only possess as much of what He has for me as I am willing to secure with my obedience.

Taking the initial step of making Him Lord over your life is the same for everyone. Saying yes to God every day is an individual matter. God gives you personalized direction. He may ask you to do something He is not asking anyone else to do. For example, He may be directing you to leave a specific job or move to another city. You have to trust that God has your best interests in mind and be willing to do what He asks of you, even if you don't understand why at the time. Obedience starts with having a heart that says yes to God.

Releasing Your Dreams

I always wanted to be a successful entertainer. It sounds embarrassingly shallow even to mention it now, but it was a desperate drive at the time. I desired to be famous and respected, never mind the fact that I possibly didn't have what it might take to attain either. After I received the Lord and had been married just a few months, God clearly impressed upon my heart that I wasn't to be doing television or commercials anymore. I wasn't sure why, but I knew it wasn't right for me. Whenever my agent presented me with an interview I once would have died for, the thought of it gave me a hollow, uneasy, deathlike feeling. Because the peace of God did not accompany the prospect of doing it, I turned down every job that was offered.

Yes, God, I won't do that commercial. Yes, God, I won't accept another television show. Yes, God, I won't sing in clubs anymore. Yes, God, I'll leave the agency.

Gradually, all my work was gone. God had closed all doors and asked me to stop knocking on the ones that were not in His plan for me. The experience was scary, but looking back now I clearly see the reasons for it. Acting was an idol for me. I did it entirely for the attention and acceptance it would bring me, not because I loved the work. My identity was totally wrapped up in what I did. For God to change that, He had to take away my means of defining who I thought I was and help me to establish my identity in Jesus. He knew

I couldn't be healed of my deep inferiority feelings if I was daily putting myself in a position of being judged by superficial standards.

The part we don't want to hear is that a time comes when each of us must place our desires and dreams in the hands of God so that He might free us from those that are not in His will. In other words, you secure your future by allowing your dream to die and God's plan to replace it. If you've always had a certain picture of what you think you should do, you have to be willing to let the picture be destroyed. If it really is what God has for you, He will raise you up to do that and more. If it isn't, you will be frustrated as long as you cling to it. Often the desires of *your* heart *are* the desires of *His* heart, but they still must be achieved *His* way, not yours, and you must know He is accomplishing them in you, not you achieving them yourself. *God wants us to stop holding on to our dreams and start holding on to Him so that He can enable us to soar above ourselves and our own limitations.* Whenever we let go of what we long for, God will bring it back to us in another dimension.

The Art of the Quick Response

Saying yes to God means being willing to obey *immediately* when we hear His voice, and not waiting until all else fails or we feel like it or we're at the end of ourselves. For God to transform us into whole people, we have to be totally available to Him. If He is saying to us to "Do this," then saying, "Yes, God" immediately, will bring the desired results more quickly.

Again, this is done a step at a time. If you can't trust God enough yet to say, "Anything You ask of me, I'll do," then keep working at it. I must admit that saying yes to God was difficult for me until I read God's words in the Scripture, "When *I* called, *they* did not listen; so when *they* called, *I* would not listen" (Zech. 7:13 NIV, emphasis added). That puts it all in perspective, doesn't it? If we want God to hear our prayer, we need to listen and respond to His voice.

Being willing to say yes to God made me a candidate for much healing and blessing. Of course, I don't always hear Him and I don't always say yes immediately, but my desire is to do that. Saying yes to God without reservation is the first step of obedience that begins to build the superstructure for emotional wholeness on the foundation you have laid down in the Word, prayer, confession, praise, and ongoing forgiveness.

Live in Obedience by Fasting and Prayer

She wants me to fast? I gasped to myself upon hearing Mary Anne's assignment for me the very first time I met her in the counseling office. I'd heard about fasting from Pastor Jack, and the whole church was fasting every Wednesday, but I wasn't ready for that. Besides I was afraid of being hungry since I'd gone to bed too often that way as a child.

"There's a certain kind of release that will not happen without fasting and prayer, Stormie," Mary Anne explained. "It's an act of denying yourself and placing God at the center of your life, which breaks any hold that Satan has on you and destroys the bondage resulting from sin."

I need that, I thought to myself as I listened, *and if it might not happen unless I fast, then I've got to do it.*

Mary Anne suggested that I fast for three full days, drinking only water, and then return to her office with the list of sins I felt I needed to confess. I did as she instructed, drinking water and praying every time I felt hungry. After the first day the hunger pangs weren't bad. In fact, it was much easier than I had anticipated. When it was time to see Mary Anne, she called to cancel our appointment and reschedule it for the following week. That meant I needed to fast three days again.

Nothing's going to happen, I thought. *I've been depressed for twenty years and it's never going to be any different. I was foolish to hope otherwise.*

Through the week, my depression grew in degree and intensity. The fasting was harder this time and I wanted to give up, but I obeyed anyway. On the day of my counseling appointment I prayed for a miracle, but I was afraid to really hope for one.

From the moment I entered the counseling office something was different. My mind was somewhat clearer, but most of all I sensed the presence and power of the Lord far more profoundly than ever before. After I confessed my sins and forgave my mother, Mary Anne and another counselor laid their hands on my head and shoulders and prayed for my deliverance from depression. As they prayed, a source of energy like electricity coursed through my body. The counseling session lasted two hours, and when it was done I felt tired but relieved and peaceful.

The next morning, I woke up without depression. Day after day I waited for it to come back, but it didn't. In fact, even though I was depressed at times later on, it was never that intense, nor was I ever controlled by it again. I believe that fasting helped me to be set free with greater speed and completeness.

Who, Me? Why Should I Fast?

God designed fasting to bring us into a deeper knowledge of Him, to release the Holy Spirit's work in our lives, and to bring us to greater health and wholeness. Fasting blesses every area of our mental, physical, spiritual, and emotional lives. It breaks down strongholds that we are not even aware the enemy has erected against us. In fact, the Bible says certain spirits can be broken only through fasting. When Jesus' disciples asked why evil spirits didn't submit to them, He replied, "This kind can come out by nothing but prayer and fasting" (Mark 9:29).

Fasting is like getting a holy oiling so the devil can't hold on to you. It's designed

"To loose the bonds of wickedness,
To undo the heavy burdens,
To let the oppressed go free,
And that you break every yoke." (Isa. 58:6)

If fasting accomplished no more than that, anyone seeking emotional wholeness would want to take that step of obedience.

Who doesn't desire to be free from any hold of the devil? Who doesn't need the power of God to penetrate his circumstances? Who doesn't want to be released from at least one negative emotion? We all do. So what's holding us back? Ignorance and fear. We are ignorant of what the Bible says about the subject, of what God wants from us, of what fasting can accomplish, and of the wonderful benefits. We are also afraid we'll die in the night if we go to bed without dinner. Or at least we fear the hunger, headache, nausea, weakness, and dizziness that often accompany infrequent fasts. But there are many good reasons to put up with this discomfort.

There are over eighty references to fasting in the Old *and* New Testaments. Jesus Himself fasted. If fasting was dangerous or something to fear, why would it be mentioned throughout the Bible? Why would the greatest people of biblical history have done it, and why would Jesus have fasted for forty days?

Fasting is a spiritual exercise and discipline during which you give yourself completely to prayer and close communication with

God. Discipline always has its rewards. A physical discipline, like exercising, has physical rewards. A spiritual discipline, like fasting, has spiritual rewards. (Fasting has physical benefits also, but for the purpose of this chapter I will only emphasize the spiritual.)

You don't fast to get God to love you. He already loves you, and He will love you just as much whether you fast or not. It is also not a time to get what you want from God. It *is* a time to draw closer to Him, to sensitize your soul to His Spirit, and see Him work mightily on your behalf.

How Should I Fast?

Once you are convinced of the rightness of fasting, you need to take the first step. Begin by simply skipping a meal, drinking water, and praying through it. Say, "God, I fast this meal to your glory and to the breaking down of strongholds in my life." Then lift up in prayer all the areas where you know you need freedom. Say, for example, "Lord, I fast this day for the breaking down of strongholds the devil has erected in my mind in the way of depression, confusion, unforgiveness, or anger."

The next time you fast, try skipping *two* meals, drinking water and praying through each one. See if you can work up to a full twenty-four- to thirty-six-hour water fast once a week. I do this every week and actually look forward to it as a time to hear God more clearly. Fasting is just like any other discipline in that if you fast regularly, it becomes easier. Also, the better you treat your body between fasts, the more pleasant the fast will be.

When you are able to do a thirty-six-hour fast without problems and are willing to try a three-day fast several times a year, then do so. If you have a physical limitation and cannot water fast, then go on a vegetable or fruit fast, denying yourself all else but vegetables or fruits for a day. Most people can do that.

If you are afraid of fasting, read a good Christian book on the subject. My own book, *Greater Health God's Way* (Sparrow), has a chapter on fasting to help you move into that discipline.

The Fasting God Chooses

In Isaiah 58, God describes the benefits of fasting. I recommend reading the whole chapter each time you fast to remind yourself of exactly why you are fasting (to be free), what you are to do (give of

Twenty Reasons to Fast

To purify and cleanse the spirit, soul, and body
To receive divine guidance and revelation
To seek God's face and have a closer walk with Him
To hear God better and to understand His will more fully
To invite God's power to flow through you more mightily
To establish a position of spiritual strength and dominion
To break any bondage that is on you
To receive clarity of mind
To be free of evil or debilitating thoughts
To break through depression
To weaken the power of the devil in your life
To stabilize you when life seems out of control
To be strengthened in your body and soul
To break the lusting of the flesh after anything
To discover gifts God has placed in you
To be released from heavy burdens

*To establish a clean heart and right spirit
within you
To be set free from negative emotions
To find healing
To gain strength for what you don't have the
ability to do*

yourself), and what your rewards are (healing, answered prayer, deliverance, protection).

Be sure to accompany your fast with prayer. Fasting without praying is just starvation. This is a time to be close to the Lord and allow Him to guide you where you need to go. Sometimes you will have the clear leading of the Holy Spirit as to why you are fasting; sometimes you won't. Whether you do or not, it's good to have a prayer focus in mind.

God calls all who are able to fast and pray—not just pastors, not just elders, not just authors or teachers, not just men and women over fifty, but all adults who acknowledge Jesus as the Son of God. Ask God what He is saying to *you* about fasting, for he *is* saying something. Remember that "no discipline seems pleasant at the time, but painful. Later on, however, it produces a harvest of righteousness and peace for those who have been trained by it" (Heb. 12:11 NIV).

Because fasting is an instrument for defeating the enemy, it's a key to deliverance and emotional wholeness. Don't neglect it. Even after you have been set free, Satan will be looking for ways to put you back into bondage. Be determined to slip through his fingers by walking ongoingly in this step of obedience.

Live in Obedience by Giving Yourself Away

When I was ten years old, I lay awake in the middle of a cold, pitch-black night because I was too hungry to sleep. The pangs in my stomach were magnified by the knowledge that there was no food in the house and no money to buy any. My mother was asleep in the only other bedroom, on the opposite side beyond the service porch, and I felt isolated, alone, and afraid.

"There's nothing to eat," I had said to her earlier that evening after I searched the tiny kitchen. All I saw in the refrigerator were half-empty bottles of ketchup and mayonnaise. She had thrown remnants of old leftovers on the table for dinner—none of which went together in any appealing way—and made no apology for the fact it wasn't enough to sustain either one of us.

"Stop your complaining—we don't have money for food," she snapped and went back to talking to herself the way she often did for hours at a time. She hated it when I intruded on her imaginary world.

Now, as I lay in bed, my mind reeled with fear about the future. I feared I could starve to death and no one would care. I felt old.

Going hungry was terribly frightening. Having to be totally dependent for life and sustenance upon someone I couldn't depend on bred deep insecurity. I'm sure now that my mother knew Dad would bring money when he came home, but she told me there was nothing at all to eat and no way to buy it and that was that. We had no friends and Mother always made it seem as if we had no family either, since she considered them all to be her enemies. I had *nowhere* to turn and *no one* to help. We had nothing to sell, and as far as I could see we had no prospects for making any money. I became desperately afraid for my future.

Once I was out of school and self-supporting, I handled money very carefully. I felt the weight of being entirely responsible for my life, and the horror of someday starving to death always bubbled just below the surface of my mind. After I came to know the Lord and started going to church, I put money in the collection plate according to what I had with me—a couple of dollars at first, then a five, a ten, and later a twenty. It was more like donating to a good cause or tipping the piano player than having any thought of actually giving to God. But when I heard Pastor Jack teach on what the Bible says about giving, I knew I had far more to learn about the subject than I ever dreamed.

A heart ready to give makes room for all God has.

I learned first of all that giving was actually giving *back* to God from out of what He had given me, and by doing so I would never lose anything. In fact, I would be enriched. I also learned that the Bible teaches we are to give a tithe (10 percent) of our income to the Lord. When I started doing that, I found that my financial blessings were greater and the drains on my finances were fewer. I found, too, that the more I gave, the less fear I had about not having enough. My future felt more secure. Because I experienced such a flow of God's blessing in my life, the thought of *not* giving became more frightening than giving.

Giving is a step of obedience that brings life, health, healing, and abundance. Not giving will stop up our lives and our bodies and eventually lead to emotional and physical sickness and poverty. The Bible says that a person who gives will have a secure heart and will triumph over his foes. Giving is linked to protection and deliverance. There are two types of giving that are important: giving *to the Lord* and giving *as unto the Lord*.

Giving to the Lord

Because we can't separate our money from our lives, God must be made Lord over our finances, and we must obey Him. God says in His Word that we need to give a tenth of our earnings back to Him for His purposes. When we realize that every cent we have comes from God in the first place, that's not such an unreasonable request. A good steward of money realizes he has nothing on his own, but only manages what he has been given.

If we tithe, the Bible promises we will receive a multiplied return of God's abundance and His power. The Lord asks us to try Him and see if He is not faithful to pour out more blessings than we can contain. When we cut ourselves off from this life principle, the devourer comes in to eat up everything we have. I see people who don't give and then lose what they could have given in medical bills, appliance and car repairs, and a general lack of power to change their lives. God still loves them, but they've stopped up the flow of His blessing to them. The only way the storehouse of God's abundance can be opened is for them to start the process by opening themselves up to giving.

We often feel we will lose something if we give. We think, *If I didn't have to give this, I would have more for myself.* But actually that attitude will cause us to lose. The Bible says that if we give to the Lord, we will have everything we need in our life. If we don't, we won't.

If you have a hard time with this, tell God. Say, "Lord, I want to do what's right, but 10 percent of my income seems like too much to me. I feel I won't have enough if I do that. Help me to learn how to give the way You want me to. I want to receive all You have for me and become all You made me to be." Then, give as you are able and watch God move you into His ways.

Giving as Unto the Lord

Besides giving *to* the Lord, we need to get into the habit of giving to others as *unto* the Lord. This means we are to bless others because it blesses God—without expecting something in return. What-will-I-get-back thinking sets us up for disappointment and unhappiness, but when we give and expect nothing, the Lord will reward us.

Giving is a principle of release: "Give, and it will be given to you: good measure, pressed down, shaken together, and running over will be put into your bosom. For with the same measure that you use, it will be measured back to you" (Luke 6:38). To receive things that last you must give from what you have. If you need release in any area, give something away of yourself, your possessions, or your life, and you will see things begin to open up to you.

There is much to give besides money or store-bought gifts. We can give food, clothing, services, time, prayer, assistance, a ride in our car, or any possessions or abilities that could help someone else. It's important, however, to ask God for wisdom and direction about giving. Once my husband and I gave money to a person in need and, instead of feeding his family and paying his rent, he spent it on drugs. We've never made that mistake again.

You may be so depleted that you feel you have nothing to give or so overwhelmed by circumstances that giving of yourself seems monumental. If so, say, "I don't have anything to give, Lord. Provide me with resources beyond myself." As long as you have the Lord in your life, you will always have at least one thing to give—His love. People need someone to love them, to listen, to encourage, and to pray for them. You might say to someone, "My gift to you is a promise to pray for you every day for a month." Who wouldn't love that gift? I know I would.

When we live in fear that we won't have enough, it's hard to give. But the truth is, the more we give to others, the more will be released to us. We will reap a spiritual as well as material harvest. While it's good to save and plan wisely for the future because extreme poverty is also emotionally crippling, giving to the Lord and to others must not be excluded. If we don't give as the Lord directs, we end up losing what we think we're saving anyway.

My mother never gave anything away, and I believe that was part of her mental and emotional illness. She hoarded everything out of fear that she would someday need it. Her closets, sheds, rooms, and garages were full of "stuff." The Bible says, "He who gathered much had nothing left over, and he who gathered little had no lack" (2 Cor. 8:15). The sheer volume of my mother's stuff rendered it unusable.

Whenever my life seems not to be moving in any direction, deliberately giving of myself always brings breakthrough. It's not a matter of giving to get but of taking this step of obedience to release the flow of all God has for you. It's not that you can't receive any of God's blessings unless you give but that you can't receive *all* of them and life becomes more of a struggle. A heart ready to give makes room for all God has.

PART FIVE

I Am Related

Just for Fun

A Very Short Play in Two Acts

Cast of characters: WELL-KNOWN PREACHER and WIFE
Place: Interlaken, Switzerland. A balcony on the Hotel Victo-ria-Jungfrau
Time: Ten o'clock on a warm summer morning

Act 1

WELL-KNOWN PREACHER (*gazing pensively at the Jungfrau, which happens to be obscured by clouds*): "You know, I have an idea. But I'd better not tell you what it is, because you wouldn't approve."

Expectant silence. Wife, who is knitting, says nothing.

WELL-KNOWN PREACHER: "Did you hear me? I said I had an excellent idea. But I'd better not tell you about it, because it would just upset you."

Wife knits on placidly.

WELL-KNOWN PREACHER: "Do you think I ought to tell you? Or would you rather remain happy and undisturbed?"

WIFE (*calmly*): "Whatever you think best, dear." (*She puts away her knitting.*) "I think the sun is going to come out. Why don't we go for a walk around the meadow?"

WELL-KNOWN PREACHER (*wistfully*): "Don't you want to know what my idea is?"

WIFE: "Certainly. But only when you're ready to tell me. Oh, look you can see the mountain now. Come on, let's walk."

Act II

It is thirteen hours later. The well-known preacher and wife are getting ready for bed.

WELL-KNOWN PREACHER: "You know, I think I'd better tell you about the idea I had after all. It will upset you, because it involves changing plans, and I know how you hate changing plans once they're made. But I've been thinking. Instead of going to Hamburg as our itinerary calls for, and shipping the car home from there with all that bother and red tape, why don't we drive back to Stuttgart where we got it and let the manufacturer worry about shipping the car? We could fly home from there. It really makes a lot more sense, don't you think?"

WIFE (*cheerfully*): "Yes, I do."

WELL-KNOWN PREACHER (*incredulously*): "You mean, you're not upset?"

WIFE: "Why, no. Not at all."

WELL-KNOWN PREACHER: "Well, that's fine. I was afraid you would be. Are you *sure* you're not?"

WIFE: "Quite sure."

WELL-KNOWN PREACHER: "Well, that's great. Because if you had been upset, then I'd have been upset. It's all settled then. We'll go to Stuttgart, not Hamburg, right?"

WIFE: "Right."

They climb into bed, switch out the lights. Silence. But not for long.

WELL-KNOWN PREACHER: "Ruth, are you sure this change of plans doesn't bother you?"

WIFE: "Quite sure."

WELL-KNOWN PREACHER: "Positive?"

WIFE: "Positive!"

Long pause.

WELL-KNOWN PREACHER: "But *why* aren't you upset?"

WIFE: "Well, dear, I don't want to depress you, but that idea wasn't exactly new."

WELL-KNOWN PREACHER: "It wasn't?"

WIFE: "No, it wasn't. It's exactly what I suggested to you three weeks ago in New York."

WELL-KNOWN PREACHER (*weakly*): "You did?"

WIFE: "Yes, I did. We were sitting in the kitchen at the Hill Farm, and we were planning this trip, and I said we ought to have the car shipped home from Stuttgart and then fly from there. But you said you wanted to go to Hamburg."

WELL-KNOWN PREACHER (*amazed*): "I did?"

WIFE: "Yes, you did. Don't you remember?"

WELL-KNOWN PREACHER: "Well, now that you mention it, I do seem to recall some sort of discussion along those lines."

WIFE: "It's still a good idea. There's nothing wrong with having it twice."

Silence. Finally . . .

WIFE: "Good night, dear."

WELL-KNOWN PREACHER (*in small voice*): "Good night."

Ruth Stafford Peale
Secrets of Staying in Love

Intimacy: Building Close Relationships

Intimacy—supreme sharing—the top rung on the ladder of communication. It's something all human beings crave. In fact, we develop relationships in search of this true intimacy—a person with whom we can risk being who we truly are. True intimacy is not reserved only for marriages, happens only with the opposite sex, or is guaranteed with any friendship. This chapter from my book, Starting Over Again, *gives the basics for true intimacy in a relationship, whether it be with a friend, a spouse, or a mother-in-law.*

Joanne Wallace and Deanna Wallace Early
Starting Over Again

When I lived in Oregon I was only an hour's drive from the gorgeous Oregon coast where I often vacationed. I loved to take long, solitary walks along the wide, sandy beaches. The smell of the salt air, the sand between my toes, and the overwhelming beauty of my surroundings always helped put my problems into perspective. To think that the God who created the oceans also loved and created me!

I've noticed, though, that solitary walks along the beach often have a way of emphasizing loneliness. Even though I enjoy the chance to be alone and hear myself think, I also miss having some-one with whom to share the beauty around me. At those times I'm made aware of the basic human need for companionship. Whether it's to share an ocean view, or just to share our daily lives, we all want an intimate relationship with at least one person with whom we can share our thoughts, feelings, and the world around us.

Real intimacy requires a certain level of communication. Al-though we communicate with people every day, it is usually not on the intimate level we crave. There are several rungs on the communi-cation ladder, and most of the time we find ourselves conversing on one of the lesser rungs. To understand this, look at a brief description of each rung:

Superficiality is the first rung. On this level you communicate with someone through standard conversation such as, "Have a nice day" or "How are you?" On this rung you say what is expected of you. Even if you are having a rotten day, you say you're "fine." This is the lowest rung of the communication ladder because you're not even required to tell the truth.

Storytelling is the second rung of the communication ladder. On this level you share facts and newsworthy information such as, "I read an article in a magazine about making quilts and it said . . ." or "When I traveled to Europe, I learned that. . . ." This is often the conversational method you use with someone you've just met be-cause it doesn't require you to share anything personal.

Sharing sentiments is the third rung. On this level you start to reveal yourself. Sharing your sentiments means stating your opinions or disclosing your ideas. At this point you start to risk peeling back your mask, although on a small scale. If the other person slams the door on your idea or opinion, you can easily move back to one of the first two rungs of the ladder.

Sharing sensations is the fourth rung on the communication lad-der. On this level you can share your feelings and emotions. At this point you expose your inner thoughts and hopes, and the other per-son reciprocates. If you've reached this level with someone, you know how wonderful it feels.

Supreme sharing is the top rung of the ladder. This is the ultimate form of communication because along with sharing your feelings and emotions, you are also able to risk exposing your faults and shortcomings, assured in the knowledge that the other person will still accept you. On this level you can risk revealing your mistakes without fear of judgment. You and the other person share a personal commitment to each other, one that brings complete freedom in communication. We all need and desire this freedom in communication. On this level true intimacy is achieved.

Each rung on the communication ladder serves a purpose, but most of us desire at least one relationship that reaches the supreme sharing level. If this is true, why don't more of us have it? Often we've been misled about the nature of true intimacy. Possibly we've been searching for this intimate form of communication in all the wrong places. Many of us believe these five things about intimacy:

1. Intimacy is with the opposite sex only.

2. You're intimate if you live with someone.

3. You're intimate if you spend a lot of time with someone.

4. You're intimate if you're married to someone.

5. You're intimate if you've had sex with someone.

All of the above statements are false. They are not accurate measures of intimacy. If you've been looking for intimacy through sex, marriage, or quantity time spent with someone, you'll be disappointed. True intimacy doesn't require any of these things. How then can you achieve intimacy? By embarking on a journey in which you'll learn to reach out to others, hold a confidence, be a good listener, and be an encourager.

Reach Out to Others

If you're hurting or feeling lonely, it's your responsibility to let someone know. Since another person cannot read your mind, you've got to take the first step and express how you're feeling.

When I am having a particularly bad day it's important for me to tell the people around me. Otherwise they might think that it's their fault. If I'll just say, "I'm feeling grumpy today. It's not your fault, I'm just feeling stressed," it can make all the difference. By reaching out and letting others know how I'm feeling, I'm keeping the lines of communication open.

If you are hurting, you've got to let people know.

We close communication lines with our anger or bitterness. I have a friend, Sally, who is consumed with bitterness because she feels fellow Christians rejected her when she went through a divorce. She has said on more than one occasion, "Everyone deserted me. When I was in the worst pain and needed someone, no one was there." Since I know Sally, I also know that her story could have had a different ending. Sally never *told* anyone that she was hurting or that she needed friends. In her pain she often lashed out at people, driving them away, although it was the last thing she meant to do. Then, when she found herself alone, she was bitter that no one had read her mind or mystically understood that her anger was a mask for her pain.

If you are hurting, you've got to let people know. This doesn't mean that you hold a pity party and invite all your friends, but it does mean that you give people an opportunity to help you.

I often had to force myself to reach out to others. In the midst of my pain and confusion I had to *choose* to get involved in a women's Bible study group. Once I joined, I then had to swallow my pride and admit to the women there that I needed them. At first it wasn't easy, especially since I was used to being the counselor, not the counselee. After all, I was the one who traveled every weekend speaking to women's groups. What would people think if they knew that I was hurting and didn't have all the answers?

The women in my Bible study group came through for me like troopers. I have nothing but gratitude in my heart when I think of them. Although I have since moved to California, they are a big reason why part of my heart is still in Oregon. They helped to heal the wounds in my spirit so that bitterness could not creep in and destroy me, as it did my friend, Sally. And it all started when I was willing to risk sharing my feelings with others.

Possibly, you're ready to tell someone about the pain you're feeling, but you feel isolated. Maybe you feel you don't have anyone you can trust with the information. In my experience one of the most isolated groups of women are pastors' wives who are often pressured to perform on a certain level at the church, are expected to be nearly perfect, without problems, and to be giving to others. If they experience problems with their family or husband, who can they tell? Usually their friendships are based in the church congregation, and for obvious reasons they feel unable to share on a personal level with other church members. What can be done in this situation?

I know of one pastor's wife who was confronted with just such a problem. She couldn't share her innermost feelings and difficulties with women in her congregation, but she didn't throw up her hands and resign herself to isolation. Instead, she decided to instigate her own fellowship group made up of other local pastors' wives. Together these wives formed a bonded group for fellowship and sharing. What a great idea!

When I first moved to California I also felt very isolated. I didn't know anyone in the city of Fremont, where I now live. I had learned enough in my healing process, however, to know that I would have to make the effort to develop friendships. I couldn't just twiddle my thumbs, hoping that someone would miraculously call me up and ask to be my close friend. One of my former Image Improvement teachers, Rita Lamphere, an old and good friend, lived nearby, so I called and asked her to lunch.

The lunch with Rita was a wonderful time of further developing our friendship. Rita was very supportive and loving, and we made a commitment to continue to develop our friendship. As time went by Rita and I grew closer and closer. She proved to be an encouraging, trustworthy, and loving friend.

A few months later, Becky Martin, another former Image Improvement teacher, moved to Fremont, and she began joining us for times of sharing. Together the three of us made a commitment to meet once a month for a whole day of prayer and sharing. We had an agreement that whatever we shared would not be passed along to anyone else, and our trust in each other grew. At a time when I really needed it, I developed two close friendships; all because I decided to risk reaching out to others.

If you're feeling isolated, try to expand your horizons. Make the first move, take the first step, explore all the different avenues that may lead you to a sharing, intimate relationship. Let others know you need them.

Another reason it is important to reach out to others is that you need to be accountable to someone else. If you're grieving over a loss, struggling with an addiction, or just trying to put your life back together, you need to be accountable to someone else for your progress. This person may be your pastor, close friend, professional counselor, or possibly a group of people such as a church Bible study or fellowship group. The important thing is that you meet on a regular basis with at least one person and talk about how you're doing.

The reason for accountability is simple. If you don't have someone with whom to "check in," it is too easy to stagnate and never grow at all. Being accountable to someone means that you're conscious of making improvements in your situation. The idea is to move forward, not slip backward. With help, any backward steps can be corrected. Without help, chances are you'll just keep slipping.

During my crisis experience, I was accountable to the women in my Bible study group. Once a week we met and shared our progress. Knowing I was going to be seeing them each week helped me continue to improve my situation.

If you don't have someone to whom you are accountable, it's up to you to change the situation. Start by checking out the available support groups at your church. Or, make an appointment to talk with your pastor. If your church is small, you may want to call a larger Christ-centered church in your area. Many of the larger churches offer specialized support groups for various problems. Others have small "covenant" groups that meet on a weekly basis. Just make sure that you're accountable to someone so that you'll be encouraged to keep going, growing, and making progress.

Hold a Confidence

As you reach out to others you'll most likely find that they are also reaching out to you. When this happens, and you're making progress toward developing an intimate friendship, it's crucial that you keep a confidence. Nothing will ruin a potential relationship quicker than a loose tongue. If someone has shared inner feelings and problems with you, it's vital that you keep the secrets. This holds true in any sort of friendship, but especially if you want to develop trust and intimacy. The only information you should be revealing to a third party is the type that passes the following criteria:

1. Is it true?

2. Is it kind?

3. Is it necessary to tell?

4. Is it beneficial to all concerned?

5. Do you have the other person's permission to share the story?

Use these five questions as your rule of thumb when you're tempted to divulge someone else's business. If the answer to any or all of these five questions is no, you're just asking for trouble if you pass it along.

It is imperative that you learn to keep a confidence, but to be fair, I must mention one exception to this rule. Breaking a confidence is justified if the people involved have violated the law. If someone confides in you about something criminal, you could be held accountable if the truth comes out. In this case breaking a confidence is the best alternative.

I was faced with this very difficult choice this past year when a twelve-year-old girl at my seminar wrote on her prayer request that her stepfather was "slipping into her room at night." I always assure my seminar attendees that their prayer requests are kept confidential, and up until that point, I had always kept my word. This time, however, I was confronted with a situation that I couldn't repress. Since the girl had signed her full name to the prayer request, I was able to get her telephone number. I phoned the young girl and told her that I was going to have to let someone know what was happening in her life. I told her that the abuse had to stop and I would do whatever I could to help. After talking with her she decided to tell her mother. Her mother then talked with me and I let the mother know that I was calling the Child Protective Services department in their area so that they could get help. As far as I know the girl is now safe and the family is in counseling. Although I hated breaking a young girl's confidence, I know it was the right thing to do. She was crying out to me for help.

Barring criminal involvement, however, breaking a confidence is a major taboo in developing intimate relationships. There are good reasons why the Bible often refers to keeping control of the tongue. In Proverbs 21:23 it says, "Whoever guards his mouth and tongue keeps his soul from troubles."

My friend, Connie, is a pastor's wife and several years ago she confided to a close friend about a minor personal problem that concerned her husband. Once Connie and her husband moved to another state to pastor a new church, her friend decided to pass along Connie's confidential information to a third party—with a few embellishments added to the story! By the time it got back to Connie, after making the rounds of several people, the story was blown completely out of proportion and didn't have much truth left in it. Connie's husband was hurt by it and the relationship between Connie and her friend was damaged. When Connie confronted her friend about spreading the information, her friend said she didn't know why she had done it and she was extremely sorry about it. Unfortunately, it was too late. Although Connie and her husband are continuing with a thriving ministry, she now feels leery about sharing herself with anyone.

Spreading gossip is no way to develop an intimate relationship. Any time you share someone else's story or situation without their permission you're spreading gossip. In almost every case what you pass along about someone else will eventually get back to them. The grapevine works in two directions! Do you want the other person to know what you're saying?

Be a Good Listener

One way to avoid having a loose tongue is to close your mouth. I don't mean to sound flippant, but most of us need to concentrate on being good listeners. Sometimes consciously making sure our mouths are closed is the right place to start. In learning to develop intimate relationships good listening skills are invaluable.

A few years ago I was having dinner with an acquaintance of mine. We hadn't seen each other for quite some time, and as we chatted over dinner she said to me, "So how is your husband doing?" For a moment I froze. I wasn't sure what to tell her. I had assumed she already knew about the divorce. Obviously, she didn't.

Gathering my courage, as I was still in the midst of a painful situation, I began to talk about the tragic events of the past few months, culminating in the recent signing of divorce papers.

"Oh, well, that's too bad," she replied, as she then changed the subject. Several minutes later she asked me, "So what have you been doing the past few months?"

I almost gasped audibly. In a quiet voice I said, "I've been going through the process of a divorce." Seemingly unaware of her insensitivity, my friend kept on chatting. At that point any chance for rewarding communication was lost.

My daughter, Deanna, had a similar experience several years ago, on the day she found out that her then five-year-old daughter, Kimmi, was going to be attending a school for multihandicapped students. Kimmi, adopted from Korea, has cerebral palsy and is also mentally retarded. Although Deanna was aware that Kimmi had special needs, the news that Kimmi would never lead a normal life was hard for her to assimilate. That afternoon she was visiting with a good friend and began to share what Kimmi's teachers had told her. Fighting back the tears, Deanna said, "It's just so hard to let go of my dreams for Kimmi's future. I feel so sad right now."

As Deanna finished speaking her friend was quiet. She literally didn't say *anything*. Then, without even acknowledging that Deanna had spoken, her friend changed the subject and started talking about her own problems. Deanna was stunned. Although they are still friends, a chance for real and intimate closeness disappeared that day.

Being a good listener requires that you concentrate on the other person, not yourself.

What caused Deanna's friend to ignore the pain Deanna was feeling? What caused my friend to gloss over the painful information I had shared about my divorce? Were they both so shocked that they didn't know what to say? Or were they so anxious about their next sentence that they couldn't hear what we said? I suppose we'll never know for sure, but I do know that heart-to-heart talks died because these women were unable to listen.

I have to admit that there are times when I've been guilty of poor listening skills, usually when I'm extremely busy and in the middle of trying to meet a deadline. One day Deanna called during my busy time, and I kept right on working while holding the phone to my ear. Suddenly, I was aware of dead silence on the other end of the line.

"I'm sorry. What were you saying?" I said.

"Nothing," she replied. "I guess I must be boring you."

Fortunately, Deanna understood the pressure I was under. I realized, however, that I needed to stop working for the short time that I was on the phone with her.

Listening is a skill that many of us find difficult to master. Being a good listener requires that you concentrate on the other person, not yourself.

Good listeners:

- devote their complete attention to the person talking.
- keep listening even when they disagree with the person talking.
- avoid giving unsolicited advice.

If you're not naturally a good listener, you can become one. Each one of the characteristics of good listening can be learned. While good listeners may be difficult to come by in this self-absorbed age, the reward is worth the effort: good listeners usually have deeper and more satisfying relationships.

Give Your Undivided Attention

Whenever I get the chance to visit with my sister-in-law, Marilyn, I'm always charmed by her wonderful listening skills. When you talk with Marilyn her body is always leaning slightly toward you, as if she can't wait to hear what you have to say next. Her face shows under-standing and empathy. She looks right at you, not over your head or out the window. She asks pertinent questions that show she is really interested, and she doesn't interrupt in the middle of your thoughts. Marilyn has always been my model for good listening skills.

Give someone your undivided attention by making sure your eye contact and body language communicate your interest. When some-one else is talking, maintain eye contact. This doesn't mean that you stare at them, but it does mean, for example, that you put your book down, turn the television off, or stop writing your grocery list. It's just too hard to concentrate on two things at once. If your eyes are look-ing down at your lap, reading the newspaper, or wandering all over the room, the other person will get the unspoken message that you're not interested. Also, lean forward slightly, *toward* the person who is talking. Leaning back or away from the person indicates that you're wanting some distance between you.

Instead of thinking how you'll respond when the other person stops speaking, concentrate on what the other person is saying. This way you'll be able to ask intelligent, meaningful questions that will indicate how well you've been listening. Asking pertinent questions will also stimulate the conversation and deepen your communication.

Keep Listening Even if You Disagree

One of the truest tests of an intimate relationship is the ability to disagree and still maintain the relationship. When you can listen to someone else without interrupting or arguing, even when you don't agree with what that person is saying, you're well on the way to intimacy.

When Deanna and I have an intimate talk I sometimes find that I don't agree with her feelings. Since we come from two different generations, our opinions don't always coincide. Not that either of us is wrong, it's just that we don't see eye to eye. When this happens, my old childhood programming wants to say, "Deanna, you shouldn't feel that way. Snap out of it!" I really have to take a mental step back. I know that imposing my opinions on Deanna will only alienate her, and I'm learning to respect her opinions, even though they may be different from mine.

Too often we have the tendency to shut our ears when we hear something with which we disagree. Sometimes we even exclude that person from our lives. In very rare instances this has happened to me when I've shared with a church leader the fact that I have been divorced.

Sometimes I have felt hurt and rejected, but I try to remember not to do it to someone else. When I disagree with someone I usually try and keep the lines of communication open. *It is not my place in this world to judge.* Only God has the right to judge. When you or I cease communicating with someone because we disagree with that individual, we assume God's job and, confidentially, we just don't have His qualifications!

Sometimes when we judge, we jump to the wrong conclusions, and we end up looking very foolish. There are times when appearances can definitely be deceiving. To illustrate this, let me tell you about an experience that happened to my daughter.

Deanna, and her husband, Dean, have a unique, "rainbow" family. Robby, the oldest, is adopted from India and has beautiful, dark-brown skin and straight black hair. Aron, their birth son, has curly blond hair and blue eyes. Kimmi, adopted from Korea, has deep olive skin and Asian eyes. Jameson, adopted from Illinois, is of Cherokee Indian heritage and has medium-brown skin and black wavy hair. Shaina, adopted from Maryland, is of African-American heritage and has light-brown skin and curly brown hair. The baby, Fallon, their birth daughter, is very fair complected and has reddish-blonde hair. As I said, they have a rainbow family!

You can imagine what it's like when Deanna takes all the kids to the store with her. People tend to stare, not just at all the ethnic groups represented, but at the sheer number of children! While most people make very favorable comments about such a diverse family, there are exceptions. One day, a woman approached Deanna in the store and said, "Are these all your children?"

"Yes," Deanna replied.

"How could you?" the woman continued.

"Well, I just love children. They're all great kids," said Deanna.

The woman then became irate and started an angry tirade. "I just don't understand how you can sleep around like that. Don't you have any moral character? How many different fathers do they have anyway?"

Stunned by this woman's vehemence, Deanna could hardly believe her ears. Obviously, the woman had judged Deanna without bothering to know or understand the situation. Overcoming her momentary shock, Deanna then took great pleasure in letting the woman know that four of her children were adopted. You can imagine how embarrassed the woman was by her blunder. Deanna has been chuckling about it ever since.

When you judge without trying to understand, intimacy is impossible to achieve. Allow yourself the opportunity to really listen to someone else's unique circumstances without judging. Just like the woman in the store who confronted Deanna, you may find out information that will help you to understand the other person, even if you don't agree. Remember, a good listener respects another person's opinion.

Avoid Giving Unsolicited Advice

While working on this book, Deanna and I have had more than our usual share of heart-to-heart talks. Although we've always been close, working together on the material for this book has caused us to examine our relationship more carefully. Just a few weeks ago, while discussing the information for this chapter, I said to her, "I really want to share what I've learned about not giving unsolicited advice. It's so important not to tell someone else what to do."

"Hmmm, that's interesting," Deanna replied. "So why do you still try and fix my problems?"

I didn't realize what I was doing! I'd been working on using all the right communication skills with other people, but somehow hadn't translated them to my relationship with Deanna. Instead of listening to Deanna share her feelings, I naturally wanted to protect and mother her. I told her what she could or should do in each situation, trying to give her a pep talk when what she really wanted was a listening ear. I now realize that I have to downplay my natural instinct to mother her. After all, she's a married woman and the mother of six children! I guess if she really needs my advice, she'll ask for it!

Learning to listen without giving unsolicited advice will make you one of the most sought-after people in the world.

I've learned that unless someone asks for your opinion, it is best to keep your advice to yourself. Usually people can sort out their problems on their own. They just need a chance to voice their concerns aloud to a sympathetic listener.

When someone is sharing with you, remember that words like *should* or *ought* need to stay out of your vocabulary. Saying, "You should do this . . ." will only alienate your friend. Don't try to coax, badger, or cajole a person in crisis to "Get counseling," "Quit smoking," "See a doctor." Although these may be good suggestions, they are not what someone in crisis needs to hear. The best thing you can do is listen without judging. Let the person cry or sound a little crazy without trying to fix the problem. Say things such as, "You mean so much to me and I'm sorry you're hurting," or "I'm behind you on this and I'll always be on your side," rather than giving advice. Better yet, try "I know you're hurting. . . . Let me know if I can help in any way." This lets the other person know you're ready to help or give advice, *if* she wants to ask for it.

The following poem expresses this idea so beautifully:

I Am Related

When I ask you to listen
And you start giving advice,
You have not done what I have asked.
When I ask you to listen
And you begin to tell me why I
shouldn't feel the way I do,
You are trampling on my feelings.

When I ask you to listen
And you feel you have to do something
to solve my problem,
You have failed me,
strange as that may seem.

Listen,
All I asked you to do was listen,
not talk, or do.
Just hear me.

I can do for myself;
I am not helpless . . .
perhaps discouraged or faltering,
But not helpless.

When you do something for me
that I need to do for myself,
You contribute to my fear and weakness.

But, when you accept as fact
that I feel what I feel,
no matter how irrational,
Then I can stop trying to convince you
and get on with understanding
What's behind that irrational feeling.

And, when that's clear,
The answers will be obvious,
And I won't need any advice.[2]

Learning to listen without giving unsolicited advice will make you one of the most sought-after people in the world. But keep in mind good communication is a two-way street. There will be times when you'll need to express yourself. At those times your words of encouragement will be necessary.

Be an Encourager

Along with being a good listener, you also need to be an encourager, one who uses the power of words to help, not harm, someone else.

When you were small you always looked to others to affirm your abilities. When you tied your first shoe, got an A on your math test, or learned how to ride a bike, you looked to someone else to praise your accomplishments. Hearing words of praise from those people, usually your parents, made you feel like a capable person.

Possibly you didn't hear words of praise. How did it make you feel? Unloved? Worthless? Charles McCabe, a newspaper columnist, once wrote a vivid account of his own feeling of unworth.

> I don't know about you, man, but I was brought up to feel unworthy. Maybe worthless. . . . At home I would do this or that or the other thing, or be thought to be doing this, that or the other thing (which was equally bad) and my mother would make her usual statement. It was generally toneless and without emphasis, because it had been repeated so often and because it had the ring of revealed wisdom: "You'll end up in Sing-Sing. . . ."[3]

Somehow Charles McCabe overcame his mother's dire prediction. He learned to be a responsible and contributing member of society, no thanks to the unaffirming childhood he endured. But you can be sure he has an overwhelming need to hear words of praise, even to this day.

We all need to hear words of praise. You may not have heard them in childhood, but you can start to give and receive them today. In developing an intimate relationship words of praise and encouragement are essential, enabling you to see yourself as a capable, valuable person.

If giving praise is difficult for you, start off by giving compliments. Compliments are words of love. A sincere compliment goes to your very soul, your essence.

Recently, I was preparing for a seventeen-day speaking trip in Germany. I was especially nervous because it would be the first time I had ever spoken with an interpreter. The week before I was to leave, my son, Bobby, called me from his home in Holland. After I explained how nervous I was he said to me, "Oh, Mom, I know you'll be great. You're such a good speaker. You're the best!" His enthusiastic compliment made all the difference in my attitude. Although I know he's biased in my favor, his words of love are good to hear!

In our homes words of praise should be heard at least three times as often as words of criticism. People usually hear all about their failures, but their successes are overlooked. My friend, Terri, was determined not to let this happen in her family.

Terri's son, Benjamin, then thirteen, was having trouble with his schoolwork. One day he brought home a D on his report card, the first one he'd ever received. Looking very forlorn, Ben assured his mother he'd try harder next time. Instead of berating him, Terri smiled, hugged, and encouraged Ben by saying, "I'll look forward to next time."

The next semester, Ben brought home his report card and his D grade had now become a C. When Terri saw it she didn't say, "Well, now you can try for a B." Instead, she started jumping up and down, shouting "Hooray! Let's have a party!" That night the family went out to dinner and celebrated Ben's improvement! What a beautiful way to show love and encouragement.

In our homes words of praise should be heard at least three times as often as words of criticism.

You can also show your love and encouragement by writing and sending thank-you notes. Too often we take people for granted. In our minds we may say, "Well, they already know we had a good time when we visited them. Why write a note?"

Writing thank-you notes is an important way to show someone that you really care. In our society, where everybody is on the fast track and no one seems to have time for anyone else, taking the time to jot a note to someone can have a powerful effect. Several years ago, when I was still personally teaching the Image of Loveliness course, I sent one of my students an encouragement note. After receiving my note this student phoned me and said, "You'll never know what a difference your note made. I was ready to commit suicide this morning. I believed that nobody cared about me. When I received your card in the morning mail I couldn't believe it. Thank you for making the difference between life and death for me." Since that time you can be sure I've never forgotten the importance of sending notes of love and encouragement to others!

Since I really believe in taking the time to jot notes, I often send short postcards to my son, Bobby, in Holland. Usually I write these notes while I'm on an airplane or waiting for my flight at the airport. Frequently I am in a hurry to get the note written, but I feel so good about being able to send off a word or two. Last year, however, my son informed me that although he loved hearing from me, my notes left him feeling he was somewhat second-rate. Frequently my notes started out saying, "I'm in a rush . . ." or "I'm so busy and I just have a minute. . . ." To him, this implied that he was not important enough for me to stop what I was doing to really communicate with him. I'm so glad he told me! I hadn't realized what I was implying, and although it was never what I really felt, I now know better than to use the "I'm in a rush" phrase.

Nobody wants to feel second-rate: we all want first-class treatment! Part of giving first-class treatment is learning to express words of love, but you must also learn how to receive words of love from others. Remember, a compliment is a word of love and you squelch a word of love when you don't accept it.

How many times have you heard someone say, "You *like* this blouse? I got it at a garage sale . . ." or "What do you mean I look good? I need to lose twenty pounds!" Many of us need to be taught that the correct way to accept a compliment is to say, "Thank you." That's all that's necessary. Just, "Thank you."

It's rude to contradict or insult those who go out of their way to speak well of us. If you want to add something to your "thank you," make sure it's positive. For example, if someone compliments you on your red dress, don't say, "Thank you, but I think it's the wrong color for me." A much better response would be, "Thank you, I wasn't sure about the color, but knowing you like it makes all the difference."

You must learn how to receive words of love from others.

We all love compliments, so why do we sabotage our chances of getting them? When a loved one says, "You look beautiful today," a good response would be, "Thank you, you've made me feel so good. Now I'll think about what you said all day long." Let others know that you care by learning to accept compliments graciously.

You can also be an encourager by using nonverbal language. To share your joy, show your support, or let someone know you understand, say it through your facial expression and touch.

Your smile can be a great encourager. Do you know that we all smile in the same language? Let others know you care by letting your face show it. Most smiles are started by another smile!

Another way to let people know you care is through your touch. Hugs can work wonders! When I arrive at various cities for my speaking engagements, I'm usually met at the airport by the women's ministry director or whoever is in charge of the seminar. Since I've spoken on the phone to this person and I feel like I already know her, I always reach out and give her a hug when we meet. This hug often sets the mood for the whole weekend.

Some people say that they don't like to be touched, but most of those people will never forget it if they're hugged in the right way. A hug is so affirming—it lets you know someone cares. Sometimes, even when we know the appropriate words it's difficult to say them out loud. At such a time hugs can help to bridge the communication gap.

While we may need to be careful about hugging members of the opposite sex (depending on the situation), the main idea is to show your love through affirmative touch. If hugging makes you feel uncomfortable, try giving a squeeze on the arm or patting someone on the back.

Your aim is to develop more loving communication with another person. Don't force someone who is obviously uncomfortable with physical contact. Keep in mind unique feelings and needs and you'll always keep the lines of communication open.

By working on deepening the communication with the people you love, the pain in starting over will be considerably lessened. Rebuilding your life after a crisis experience can be extremely difficult, but developing new or improved relationships can make the future look bright again. By communicating with others on an intimate level you'll find a terrific reward in increased love, cooperation, good feelings, and better relationships. As Dinah Maria Mulock Craik expresses in this poem:

Oh, the comfort—the inexpressible
comfort of feeling safe with a person,
Having neither to weigh thoughts,
Nor measure words—but pouring them
All right out—just as they are—
Chaff and grain together—
Certain that a faithful hand will
Take and sift them—
Keep what is worth keeping—
And with the breath of kindness
Blow the rest away.[4]

* For information on seminars by Joanne, please write JOANNE WALLACE SEMINARS, P.O. Box 2213, Fremont, CA 94536, (510) 797-2785.

Blessed are they who have the gift
of making friends,
for it is one of God's best gifts.
It involves many things, but above all,
the power of going out of one's self
and appreciating whatever is noble
and loving in another.

—Thomas Hughes

Do I Need to Confront My Mate?

For women, confronting another per-
son, especially a spouse, can be one
of the hardest things to do. But sometimes, in homes with serious
problems, confrontation is the only thing left to do. If you have an
immature mate who is not willing to consider himself part of the prob-
lem and work honestly to improve the relationship, perhaps it will be
necessary to confront him, even if it's only in an effort to get counseling
for the marriage.

First, take the evaluation in this chapter to determine if confronting
your mate is a necessary step. If it is, work through the steps to prepare
yourself to confront. It will be easier if you can find strength in knowing
that you are doing this because you want to work on a better life
together.

Fred and Florence Littauer
Get a Life Without the Strife

Is it possible that you are living in a situation that desperately needs
some changes? Some women think that if they are submissive
enough their mate will stop abusing them. They don't realize that the
victimization has little to do with their behavior and much to do with

the abuser's past. Because of his inner turmoil he has a compulsion to take it out on someone else—and that someone happens to be you. It's not a sign of spirituality to accept abuse from your mate. No matter who tells you, "This is your cross to bear," you are not required to be beaten up or verbally abused to get into heaven.

God's plan for marriage is mutual respect and love. If neither of these is in your home right now, perhaps it is time to confront. Don't say, "If you don't shape up I'm out of here." Instead express clearly, "We can't live like this any longer." Consider the questions below in deciding whether you need to confront and if the time for it is now:

ASSESSING THE NEED TO CONFRONT

Check each line to which you would answer Yes.

1. _____ Has your situation become unbearable?
2. _____ Is there a relationship that's out of control?
3. _____ When you look ten years down the line does it depress you?
4. _____ Is this relationship one-sided?

Do friends ask:

5. _____ What is the matter with you?
6. _____ When are you going to wake up?
7. _____ Can't you see what he or she is doing to you?
8. _____ Why aren't you fun anymore?

Ask yourself:

9. _____ Do you feel physically ill when trying to deal with a certain person?
10. _____ Do you feel exhausted much of the time?
11. _____ Do you feel as if there is no hope?
12. _____ Has your mate had affairs?
13. _____ Is he or she always looking at or commenting on the opposite sex?
14. _____ Do you feel submission means being a doormat?
15. _____ Are you being verbally or emotionally abused?
16. _____ Does your mate (or children) put you down?

17. _____ Has your mate hit you or threatened you?

18. _____ Are you in a financial bind?

19. _____ Is your mate irresponsible with money?

20. _____ Do you fear being alone or on your own?

21. _____ Do you rationalize, *This is my cross to bear?*

22. _____ Do you soothe yourself with the thought, *Oh well, everyone has problems.*

If you checked five or more statements, you are not happy with your current situation. If you checked ten or more, you need to consider options for future action. If you have checked fifteen or more, you need to confront this person or situation as quickly as possible.

No one has the desire to confront touchy or abusive situations head-on. We would all rather look the other way and hope the problem disappears. Not all marriage problems involve abuse or affairs; some stem from chronic emotional problems or repeat business failures.

Florence remembers, "One of the hardest things I ever had to do was to tell Fred that I could not handle anymore financial problems and that I didn't wish to live under the threat of his anger that I felt loomed over me. I knew it would be hard for him to understand since he had always kept us in better-than-average houses and really never exploded or yelled at us. He was always a gentleman and I knew he meant well."

Some of you might ask Florence, "What did you have to complain about?" We understand that your situation may be far worse than Florence's ever was, but she wanted the best marriage possible and she was willing to take a chance.

As Florence did, you may need to examine your own life and your situation. Don't wait until there's no love left between you. Perhaps you and your spouse need to seek counsel. If there is resistance or if he thinks you are the whole problem there may need to be some personal confrontation. We suggest a few guidelines based on what we did.

1. Determine If There Is a Need to Confront. Is the behavior of the individual in question threatening the emotional health of at least one family member? Is any physical abuse occurring? Is there an addiction—drugs, alcohol, gambling, pornography—that shows no signs of stopping? Are there continued business failures or other patterns that are damaging to the family? Is there a fear of blowups, temper tantrums, fits of rage?

If any of these types of problems exist now and are getting worse and not better, there may be a need for confrontation. We have talked with women who have been beaten and abused by their husbands who felt that if they were submissive enough their husbands would stop the abuse—tomorrow. In our experience, women who tolerate this treatment in a marriage over a long period of time do so because they were abused as children. They have learned to "take it." Be sure to check your own emotional stability before attempting to confront someone else.

2. Seek the Lord's Direction.   Do not hastily jump into a confrontation or you may end up defeated. Write to the Lord in daily prayer, asking His guidance in the situation. Make sure you are spiritually ready and divinely inspired. Don't confront just to get your own way.

3. Read at Least One Book on Confrontation.   This can better prepare you for what may happen. The victimizer may not agree to what you have in mind, so it's helpful to have studied all the background available to you.

4. Find an Independent, Outside Person.   He or she should be someone who is willing to stand with you as a mediator, not an attacker. Explain the situation as objectively as possible and have this individual ready to do the confronting if necessary. This person can be a professional counselor, a pastor, or a friend who is known to be fair by the one being confronted. Florence asked a counselor/friend.

5. Enlist Family Support.   It's almost impossible to implement family change if your family members are not with you. If they all feel you are off balance, you will need some family counseling first. It would be devastating to go into this risky situation only to have the entire family turn against you and support your mate.

6. Develop a Plan for Possible Solutions.   Before Florence expressed to Fred that she felt he would benefit from counseling, she had talked with a therapist about the situation and knew when the counselor had a block of time available. Don't go into any confrontation until you have looked into possible solutions and have the phone numbers of professional help in hand. This meeting is not to cause trouble but to lay out a plan for a better future. Be sure to have one!

7. Be Willing to Hang Tough. No confrontation is easy and the person may turn on you and try to browbeat or reason you into changing your mind. He or she has probably already done that many times in spontaneous confrontations you've had in the past. You must be ready and willing to hang tough because if you don't enforce what you agree upon, your mate will never take you seriously again.

8. Be Prepared for the Worst. You don't want to approach this meeting with a negative attitude, but you must be alert to the possibility that the person might pack up and leave. Consider what is the worst that can happen. Will you be out of money or out on the street? Do you have a Plan B?

9. Set an Appropriate Time. No time is perfect for a confrontation, but make sure you choose a time when the person to be confronted will be under the least amount of stress and when he or she is not under a time pressure to leave. Florence chose a vacation time where there was no excuse for running off to work.

10. Approach with Love. Don't make the confrontation an attack. It is shocking enough for the person to find himself or herself in a position where everyone seems to have suddenly turned against him or her. Continue to say, "We love you. We want the best for you, but we need some changes made." Be willing to modify your own behavior and compromise in minor areas as long as the confronted person is willing to take major steps. Set timetables for changes and hold your mate and yourself accountable to a third person.

Our time of facing reality was not easy, but it was necessary and the changes over these many years have been remarkable. Because we were both willing to adjust and Fred was willing to find the root of his problems, God has blessed our ministry and given us a new depth and understanding. We can both say in unison, "We are more in love today than we have ever been before." We have a new life with a lot less strife!

Chapter

19

The Healing Art of Absorption

A re there really secrets to staying in
love?

*I was traveling to California to join my husband, Norman Vincent
Peale, at some of his speaking engagements there, when I began talking to a young woman beside me on the plane. Many times I think
God arranges coincidental meetings such as ours. She was in distress
over her marriage, and I listened to her heartfelt story of how she felt
she and her husband were falling out of love. She had read the book I
had written about marriage and she implored me to tell her some
secrets of staying in love she could take home with her, pin up on the
refrigerator, and learn to help save her marriage. The results of our
continuing correspondence were incorporated in a new book,* Secrets of
Staying in Love. *It is from this book that I would like to share this
chapter on one of the finer and perhaps lesser known arts of staying in
love—the healing art of absorption.*

Ruth Stafford Peale
Secrets of Staying in Love

Sometimes I think the best epitaph a wife could hope for would be
just six words: "She was a wonderful shock absorber." Carved on a

headstone, that might not look very elegant or very spiritual, I know. But to go through life cushioning shocks or blows for other people calls for a set of characteristics very close to the Christian ideal. It calls for selflessness, service, compassion, and kindness—just as religion does.

Being a shock absorber comes easily to a mother, because it's reinforced by instinct. Your toddler falls and bangs his forehead; your second-grader burns her fingers on a hot stove; your teen-ager is in tears because her feelings have been hurt by some thoughtless friend. Here the protective instinct is swift and sure: you dry the tears, you say the consoling or comforting thing, you put the right medicine—physically or emotionally—on the hurt.

But it's more difficult for husbands and wives to respond so automatically to each other's needs. Here two adults are involved, two separate and sometimes demanding egos. In dozens of marriage situations, affection whispers: "This is my man (or woman). I love him. Therefore I will try to spare him and protect him." But there is also a contrary voice, a churlish sort of voice that grumbles: "Well, he's a grown man, isn't he? He ought to be able to cope with his own problems. Besides, I've got my own difficulties . . . and what's he doing to help me?"

In other words, where marriage is concerned, no one is a natural, ready-made shock absorber. It's an art—and you have to learn it, just the way you learn any other skill or art.

What does it take to learn it? It takes intelligence, discipline, practice at anticipating trouble, adroitness at moving to head it off or minimize it. Above all, it takes motivation. You have to be able to see clearly that the more you can spare or shield your marriage partner, the stronger and deeper will be his gratitude and his affection for you.

It doesn't matter whether your husband is a bus driver or the president of the United States, there are always ways in which a wife can ease the burden, reduce the tension, eliminate unnecessary worry.

Speaking of bus drivers, let me tell you about two good friends of ours. Fred and Betty are strong Christians, good citizens, the salt of the earth. Fred is a New York City bus driver. He is a sensitive, high-strung person. But he didn't always think highly of himself; in fact, he thought he was a failure. He looked upon bus driving as an unimportant task. But he had been at it for so long that changing jobs would have been difficult. He wasn't really trained for anything else.

This sense of personal inadequacy kept gnawing away at Fred until one day his wife could stand it no longer. She sought out Norman and me and asked, "What on earth can I do to bring happiness into Fred's mind? What can I do to make him feel that his job is important? I'm convinced that it is. He helps people who ride in his bus by being cheerful and patient and friendly. He watches older people and young children to see that they don't get into trouble. But still he feels inferior. Do you think you could possibly talk to him? He doesn't really listen to me."

We said we would, and Norman did talk to Fred. "I tried," he told us later, "to make him see that if you're serving people—which he is —you're serving God. And if you're serving God, one form of service is as honorable and worthwhile as another."

"Did you get through to him?" I asked.

Norman shook his head doubtfully. "I don't know. He agreed with everything I said. But I had the feeling that he was just being polite. I also had the feeling that until Fred is able to straighten up and look people in the eye with pride and confidence and *say* he's a bus driver, he'll never be at peace with himself."

"I'm afraid you're right," I said.

It doesn't matter whether your husband is a bus driver or the president of the United States, there are always ways in which a wife can ease the burden, reduce the tension, eliminate unnecessary worry.

Fred was an expert driver of any kind of car, and quite often he would offer to drive us to a dinner or a speaking engagement out of town. This suited me fine, because Norman never liked to drive when he had a speech on his mind, and I found it easier and more pleasant to relax with him instead of battling with the traffic myself. On these expeditions, Betty usually joined us, and the four of us always had a fine time riding out and riding back.

One rainy night Fred and Betty drove us out to a country club in New Jersey where Norman was to be the after-dinner speaker. It was quite an elaborate affair, with important men and women from all over the state—politicians, business tycoons, high-ranking military people, and so on. Fred and Betty had planned to go to a restaurant for dinner, and then come back for us. But on this occasion, at the last minute, two guests were unable to come, and Norman asked the host if the two friends who had driven us out from the city could take their places.

The host was very gracious and said he'd be delighted. But Fred hesitated. When we kept urging him, he mumbled, "I'm just a bus driver. I don't belong with those people in there."

Then up spoke Betty, lovingly but firmly. "Fred," she said, "you're my husband, and I love you, and I'm proud of you, and as long as I feel that way I don't see any reason in the world why we couldn't accept these good people's invitation."

Fred looked at her for about half a minute without a word. "All right," he said finally, "if that's the way you feel, we'll do it."

They took the two seats at our table and everything seemed to be going fine until suddenly, in one of those unexpected lulls that always seem to happen at dinner parties, I heard a man across the table from Fred—he was an international banker, a very prominent man—say, "And what line of business are you in, sir?"

I held my breath, because the whole table seemed to be listening, and I knew Betty was holding hers, too. Then all of a sudden Fred smiled a friendly, relaxed smile. "I drive a bus," he said. He said it loud and clear, but the banker was so taken aback that he evidently thought he hadn't heard Fred correctly. "You do *what?*" he said incredulously.

Fred gave Betty just the flicker of a grin, and then looked across the table at the banker. "I drive a bus in New York City," he said. "I'm a bus driver."

"Well, my goodness," said the banker, "that's marvelous! I've always envied the job you fellows do. Tell me, don't you ever lose your temper with all that traffic and all those people pushing and shoving?"

He wasn't being condescending or merely polite. His interest was completely genuine. And that was only the first question. Other guests joined in with real interest, real curiosity. And suddenly there was Fred the bus driver talking easily and naturally about his work with no hesitancy, no apology, no sense of inferiority. Norman looked at me and I looked at Norman and I think we both said a little prayer of thanksgiving. Because faith had worked a small miracle, as it so often does—and the faith that did it was Betty's.

Sooner or later in most marriages a situation is likely to arise in which one partner is threatened, upset, driven to extreme action that may or may not be wise. And this is precisely the time when the other partner can salvage or retrieve the situation by keeping calm, praying for guidance, and above all by taking some of the shock—absorbing it—until the worst of the crisis is over.

I remember very well the time in a midwestern city when we were staying in a very large hotel, one of the key properties in a very important hotel chain. We had stayed there before, and had become friendly with the assistant manager and his wife, both admirable people. On this occasion we got a telephone call from this man asking us to have lunch with him and his wife, saying they would like to talk to us. It was a personal matter, he said—and to them an important one.

I'll never forget how they looked when they came into the dining room. The man was pale, tense, obviously much upset. The woman was upset, too, but I could see that her whole concern was for her husband. She was not thinking about herself.

What had happened, it seemed, was the manager of the hotel was retiring. This had been expected for some time, and the assistant manager had hoped that the job would be his. He had practically been told as much, he said, by a high official of the hotel chain. But that very morning word had come down that a manager was to be brought in from outside. Our friend was not to get the job after all. He was so disappointed, hurt, and angry, that he had decided to resign. He had been on the point of calling up his superiors and telling them just what he thought of them when his wife remembered that we were in the hotel. She had persuaded him to talk to us first.

Now, if anything, the wife was angrier than her husband. She loved him, believed in him, hated to see him hurt. Her first instinct, I'm sure, was to strike out at the thing that was hurting him—which in this case was the impersonal management of a great hotel chain.

But she also knew that at the moment her husband's judgment was impaired, that he was capable of doing something he might regret later. Also, the practical, sensible homemaker inside the angry wife knew that she and her husband were both middle-aged, that jobs as good as the one they had did not grow on trees, that they had two children to think about—one in college. She knew her man well enough to know that in his present state of mind nothing she could say would have much effect. But she also knew that he admired Norman and might listen to him. So here they were.

In a case like this, Norman never says much at first. He always encourages the person in trouble to pour it out, ventilate all the anger, the frustration, the bitterness, whatever (as he puts it) is "heating up the mind." So the assistant manager talked for some time, reviewing all his past contributions to the hotel, marshaling all the arguments why he was perfectly capable of taking over the top job, occasionally appealing to his wife for reconfirmation—which she always gave.

Finally, when he had talked himself out, Norman began to place "cool" ideas in the vacancies left by all the "hot" ones that had come sizzling out of the man. He started out by saying calmly that while this disappointment was hard to take, maybe God had some plan in mind for both of them and that this could be a part of that plan. He said he thought it would be very foolish, though understandable, for the man to quit his job in a fit of anger. "The work you do here is important," Norman said. "You make tired people comfortable. You make dispirited people cheerful. You're a warm, welcoming sort of person. People sense that, and they like it. I think you're in the business God meant you to be in, even if the rung of the ladder you want is still out of reach."

The man stared at the tablecloth and said nothing, but I could see that he was listening.

"Now," said Norman, "you are an intelligent person and a big person, so I am going to make a suggestion that a small person or a stupid person could not follow. I suggest that you make yourself swallow your injured pride and your sense of injustice and treat the new manager with great courtesy and respect. As you know better than anyone, you can make his new assignment hard, or you can make it easy. I hope you will make it easy by cheerfully helping him in every way. After all, he hasn't done anything unfair. I don't think you should focus your resentment on him."

Then he turned to his wife. "And I have the same suggestion for you. Treat the new manager's wife as nicely as you possibly can. After all, she's in a difficult position too. Everyone will know that you hoped the job would go to your husband. Everyone will be watching for you to show resentment or hostility. Don't give them that satisfaction. Treat the new boss just the way you'd want him to treat you, if you were in his shoes."

I remember how the assistant made a wry face and gave a reluctant laugh. "I can see we made a mistake inviting you two to have lunch with us," he said. "You're telling us to act like Christians. And that's just the way we don't feel like acting."

Norman and I laughed, too, because we knew we had gotten through to him. Oh, he still took some convincing. But his wife swung around to our side (she had been there all along, really) and began to point out various ways in which he could be of enormous value to the new man. "You'll be a lot more important to him," she said, "than you were to our old boss, who knew all the ropes. I'll bet you'll have more responsibility, more authority than you've ever had before."

Which is exactly the way things worked out. The new manager was so grateful and so impressed that three years later, when he moved on to yet another job, he recommended our friend so highly that he moved into the top spot with no trouble at all.

There was a kind of postscript to the story, too. Norman happened to meet a man who was on the board of that hotel chain. The talk came around to our friend. "You know," the board member said, "the reason we didn't promote him the first time was that we weren't quite sure how he could handle himself under pressure. We were always afraid that in a tough situation he might let his emotions run away with him. But when he took that disappointment with so much grace and self-control. We decided we must be wrong about him." Then he gave Norman a suspicious look. "You didn't have anything to do with all that, did you?"

"His wife was the key," said Norman cheerfully. "She deserves the credit."

And of course, truly she did!

Chapter 20

The Continuity of Life

My book Common Sense Christian Living *was written to flesh out a series of my lectures and conversations that were filmed for use in homes and churches. I have chosen this chapter to share with women my thoughts that all humans need continuity in life. It is my belief that continuity is preserved by marriage; and it is, therefore, of utmost importance to preserve the marriage in spite of harsh words that might be spoken. Perhaps the ideas that I have spoken of here will help you work toward the preservation of continuity through your marriage.*

Edith Schaeffer
Common Sense Christian Living

More than twenty years ago, a ten-year-old girl said to our daughter Debby, "When I grow up, you know what I'm going to do?"

"What?" asked Debby.

"I'm going to stay married to my first husband for ten years, then I'll marry a lot of different men for short times."

This was a child staying in a Swiss boarding school while her parents went through their current divorce. She was calmly stating her ideals. To stay married to one man, then to marry a succession of men sounded to her like quite a natural goal in life, similar to traveling and trying different climates for short periods. Why not? She obviously had not been taught by example or careful explanation how priceless continuity is and how valuable and central it is to a balanced human life.

This little girl is in her thirties by now. One wonders whether her dreams have come true, and how satisfying her attempts to taste happiness have been. Thousands and thousands of people have never discovered what a lasting human relationship is like, some because of having had all their relatives and friends killed in war, or drowned or starved in a disaster. Some refugees have been torn, time after time, from every relationship. Other people are as ignorant of the value of lasting human relationships and how to treasure and protect them as poverty-stricken people would be if they might happen upon some rare china, using the Spode cups to mix paint or weed killer.

To live from birth in a refugee camp in tents of flapping fabric, or in makeshift shacks made of bits and pieces of any available material, and never to know that the words *home, village, country, school,* or *community* have any other shades of meaning beyond what has been experienced in that refugee camp is to be ignorant of what some other people in the world think of as "normal life." To be deprived by circumstances of growing up in a family that feels a part of several generations because of old photo albums, yellowed letters, stories passed down, or personal contact with grandparents and great expectations for the youngest generation ahead, is to be so ignorant of the experiences of the continuity of family relationships as to be unable to picture a "normal life."

Whether we are talking about the refugees of Cambodia, the Near East, or Somalia, or children who live in broken homes, going to school with other children from broken homes, getting explanations of life from those who believe there are no absolutes, no patterns, no norms of any kind, no permanency of ideals, no patterns for the shape of dreams—in both kinds of deprived childhoods there are two tragic problems in the area of dreams for the future.

First, the dreams are likely to be shaped by the only reality known, as the ten-year-old girl's were, or the dreams might be of a better tent in another refugee camp with more food and water!

Second, the dreams are also likely to be so unrealistically of perfection that the dreamed-of "perfect life" would have to be lived with perfect people (who do not exist), in a perfect town or village (which does not exist), in a perfect country (which does not exist), and governed by unfailingly wise and perfect people in government (who do not exist). The dreams of utopia—whether dreamed by children concerning a mate, a home, a place to live, or a country to live in, or dreamed by young adults concerning what a relationship should be like and what a breakfast conversation should consist of, or dreamed by management concerning what labor should be like, or labor as to what management should be like, or dreamed by Parliament or the House of Representatives concerning what the prime minister or the president should be like, or by the prime minister or the president as to what Parliament or the House should be like —are so often unrealistic.

But, the problem is that people are always sure that all that needs to be done is to change to the choice of another person, or people, and *then* all will be perfect. The problem is that agnostics, or secular humanists, or people in the midst of a variety of false philosophies or religions, do not know about the Fall and have no explanation as to what is wrong with the world or the people in it. And very often, believers in God's existence, those who *say* they base their lives on His Word, do not recognize the central place of the Fall in their own practical lives. We who are believing Christians are *still* imperfect. We live with imperfect people at home, in our work, and in our churches, as well as in the world!

Is there a common sense factor in Christian life as it relates to continuity being a practical possibility? Is continuity an airy fairy, unthinkable, absurd concept? Is it so unattainable as to be cruel to even talk about it at all? What about people who are half way through life and because of their own, or other people's choices, have had nothing but brokenness?

In many circles in today's history, expectation of continuity in relationships is almost unheard of. "I really don't think *any* marriage can last, do you?" is a common question expecting only the answer, "Oh, of course not." The concept of continuity is misunderstood as being a barrier to personal freedom and happiness.

Relationships are thought of as only for really short periods of time. The popular opinion of a relationship, expressed in all the media, is that it is something that should provide "fulfillment," "satisfaction," "happiness," "enjoyment," "pleasure," "understanding," "contentment." How quickly must all these positive things take place in a relationship? In the "NOW"? All too often, the immediate moment's desire or hunger tempts us all to make an incredible exchange. The possibility of everything that continuity has to offer for generations, as well as for a lifetime, is kicked aside for the *now* of an immediate or imagined satisfaction.

Do you remember Esau's choice?

> Now Jacob cooked a stew; and Esau came in from the field, and he was weary. And Esau said to Jacob, "Please feed me with that same red stew, for I am weary." Therefore his name was called Edom. But Jacob said, "Sell me your birthright as of this day." And Esau said, "Look, I am about to die; so what profit shall this birthright be to me?" Then Jacob said, "Swear to me as of this day." So he swore to him, and sold his birthright to Jacob. And Jacob gave Esau bread and stew of lentils; then he ate and drank, arose, and went his way. Thus Esau despised his birthright.
>
> Gen. 25:29–34

Esau sold his birthright which meant affecting other human beings for generations to come! He sold a continuity of life and events —threw away a precious possibility of a different life for himself and his children and children's children, right down to the descendants of Esau today! Repercussions, consequences, ripples in history still going on today, were effected by Esau's choice at that time. Human beings are not pebbles that fall into the water and cause no ripple; our choices cause unending ripples. Esau chose to satisfy his immediate hunger as the fumes from a red lentil stew hit his nostrils! What an exchange for a birthright!

Human beings are not pebbles that fall into the water and cause no ripple; our choices cause unending ripples.

But, day after day, thousands of people choose a totally selfish search for personal happiness, some form of immediate fulfillment, freedom to "do what feels good" or to kick anyone who might get in the way, exchanging *continuity* for one's self and for one's children and grandchildren for a terrific variety of that "mess of pottage." What "mess of pottage" has tempted you, or me, and how can we see things clearly in the light of the whole of history, rather than in the immediate now?

Pressures are terrible at certain crisis moments of life, converging with the force of the winds that come together in what is known as "the wind shear factor." Such pressures can rip apart a relationship like the winds can rip apart a plane in the air! We each have a varying amount of selfishness that is a pressure from within. Pressures come from without on the part of people who find their pleasure in other people's failures as a form of self-justification for failures in their own lives. When selfishness hits hard, wiping out all thought of future results in history and the effects on a wide circle of people, and when friends whisper in your ear, "You deserve freedom . . . you deserve a higher salary . . . you are too good to take any more of this. . . ." Then the "wind shear pressure" builds up! As a Christian you have another pressure added, since our accuser has not yet been cast down (see Rev. 12:10).

Satan is attacking God as he accuses each Christian of loving something far more than God, and so in every case Satan is eager to see us put self first at any cost! That "at any cost" includes the cost of disregarding our opportunity to show the Lord in this present life the reality of our love and trust of Him in practical ways.

Someone might ask here, "Hey, aren't you mixing things up? What has the continuity of a marriage relationship, or family relationship, or other human relationships to do with our relationship with God? Isn't there a wall of division here that puts these two parts of our lives into different rooms with no connection?"

As we go on, the answer will be given. In brief, however, our understanding of what is involved in working at continuity in human relationships and our understanding of what is involved in working at *our* side of our relationship with God have a lot in common. There is a blending and exchange of the lessons learned. We grow in understanding as time goes on. We grow in the understanding of what God made us to be capable of in the area of continuity on a finite level during the limited confines of one lifetime. We also grow in the understanding of what is ahead of us in both continuity of an eternal relationship with God and with other perfect human beings in heaven!

When we hear statistics of the ratio of divorces to marriages, we must realize that many, many people have never been a part of relationships that last a long time. Children are growing up in an atmosphere in which temporary relationships are the "normal" way of life. The dividing of a child's time between "a weekend with father" and "weekdays with mother" is more confusing than simply the broken unity of the together names "Mother and Father." The breaking up of the name "Mom and Dad," which is a couplet that spells solidity, a solid home to which to return after physical or mental travel, is confusion enough. But the confusion is compounded when the short weekend with father includes another woman whom the child is supposed to "relate to, Dear." And the multiplication of confusion comes in the man that now has taken Father's place with Mother, and the added grandparents, sisters, and brothers who have *no* blood ties, and new babies that are half-brothers or half-sisters. No wonder a little boy of seven in such a situation sighed deeply and exclaimed, "I can't wait until I grow up and can have a home of my own!"

Why is it that relationships are being gloomily regarded as something that can not ever go on and on? Is it a twisted understanding of what a human being is capable of? Is it a lack of knowing that there is *anything* in the universe that continues? Is it a loss of observing any two people or a family working at the upheavals that come day after day in their living under the same roof with a feeling that there *is* something worth working for?

The capability of human beings having lasting relationships that span several generations has been shoved aside, not believed possible, not prepared for, not expected to be demonstrated! Relationships that go on through unpleasant incidents—disagreements of a variety of sorts, difficulties big and little, hurt feelings, unfair treatment of each other, unthoughtfulness, forgetfulness, silence and lack of communication for a period, moods, and sudden anger—are considered to be archaic, old-fashioned and something to be scorned . . . not something that can be worked on and improved.

There is an oft-repeated statement these days: "Children are better off if their parents divorce because a home where there are fights and constant disagreements is very bad for them." Period!

What is ignored all too often is the fact that children discuss with other children the signs of an impending divorce and what terrifies them, and brings tears in the night, is the fear that the fights they are overhearing mean a split is on its way. No one of any age feels comfortable when people are shouting at each other, but there is a measure of comfort in being assured that although this disagreement may *sound* fierce, there *will* be a solution. One of the two who are arguing will have enough imagination and ingenuity to work out a solution concerning the day off or the vacation about which there is such a difference of opinion! Is the soup burned? A resourceful cook will hurry and make a substitute without continuing the argument that, "it can't be tasted." Children need to see *solutions* take place, not only as a reassuring factor in their present home lives, but as an example for the future.

Children need to be able to say to other children, "Well, my mother and dad get a little upset at times. One or the other gets very angry at other times. But they do love each other really, and they love us, and they have lots of imagination and many ideas as to how to make it all up and do something pleasant together after the fight is over!" Sadly, very few children today have seen the pattern of living *through* differences, coming out the other side of them, of someone's apologizing to someone else—or both apologizing—and then one of the two having a brainstorm about going for a picnic, eating supper in front of the fire, having watermelon out under the lilac bushes, playing a game after supper, reading two chapters of the current book while nibbling on popcorn, or getting out a map and planning a "someday kind of a vacation." And very, *very* few children have friends who can tell them how it works!

*There is a desperate need for patterns of how to cope, not just seminars on the subject. There is great value in **hearing** someone keep quiet, or in **watching** patience work!*

Facing the reality of being imperfect—explaining to children that the family is made up of a number of imperfect people of different ages, living together under often difficult circumstances—puts things into a different perspective. There is a desperate need for patterns of how to cope, not just seminars on the subject. There is a need of seeing a compromise work out in a real-life situation. There is great value in *hearing* someone keep quiet, or in *watching* patience work! The skill of changing the subject without doing so obnoxiously needs to be observed. Children need to recognize how mother prepares ahead of time to relieve strain. "Daddy wanted this done before he came home, so let's surprise him. You cut up the bananas and this grapefruit and a piece of watermelon into squares this size. And I'll finish this letter I said I'd type for him [or sew the button on the shirt, or whatever]."

In today's world mother may be at the office and dad may be preparing dinner. If so, he must be the one to be sensitive enough to realize the children are hot and cranky and need a relaxing time in a bubble bath before mother gets home. Perhaps the children are low on blood sugar and need a scrambled egg on toast points, a glass of milk, and a fruit yogurt before daddy (or mommy) gets home. It's not a bad idea to point out, "People get cranky and unreasonable some-times just because they are hungry. Human beings are so compli-cated!" This is the school for human relationships: the home, the family!

Faithfulness, dependability, reliability, steadiness, trustworthi-ness, ability to understand and get along with other people are quali-ties looked for among businessmen, farmers, educators, government officials, and so on down through the list of possible careers. From where are these and other qualities that lead to treating other people as human beings to come? When children or adults hear a constant barrage of "I want my rights"; "I want happiness"; "I want to do my thing"; "I want to go out and get what I deserve in life"; "I want to be fulfilled"; "I want the perfect relationship," they are constantly being taken into the area of daydreams. Selfish, egotistical daydreams? Yes, but putting that aside for the moment, the daydreams are utopian in one way or another. Perfection does not exist. There are no perfect people or perfect situations. Your or my "rights" collide head on with another person's "rights."

In the search for what does *not* exist, what could be a growing, changing situation, with continuity as a framework for growth, is smashed into pieces. Think of continuity as a trellis for a vine. Gradu-ally the plant puts out tendrils that cling to the trellis and take its shape. The ivy or the flowing vine needs years to become what it can be on *that trellis*. To transfer it to another garden sets it back, or kills it altogether. The vine can take storms and blights, or the baby pull-ing at it, or a child cutting parts of it, if it has care in replanting, fertilizing, and watering. In this picture, the same trellis is the con-tinuity, a familiar framework.

No illustration is perfect. But we need to understand that the insistence on having what does not exist and the insistence of smash-ing through all that human beings really *are*, to try to find fulfillment in what they are *not,* bring sorrow. Esau was not very satisfied with the memory of that red lentil stew. Hunger came again. A birthright such as he gave up was intended to be passed down from generation to generation. He had smashed his own *true* rights by grabbing for something in search for a temporary fulfillment. The shout for rights is so loud, and the beat of the drums is so in rhythm with that shout, that common sense is drowned out! Common sense is meant to help us think through the waves of anger or temptation. It helps us realize that we are in danger of losing what is priceless, that which is not worth swapping for a bowl of lentil soup.

There is a factor in our relationship with God that is totally different from our relationship with husband or wife, mother or father, children, sisters or brothers, cousins, aunts, grandparents, friends, fellow workers, neighbors, church members, and so on. That factor is that God is perfect. Our Heavenly Father, our Friend and Shepherd; our Intercessor Jesus Christ; our Comforter the Holy Spirit are each perfect!

God's side of His relationship with us is absolutely perfect. He is so tremendous in His infiniteness and His diversity, that we will never get to the end of coming to know Him. But the gradual progress of knowing God will never be on the same level as knowing a finite, limited ever-changing human being. God tells us that He does not change. He will be tomorrow as He was yesterday. We can depend on Him to be faithful, reliable, trustworthy. He has said He understands us. We are told that the promises He made centuries ago are just as true today—not just true in the academic sense of truth, but true to you and me personally. His truth makes a difference to our present lives, as well as to our part and place in eternity.

Let's consider for a moment our relationship with God, and the factors needed to make it a growing reality, since our side of that relationship is imperfect. Continuity of any relationship needs verbalized expression of love and trust, as well as actions that show forth love in a variety of practical ways day by day.

God has carefully given us His Word, which expresses His love clearly, so that we can reassure ourselves constantly as we read. When we read, "God so loved the world" (John 3:16), it is not meant to be impersonal, but it is in reality a precious verbalization to each of us personally. God carefully expresses His love so that there is no shadow of doubt. We are meant to take His Word as true to us personally and actually bask in His verbalized love. When we read in Jeremiah 31:3, "Yes, I have loved you with an everlasting love;/Therefore with lovingkindness I have drawn you," we are meant to respond not only inwardly, but also with a verbalized response. When we read in 1 John 4:10, "In this is love, not that we loved God, but that He loved us and sent His Son to be the propitiation for our sins," we are meant to accept that love as if we were reading God's letter written just to us, each one personally. God has carried out His love in action, in the most perfect way. But He also has verbalized His love in words we may read over and over again, sing, hear in our own brains. For this reason, we are meant to read the Bible frequently so that we may have the communication of the continuity of God's love in the midst of a broken world full of hate.

Human beings are affected by what they hear spoken in their own voices!

Just so, we need the help of verbalizing our love for God over and over again. Words have an effect upon us. The words coming out of our own mouths influence us! Never forget that. We affect ourselves, we influence ourselves by the things we say with our tongues which then enter our own ears. The phrases and words may form in our brains, but as we speak aloud there comes an underlining, making them stand out in our own thinking and understanding. Human beings are affected by what they hear spoken in their own voices! We can consciously and deliberately reject ideas or words that are suddenly in our minds and deliberately *not* say these things, turning away from them. Speaking and declaring repetitively, *not with a mindless kind of repetition,* but with serious consideration, can affect us amazingly.

How can I help my love for God my Father, Jesus my Savior and Lord, the Holy Spirit my Comforter, to become more real, to grow with a consistent growth? One necessary means of growth is verbalization of that love and trust in thoughtful and constant words. Our own ears need to hear our own voices telling God we love and appreciate Him. Our own minds need to think of the endless reasons why we love God, but those reasons need to be put into words and spoken.

"I will bless the Lord at all times; His praise shall continually be in my mouth" (Ps. 34:1) is translated "I will extol the Lord at all times; his praise will always be on my lips" in the New International Version. This psalm of David's should be enlarged upon over and over again with fresh words of our own: "Oh Lord, right now I want to wipe out complaining thoughts and words from my mind. I need Your help to make real and true my praise of You. As I sort out these clothes to wash, I thank you that you have provided a cleansing for me. I thank you for washing me and making me clean in your eyes. I do want to praise You, O God, with a praise that will bring joy to You, and I want my love to grow during my short lifetime. Please don't let me waste the time that I have to praise You with my lips. As I tell You I do really love You, may these words be acceptable to You because they are more real to me day by day. O Lord, I love You. Please help my lack of love, and open my eyes to my blind spots in this area."

Constantly during the day we need to verbalize to the Lord our expressions of love, dwelling on the reasons for that love, whether it is the titanic reason of His providing eternal life, or the recognition of the wonder of His design of the first snowdrop or violet found in the woods in spring.

> My soul shall be satisfied as with marrow and fatness,
> And my mouth shall praise You with joyful lips.
> When I remember You on my bed,
> I meditate on You in the night watches.
>
> Ps. 63:5–6

With David, we, in our own century, our moment of history, are to verbalize with our lips our satisfaction with our compassionate and wonderful God. In the night when we lie awake, when it is easy to fret or become full of fears, we are to think about God and meditate upon His goodness to His children. We are to trust Him by verbalizing that trust and to love Him by expressing that love. This expression of love can be combined with crying for His help in a moment of trouble and deep need. Our lack of understanding of our circumstances, fears, and distresses does *not* cancel out the possibility of expressing love. The expression does not have to be false because we are in physical pain or in the middle of a shock. The very verbalized recognition of the continuity of our love for God . . . in the imperfect manner of our human love, coupled with acknowledging that we appreciate His verbalized assurance of His love for us . . . helps us in the very "eye of the storm," time after time in life.

"Whenever I am afraid,/ I will trust in You" (Ps. 56:3) is not just David's declaration to God. It must be our spoken declaration too.

In our human relationships, we need to practice verbalizing our love for each other. Husband and wife need to hear each other's expressions of love with a flow of continuity. If you find it hard to speak, then write that love into a poem or ditty or note to stick under the pillow, or in the pocket of the other person. Do not just do it for a birthday, but on an ordinary rainy day! "I love you" should ring in the ears of the other person, after he has hung up the telephone. The sound of the spoken words is a help to the ears, mind, and emotions of the one speaking them. The very words remind the speaker, as well as the hearer, of the reality of what has happened in past weeks, months, years. Memories of what caused that love to take place, to grow, to be real at other moments in history come flooding back. Spoken words can cause negative or positive incidents in the continuity of relationships. We influence reality by our spoken words.

Another dimension of the expression of love is the sexual relationship. It is meant to be a communication. However at any time in life, even when the "fires burn low" the physical touching of each other in response, the holding of hands when walking along in silence, communicate a great variety of things. Love or joy, appreciation or sympathy, agreement or impatience, "let's go" or "let's stay" can all be expressed with a squeeze of the hands . . . with no words spoken. It is true too that eyes can communicate nonverbally, as well as can gestures. But the words "I love you" are still important —growing even more important as life goes on and we grow older.

Does this mean that two people in any relationship in life can simply say, "I love you" without any feeling of love? Giving even a trivial reason for having an appreciation of something about that other person right at that moment helps.

"I love you."

"Why?"

"Oh, I love the way your hair looks right now since you washed it . . . so shiny and squeaky clean."

Trivial? No, practical, and sensible, and the stuff of response!

Are we all, then, to be capable of giving a "soft answer" when the crystal water pitcher, hot out of the dishwasher, is filled with ice water and cracks? Are we to be *so* controlled and calm that we think up a lovely thing to say when mud is brought in on the freshly cleaned rug, or the toast is burned, or the chicken is turned into charcoal in an oven left too high during church? Can we look at shirts, underwear, handkerchiefs, and a teacloth all shades of pink because red socks were put into the load of wash and washed at too high a temperature, and say an appreciative word about the good sponge cake from last week? When bills come in and one person has overspent, or the tax money has been used for another purpose, does the strain drain away immediately to provide a pleasant exchange of ideas with *no* unpleasant words?

In other words, can we give a nice little list of sentences that are to be mechanically recited at the appropriate times? The answer to all these questions is a resounding *no*. As human beings we are imperfect, sinful, affected by the Fall, affected by our own weaknesses and the quirks of our own individual personalities. We are not like each other, and we cannot predict our own flare-ups, let alone those of others. We are also affected by physical stresses such as coming down with the flu, or by low blood pressure, or by a drop in blood sugar, or by a headache, or by just plain fatigue. We get angry, furious, upset, or simply irritated, and we blurt out something that then stirs up a quick retort on the part of the other person. Back and forth words fly. However, there are some ground rules to be resolved early in married life, concerning relationships with our children and others. I feel that allowing ourselves (and I include myself in that) to say harsh things to each other *beyond a certain point,* is very, very dangerous. It will affect getting things back together again and going on in our continued relationship and our growing love. Because we know someone very well, we can say things that are so cutting, and hurt so thoroughly at the most tender spots that the memory of these sentences penetrates like a surgeon's knife.

You know each other—you and your friends, your spouse, your parents, your children, your grandparents, or your aunts and uncles. You know the most vulnerable spot, the Achilles' heel of another person's emotional and psychological make-up. You know what makes that person feel uncertain, inadequate, or unimportant. You know exactly how to pull that person down. Therefore in the middle of a disagreement, a knockdown, drag-out fight, you know that there are certain subjects and certain inadequacies in the other person that, if you talked about them, would produce a drastic effect. That effect would be *so* drastic that it would harm that person emotionally and cut him down so that it would be a long time before confidence could be built up, even if you said, "Sorry."

The extremely important thing to sort out early in a relationship is what things are off limits.

⊱~⊰~⊱~⊰

After that kind of a diatribe, sarcasm, accusation, or tongue lashing, the "sorry" would bring inward doubts: *Did he or she or the children or grandmother really feel that way about me? Was it anger, or just the true opinions bursting forth?* At that point it is hard to get things together again. The extremely important thing to sort out early in a relationship is what things are off limits. The first requirement is to acknowledge that indeed there *are* things off limits.

Some people are sensitive about a physical handicap, a difference in family background, a lack of formal education or natural talent, a tendency to make repeated mistakes whether in speech or in choices, or a family background that makes the person embarrassed. There could be many examples that would be totally opposite from each other in what would hurt if thrown in a person's face. When the decision is made, and the choice has been voiced "for better or for worse," these peculiarities in each other's sensitivities—what I call off-limit areas—should be indelibly written in each other's memories, to be avoided when the flare-ups come!

Continuity is to be expected—and preparation for continuity is necessary when we realize that in any relationship between two imperfect people, there will be imperfect situations, imperfect conversations, and imperfect arguments! We must not think the relationship has to come to an end because we have shouted unkind words or whispered blame and accusations in big or little situations. However, in the midst of this practical preparation for coping with and weathering difficulties, it is very necessary to try to decide what will be always off limits. I know this is possible because after forty-seven years of married life, both Fran and I have maintained our own personal decisions not ever to throw certain accusations at each other. This does not say we have not hurt each other many times, but simply that there is possibility of establishing a line for one's self and stopping at that line.

Although God is perfect and does not make mistakes, human beings are even prone to go off limits in making judgments of God's perfect compassion, love, goodness and wisdom and criticizing God or declaring that God has done something He has *not* done at all.

As God's children, through having accepted Christ's work for us, accusations are definitely always off limits. As we stand before the Creator of the universe, the all-wise, perfectly holy, mighty God, who made us in His image, who upholds the universe, who understands all things, who has shown His compassion in providing a way for us to come to Him through the Messiah, the Lamb . . . how dare we shake our fist in His face? How dare we question God and say, "Why did you do this to me?"

Jesus was angry at the results of the Fall as He stood before the tomb of Lazarus. As my husband has so often said, "Jesus could be angry at death and abnormality and not be angry at Himself as God." Death is a result of the Fall. Death is that which Satan has brought into history. We can be angry at a person when we are caught in the awful results of cause-and-effect history following the Fall, or following attacks of Satan, or following human choices of one kind or another—but that person is never God. We may not understand our tragic situation. We may not feel we can face life after a terrible shock. We may not feel that we know how to cope in the midst of a war, or avalanche, or earthquake, or famine. But it is always off limits to blame God. We are not to run away from God, shaking our fist at Him and screaming. We are to run *to* Him when we are shaking with grief or trembling with fear.

He is our refuge and strength; a very *present* help in trouble. Our help is to come from Him as we run into the shelter of His arms, away from the noise of the battle, or the storm. He has promised us comfort, and we need to climb on His lap as a weeping, hurt child, not to kick at Him.

We can look into His Word and see what He has said we are to do when we face a hard moment. We can come with appreciation of that Word and thank Him even as we search for His verbalization to us for the moment of need. He has prepared a verbalized careful explanation to fit our various times of need.

In the very midst of the most difficult times filled with anxiety, God has given us *His* pattern for the continuity of our relationship with Him. He does not leave us without explanation of what to do.

Rejoice in the Lord always. Again I will say, rejoice! Let your gentleness be known to all men. The Lord is at hand. Be anxious for nothing, but in everything by prayer and supplication, with thanksgiving, let your requests be made known to God; and the peace of God, which surpasses all understanding, will guard your hearts and minds through Christ Jesus.

Phil. 4:4–7

There is value, of course, in being honest and not plastic in our rejoicing. But God has made it clear that the path to praising and loving Him in an anxious time is through reviewing what He has done in the past. "With thanksgiving" (v. 6) refers to a reality of reviewing what one is thankful for. As these instances and realities are verbalized, the immediate need can be measured by the wonder of who God is, and what He has done in the past. But it is after the requests have been made and with trust as to God's wisdom in dealing with those requests, that the peace that passes all understanding flows in. It is not automatic—God sets forth conditions which help us to have such a reality.

Of course any words can be said with falseness. Do you try to analyze whether you really love God or love another person *before* you ever say the words, "I love you"? We are so pulled in to self-analysis today that we are in danger of being like the thousand-legger. Do you know the old story of the thousand-legger bug? Someone said to the bug, "You've got to learn how to put one foot in front of the other." When the poor bug tried to sort out the complicated process which had been so natural before, it fell on its back with its thousand legs in the air! So ended its walking naturally!

Self-analysis and introspection can be so harmful. It can be like pulling off the wings of a butterfly to see how they were fastened. The analyzing of what is meant by "I love you" while trying to analyze all of one's feelings can be really horrible. That kind of so called "honesty" is not always helpful.

You may say, "What in the world are you talking about? Aren't we supposed to be honest in all our statements and always speak the truth?"

I would reply, "Let us be really very careful as to whether we are rationalizing our motives for making hurtful criticism." We have been told that the tongue is the most dangerous portion of our whole body. James 3:5–12 warns us of the slippery traps into which we can fall when we use our tongue in criticism to tear down relationships, and cause destruction in the church or other groupings in life, right up to the country's government. "Honesty" is often used as a cloak to cover up a spiteful lashing out at someone close to us, or in a wider circle.

Human beings can tear down the person they have promised to love and cherish for life simply in order to free themselves for another person to whom they have consciously or unconsciously been attracted. When God says that the human heart is deceitful, it is a warning to each of us that we are to be careful not to deceive ourselves. An old pastor I used to love to hear preach frequently said, "What is deep in the well of the heart comes up in the bucket of the mouth." The deceit starts in the heart, and spills forth in a rush of rationalizing criticism. Then the spoken words convince the speaker and it can begin a vicious circle of destruction of a relationship that did not need to be destroyed.

As James talks about the tongue, he begins with a description of how a bit in a horse's mouth is used to turn the horse in one direction or another, and how a small rudder steers a ship through storms (see vv. 3–4). Then he says:

> Even so the tongue is a little member and boasts great things. See how great a forest a little fire kindles! And the tongue is a fire; a world of iniquity. The tongue is so set among our members that it defiles the whole body, and sets on fire the course of nature; and it is set on fire by hell.
>
> James 3:5–6

Strong words? Yes, God's warnings are strong. I have written at length in my book on the Ten Commandments, *Lifelines*, about the tongue. Throughout His Word God explains what being a false witness involves. The important factor that needs to be considered in the midst of every relationship in life is that the tongue, or words formed on the tongue and spoken audibly into the ears of another person, have the potential to accomplish marvelous things in the continuation of a relationship—or horrible things in splitting that relationship into bits and pieces.

The tongue is dangerous. Why?

Because with a few words, we can destroy something we have taken months or even years to build up. We go along building, sometimes destroying bits that have to be rebuilt, but we keep on building. Then, we tear down!

Proverbs has a lot to say in warning and in teaching us to think before we pour out harmful sentences.

Every wise woman builds her house,
But the foolish pulls it down with her hands.

Prov. 14:1

A soft answer turns away wrath,
But a harsh word stirs up anger.
The tongue of the wise uses knowledge rightly,
But the mouth of fools pours forth foolishness.

A wholesome tongue is a tree of life,
But perverseness in it breaks the spirit.

Prov. 15:1–2, 4

Women and men are in danger of pulling the beautiful continuity of a family—generations of togetherness, reunions made up of a flow of generations, the most preciously fulfilling things of human life—down around their ears. In so doing, they cause themselves and others to live among broken pieces of memories, and the ugliness and desolation of living in the midst of broken continuity.

People shudder at pictures of the smashed and smoldering ruins of Beirut, where human beings wander aimlessly. Yet people "bomb" with harsh and dangerous words the treasures of their home, their children, and their personal continuity—that which should be protected with gentle, sensitive words expressing that reality of "Love suffers long and is kind" (1 Cor. 13:4). The ruins of Beirut are no more ugly than the ruins of families divorced from each other and divorced from the realities of what God made human beings to know in the fullness of lives that have some measure of continuity.

Dissecting and analyzing each word destroys freedom of expression, and makes it impossible for some people to say "I love you." It takes them months to come around and say, "Well, I do love you." And if the question "Why?" comes, does the answer have to be a profound analysis of the whole gamut of possibilities that the word *love* covers? There are lots of reasons we love each other, and we can use those words to express very *simple* everyday things. It is the critical analysis of every word, or every feeling that you are expressing that can be destructive to a relaxed and warm natural relationship.

There is also danger of being honest in the negative or opposite direction, or rationalizing harsh criticism by saying, "I have really got to tell him what I think of him" or "I'm going to be honest with her and tell her right down the line what I think about her." As harsh words spill out, exaggeration so easily underlines it all, and adds word after word. There is no way of your seeing from the outside what effect your criticism is having inside another person.

Creativity can be stopped by harsh criticism. A person's freedom for creativity can be a very delicately balanced thing. The creative mental work of a sensitive violinist, a talented composer, a painter, or an architect cannot be "seen" in the traditional sense of the word. Crash in on creativity, and something may die! The birth of creativity may end in miscarriage. An individual piece of creativity means a great deal to an individual.

A child can be planning a play with mother or dad. He may write the script in a crooked handwriting, he can bring in neighbor's children to be the bride and bridegroom or other characters, and he can direct the play. And as this creativity is in the midst of taking place, someone shouts out and begins to criticize, saying harsh, cutting things. Suddenly the sensitive young artist, or cook, or musician, or playwright, or poet, or gardener stops enjoying the creativity and the flushed excitement over the lovely unfolding of beauty, and crushed embarrassment floods him or her. Creativity has been stepped on, squashed.

Just as there are limits to the areas of things that are never to be referred to in anger, so there must be limits to the *timing* of criticism. Creativity should not be crushed through scolding, no matter how legitimate, just because a family member or friend is angry. *Time* can be chosen carefully . . . and that kind of a setting up of limits should be done when we are not angry.

No, we are *not* talking about perfection in relationships. But if we are to fight for reality in the continuity of our relationships while things are falling apart around us, we need to go to the source of wisdom. We must discover the common sense danger signs as well as the trail marks on the paths God has laid out to fulfill the reality of our being human beings, made in His image, to whom continuity is basically important. "It is not good that man should be alone" (Gen. 2:18) coupled with "till death do us part" speak of lasting togetherness, even though imperfect since the Fall. The rules or commands of God are given in the Bible to help human beings be human. Inhumanity of one human being to another fills our newspapers with a variety of horror tales. Human beings need help in the way of finding true patterns for life.

"Set your hearts on all the words which I testify among you today, which you shall command your children to be careful to observe—all the words of this law. For it is not a futile thing for you, because it is your life, and by this word you shall prolong your days in the land which you cross over the Jordan to possess."

Deut. 32:46–47

Commonsense Christian living, in the framework God Himself has given, is the path to life *now*, as God means it to be.

Eternal life is for later in the perfection that will be God's future for us. But—at present—God's words to us in His Word are profoundly important and urgent: "[They are] your life" (v. 47).

Another aspect of creativity in relationships with husband, children, relatives, friends, is an honest look over the past (in privacy) to discover your most irritating habit—the one that has most often preceded a tense situation, or an argument. This kind of a check-up can become a creative challenge to yourself. As you plan a skeleton outline of your week, do a very attractive poster or chart, for your own encouragement, using whatever artistic ability you have, and listing what you hope to get accomplished in addition to the essentials. In this reminder to yourself, try to fit in the *timing* of things you have always been too late doing. Put a star, a candle, a flower, or some sparks, beside items like "pack suitcase," "make the pumpkin pie for Thanksgiving," "sew buttons on pajamas," "write the promised letter," "take clothes to the cleaner," "prepare for the committee meeting with refreshments made and frozen, and the outline of business"—whatever things have been often forgotten, or done in great haste too late, and have caused continual outbursts in the past.

This is a creative way of preparing for situations long enough ahead to avoid the old patterns of difficulties in your relationships. The *timing* of what to do first should include not only a rearrangement on your list of things to do, but a rearrangement of your attitudes, a self-discipline consciously concerned with the fact that we have ridiculously ignored the common sense recognition of danger points in our relationships. Perhaps it will be maddening to prepare your suitcase ahead of time, and have it ready by the front door, and to have no one notice with praise that change in timing. But your reward is in improving a situation by avoiding the habitual mistake. Your reward is in seeing the artwork of relationships begin to take a new shape here and there, like a painting the great artist improves with each brush stroke.

The beauty of preparing an artistic colorful list or poster—"TEN SPECIAL DAYS from OCTOBER 24 to NOVEMBER 4" or "WORK TO BE ACCOMPLISHED AND EVENTS TO OCCUR BEFORE CHRISTMAS" —is that you are really being your own helper and inspiration. You encourage yourself with incentive, ideas, and originality and treat yourself as significant enough to receive creative help! It is my own secret weapon. Childish? I really don't think so. It encourages you to improve without nagging. It is never too late to work on your own irritating habits, your own weaknesses in down to earth, practical, and creative ways.

Before finishing a chapter on continuity in life, it is imperative to remind ourselves that as human beings we have a need for continuity in the area of familiar physical surroundings. God's promises to His people in the Old Testament strongly emphasized being brought to a land that would be a good land and would be handed down from generation to generation. Land to build homes on, to plant trees that last from one generation to another, to fertilize and grow crops on, to landscape with artistic care for others in the family to enjoy, is something God has pointed to as good.

> And you shall do what is right and good in the sight of the LORD, that it may be well with you, and that you may go in and possess the good land of which the LORD swore to your fathers.
>
> Deut. 6:18

> Honor your father and your mother, as the LORD your God has commanded you, that your days may be long, and that it may be well with you in the land which the LORD your God is giving you.
>
> Deut. 5:16

The Creator speaks of that which is good for those whom He has made to be finite, yet with needs He understands perfectly as He made them in His image. The created earth was made to be inhabited—to provide families a familiar home, familiar trees and grass, familiar hives of bees or flocks of sheep, familiar looms on which to weave, familiar wood to cut and season and carve into art objects or musical instruments, or build into another dwelling place on the land. God is describing as good and natural for His people, the possession of a piece of land to supply shelter, food, and creativity, as well as fulfill a need of security.

Yes, God makes it clear to His people that the world has been spoiled by the Fall, that history is abnormal, and that He is preparing perfection for us for all eternity in a heavenly land, a home He is getting ready for us. But while we are in the land of the living, we are still human beings who have a need for continuity of some familiar things. Material things do affect us. To have to change geographical location every day, or week, or even year, and to have *nothing* familiar in sight, is something that can have an effect not only on children, but on adults.

But so many of us are unable to have a piece of land with a home which is our familiar dwelling place for our lifetime and which is ours to hand down to the next generation. Perhaps one day the Lord will give you and me a comparatively lasting piece of land or house, tent, or tree house that we can have as home, and prepare for someone to follow us. But if not, we can still be surrounded with familiar things even in unfamiliar geographical locations.

There are many reasons to move about—floods, famines, wars, earthquakes, volcanos, fires, as well as changing jobs. For those who can move a household of furniture—chairs that belonged to a grandmother, a bed that "daddy slept in as a child," dishes that bring back memories of day-by-day meals as well as a stream of Christmas dinners—it is important to do so. It is a mistake to believe it is possible to buy all new things because of an increase in salary, and to start out without any of the memories that are bound up in things that have lived with the family for years. Other people may not be able to take a large number of things, or anything as big as chairs and beds and barrels of dishes because they have been burned or stolen!

I feel so very strongly that human beings were made for continuity, and that continuity makes a difference to us emotionally, psychologically, intellectually, and spiritually. I believe we all need to work at taking things along with us from one location to another! Memories and a feeling of reality go along with the material things, across mountains, land and sea!

Babies need a "security blanket," the same bed, familiar toys and the favorite dishes in order not to feel uprooted and bewildered. Children's needs of the familiar should always be taken into consideration if parents are in diplomatic or military service, or any other kind of work that makes frequent moving the pattern of life. Books are important—not just the same titles, but the actual books themselves with their smudges and markings as well as content. It is important to fill the new home with the music that was always played on Sunday or on Friday night! Candlesticks, the shell collection, tablecloths or mats, pictures, other art objects need to be placed lovingly to turn a bleak, unfamiliar place into a set of familiar surroundings. It isn't just the children who need to see the familiar old things come out of boxes and trunks to make the strange place "home." Adults need this just as much.

One does not need to be apologetic about taking things that are familiar across the world. It is a way of taking along the only part of "the land" that can go with you.

A very creative and wise niece of mine just put together an ingenious and practical piece of continuity to be put into her son's trunk as he went off to college for his first year away from home. She carefully made a quilt with pieces of corduroy from all the past years —from jeans and skirts of brothers' and sisters' clothing as well as from his own. These recognizable parts of years of incidents, celebrations, school life, home life, made a practical bridge, and helped the continuity to be real.

Each of us should use our imagination to prepare things for each other in our families, or to tuck things into suitcases that help to substitute for the continuity a family homestead is really meant to give us. In a torn and broken world, fast becoming unfamiliar in tragic ways, nothing is too trivial to carry out our own and other people's need for help in our feeling at home in strange situations and places. Be sure to record as much as possible in diaries, or in photograph albums, in treasured recipes of grandmother's pumpkin chiffon pie, or Aunt Elsa's sponge cake, or Prisca's rose hip jam. Recipes carry flavors and smells from one generation to another in families who cannot live on the same land!

The smell of Thanksgiving, of pine freshly cut, of a wood fire, of roasting turkey, of currant jelly bubbling on the stove, of fresh bread baking, of leaves burning in the fall . . . these help not only to bring back memories, but to give a security of continuity! It is common sense to live in the light of who we are as human beings . . . made for continuity . . . in life.

The Pursuit of Excellence

O n the twenty-ninth anniversary of my marriage to my husband, Joseph Dillow, I began a series of letters to my two daughters to share my thoughts about marriage as I had lived and learned them through those years. I wrote for a year, and the letter I would like to share with you is the last one I wrote. It holds for me, I think, the essence of what I wish to convey to them and to you about really loving your man.

Linda Dillow
How to Really Love Your Man

Dear Daughters,

In the first letter I wrote you about loving your man, it was your father's and my anniversary. Amazingly enough, it's anniversary time again. God gives us anniversaries as milestones, significant points in the passing of time, specific yet mute reminders that more sand has passed through the hourglass. God builds them into our calendars once every year to enable us to make an annual appraisal not of the *length* of time we've been married but the *depth* of our intimacy, not just to remind us we've been married *longer* but to help us determine if we are now married *deeper*.

Anniversaries do, however, give us a handle on the measurement of time. Another year has passed for me. It truly seems unbelievable that I've been writing these letters to you for a year! The minutes of marriage pass so quietly, so consistently, that we fail to realize the time is ticking away. We have only this year, this month, this moment to love. Picture your life of seventy years as a clock with the hours of a single day from seven in the morning until midnight.

You, my daughters, are almost at noon, in the sunlight time of life. I'm just past 6:00 P.M., headed toward evening. Yet, how clearly I remember my wedding day. Was it really twenty-nine years ago? How quickly the hands of the clock move around the circle. We must not move about in a cloud of ignorance, spending and wasting time as though we had a million years. We must be women who realize life while we live it!

> Four things come not back,
> The spoken word, the sped arrow,
> Time past, the neglected opportunity.

We can't bring time back, but we can seize the opportunity today to live each day as a gift of God: seeking to love, seeking to encourage, seeking to give, seeking excellence.

We Must Live with the End in View

To begin with the end in view means to start your marriage with a clear understanding of your destination as a wife. By keeping that end clearly in view, you can make certain that whatever you do on any particular day does not go against the criteria you have defined as supremely important, and that each day of your life contributes in a meaningful way to your vision of your life as a whole.

To help you think about the end at the beginning, I took you on a journey to your own funeral fifty years from now and asked you these questions: What would you like your husband to say about you after fifty years of marriage? What kind of wife would you want his words to present? What character qualities would you like him to have seen in you? What kind of love relationship would you want him to describe? What kind of love would you want him to have received from you during all those years?

In Proverbs 31, we have a beautiful example of a woman of

excellence, the virtuous woman. Her husband praised her after thirty or more years of marriage. And what a tribute his praise was:

> Many women have done excellently,
> But you excel them all. (Prov. 31:29 paraphrased)

It's as if her husband said, "For thirty years I've watched women, seen the wives of my friends, I've intimately known you, my wife. I've seen your strengths, your weaknesses: but after observing all women, it is very obvious to me, *you* excel them all."

Aristotle said, "We are what we repeatedly do." Excellence, then, is not an act but a habit. Our character, who we are *becoming*, is basically a composite of our habits.

> Sow a thought, reap an action;
> Sow an action, reap a habit;
> Sow a habit, reap an attitude;
> Sow an attitude, reap a character;
> Sow a character, reap a destiny.

A personal marriage statement can set us on the right path to becoming women of excellence. Adhering to it determines where we are headed, who we will become. Our secret choices determine our thoughts, which determine our words, actions, habits, attitude, character, and destiny; who we become. The Proverbs 31 wife became the most excellent of all, and the reason is clear; it is visible for all to see:

> Charm is deceitful and beauty is vain,
> But a woman who fears the Lord,
>   she shall be praised.
> Give her of the fruit of her hands,
> And let her own works praise her in
>   the gates. (Prov. 31:30–31)

The excellent wife had as part of her personal marriage statement to view her marriage with an eternal perspective; she lived in fear and reverence of God, and she lived to be faithful to her God. Her eternal focus plus her secret choices determined her destiny.

We Must Live to Be Faithful to Christ

Paul wrote, "I press toward the goal for the prize of the upward call of God in Christ Jesus" (Phil. 3:14).

Chuck Swindoll puts this verse in perspective:

> Our ultimate goal, our highest calling in life, is to glorify God, not to be happy. Let that sink in! Glorifying Him is our greatest pursuit. Not to get our way. Not to be comfortable. Not to find fulfillment. Not even to be loved or to be appreciated or to be taken care of. Now these are important, but they are not primary.
>
> As I glorify Him, He sees to it that other essential needs are met . . . or my need for them diminishes. Believe me, this concept will change your entire perspective on yourself, your life, and your marriage.

As I look at the hands of the clock of life and see that my life is more than half over, that I am headed down the home stretch, I realize that I desire two things above all else:

1. To hear my Lord say to me, "Well done, good and faithful servant."

2. To know that during all the years of my marriage I have strived to live my personal marriage statement.

W. Nathaniel Howell was ambassador to Kuwait and withstood four and one-half months of virtual imprisonment at the American embassy during the Gulf War. People frequently ask him, "Were you afraid?" Howell's answer:

> We would have been fools if we hadn't been afraid at times. But what it taught me about myself was that I was a whole lot more afraid of not being able to live with myself if I didn't do what was right, than I was of Saddam Hussein and his troops. You only die once, but you live with yourself a long time.

My daughters, for you, for me, I desire that we will not only be able to live with ourselves, but that we will live with peace and joy knowing that we have made the secret choices that are honoring to God, and that build an intimate oneness with our husbands.

This week, your father and I were at a dinner party, and a man said to me, "Linda, I hear you are writing another book on marriage. There are so many books on marriage in Christian bookstores, how is this one unique?" Before I could answer, your father answered for me and said, "My wife's book is powerful because she has lived what she is saying." I was very humbled by his comment because I know how far I still have to go to become the wife I desire to be.

My prayer for you, my daughters, is that you, too, might be praised by your husbands after many years of marriage and hear the beautiful words:

> Many women have done excellently,
> But you excel them all!

I love
you,
Mom

PART SIX

I Am
Professional

Women's Work?

APRIL 1919

Flaring headlines in the papers have announced that "women will fight to hold jobs," meaning the men's jobs which they took when the men went to war. What to do about the situation seems to be a very important question. One would think that there must have been a great number of women who were idle before the war. If not, one wonders what has become of the jobs they had. To paraphrase a more or less popular song—I Wonder Who's Holding Them Now?

With men by the thousands out of work and the unemployment situation growing so acute as to cause grave fears of attempted revolution, women by the hundreds are further complicating affairs by adding their numbers to the ranks of labor, employed, unemployed, or striking as the case may be.

We heard nothing of numbers of women who could not find work before the war. They were all busy apparently and fairly well satisfied. Who is doing the work they left to fill the places of men who went into the army, or is that work undone?

It would be interesting to know, and it seems strange that while statistics are being prepared and investigations made of every subject under the sun, no one has compiled the records of "The Jobs Women Left or Women's Work Undone."

But however curious we may be about the past, we are more vitally interested in the future. Will these women take up their old work and give the men a chance to go back to the places they will thus leave vacant? The women say not.

Other women, also, besides those who took men's jobs, have gone out of the places they filled in pre-war days, out into community and social work and government positions which were created by and because of the war. Will these women go back? And again we hear them answer, "Never! We never will go back!" All this is very well, but where are they going and with them all of us?

I think this query could most truthfully be answered by a slang expression, which, though perhaps not polished, is very apt: "We don't know where we're going, but we're on our way."

It makes our hearts thrill and our heads rise proudly to think that women were found capable and eager to do such important work in the crisis of wartime days. I think that never again will anyone have the courage to say that women could not run world affairs if necessary. Also, it is true that when men or women have advanced, they do not go back. History does not retrace its steps.

Laura Ingalls Wilder
Little House in the Ozarks

Combining Success and Femininity

Yes, as Laura Ingalls Wilder wrote over seventy years ago, we may not "know where we're going, but we're on our way!" We've gained a lot of ground in these past years as millions and millions more women entered the job market. But mistaken attitudes and early programming of both men and women have made us women limit ourselves and not achieve our full potential in business. I wrote Equal to the Challenge because I was tired of seeing women self-destruct or give up becoming a respected, top-level professional. I hope this chapter from my book will help remedy any faulty ideas you may have about being successful and feminine at the same time. There may be prices to pay for our new found freedom—but our femininity is not one of them!

Diane Lewis
Equal to the Challenge

Recently it was my pleasure to be a guest at the swank Union League Club in Chicago for a dinner introducing a number of African businessmen to the American market. It was the kind of affair to which a lot of notable people were invited, the kind where you keep whispering to your escort, "Hey, see the tall guy in the corner? Isn't that so and so?"

Among the bejeweled women was one very attractive young woman who was with one of our more prominent local politicians. I was sure she was a model or a movie star or something like that. She had the kind of poise, of total self-confidence and self-assurance, that women in those professions often seem to have.

Even though most of my time these days is devoted to my trading business, I'm always on the lookout for women who seem to be self-reliant. They tend to do well in the personnel business, and I never miss the chance to recruit one. So I struck up a conversation with Eleanor during the reception that followed dinner.

"So, Eleanor," I said, "where do you work?"

She named one of the air freight expediting companies.

"What do you do there?" I asked, assuming from her age that she might be a secretary or receptionist.

"I drive," she said brightly.

"Drive? You mean you drive a truck?"

"Sure. It's a great job. It pays two or three times what my friends make doing office work."

"Forgive me for being so surprised," I said. "It's just that one doesn't normally think of women being truck drivers. Especially ones as pretty as you."

"Actually, the job helps me keep my looks—plenty of exercise. But the company has a weight limitation on all packages, so it's never too much for me to handle. Maybe in the old days it required a lot of upper body strength, more than most women have, in fact, but not any more."

So she made good money and enjoyed the work. But what about the *real* reason most women would be reluctant to look for that kind of job? It's a difficult topic to ask about, especially on such short acquaintance.

"But doesn't driving a truck make you feel a little, well, 'mannish?' A little less attractive as a woman?"

She gave the only possible answer as yet another handsome man came up at that moment to ask her to dance. "Haven't had any complaints yet," she said.

Eleanor is an example of the modern woman who can take any job that she chooses to take and still be confident about her own femininity. Thankfully, she's not unique. More and more of us women are realizing that our "gender identity" need not depend on what we do to earn a living. Another example is a California woman named Gwen Adair. She looks to be about thirty and is very attractive, with a feminine mass of long hair. As far as anybody knows, she is *the only woman in the world* to practice her particular trade, even though her job pays well and looks like a lot of fun. She's the first woman licensed to referee professional boxing matches.

It would be difficult for me to believe that her job has hurt her self-confidence. I would rather think that her work has probably enhanced it. After all, a 120-pound woman who steps in between two heavyweight prizefighters and says, "All right, boys, I want a good, clean fight," is likely to develop the ability to seem at ease in most situations.

Threatened Femininity

We women often feel we aren't equal to the challenge of exciting work because, unlike Eleanor and Gwen, we perceive a threat to our sense of femininity from nontraditional work. Here's how that mistaken perception comes about. There is an image inside you of what it means to be feminine. It's like one of those props they use for trick photos—the kind where you rest your chin on a headless cutout and the photo shows the body of a cowboy or a bathing beauty with your head on it.

The root of the problem is that the picture of femininity many of us have learned corresponds poorly to the new reality for women who work.

Every time you think about yourself, you see your head on top of that feminine image stored in your mind. The image may or may not be an accurate depiction of you. It may or may not be an accurate depiction of women in general. But it *is* the programmed filter through which you always see (and *judge*) yourself as a woman. Your picture of what constitutes femininity is another result of your early programming. Of course, if it remains unspoken and hidden, it can be just as insidious and just as hard to change as are all those other images your programming has given you.

The root of the problem is that the picture of femininity many of us have learned corresponds poorly to the new reality for women who work. Thus, we find ourselves suffering today from a kind of "gender confusion." That is, for most of us the image of the feminine ideal with which we've been programmed does not include the picture of the strong, powerful woman in charge. In fact, it almost always includes just the opposite picture: the weak, passive, dependent woman.

The error that results comes about because we cherish our frilly notions about the feminine ideal, so much so that one of our greatest fears is losing our femininity. As a result of this fear, many of us women find it necessary for our peace of mind to make an uncomfortable choice between who we *can* be and who we *let ourselves* be.

In order to continue to feel confident about our femininity, then, many of us sacrifice our potential and become less than we might have become. That is, some of us subconsciously hold ourselves back, fearing success because it seems to be at odds with all that we've been programmed to appreciate as feminine. And who of us wouldn't want to feel secure about her femininity? It's a perfectly normal reaction.

The irony is that no such choice between femininity and achievement is really necessary. Being successful, being an achiever, and being the boss are not conditions that are at odds with true femininity, but only with our warped and lopsided picture of weak and ineffectual femininity. You can be both securely feminine and enormously successful at the same time. You can be in charge of hundreds of subordinates and millions of dollars of budget and still not be thought of as "mannish."

The error, therefore, is grounded in the distorted *perception* many of us have been given of what it means to be an ambitious, assertive achiever. We wrongly perceive it as unfeminine. One basis for this error, of course, is the early, girlish programming that has caused us to think of femininity the way that we do. I'm sure that by this time that statement doesn't surprise you, because I've identified early programming as a culprit so many times before. This time, however, there's another culprit as well.

Femininity and Men

This time it's necessary to specifically indict *men* as being partially responsible for one of our mistaken attitudes. What leads to their culpability in this case is the male ego, which is so fragile that it makes Wedgewood seem like Tupperware by comparison.

The modern Western male is often terribly insecure. The only way he can be sure of keeping his place is to keep you in yours. Then he knows that he *always* has *someone* to look down on, even if it's *only* you. (Don't blame me if the last sentences seem offensive; it's the way many of them feel, isn't it?)

The need to accommodate a man's ego may be one of the reasons you limit yourself. You become afraid to be too good at anything, afraid that your man's ego will be bruised if he's confronted with your competence.

Then, of course, he might leave (or at least distance himself emotionally). And one of the things we've been programmed to be very, very bad at is being alone. Most of us would rather have him with all his faults than be alone. So we let ourselves be less than we can be in order to avoid causing him to doubt his unjustified feeling of automatic and inherent superiority.

I know what I'm talking about because of my firsthand experience with the male ego. My second husband was an ex-Marine; that's strike one in the male ego game. He was also a pilot (strike two). And his hero was Ernest Hemingway; strikes three, four, and five.

I was married to him when I first decided to start my own company. He wailed like a siren when I told him. He recited every reason in the book why I was wasting my time. And you know what? Most of his arguments against my attempts to find success had no factual basis. His most effective arguments (the ones that had the most effect on me, anyway) were those that were personally belittling rather than logical.

*There **are** supportive, secure men out there;*
it's just that there are more women who want
to develop themselves than there are strong,
enlightened men willing to see and help their
women succeed.

355

He said a lot of the same things we women so often hear when we announce an intention to try to move ahead on our own. *"You can make a go of your own business? Don't make me laugh." "You can become a lawyer? Who'll take care of the kids?" "You want to go to night school? Over my dead body!"* Those are the kinds of arguments many a woman hears from her "significant other" when she endangers his self-assigned supremacy by asserting her independence of both thought and action. There *are* supportive, secure men out there; it's just that there are more women who want to develop themselves than there are strong, enlightened men willing to see and help their women succeed.

In fairness, though, it must be noted that our men today are in a quandary of their own over gender expectations, just as we are. Especially confused are those men in white-collar businesses who work right alongside the pink-collar work force of women. Corporate affirmative action programs have required that these men be democratic and liberal in their thinking. So, outwardly, male executives have to display what I like to call the "Sesame Street Syndrome": the loud, ringing assertion that everybody is equal and everybody is the same, just as is frequently proclaimed on the TV show. It's a beautiful philosophy.

But how much do they really mean it? How deeply have they accepted this philosophy of equality? Many men of an age to be important executives today have grown to adulthood under a culture in which women were considered inferior. We've required them to make a complete about-face in their basic beliefs in a fairly short period of time. As a result of trying to obey laws that conflict with their own early programming, some of these men have come to sound like "Sesame Street" on the outside. But on the inside, they may feel less like "Sesame Street" and more like George Orwell's *Animal Farm*, the fable about the barnyard where all the animals were equal—but where the pigs were a little more equal.

Men's Programming

Let's be fair to them: men are victims of their own programming, just as we women are of ours. They can no more help wanting to feel "a little more equal" than those pigs could. But even though we understand how they got the way they are, it's past time for them to alter their programming and come to grips with the new reality.

The programming of men that makes them demand supremacy is

universal. There is a sheikh, for example, with whom I have worked closely for nearly ten years now. His wife, the sheikha, and I have become closer than I would have thought possible for women of such different cultural backgrounds. Nonetheless, only recently did I tell her that one of the reasons for my divorce from Smilin' Jack, the "Terror of the Skies," was that he'd been having an affair with another woman.

Khalila stared at me for a while after this revelation. Then she looked quizzical, as if she expected more, and said "Yes?"

"That's it," I said. "He was seeing another woman. And she was a real drip, too. Joan Collins I might have understood. But a drip!"

Again she looked puzzled. "Of course she was, as you say, a 'drip.' That was the kind of woman he needed for his mind."

"His mind? I don't think it was his mind that was his number one concern."

"Oh, but of course it was," she said. "We take a different view of men here. Men have to feel they are commanders. So we let them command. But some of you Western women can command men. So then the men must find other women to command. But they fear the strong women. So what women are left to make them feel like commanders? Ones who are 'drips.' "

I love the sheikha like a sister. But in this one instance, I wasn't sure her pragmatic viewpoint could be easily adopted by a Western woman. She's a victim of her own kind of programming, one that causes her to willingly limit her prerogatives in life in order to accommodate somebody else's wishes: ". . . we *let* them command."

Don't be misled into believing that Middle Eastern women must be subservient because they have no say in the matter. While that's true, it's also true that their system is one that the women themselves accept and help to perpetuate. The Middle Eastern women know they're not helpless and inept. *But they've learned to act as if they were.* And that's the fondest wish of Western men: to get us to behave subserviently. Our fear of violating that wish is what makes us cling so tightly to our outmoded picture of soft femininity.

Understand that men are concerned purely with outward behavior rather than with internal belief. It's not important to men what we women believe about ourselves so long as we behave meekly. The truth has nothing to do with it. Whether or not a woman is as inept as her image makes her appear to be is not the point. The system is just like the Middle Eastern system in this respect: it requires us women only to *behave* as if we're inferior. That's why women so often hold themselves back from maximum effort in their careers. Obvious success would make it impossible to maintain the fiction of female inferiority.

That's where the notion of losing our femininity begins to play such an important role among us Western women. Our men have the same need to be commanders as do the Middle Eastern men. They expect us to behave as if we were their subordinates. But society has recently acknowledged that we women are free to develop as persons in our own rights. Naturally, that makes our men nervous.

Which, in turn, makes *us* nervous.

In fact, this confusion makes us so nervous that many of us simply abdicate our rights to personhood and behave as "the old man" wants us to. Behaving the way he wants you to behave almost never results in your becoming at least as successful as he is in the workplace. That level of achievement would be too threatening to his fragile ego, and you both know it.

These are not radical ideas, of course. Many women have written on the subject of how the need to appease the male ego acts as a depressant to us. It's helping us finally to recognize that success is not at odds with femininity, only with somebody else's faulty idea of femininity. It would be best if some man could explain the same things to your man, to help him change his outmoded concepts about your success. Regrettably, until that happens he'll just stay tense, because there's not much *you* can do to calm his fears when he sees you usurping his position of supremacy. As they say, *he* owns the problem. Therefore, *he* has to solve it.

And, so far at least, nobody seems interested in helping him. In fact, my biggest criticism of the feminist movement (and I have many) is that nobody is explaining to our men what's going on. Nobody is calming their fears. Nobody is soothing their egos and saying, "There, there" when they have to begin reporting to us women on the job. Nobody is helping them get used to us. Nobody is informing them that we're still women and not men in skirts, and that everything is just the same as it always was.

Except that we're equal to them. Equal in the "Sesame Street" sense, not the *Animal Farm* sense.

Is Business Unfeminine?

If there's not much we can do to get men to appreciate an ideal of femininity that stresses equality and that includes strength, at least we can be sure that *we women* avoid misunderstanding the feminine ideal. But I'm not at all sure that we've reconciled success with femininity in our own minds yet. I'm doubtful because of that remark I heard so many times while compiling the reactions of other women for my *Equal to the Challenge* book: "A woman shouldn't act like a man." I'll bet you've heard women say it yourself.

So, how does a man act in the business world? It seems that many of us believe male business behavior to be synonymous with brutality and cruelty. Otherwise, why would we be so worried about coincidentally "acting like a man"? And if this is really the way men behave, does that mean that fascism is a necessary personality trait for getting ahead in the working world?

In truth, neither men nor women who are respected achievers in business can afford to indulge in vicious, unstable behavior. On the contrary, the higher you go in business, the more you need such traits as diplomacy, integrity, and compassion. For example, it's typical of successful managers, whether male or female, to understand that one gets a job done *through* people and that people must be treated as though they were important, which they are. That means that getting to the top levels of most corporations is more likely to happen to a well-integrated personality than to a bully.

How is it, then, that so many of us have developed the erroneous idea that business success requires a domineering, uncaring personality, and that pushing ahead vigorously in business therefore entails a risk to our femininity? It's because of the way in which we women who work have built up experience with male bosses. What happens is that we work for the worst male bosses at the worst possible time, when we're just starting out. It's what may have happened to you on your first job. Was your immediate supervisor a man? Was he arrogant? pompous? tyrannical? It's easy to see how you might have gotten the idea that such unpleasant characteristics are the reason men are in charge.

Here's what really happened to him, however. He planned to be a top-level manager. But most upper-level managers start as "first-line supervisors" in charge of some entry-level operational area in an office or plant, right where many of us women are most likely to bump up against them. The successful men, just like the successful women, move on to the next level. But the ones who are short of people skills get frozen where they are. The reality is that men who behave inhumanely toward their subordinates are those who stall out early on the career ladder. As a result, they are clustered around lower management levels, pretty close to where they started.

Most of us women, therefore, are supervised by males in our early, entry-level, start-at-the-bottom jobs, and those males, by definition, are often the ones who didn't make it. They're cranky, and they take it out on us. They're the "secretary bashers" who burn out three secretaries a year. They're compensating for their own lack of competitive success.

The point is, that's not the way *really* successful men behave. I've met lots of them. Although most are admirable, adult role models of the Lee Iacocca type, a few have impressed me as dreadful people. So, of course, the expression "The bigger they are, the nicer they are" is somewhat of an overgeneralization.

As a general principle, however, it's true that the person, male or female, who's made it to the top behaves better toward subordinates, associates, and customers than do some of the male, first-line supervisors with whom so many of us have experience. In fact, the top executives of our top corporations tend to display qualities such as compassion and concern for their employees, which some people would classify as feminine virtues. I contend, in fact, that those "feminine" virtues are *essential* for any person, regardless of sex, who plans to rise to the top. They're *in addition* to all those so-called masculine qualities of toughness and assertiveness and so on that are also necessary to business success.

I've seldom met a senior male executive at a big company who was not mentally and emotionally tough, for example. But most of them were also fair, as far as I could tell. They weren't the fascist bullies that most women seem to think of when they talk about the way men act in business. As a result of their toughness, some of the top men I've met are feared. As a result of their fairness, some of them are loved.

But whenever they possess both characteristics, they are *respected*.

Any woman who's concerned that business might tempt her to "act like a man," then, might want to reconsider. Maybe the error of letting your femininity be threatened is really committed by the woman who tries to act "macho." In other words, it's true that being aggressive and combative and pugnacious and all those other "macho" behaviors will detract from your appeal as a woman. However, if you're honest about it, you'll have to conclude that they're behaviors that detract from a man's appeal, too. They're behaviors that have no place in business in any event.

Don't limit your rise in business because you think you have to sacrifice your femininity. Your femininity is *not* one of the prices you have to pay for success in business.

The Working Wounded

*W*hy is the American Success Cult that Thomas Pike and William Proctor talked about so widespread today? I would like to present what I feel may be one of the largest contributing factors.

I have read statistics that over 90 percent (as high as 98 percent) of our families today are dysfunctional. Many times the Hero emerges from the dysfunctional family. The Hero (often the firstborn) is the child who figures out that there's something wrong with his or her family and tries to save the family face by being good and overachieving in her efforts to make her family appear normal. The role she plays in her family is often repeated as she makes her way into the workplace. Work then becomes another way to avoid or control the pain. I believe that many members of the American Success Cult are working wounded.

I hope this chapter from No Longer the Hero may bring some understanding and help—either to you or someone you know. It is time for our generation to heal our working wounded.

Nancy LeSourd
No Longer the Hero

When our Hero enters the workforce, he carries with him the wounds of his childhood. The survival techniques that served to protect him as a child continue to operate as he selects a career, engages in meaningful work, and relates to others in that environment. As a result, he is troubled. He is never satisfied—either with his personal performance or his choice of work.

Something just isn't quite right, but it may be difficult for him to define. After all, our Hero's overachievement in school translates well in the workplace. Often he is a very responsible, dependable, and accomplished worker. Society applauds competition and achievement, and the Hero's success is rewarded by promotions, salary, and prestige. Any success he achieves, however, is often bittersweet. He feels driven to perform but unable to enjoy the benefits of his hard work. Compliments are downplayed; criticisms replayed.

Job satisfaction is elusive. He feels constricted in various job situations, often changing positions or jobs frequently. There is an uneasiness with coworkers. He is often driven by perfectionism. He is one of the working wounded with whom we associate daily. He may even be one of us.

Work was intended by God to be deeply satisfying. God was able to stand back from His endeavors, evaluate them, and find pleasure in them. Adam and Eve, before the Fall, were given a work assignment: the commission to tend the Garden. "The Lord God took the man and put him in the garden of Eden to tend and keep it" (Gen. 2:15). It was only after the fall that work and sweat became related (3:17–19).

Why, then, is work so often a difficult place for us to experience satisfaction? This is a perennial question for many, but even more so for the adults from dysfunctional homes. We seem to keep repeating negative patterns over and over. We move on to different jobs, different cities, different careers, and yet the same problems plague us in the workplace. What are we doing wrong? Where is that ability to stand back from our work and pronounce it good? Where is our ability to rest from our work?

Overwork: The Hero's Acceptable Addiction

When our Hero was a child, he learned especially during the school years that achievement provided two important requirements for his survival. First, it deflected attention away from the family problem and onto his accomplishments. For a while, at least, the family appeared happy and proud. Often, if the dysfunctional parent placed a high value on education or success, this was the only time he received any affirmation or validation from that parent.

Second, achievement provided a way to protect the family secret. Perhaps no one will suspect that there is anything wrong with his family if he just achieves enough success in his school or social setting to cause others to assume he comes from a loving, nurturing environment. After all, if he can accomplish this or that feat, then the stock he comes from can't be all bad, can it?

These motivations, unrecognized and unchanged, compel the Hero just as forcefully when he enters the workforce. He overachieves there as well, often becoming driven. Particularly, in the late twenties and thirties, as psychological defense mechanisms such as repression begin to lose their ability to keep childhood pain down, he may work to dull the pain of what he is really feeling. He is troubled, but denies the pain by throwing himself into his work.

It's round and round the carousel, grabbing for brass ring after brass ring. One achievement mastered, it's on to the next. No time to sit back and enjoy the accomplishment. No time to dream and let creative intellect pursue perhaps uncharted territory. The Hero needs defined goals, outlining his path to success. Rung after rung he climbs the ladder, each step a forerunner to the next, the never-ending staircase to success.

Catch your breath, perhaps. Evaluate the next step, perhaps. But ever onward, ever upwards goes our Hero. For what? What is he looking for? What does he need so desperately from his work?

My first teaching job was at a small Catholic high school in the Boston area. The demands by the administration for teacher involvement in extracurricular activities were very minimal. I could have been home each day by 3:00 P.M. Instead, in the two years I was there, I created a joint American history/American literature teaching program, became Social Studies department chairman and revamped the entire curriculum, started a scholarship award program for the study of Congress, and coached the cheerleaders. I was also in my final coursework and completion of my thesis for my master's degree. If that were not enough, I had a burden for these kids to have a personal relationship with Jesus Christ, so I began a Young Life club at the school, creating a need for fifteen to twenty more hours a week in planning club activities, meeting with leaders, and contact work with kids.

My next teaching job required overinvolvement from the beginning; it was at a boarding school. The demands on a boarding school teacher are high by nature: teaching, coaching, and living in a dorm provide a round-the-clock work environment.

Then it was on to Georgetown law school. I chose a highly competitive, highly expensive school, necessitating long hours of study and many hours of outside work to pay bills. Again, overwork was no stranger. The old adage about law school is true, "The first year they scare you to death; the second year they work you to death; and the third year they bore you to death." The first two years were jam-packed. Thirty to forty hours of work at a law firm were crammed into non-class hours. Law review and litigation clinic hours ate up more time. Then, of course, my outside interest in religious freedom cases and involvement with the Christian Legal Society needed their measure of time.

By the third year, a time to relax perhaps and be "bored to death," I was heavily in debt. I pumped up my work hours as a law clerk, often spending the night at the firm to complete a project. I was at Georgetown Law Center by 5 or 6 A.M. and at the library or work until midnight most nights. I thought nothing of this. After all, it's law school—the paper chase years.

The law firm experience is set up to capitalize on this pattern of long hours and hard work in law school. As an associate in a law firm, you must work long hours for a number of years to demonstrate a commitment to the firm if you want a chance for partnership. With the increased financial pressures on firms in the eighties to offer larger salaries to young associates, this translates into 2,000-plus billable hours per year, which makes it difficult to maintain a personal life as well.

Why did I do this? Why did I select a career that blatantly puts such a premium on hard work and long hours? Why did I take a reasonable teaching job and fill it with unreasonable hours and multiple projects?

Dr. Bryan E. Robinson has called work the "drug of choice" for many adult children from chemically dependent and dysfunctional homes.[2] He claims that excessive work anesthetizes the childhood pain and yet can create many of the same patterns of a drug- or alcohol-addicted person. Many times I have thrown myself into my work to seek stability when my personal relationships felt out of control. I could become self-absorbed in work that society or my church pronounced worthwhile—all the time running as fast as possible from my inner pain. Being away from work can make you feel uneasy. What do you do with yourself? Saturdays, if not spent at work, were certainly not spent at play. Projects! Weekends were times to see how many things I could cross off of my "to do" list.

Many times Heroes, especially those from alcoholic homes, pride themselves on not succumbing to alcohol or drugs like their parents or siblings. More insidious, however, is becoming dependent on work to create your sense of self-worth and to mask the pain. Like an addictive agent, however, this kind of working may create more problems for the worker than it solves:

> The irony of the disease is that work addicts suffer more problems on the job than their colleagues. Work addicts are generally not team players and often have difficulty cooperatively problem-solving, negotiating, and compromising. Because they are over-invested in their work, they tend to suffer extreme stress and burnout, and subsequently their efficiency declines.[3]

The twenties and thirties are years often spent building up one's career, trying out different career paths, and working hard. Why should that be any different for the Hero? The two central issues for the Hero in evaluating whether he is overworking are his motivations and balance. The Hero finds himself running from one project to the next, even one job to the next. Is his hard work primarily motivated by enjoyment of what he does? Is he called to that work? Or is he driven? The Hero should also look at the question of balance. Hard work is not to be condemned. Hard work, to the exclusion of the time spent alone, with God, or with others, should be examined, however. If the Hero spends inordinate amounts of time in the workplace because it becomes a place to hide from oneself and others, then it is not healthy. Busyness becomes a catch word for avoiding relationships. "Wish I could join you, but I have to finish this project." "Sorry, son, I know I said I would come to your baseball game, but this emergency came up." "Honey, we'll celebrate our anniversary next month; it's just a bad time at work right now." Adult children were such loners as children, never feeling like we fit in no matter how successful we appeared, it is easy to duplicate this pattern in adult life. It feels so right, so comfortable.

Douglas LaBier, author of *Modern Madness* and a psychotherapist whose practice is made up of patients whom he calls "troubled winners," notes that oftentimes a spiritual vacuum is created as individuals make compromises for success in their careers: "I found that the drive for success—and its criteria of money, power and prestige —exists alongside a parallel, but less visible, drive for increased fulfillment and meaning from work."[4] He hints that meaningful work, such as an investment banker who can use his skills to help develop low-cost housing, is the panacea to this spiritual vacuum. However, Pascal noted that each of us has a God-shaped vacuum in our hearts, and we have been scurrying around trying to fill that aching void.

For the Hero who has developed a self-identity circumscribed by his achievements, it can be very easy to allow success, work, and achievements to become an idol. Meaningful work, even that which advances the causes of Christ such as ministry, is only an attempt to fill this aching void. Our Hero, who so desperately needs to know he matters—to his father or mother, to his heavenly Father, to himself— drives himself to achieve. Until he has found his call first in the love of God for him and then in expressing his unique gifts and talents in the professional realm, he will be frustrated. Done backwards—seeking affirmation of self and validation of worth by God through his work—his accomplishments become less and less fulfilling. He begins to recognize how inadequate success is to provide him the love and wholeness he has yearned for his whole life.

What are some of the characteristics of the working wounded? How can you know if unresolved childhood issues are a part of your current struggles in your job?

Burnout

Many adults from dysfunctional homes suffer from periodic burnout. Their inability to express their frustrations and their high level of intensive work combine to produce depression and burnout. Much has been written on corporate burnout as experts review the eighties' focus on work to the exclusion of other relationships. Recently, *USA Today* cited the high employer costs of burnout. Employers were surprised to learn that one of the main reasons for rising health care costs is mental health expenditures. The National Institute of Mental Health estimates 5.8 percent of Americans suffer from depression and burnout, costing more than $27 billion in lost productivity, $17 billion just from lost workdays.[5] Douglas LaBier found in his research that 45 percent of career professionals suffer from work-related emotional problems, such as stress, burnout, malaise, and value conflicts.[6]

Dr. Herbert J. Freudenberger, in his book *Burn-out: The High Cost of High Achievement,* defined burnout as wearing oneself out by excessively striving to reach some unrealistic expectation imposed by oneself or by the values of society.[7] As a child, our Hero learned to emphasize his capacity for achievement and activity to receive the attention or love he needed. He also learned that his accomplishments deflected family pain, at least temporarily. When he enters the workforce, he carries these patterns of relating to the task at hand into his work. Hardly ever questioning the wisdom of piling yet another responsibility on his already full plate, the Hero manages to draw from within the ability to sustain yet another commitment. As typical with the Hero, he will usually do all things quite well.

Heroes have an enormous capacity to handle many things at once, often amazing friends and coworkers with their abilities. However, this energetic approach to all of life may be a facade. When the burden of sustaining this facade becomes too unbearable, the Hero can face a burnout. Burnouts most often occur in the workplace, but they can occur in the home as well. The Hero typically will take on more and more responsibility for the home and family as well. He will care for home and hearth, managing the home corporation and its attendant organizational and financial responsibilities, as well as the very important interpersonal needs. Rush Susie to swim practice and then drop Jimmy off at his soccer game. Swing by the grocery store. Don't forget Aunt Ellen's birthday card. Tonight is family night; have you planned that game yet? Stop by the gas station, the dry cleaners, the photo shop. Got to get these pictures in the album by Saturday when Grandma gets here.

Another time to observe this overcommitment is at Christmas. Typically a season of many activities, our Hero goes into high gear. Why? More than likely, holidays were a tense time in his childhood home. When he has his own family, these holiday periods are imbued with larger-than-life expectations. Everything must be perfect. Cookies must be homemade. The home must be decorated splendidly, inside and out. Christmas cards written. Activities planned. Parties attended and given. The presents must be perfectly selected for each family member and tied up in ribbons and bows. He races around throwing all of these responsibilities into his already overscheduled mix of duties. By the first of the year, he is depressed. He is burned out.

Dr. Freudenberger notes that not every personality type experiences burnout. Typically burnout occurs in "dynamic, charismatic, goal-oriented men and women or determined idealists who want their marriages to be the best, their work records to be outstanding, their children to shine, their community to be better."[8] When we look to our work—whether in or out of the home—to sustain our vision of an ideal family and to make up for a lost childhood, we suffer. Not only do we suffer burnout, but we suffer repeated disappointment. No job, no amount of effort placed in our career success, no solicitation from our current family is going to make up for the past. The past must be healed for the present to be freely lived.

A burnout in work, like a failed relationship, however, may be just what the Hero needs to shake up his patterns enough to ask significant questions. It is only in asking the questions of why self-destructive patterns continue to exist that one can get beyond the seeming failure of his coping mechanisms to the root childhood issues. Seven questions we need to be asking are: Am I always trying to be safe? Do I tend to be rigid? Do I tend to try to flee rather than fight? Do I tend to avoid conflict? Do I prefer working alone? Do I tend to avoid criticism and reject praise? Am I able to take a break?

1. Am I Always Trying to Be Safe? I have been drawn to friends who take risks when it comes to work. One friend thought nothing of taking her medical skills from the hospitals in Boston to the Cambodian refugee camps in Thailand. Another started his own law firm in Manhattan. Another friend left a thriving legal practice to manage a struggling publishing company. When I left teaching to go to law school, you might think that I, too, was taking a risk. Underlying this change, however, was my great need for safety.

One thing I knew I did well was academics. I rolled right out of college into graduate school because I knew I could succeed there. Later, when I was trying to determine what track to take after teaching high school for five years, I looked at three avenues—school, school, or school. I examined a graduate program in counseling at a seminary, a doctorate in education, and law school.

Why didn't I look at a variety of new job options? Why did I return to school instead? I knew I could succeed at school, and if I was to embark on a new endeavor, I would learn the skills for that through my safe haven. No need to maximize any chance for failure.

One of the hazards of growing up as the Hero is that success comes with such a high level of expectation for what it can do for family harmony that you dare not engage in suspect activities—those with a possibility of failure. Rather than try new avenues of work, the Hero may cling tenaciously to those jobs in which he can do well, even if it is limiting his current growth. He may stay in a job that has predictable, safe requirements long past the time that job has provided him any challenge and stimulation. Dr. Patrick Gannon, clinical psychologist, observed that many survivors are in jobs that fit their fears and not their talents.[9] Safety, even predictability, is what the Hero seeks.

2. Do I Tend to Be Rigid? However, this predictability can lead to rigidity in an adult from a dysfunctional home and create a problem in the workplace. The needs of most businesses require individuals to be open to change, willing to learn new skills, and adapt to new programs. A person seeking predictability and safety can exhibit an extraordinary amount of resistance to change. A new computer program is introduced. Four of the employees are interested in learning the new software; two sit stone-faced, arms crossed as the supervisor explains the new program. They are not reacting to the computer program; they haven't even tried it yet. Instead, they are reacting to change.

The business has hit a down period. To avoid having to downsize, the company streamlines some procedures that will make the work more efficient. The end result should be to protect everyone's job. However, a number of the employees are subtly sabotaging these procedures. They know that they could lose their position if the company has to downsize, but they just can't seem to accept these new methods.

Rigidity also works against creativity. Effective problem-solving requires an openness to discussion, an expansion of possibilities, and objective evaluation. When one of our working wounded gets involved in problem-solving, he may view any evaluation of his avenue of expertise or sphere of authority as a threat to his self-worth. He may limit the discussion of possibilities because he seeks closure, predictability, certainty. He may also be unable to evaluate objectively the various possibilities. His agenda becomes primary, and his need for control can cause him to steer discussion, either overtly or indirectly, away from objective evaluation.

3. Do I Tend to Try to Flee Rather Than Fight? Ever since I was a little girl, I wanted to be a lawyer. Both grandfathers had been lawyers. My parents were both lawyers. As the eldest, I loved arguing my case for greater expansion of childhood privileges, such as staying up later. Extremely idealistic, I was drawn toward politics and the

chance to change society. It appeared to me that it was the lawyer/
legislator who was best equipped for that. But when my mother died,
my dreams died.

I determined to make a radical shift in the direction my life was
taking. Up to now it strongly paralleled my mother's life. So, put the
brakes on my career drive, and surely then I wouldn't be quite like
her. I squelched the desire to take the law school admission test with
the rest of my college classmates. "I know," I thought. "I'll be an
American history teacher. I'll help high school students learn about
the laws of our land instead."

So I escaped into the safety of a teaching position, which would
provide meaningful work, I thought, while protecting me from any
similarities with my mother. I literally hid out in the teaching field for
five years, thinking that this decisive action on my part cut any tie I
might have to my mother's life.

Adults from dysfunctional homes may find that they have fled
into a career rather than chosen a specific field. It may not be a
conscious decision, as mine was, but it will be driven by a need to
protect themselves from what they perceive as possible harm. Some
adults select careers in the same way they discovered hiding places
as children. They find a comfortable, womb-like place to earn a
living. It may be as subtle as investing yourself in a job that requires
minimal effort from you so that you can be assured of success or
discovering an insular environment for anonymity, such as the government or a large corporation.

Flight-or-fight responses to stress at work have been documented
by numerous organizational behavior analysts. Both these underlying
issues were present in the Hero's childhood. When the family got too
crazy, the Hero would go into high gear trying to order the circumstances of the family so that the chaos was manageable. His intense
need to control both circumstances and people later in life can be a
pattern created by the conditioned reflex to the chaos and unpre-
dictability of his childhood life. The other conditioned survival response, flight, caused him to escape into fantasy or activity to cope
with the family problems.

When he enters the workforce and confronts job stress, his tendency is to respond with the same two conditioned responses, particularly if the job stress is prolonged and seemingly unrelenting. The
Hero may exhibit a flight response through (1) conflict avoidance or
(2) leaving the position or the job. Instead of fleeing, the Hero may
fight the source of the stress by trying to control his environment,

assignments, or personnel or by revamping the organization. The method he uses depends on how much latitude he has within the scope of his authority to effect those changes.[10]

4. Do I Tend to Avoid Conflict? An adult from a dysfunctional home has spent a lifetime in conflict avoidance. This pattern may follow him into the workplace. Rather than confront a recalcitrant employee or coworker, he may avoid them. He may also attempt to avoid conflict by restructuring his work environment so that his interaction with those individuals is minimal. Why, I even structured my entire legal career to avoid conflict!

I had opportunities when I joined my firm after law school to pursue litigation in administrative agencies and federal courts as well as corporate work with nonprofit corporations. The combatant nature of most litigious proceedings was too close to home for me. Word wars. I had had enough of that as a child. I began subtly seeking more and more assignments in the nonprofit and preventive law side of the firm so that I could say, "Sorry, I've got more than I can handle right now" when the litigators came by my office seeking assistance.

Nonprofit corporations, needing counsel on various business or ministry issues—that's for me. Working to solve problems. Working together to advance their ministry objectives through the application of legal principles. Preventive law—establishing policies, procedures, and strategies that could minimize or prevent legal problems and conflicts from arising—was my chosen field. This felt right. No need to wage war here. Leave that to the litigators.

One of the most difficult areas in conflict avoidance is asking for a promotion or a raise. Issues of worth surround that request ordinarily, but for an adult from a dysfunctional home, it is easier to continue producing rather than rock the boat. This can create a potential for abuse. Patrick Gannon, in *Soul Survivors: A New Beginning for Adults Abused as Children,* found that

> many of you who have continued the caretaker role into adult life may have found that applying the same high control, problem-solving acumen used to survive your family ordeal has made you a manager's dream. You are used to hardship, so no task is too difficult. There is less fear of being abused, although the possibility for exploitation may exist in not being fairly compensated for all you do.[11]

5. Do I Prefer Working Alone? Adults from dysfunctional homes are more comfortable working alone, and they typically have little skill in working together to resolve problems or accomplish an objective. They rarely, if ever, saw effective teamwork modeled in their homes. Yet teamwork is necessary in most businesses.

> *When you find yourself unable to work with others when necessary, you may be reacting to unresolved childhood issues.*

The Hero deals with this dilemma most often by avoiding businesses or career opportunities that require much teamwork. He is used to being a lone ranger and yet in so doing, accomplishing a great deal. He feels more comfortable working alone. After all, he can count on himself. The Hero may choose a field that allows him to work alone or that allows him a great deal of independence and autonomy. Instructors, doctors, lawyers, accountants, writers, editors, entrepreneurs all can work in an independent fashion.

I spent five years as a high school teacher thoroughly at peace in the classroom—my domain. Here I had total control and authority over all that was to transpire in six fifty-minute segments each day. I could plan out the course and each day's lessons. I executed those plans and I, alone, was responsible for the outcome of my efforts.

Law is not that much different. It requires long hours of solitude in work. Pouring over documents, reviewing cases, planning strategies are often done alone. Here, too, you could easily lose yourself in lone ranger thinking.

Fortunately, for me, I joined a small firm where my growth as a lawyer could take on a more apprentice-like relationship. I could be "teamed-up" with a more experienced, talented lawyer and work together on client matters. I often chafed at the rub that comes from that kind of close working relationship, but God was continuing to chip away at this particular aspect of my childhood patterns.

Working alone or independently is not a negative pattern in and of itself. However, when you find yourself unable to work with others when necessary, you may be reacting to unresolved childhood issues. Cooperative thinking, strategizing, and problem-solving are necessary components of any business. If the Hero is freed to operate as a part of a team, he can bring his extraordinary abilities and achievements to bear on the problem.

6. Do I Tend to Avoid Criticism and Reject Praise? No one, I repeat, no one is harder on himself than the Hero. Due to his proclivity for assuming blame, his low self-esteem, and his incredibly high, almost unachievable standards, he is constantly berating himself for average performance. He must be the best. His work product must be outstanding.

So what happens when his work is criticized? Often the Hero will be unable to view his performance objectively. His personality and self-esteem have become so entwined with his work product that criticism of the product is taken as a condemnation of himself as a person. Emotions may well up as he hears a negative report. Inside he is churning. "How could you have made that mistake? You're so stupid. Don't ever let that happen again." The supervisor or boss giving the criticism may be even-handed, temperate, and encouraging in his approach to the review. No matter. The Hero will remember every comment and find twenty more reasons for self-flagellation.

The Hero could not afford to make a mistake in childhood. He had to be excellent at whatever he did. He must be the very best, but he is rarely pleased with his accomplishments. Just try praising him for a job well done and see what happens. "Thank you, but it was really nothing." "Well, I wanted to polish that last section but there just wasn't time." "Thanks, but if I'd had another day, I'm sure the results would have been better."

Praise makes the Hero uncomfortable for several reasons. First, there is a basic sense that the praise is not deserved. After all, even though he may be receiving praise for this particular project, he knows it was not up to his high standards. He feels as though he has defrauded the praise-giver. Second, he is afraid he will be found out. If this praise-giver only knew how far short the Hero fell from his own standards, he would not be offering these accolades. Third, the Hero distrusts the praise-giver, questioning his ulterior motives. He spent his childhood in heightened alert, trying to figure out what was going on in the family. He maintains the same vigilance now, questioning the intentions of each person he must interact with, trying to evaluate that person's ability to help or hurt him.

Most importantly, we need to learn how to praise our own work.

꧁꧂

Learning to evaluate one's work is a difficult task for Heroes. So much of our self-worth is tied up in our activity at work, and yet it is so easy for us to condemn the work of our hands. We need to take our lumps, sure, and learn how to evaluate and incorporate criticism of our work. But even more difficult for us, we need to learn to accept praise—to accept our worthiness of praise. Most importantly, we need to learn how to praise our own work.

God Himself stood back from His work and paid Himself a compliment. He created day and night, oceans and land, and then He took a break and praised Himself. It was "good," He said. He created stars, the sun and moon, trees, and vegetation. Then He took another break, took a look at His work, and complimented Himself again. It, too, was good. He then created the birds and animals and took yet another break. Again, He proclaimed His work, "good." When He created man, He stepped back again, surveyed His handiwork and proclaimed it "very good." When our childhood issues are resolved, we can learn to practice this kind of evaluation of our work and in unabashed enthusiasm, praise it as "good" and "very good."

7. Am I Able to Take a Break? There is a saying that the law is a jealous mistress. Many careers have time-pressure demands and ongoing production requirements. We get busier and busier and feel good about it. The work week, with its frenetic activity, keeps us pumped up. This adrenaline high of meeting deadlines, dispensing advice, and producing results has kept us moving during the week. When the weekend comes, without work, we crash. We feel depressed if we are not accomplishing something. If not work, then some personal project.

There is a principle in the Sabbath rest. Even God purposefully refrained from working! If He needs to take a break, then surely, we might consider it. When we grew up, we filled the anxious moments of our home life with activity, diverting our attention from the pain of our families. In adulthood, we continue to deal with our anxieties by becoming operational. These patterns remain established, unless we consciously work to interrupt them.

There is a principle in the Sabbath rest. Even God purposefully refrained from working!

When we begin to set limits on our involvement in the work-place, we might feel anxious and attempt to fill up our time with activity in some other sphere. Here is where a close accountability partner can help us be honest with our use of time. When we lay our schedules before him or her and let them ask the scrutinizing questions, we come out of denial and face squarely our stewardship of our time and the motivations for our activity. Once we establish reasonable limits, we are going to need help to stay within them. We easily rationalize a few hours of work here or there, and by the end of the week, we have overworked once again.

Intense Loyalty

What happens to the Hero when he is in a destructive work environment? He stays. The Hero has amazing staying power, despite negative circumstances. When he was a child, he kept on producing those A's and honors, even though his family situation never changed. The transient interludes of peace in the family war were reward enough. When he gets into a negative work situation, he lacks the ability to evaluate when to move on. Perhaps this next project or program will be the one that makes the difference. His loyalty to the organization may keep him in a negative situation long past the time to move on.

Enjoying Success

Nothing the Hero accomplishes is ever good enough. He judges himself and his work product without mercy. His standards of excellence are tilted toward perfection, and he will demand nothing but his best. Yet he never quite seems satisfied with his work product.

There is a high cost to the aspirations that drive us. Because satisfaction of a job well-done is seldom enjoyed for any length of time, we continue to seek that which will deeply satisfy us. We set the next goal for success and soak it in high expectations. That then gives us something to shoot for, a new goal that, once reached, may fill up that aching void in our lives. When we arrive there, however, and accomplish that next level of success, we may find that we feel slightly depressed, perhaps even displaced:

> . . . An uncomfortable listlessness overtakes them. They no longer feel rooted or involved, even in situations that were so vital for them before. . . . When people paint grandiose pictures for themselves of what it's going to be like on the next plateau, more often than not what they've envisioned doesn't materialize. Not because they don't reach the plateau. They do. But once they're there, the scenery isn't too different from the scenery lower down, and disenchantment begins to set in.[12]

If this listlessness and disenchantment leads us to pursue yet another rung of the ladder, another plateau, we will continue to be stuck in a self-defeating pattern despite our obvious successes and achievements. If there comes a point, however, that we become disenchanted with the emptiness of success piled upon success, we may discover that God intended more for us and, as a result, more for our work than we could ever have imagined. Remember, work was intended to be a part of the Garden of Eden—a wondrous experience of interacting with creation and the Creator:

Super-responsibility on the Job

When we have grown up in dysfunctional homes, we learned patterns of undertaking tremendous responsibility for others' actions and behaviors. We were there to rush in and rescue when needed. We were also there to take the blame for things that were not really our fault.

When we arrive in the workplace, there is also a tendency to blame ourselves for everything—giving ourselves little room for growth and change through mistakes. If you make a mistake in judgment or performance, you beat yourself up forever. "I'm sorry" becomes a constant buzzphrase. We also assume blame for failures at work that aren't our fault.

It is easy for us to assume blame for things that are not within our realm of responsibility. We have done it for years. We took responsibility for our parents' alcoholism or dysfunction. We believed the lie that if only we could do something different, then Mom or Dad would be okay. Maybe if we were good enough, our parents wouldn't fight. Now as adults, this burden of super-responsibility follows us into our relationships and into the workplace.

This is most often demonstrated by our enabling behaviors. We often play the role of the martyr, picking up the slack for inefficiency or nonproductivity elsewhere. "I'll just do it myself" becomes our frequent response. When we delegate a task to another, we rarely let it go. We manage our work by holding it close. We delegate but we take it back. Or if we manage to let another have the assignment, we may hover over them with the expectation that we will have to step in and rescue the project. Used to the many broken promises of our parents, we distrust a coworker's commitment to follow through on a project, and we tend to that individual in often suffocating ways. Yet in our apparently super-responsible way, we limit the growth of our employees or coworkers. They never have to face the consequences of work poorly done or not done on time if we are always swooping in to rescue the project. We say we do this for the sake of the firm or the client, but are we really more motivated by our need to bear the burden for a job well-done?

The Workplace as Home

You and Your Boss

Does your place of work surprisingly mirror your childhood home? Do the relationships you have with a boss or coworkers remind you of how you related to your parents as a child? Eliza Collins, a psychotherapist with the Center for Executive Development in Cambridge, Massachusetts, contends that people tend to view their bosses as they did their parents and attempt to recreate their parent-child relationship in their boss-employee relationship.[13]

Janet Woititz, in her book *Home Away From Home: The Art of Self-Sabotage*, examines what happens when Adult Children of Alcoholics enter the workplace. She notes that an ACOA boss, who operates out of unresolved childhood issues, has an extraordinary need to control, which can result in a demand for compliance. He will often be perfectionistic and will tend to micromanage. He finds it difficult to trust that others will do what they have agreed to do or that they will do it in a manner sufficiently acceptable to him.[14]

What happens to the Hero when he goes to work and has a boss like this, a boss like his dysfunctional parent in many ways? This negative work combination plays right into his self-defeating patterns. The two will feed off of each other. He will gear up, overwork, and overachieve, attempting to get the approval of this boss. The boss's unmet needs will make it difficult for him to grant that approval. Unless the Hero has learned to stand back from his work and objectively praise himself for a job well-done from time to time, he will become increasingly discouraged. Isn't anything he does good enough? Yes, it probably is, but not if his only way of evaluating that is through the eyes of such a boss.

You and Your Subordinates

What if you are the boss? Does your high need for control and your inability to trust others create problems for you in working with employees? What if you, an adult from a dysfunctional home, are boss to employees who are also from dysfunctional homes?

In a recent *Personnel Journal* article, Dr. Michael Diamond and Dr. Seth Allcorn argued that "a better understanding of the often dramatic influence unconscious motives have on organizational behavior has become a managerial imperative."[15] In times of stress at work, perfectionistic bosses and self-effacing subordinates are caught in a double bind. The subordinates respond to stressful events by blaming themselves because they feel worthless. Perfectionistic supervisors have such high standards of excellence that they are able to blame subordinates for their inability to meet them.[16]

Manfred F. R. Kets de Vries and Danny Miller, both professors in graduate business degree programs, postulate in their book *The Neurotic Organization* that much of what has been written about dysfunctional families is directly relevant to superior/subordinate relationships in organizations.[17] The authors found that subordinates who idealize superiors are often looking for that parental approval they never had as children:

> They have faith and confidence in the leader, whom they do their very best to please. They are highly motivated and study the boss very carefully to see what they can learn in order to improve their own performance. . . . They are prone to be very flattered by a few words of praise from the leader and devastated by the mildest of reprimands. They thus become extremely dependent on the leader and very easy to control and manipulate.[18]

When the Hero is a boss and has unresolved childhood issues, he may find he attracts these types of employees. He is able to dominate them, fulfilling his own deep need for control. However, this results in a negative impact on the organization. This type of worker, although an excellent worker, has diminished independence and judgments. The employee's ability to be creative and to challenge assumptions is overshadowed by the strong desire to please his boss.[19]

Drs. Diamond and Allcorn urge bosses to be aware of the existence of these types of destructive interaction patterns:

> It is the responsibility of senior executives to recognize the effect of their behavior on subordinates. They should never underestimate the symbolic role that they fulfill for the people with whom they interact.[20]

Be that as it may, Heroes are unlikely to recognize how their behavior impacts subordinates unless they have previously recognized that their behavior itself may be motivated by unresolved childhood pain.

Whether boss or employee, Heroes may continue to recreate their home environment in the workplace or be drawn to work situations that provide an opportunity to repeat their family role. However, if we can become aware of the ways we carry our family relationships into our work, we can begin to identify the patterns, find their root causes, and change our behavior. Until we do, our work may become increasingly frustrating. We may change jobs, or even careers, but note that uncannily the same difficulties seem to reappear. At the root of our self-defeating patterns at work is our tenacious reliance on childhood survival techniques. We must be willing to lay down these once potent defense weapons if we are to find true satisfaction in the expression of our God-given abilities in work.

Working with Your Working Mate

oes it sometimes feel that the load at home is unbalanced if both you and your spouse work at jobs? How can you get your husband to understand the pressure you feel to keep the house and family going while still working full-time or part-time? Once again, we'd like to give you some "working" tools for evaluating your situation; and then, we'll see if we can't help you and your husband work to balance the load.

Dave and Claudia Arp
The Marriage Track

If we only had more hours in our days, we could balance the two-job tightrope!" commented Ed and Katie Brown. This particular Marriage Alive Workshop, filled with two-career couples, was also filled with frustrations evidenced by Ed and Katie's comment.

Telling them that they had time—in fact, all the time there is—didn't solve their dilemma. However, that particular workshop session did help them come up with a workable plan. If you are among the 58 percent of marrieds who are trying to balance jobs outside the home, we hope this chapter will help you get a better handle on your two-job team and come up with a plan that works for you.[1]

You may think this chapter doesn't relate to you because you're not working outside the home. But if your five preschoolers—give or take a few kids—make an outside job look like a vacation don't skip this chapter! You, too, can benefit from looking closer at how you can work with your working mate.

Stop, and think of all the things we blame on time. How many times have you said:

"If I just had more time . . ."
"I'll have time for that when . . .
. . . the children grow up
. . . the summer comes
. . . the summer is over
. . . I meet this deadline or finish this project (for us, when we finish this book)."

May we suggest time is not the real culprit? Time really is no respecter of persons. It's impartial. We don't have more time each day than you do. Every single person on this earth has twenty-four hours every day—no more or no less! The real issues are how we manage our time and how we work together to balance our two-job team? To help you answer this question, it's time for a "time out" to take inventory!

If you arranged all your various responsibilities on a seesaw, putting yours on one end and your mate's on the other, how would your seesaw balance?

The first step in working with your working mate is to look at where you are and assess your real situation. To help you do just that, each of you make a list of your responsibilities outside the home and inside the home.

If you arranged all your various responsibilities on a seesaw, putting yours on one end and your mate's on the other, how would your seesaw balance? For instance, if one mate is working outside the home only part-time each week and the other is working a sixty-hour week, the one who is home part-time would need to balance the seesaw by carrying more of the load at home. But for now, let's assume you both have equal commitments outside the home. The important question is, "How are you pulling together as a team at home?"

In spite of many unrealistic stereotypes today—especially of the "macho males" who don't get their hands wet—the younger generation has one up on our age group. We are delighted to see our two married couples pulling together as teams as they wrestle with grad school, jobs, and busy schedules.

On the other hand, consider Ed and Katie. They are our vintage and grew up with stereotypes of men doing this and women doing that. The traditional roles worked well for them when their three kids were little and Katie chose to stay home and be a full-time mom. But halfway through the parenting years, their circumstances changed. Ed's company took an economic slide, and their finances suffered. Although she preferred to stay at home, Katie reluctantly took a teaching job to help meet expenses and begin saving for future educational needs.

This mid-course adjustment really didn't change Ed's routine very much at all. He still was working as hard as ever at his job and came home just as tired. Katie was a different story. Now five days a week she came home tired, had lesson plans to prepare for the next day, and also had all the jobs at home staring at her—the least of which was what were they going to have each night for dinner. Ed was understanding and didn't say much about the frozen dinners, but not having clean socks was a little too much for him. Tension began to build, and by the time Ed and Katie came to our marriage workshop, they needed help!

A light seemed to go on when Ed and Katie did the above exercise and looked at their home seesaw. It looked something like this:

Responsibilities at Home

Katie

1. Prepare meals
2. Grocery shop
3. Do laundry for family
4. Keep the house clean
5. Arrange for sitters
6. Help children with homework

Ed

1. Take care of the yard
2. Keep cars maintained
3. Keep family financial records

It was evident that Ed and Katie needed to make some adjustments. Ed's home responsibilities were important and took time, but he could accomplish them on the weekends. Katie's areas of responsibility were not as flexible and daily demanded more than she could give after a day of teaching school. They needed help in balancing home responsibilities.

Maybe you're in the same dilemma. If so, let us walk you through the exercise that helped Ed and Katie.

The first step is to list on a separate piece of paper all household jobs and responsibilities (like meal preparation, cleaning the house, laundry, helping children with homework, caring for the yard).

Look at the list together and decide what you like to do best and what you like to do least.

When we Arps did this exercise, we listed all the various jobs and chores and then went through the list together from the grid of who can do the job better. Claudia immediately conceded that Dave was the best bathroom cleaner in ten states! The brutal reality is that no one will choose or want to do some jobs! Compromise is an important part of the process, and don't forget creativity. Who *is* going to clean the bathroom? When no one immediately volunteers, it's time to brainstorm. List possibilities (Humor helps the process!).

Possible solution to dirty bathrooms:

1. Husband cleans bathroom.

2. Wife cleans bathroom.

3. Husband and wife rotate cleaning the bathroom.

4. Teach the children to clean bathroom.

5. Hire it done.

6. Don't use bathroom.

7. Make a chart and let each family member have a cleaning day.

8. Each person cleans the bathroom (tub, sink, etc.) after using it.

Remember, you are trying to attack the extra pressures of having a two-job team, instead of attacking each other. You are also looking for understanding. We can all handle stress better if just one other person understands how we feel. You can be that other person for your mate.

Once Ed and Katie did the exercise, Ed became more aware of the stress Katie was experiencing and the need for his increased involvement in the home. The solution to his "no clean socks dilemma" might be to wash them himself! But the mechanics of who does what are not as important as the philosophy of a team attacking the problem together.

Katie and Ed's children were school age and were recruited for jobs around the house. They were even assigned responsibility for the bathroom! Katie was tired of teaching when she arrived home in the afternoons and loved being creative in the kitchen. She invested in some new cookbooks for easy one-dish meals. She also pulled out the crockpot and with a little planning often had dinner on the way before she left for school in the morning. Ed began to monitor homework and help with special school assignments.

For the heavy jobs around the house, Katie and Ed had a cleaning service come in once a month. They also found a high school boy who loved yard work and did the routine mowing and mulching. Ed and Katie's seesaw may still go up and down, but on any given day it's much more balanced.

Till Debt Do Us Part

One point of contention in a two-career home is finances. One wife we know went to work, as Katie did, to help with financial difficulty. But this wife's working added to their financial tension. Listen to her story:

"When I went back to work, I thought I'd have some income of my own. But what actually happened is that it all went into the same pot. My husband won't tell me where we are financially, and it's driving me crazy. I'd be better off if I just had my own bank account and helped with our general expenses."

This couple needed to take some time and figure out how to work out their finances together. They needed to come up with a financial plan they both could agree to and to decide if separate accounting would help or hurt.

At different times in our marriage, we've handled the bank account issue in different ways. When we were first married, it was all we could do to keep up with one bank account. Then as our life became more complicated, we had separate accounts we were each responsible for. Dave's account covered things like house payments or rent, utilities and other monthly bills, savings, and insurance premiums. From Claudia's account, she paid for groceries, household items, and clothing. Together we decided what our basic budget should be and how much we wanted to save and to give to our church and to others. Later we added another account that we call our "special" account. Money in our special account is for giving to others and for special needs.

For us the real concern is not how many bank accounts we have (separate or joint) or even how much money we have, but that we have a workable financial plan that we both agree to. If you function best with separate accounts and it works for you, great!

It helps greatly to have defined financial goals. These should be goals that you mutually agree on. We remember when we bought our first house—today it would be hard to buy a car for the amount we paid for our first home—but for us, it was a huge goal to come up with a down payment. Claudia was a substitute teacher in a local high school, and we were able to save her paychecks toward our house down payment.

In setting financial goals and working hard together to achieve them, let us add one caution: It is possible to end up with all the things we would like to have, but no time to enjoy them. Working with our working mate can become slavery to maintaining all our possessions. We can have it all and actually have nothing.

Dr. M. Scott Peck, author of *The Road Less Traveled,* points out that a sign of maturity is the ability to delay gratification. Yet we live in an instant world—instant oatmeal, instant coffee, and instant credit. Continually we hear that we can have it all and have it right now. If you are bored and have the right credit card, you can whisk your mate off to a romantic island—no need to get babysitters (if you have children) or even pack. We are told to "Just do it!" Many problems in marriage could be lessened if we just learned to delay gratification!

We make no claims of being financial advisors. To be honest, we don't have it all together in this area, but we are working on it, so we can share with you some things that are helping us. One of the best and most practical books on finances is Ron Blue's *Managing Your Money*™. We highly recommend using this book as a basic guide. If you use a computer, another helpful tool is the program *Manage Your Money.*[2]

Other things we have tried that have helped us are:

1. From time to time keep a detailed record of each penny you spend. We have done this for up to five or six months. Then it is easy to evaluate where your money is going and to modify spending and saving patterns, which is not so easy, but possible.

2. Limit credit card spending to what you can pay off each month. If things are really tight, we try not to use credit cards. Somehow, it's just easier to justify buying with a credit card. We sometimes say "Well, I'll probably bring it back and it'll be easier to return if I charge it." One thing is sure—it will be easier to buy—but a month later the bill arrives.

3. Don't overlook the joy of giving. Several couples we know also have a special account at the bank. Each month they place a certain amount of money in that account, and from it they support their church and several missionaries and ministries.

4. Get in the habit of saving. We used to say we just couldn't afford to save. The truth is we can't afford not to save. How much we save is not as critical as developing the habit of saving. Consider choosing long-term goals—such as retirement and your children's education. Also choose short-term goals. If you have older children, you may want together to choose a family goal to work towards. For instance you might have a family garage sale to help finance a special family vacation.

Choose Your Own Lifestyle Carefully

Only you can decide this highly personal issue for your marriage team. But the two of you should make the decision together. To help you think through different issues, you may want to talk through what your necessities are. This will be different for each couple. A starting place in evaluating this question is to think back to when you first got married and compare your living standards then and now.

Write on a separate piece of paper two lists: "What we had when we first got married" and "What we have today." What is most important to you? Consider the following areas (by no means a comprehensive list). Give each a rating, like, 3 = very important; 2 = nice to have but not so important; or 1 = can live without it.

_____ House

_____ Car

_____ Household appliances (You may want to list and evaluate each individually.)

_____ Television

_____ VCR

_____ Stereo equipment

_____ Household help

_____ Vacations

_____ Eating out

_____ Entertainment, (movies, sports, etc.)

Other things may also be necessities, but are less tangible.

_____ Time with each other

_____ Time with children

_____ Time with friends

_____ Church

_____ Sports

_____ Community service

Life Involves Choices

One young family we know was continually struggling to meet house payments and other obligations. Before the children appeared, both worked, and they really had not felt a lot of financial stress. The wife wanted to stay home with their two young daughters, but economically it seemed impossible. After working through an exercise like the one above, they listed their priorities. Home ownership was great, but higher on their list was for one of them to be at home to love and nurture their young children.

What they did was brave. They sold their house and moved back into an apartment so Pat could stay home with their children. Tough choices await each of us. But the good news is that we do have choices. There is lots of room for creativity, and in today's world we need every bit of it!

What Will You Choose?

Some of us have more choices than others, but we all have to make choices. Katie went back to work to help provide for their family in a needy time. Another chose to pursue a career. Pat chose to stay home to nurture their preschoolers. No one can tell you what is right or wrong for you.

Whatever your situation, please, oh please, look for ways to make time for each other. If you both work outside the home, do it from a united front. You'll need all the communication and negotiating skills you can muster. You will continually need to evaluate your expectations and redefine your goals. Don't be like the couple who were going to build their relationship, but there just wasn't time. Raising five kids kept them busy, but in the empty nest, they still rarely saw each other. They were both in jobs that required traveling and weren't really aware of how disjointed their lives had become. One day they met accidentally in the Los Angeles Airport. Neither even knew the other was supposed to be in California! Just then the obvious hit them: We don't even know each other; we have homes, cars, boats, but we don't have an alive marriage. From that important turning point, they looked at their lives and decided it was time to make some changes; they are now working through their necessity list and eliminating some other things. It will take a lot of work and commitment, but they are on the right track!

We often hear, "We're doing it all for our kids—to give them advantages in life." A noted child psychologist on a TV morning program said one key to successful parenting is to spend half as much money on your kids and twice as much time! Let us expand and refocus this comment: The key to a growing, alive marriage is to spend half as much money on things and twice as much time with your mate! It's up to you to work together to chart your course.

PART SEVEN

I Am Growing Older

Keep Journeying On

MARCH 1918

> Youth longs and manhood strives, but age remembers,
> Sits by the raked-up ashes of the past
> And spreads its thin hands above the glowing embers
> That warm its shivering life-blood till the last.*

Those lines troubled me a great deal when I first read them. I was very young then, and I thought that everything I read in print was the truth. I didn't like it a little bit that the chief end of my life and the sole amusement of my old age should be remembering. Already there were some things in my memory that were not particularly pleasant to think about. I have since learned that few persons have such happy and successful lives that they would wish to spend years in just remembering.

One thing is certain, this melancholy old age will not come upon those who refuse to spend their time

---

* From "The Iron Gate," by Oliver Wendell Holmes.

indulging in such dreams of the past. Men and women may keep their life's blood warm by healthy exercise as long as they keep journeying on instead of sitting by the way trying to warm themselves over the ashes of remembrance.

Neither is it a good plan for people to keep telling themselves they are growing old. There is such a thing as a law of mental suggestion that makes the continual affirmation of a thing work toward its becoming an accomplished fact. Why keep suggesting old age until we take on its characteristics as a matter of course? There are things much more interesting to do than keeping tally of the years and watching for infirmities.

I know a woman who, when she saw her first gray hair, began to bewail the fact that she was growing old, and began to change her ways to suit her ideas of old age. She couldn't "wear bright colors anymore"; she was "too old." She must be more quiet now: "It was not becoming in an old person to be so merry." She had not "been feeling well lately," but she supposed she was "as well as could be expected of a person growing old," and so on and on.

I never lost the feeling that the years were passing swiftly and that old age was lying in wait for the youngest of us when in her company.

Of course, no one can really welcome the first gray hair or look upon the first wrinkles as beautiful, but even those things need not affect our happiness. There is no reason why we should not be merry as we grow older. If we learn to look on the bright side while we are young, those little wrinkles at the corners of the eyes will be "laughing wrinkles" instead of "crow's feet."

There is nothing in the passing of the years by itself to cause one to become melancholy. If they have been good years, then the more of them the better. If they have been bad years, be glad they are passed and expect the coming ones to be more to your liking.

Perhaps, after all, the poet whose verse I have quoted meant it as a warning that if we did not wish to come to that unlovely old age, we must keep on striving for ourselves and for others. There was no age limit set by the great poet when he wrote:

> Build thee more stately mansions, O my soul,
> As the swift seasons roll!*

It is certainly a pleasanter, more worthwhile occupation to keep on building than to be raking up the ashes of dead fires.

Laura Ingalls Wilder
Little House in the Ozarks

* From Oliver Wendell Holmes's "The Chambered Nautilus."

Middle-aged Women

It seems to be that no age group is free from the possibility of depression—not infants, toddlers, or adolescents; not new parents, the middle-aged, or the elderly. Although Especially for a Woman *has touched upon depression in younger ages, I want to discuss the causes of depression in women as they begin their journey through mid-life. Many of you reading this book will be young women or young mothers who cannot anticipate the onset of menopause or the empty nest. But anticipate it you must for it happens to all women. In this chapter from* Depression Hits Every Family, *I would like to tell you about my own experience with the depression of middle-age, as well share with you the wisdom that I gained as I worked my way through it.*

Dr. Grace Ketterman
Depression Hits Every Family

The older I become, the more difficult it is to define middle age! Life expectancy is now about seventy-five years, so middle age would begin at about thirty-five—give or take a little.

There is a drop in severe depression after thirty-five years of age as measured by the decline in suicide rates. However, the members of this age group experience a great deal of anxiety, worry, and mild depression. As they try to compete in the work force, establish a marriage, and raise young children, mature adults are often too busy to take stock of their lives.

When they fail to succeed as highly as they dreamed, when income and material possessions are not as magnificent as those of their friends, when children have problems, and when marriage is not, after all, very satisfying, depression is likely to result and take its toll.

In adults, as in children, depression has its taproot in the past. Careful research by several people makes it clear that adult depression is associated with disturbed parent-child relations. These disturbances include too little parental nurturing, support, and affection and too much parental rejection.[1]

The signs and symptoms of depression in this age group are essentially the same as those for young adults and new parents. The exact symptoms will vary from person to person depending on temperament, personality, habits of behaving and feeling, and genetic and biochemical factors (that is, factors that have been inherited and are influenced by body chemistry).

By the age of forty-five to fifty, the occurrence of depression increases due to facing the inevitability of aging. In women we call this the menopause, something we face with mixed emotions. It is a relief to be free of those annoying cycles of discomfort and irritability associated with menstruation. On the other hand, as wrinkles increase and the sagging of our bodies cannot be controlled with the best of exercises, we realize that we will never be physically what we once were.

Nature prepares us women for our menopause and its inevitability from the time of puberty. Men, on the contrary, have a tougher time accepting the reality of the physical limitations of aging, and many of them experience what has come to be known as *the male midlife crisis*. Unfortunately, at this time some men choose to leave their wives of many years in favor of younger women. So, what was originally a problem for middle-aged men becomes a problem for middle-aged women.

We must add the grief and depression of abandoned older women to our list of middle-aged problems. Many of them heroically rise to their situation. They return to school, find jobs, and reestablish their social lives with dignity and strength—a great cure for depression!

Depression in Middle Age

Various researchers in both Europe and the United States show that some 18 to 23 percent of women and 8 to 11 percent of men at some time in adult life have a serious bout with depression. Many of them suffer severely enough to require time in a hospital for treatment.[2] Actually, if we were able to study the silently depressed people who cover up their symptoms, I suspect those percentages would be doubled or tripled.

Depression in midlife is complex and has many factors that combine to cause it.

1. *The body is aging.* All sorts of wear and tear on the body result in quite obvious signs of aging. Many women are entering into the menopause. Wrinkles, gray hairs, and sagging body tissues can no longer be ignored. Even the best of creams, hormones, and vitamins will not deter the effects of the relentless march of time. In a culture that values youth and beauty, the helplessness and grief women feel at losing these may be intense and may result in depression.

2. *Dreams remain unfulfilled.* Many of us have dreams about life that date back to childhood. Someday we will be rich and philanthropic. Or we will be poor but dedicated to science or to mission work. Or we will be famous for our writing, painting, or musicianship. At least we will have a family, a comfortable home, and some secure investments for retirement.

I have not come across any studies that reveal how many people, by the age of forty, have reached their goals in life. My guess is that it would be few indeed. Realizing that they have not fulfilled their dreams by midlife can create the belief that they never will do so. This belief is most likely to precipitate the helplessness, hopelessness, and sadness that are major ingredients of depression.

3. *Children are becoming independent.* By forty, many couples have at least one child going off to college or out on his own or getting married. The fabled empty nest quickly becomes a reality at this age. And mothers seem to feel it more deeply than fathers, although both parents are aware of having spent too little time with the children. Fearful of having failed to teach them how to make it in life, parents feel that they have no time to recoup these losses.

4. *Many women experience serious midlife crises.* Women are uniquely conditioned by their physiological makeup and through childbearing to accept the inevitable limits of power and to be ma-

ture enough to function realistically within these limits. But that is not to say that they avoid crises.

5. *Lost opportunities become evident.* Several of my friends have not been able to be married and yet have yearned for that relationship. There are many reasons for such a fact, but for those who do not find their wish for marriage fulfilled, there is a strong sense of being deprived or even cheated.

As these women pass their fortieth birthdays, they realize that not only have they missed out on the intimacy of marriage, but they are not likely to have children either. To those who have longed for these experiences, losing out on them is markedly depressing.

6. *Divorce may dash one's hopes.* Over the past several years I have shared with several women their heartache over divorce. On some occasions it was the wife who sought the divorce, the only logical choice to her. Nevertheless, these women may experience deep depression as they face life alone and give up their dreams of an idyllic old age shared by a lifelong companion.

7. *Ideals and values may change.* With so many opportunities for a career and the pleasure of being independent, a number of women have chosen to stay single. For some this proves a wise choice and they find life rewarding. For others, the crises of the middle years create a new sense of loneliness and a longing for something else. They may regret their earlier decision and become depressed.

Actually, there is no category of women (or men) who are not vulnerable to a period of some degree of depression.

Women, in my experience, often become depressed during the menopause and grieve over their empty nests. But at least for some fifteen to twenty years, many of them begin to rediscover themselves. They often return to college, find jobs they once dreamed about, or become involved in worthwhile volunteer efforts.

Those who, tragically, lose husbands to other (and usually younger) women after several decades of marriage suffer multiplied anguish. When they are feeling their weakest and ugliest, losing that glorified "sex appeal," and wondering what they can possibly do with the rest of their lives, the men on whom they depended are gone.

I have shared the indescribable pain, anger, and helplessness these women experience. And I have marveled at the courage they find to rebuild their lives in successful ways. These examples remind me that there is always healing for grief and recovery from depression through courage, determination, and good decisions.

Influences from the Past

In the dramatic changes of midlife both the weaknesses and the strengths of the past will reemerge. How individuals handle this critical time will depend on the balance of these characteristics. Perhaps through the story of my own midlife stress I can exemplify this fact, and you may discover some facts about yourself. I believe each of us is uniquely an individual, but I have learned, to my comfort, that I have much in common with many others.

My early childhood was hardly blemished by sadness. I was the youngest of six children (three brothers and two sisters), well-loved by all of them, happy, and secure. A friend told me a few years ago that when he worked on the farm with my father, he enjoyed seeing me play. I loved to run to my dad and jump into his arms. One day Dad commented to this friend, "Ralph, she's the best example I know of abundant life!"

I was blessed with many relatives who were close to me when I was a child. I observed them having times of merriment and laughter, but I also saw various ones become morose, quiet, and irritable at times. Periodically, one aunt would come to visit, but she would hardly talk. Even now I can picture the drawn lines of her sad, depressed face.

During the stressful times of the economic depression of the 1930s, I observed my strong, teasing father, my adored hero, become withdrawn and silent; he had those same lines of care etched deeply in his face. I became quietly anxious over the change in him and hoped he would resume his teasing and laughter.

My grandmother lived with us, and occasionally other relatives spent some weeks or months in our home. For some years we were heavily burdened by financial hardships, and the stresses of meeting the needs of such a large family were great.

When I was sick, I received unusually tender and plentiful attention. I was subject to severe strep throats and would have to stay in bed for days at a time. Mother would find time to tell me stories and bring special foods on a tray, and Dad would even manage to sit with me in the evenings to read wonderful stories by the light of the kerosene lamp.

Fortunately, the Creator who set life in motion also made it with a tendency to recover from pain and sickness.

One major event disrupted the flow of my otherwise contented and happy life. When I was five, my baby sister was born. I had never needed a younger sister and was not told of her expected birth. Her arrival suddenly catapulted me out of my position as the beloved baby of the family. Overnight I became grief-stricken and wandered about my home, feeling abandoned and displaced by this truly adorable, charming child.

My mother, furthermore, failed to understand my situation and berated me for my displeasure. I felt guilty because I could not love my new sister, hurt and angry about my mother's scoldings, and confused and helpless over such an overwhelming happening.

Fortunately, the Creator who set life in motion also made it with a tendency to recover from pain and sickness. So I, too, eventually healed from the events that left me feeling rejected and undesirable. I learned again to play and laugh, study, work, and achieve. But I had scars that left me vulnerable. I cried easily, sought comfort where I could, and often felt sorry for myself.

My grandmother became my solace. She was quite a lady, and her life was one of the healthy parts of mine. A frail, bent woman with snow-white hair neatly coiled in a bun at the nape of her neck, she was totally deaf.

In her late twenties she had fallen in love with a fervent young evangelist. She moved from her extremely sheltered life in the heart of Pennsylvania to the plains of Kansas to marry him.

As she related the stories of her early years, I sensed with wonder the courage and quiet strength inside this small woman. She was left alone for weeks as Jacob rode on horseback to the many churches he helped to organize. He performed funerals, blessed marriages, and dedicated to God the children who were born. Always he taught the incomparable love and power of the God he had come to know so well.

Hannah mourned the loss of the child who died in infancy and then her dearly beloved husband who, at age forty, died after a short illness of meningitis. Truly alone, she raised their two sons and a daughter.

Never did I see my grandmother depressed. She learned to read lips quite well, and a tablet and pencil were always with her so we could write any message she could not understand. On one occasion she said to me, "I don't mind being deaf. I've never had to hear angry comments or dirty jokes. I just talk with Jesus." Her face with its increasing wrinkles settled into a calm, peaceful expression that rarely varied.

Whenever I felt especially misunderstood by my mother or siblings, I could find refuge in Grandma's room. At the foot of her tidily made bed was a folded comforter, the softest I have ever felt. I was welcome to bury my face in it and soak it with my childish tears whenever I needed to do so. Grandma never criticized me or my family. She simply sat in her chair, piecing her quilts and being the eye of my childhood storms.

The terror and tragedy of World War II involved our world and my brother during the years of my adolescence. The war also served as the background for some unsettling episodes in my life.

My sister and I had to live some distance from home so that we could attend high school. We certainly missed the warmth and intimacy of our big family.

Then when I was only sixteen, Grandma died. She simply slipped from her sleep to her long-lost Jacob and the Father they had so dearly loved and served. My comfort was gone.

Less than four months later, my father came to the home where my sister and I were staying. It was a stormy night with the loud thunder and crackling lightning that only Kansas can produce.

His face first revealed that some tragedy had occurred. As gently as he could, Dad told my sister and me that our youngest brother had suffered a terrible accident. In his haste to finish a task on the farm before the storm broke, he jerked a rope that was to close a huge hanging door on the barn. The rope broke, and the heavy door dropped, crushing him against the wall of the barn. He died instantly.

Together, our family grieved his loss. His subtle good humor, handsome face, and his integral part in our family were gone. As much as I missed the comfort of my elderly grandmother, the loss of this vital young brother, soon to become a father, was infinitely more painful.

But life had to go on, though we wished it would stop. We all worked harder to fill the gap his death had created. Healing again began its designated process.

Only six weeks went by before my father's sister became critically ill. Unable to have children of her own, she loved her nieces and nephews, and I loved the way she laughed. Her double chins and entire body would shake when something really funny became a topic of conversation.

Aunt Tillie had encephalitis. Even now this disease is highly fatal, and then it was almost certain death. After several days of unconsciousness, however, she began to rally. She had a brief period of seemingly normal functioning, but suddenly she died. The brain, so devastated by the infection, simply stopped working.

One more loss. Another episode of grief with its inherent anger, pain, helplessness, and futility.

Looking back, I can see the strongly polarized forces that formed my life. Mainly profound love and strength surrounded and penetrated my developing young personality.

But there were losses and heartaches that my sensitive spirit had to endure, even when I felt I simply could not.

My parents' religious beliefs became a powerful force in my life. To me, God was mainly loving, helpful, and forgiving. I learned in many ways how essential He was in my life.

On the other hand, my parents followed a narrow, strict life-style that separated me by light years from my peers. I had to abide by a rigid dress code. The parties and fun of my classmates were not to be for me. I could not skate, dance, or attend movies or most of the events that fill the social lives of teenagers. And yet I had to mingle with them, feeling monstrously strange.

I survived. And I even learned to compensate for my social "differentness" by becoming a top student, a good listener, and someone who could comfort others who hurt because I knew what pain was.

When I turned forty, I experienced a sense of restlessness. I was finding the stress of working, mothering, and being a wife, friend, and community volunteer simply unbearable.

I would awaken early with terrifying, angry dreams. Struggling to an upright posture, I would look at my soft, comfortable pillow, so reminiscent of my grandmother's comforter, and say to myself, "I'll get through this day, knowing my pillow will be here tonight." And I did get through my days. I loved my family and met their needs, cared for my patients with tenderness, and handled the management of my staff with some finesse.

*Though the Bible clearly states it is more blessed to give, I now know that we also **must** receive or we become emotionally bankrupt.*

In a teaching seminar, I finally had to acknowledge some basic facts. I did not like myself. Much of the heroic work I did was an unconscious attempt to prove to myself that I was not worthless. One of my father's oft-repeated, half-teasing questions to me as a child was, "Gracie, do you think you'll ever amount to anything?" I wasn't always sure what "amounting to anything" meant, but I assured Dad that I certainly would. And so I tried harder and harder to be perfect, strong, and pleasing to everyone. I was giving far more than I was receiving. And though the Bible clearly states it is more blessed to give, I now know that we also *must* receive (blessed or not!) or we become emotionally bankrupt.

I had to face it. I was approaching emotional bankruptcy. I was depressed, and I had feelings of anger, sadness, hopelessness, guilt, and helplessness. Well, not quite helplessness because I knew where to go for help. With a great sense of failure, I prayed for guidance, but my faith was weak. In retrospect I know my prayers were answered.

As I began weekly visits with a marvelous psychiatrist to whom God guided me, I began to fit together the pieces of my past. The strength that was part of the legacy of my grandparents and parents made me say, "I will *not* spend the rest of my life in despair." The trust that I learned to have in my parents and in my God allowed me to seek the help that was beyond my own strength. The determination that had pulled our family through the losses and grief of my youth held me on course as I worked with my psychiatrist.

I learned that I had far more strength than I had felt. I discovered that seeking help was not, as I had feared, a sign of weakness or failure; it was a sign of courage and honesty. I began to understand that the way to get loving attention was not through the extremes of helpless illness (as in my childhood sicknesses) nor in giving beyond my capacity to those who sought help from me.

The way to meet my needs was through admitting that I, the strong one, *had* needs, defining clearly what they were, and asking specifically for the supplying of those needs. It was both embarrassing and frightening to have to ask, but I took that risk. To my surprise, I found that many people were delighted to be asked and that my asking helped them.

About this time in the process, I fell and broke my ankle one icy winter day. My work was demanding, but I could not drive for a while. I called a list of friends to seek their services as driver for me until I could recover.

My friend, Ellen, hesitated just a bit when I called, but she gladly agreed to drive me downtown on a Friday. She seemed a bit nervous, but we chatted away as she skillfully maneuvered through the heavy morning traffic. I was so grateful to her. Later, Ellen confided she had gathered all her courage to do this labor of real love. She was terrified of driving in heavy traffic, but for me she heroically overcame her fear. Discovering that she *could* transcend her fear became a gateway to an entirely new growth spurt in her life. Knowing she cared enough for me to combat her fear made our friendship even more precious.

Another discovery I made was that of distinguishing grief from depression. As one by one my three children left home, first for college and then marriage, I felt exactly as I had during my depression. But I learned that grief is focused on a loss that is clearly defined and easily understood. Depression is not clear. It is a heavy mixture of emotions that hang over the individual like a shroud that cannot be shaken off. Knowing the phases of grief made it possible for me to get through that sadness and return to joyful living with greater speed.

A significant, life-changing fact I unearthed was that we have the gift of the power to choose. There are, of course, many differences between human beings, created in the image of God, and animals. But one of the most important is the ability to reason, to consider information and, on the basis of facts, to make choices. It took me a long time to understand that there are two levels of choice.

The first choice is that of deciding *how we will react* to things that happen to us. Dr. Victor Frank, an inmate of the Nazi concentration camp, Auschwitz, wrote poignantly of the torture he and the other inmates endured. His very being was tormented by the cruelty of man to man, yet he refused to allow his spirit to be broken. He wrote and taught, after his release, that the ultimate power of human-kind is to choose to remain loving, compassionate, and giving even when tormented and dehumanized.

The second choice, and for me much more difficult to compre-hend, is that of deciding *how we will feel.* Choosing how we react can be mastered with willpower and self-discipline. But emotions hit us powerfully offside, as it were. Fear, hurt, anger, or excitement and joy can possess us unbidden. How, then, can we choose what we feel?

My own experience is this: I cannot prevent any emotion from welling up in me. The death of a friend causes the pain of grief. Facing serious financial problems prompts panic. Anticipating time with my grandson stimulates love and joy, which I obviously want to prolong.

When a negative, painful emotion assails me, here is what I do with it.

1. I allow its full impact to become clear to me, and I try to find the best name I can for it. At this stage, I do not try to avoid its pain.

2. Next I make sure that I understand what has caused the feeling. Sometimes it is an event that has happened today. Often it is a dim memory of crises from the past that may be like something that has occurred currently.

3. I think about the power I have, or do not have, in the situation producing my emotion. I put into effect what I can do in a carefully planned manner. I seek the help I may need to work out an answer. And then I let go of the things I cannot do.

4. If the feeling and problem are connected to a hurtful person over whom I have no influence, I work through a process of forgiving that person, and I choose to begin understanding and loving (as best I can) that difficult person.

5. If I am at fault in the problem, I clarify my mistakes, make such restitution as I can, and then forgive myself, learning to avoid that same wrong doing again.

6. I prayerfully seek the infinite wisdom and love of God and choose to give Him control over me where my own resources would fail.

I am far from perfect in practicing these steps, but the more I remember to apply the principles, the better life becomes. And I have had occasion to test them out in some extremely difficult situations.

Since learning how to practice this power of choice, I am aware that I need never be totally powerless. A big factor is thus removed from depression.

Having learned how to forgive, and having made a commitment to living in a state of forgiveness, I need not stay angry. Since anger *feels* deceptively powerful, it is tempting to want to stay a little bit angry—well, at least resentful. But as much as possible, I discipline myself to collect information, understand *why* another person did something hurtful, and then discipline myself to let go of all the anger and pain. Essentially, I stop making another person's problem mine. By giving up hurt and anger, I become free from another big ingredient of depression. By forgiving myself, making restitution, and seeking God's promised forgiveness, I am free from guilt.

The more I love, the less I fear. The Bible is concise that "perfect love casts out fear" (1 John 4:18). So you see, you can, as I am doing, learn to overcome depression. Simply consider each of its component emotions and work through them. You are welcome to use my steps in conquering depression or develop your own. You may be able to overcome it by yourself, or as I did, you may need the help of a trained therapist. I just want you to know there is hope.

Signs and Symptoms
Depression in Middle-aged Women

1. **Loss of interest** or pleasure in all or almost all usual activities and pastimes. They feel blue, sad, hopeless, or irritable and may look sad.
2. **Changes in eating, sleeping, and exercise** patterns from what has been normal.
3. **Loss of interest in sexual activity.**
4. **Loss of energy** and a sense of fatigue.
5. **Feelings of worthlessness,** self-reproach, or guilt.
6. **Difficulty in thinking** and concentrating and trouble in making decisions.
7. **Recurrent thoughts of death,** wishes to be dead, and suicidal thoughts or attempts.
8. **Tendency to focus on physical appearance** and functions. Preoccupation with even minor aches and pains.

On Being a Mother-in-Law

More than likely, you'll get your turn at being a mother-in-law. How will you do? How can you be a great in-law rather than an outlaw? Research shows that the most difficult in-law relationship is between a mother-in-law and daughter-in-law. I was lucky. From the first time I met her, my mother-in-law, Lillian, was a wonderful role model for a mother-in-law. If you have had experiences with good in-laws, like me, you can add to their example and pass it on. If, however, you have had bad experiences with in-laws, consider you have had a great example of what not to do! Here again, as we have seen throughout this book, Especially for Woman, it is time for our generation to absorb the bad, process it, grieve it, and pass on only the good to our children's generation.

Claudia Arp
52 Ways to Be a Great Mother-in-Law

"Stand Beside Not Between"

"As parents we promise to stand beside not between." That's a line from the liturgy of one of our son's weddings—the line that is most prominent in my memory. It gives a beautiful picture of how I am to relate to my sons and daughters-in-law. Remembering it, however, is one thing, actually doing it is another! Easy or not, it's the key to being a great mother-in-law!

Consider my mother-in-law, Lillian. I remember vividly the first time Lillian stood beside me. I had yet to meet her but was engaged to her only son. Lillian was living in Naples, Italy, when Dave and I decided to get married at Christmas in Ellijay, Georgia. It wasn't an easy time of the year to get a military family from Naples to the mountains of North Georgia. But Lillian's determination resulted in Dave's family's presence at our wedding.

I actually met Lillian in the Atlanta airport three days before the wedding. I discovered right away that she had purposely left her advice in Italy. From the beginning Lillian stood beside us in a loving, supportive, and noncontrolling way.

Attitude: I Want to Let Go While Remaining Supportive.

Letting go is being willing to take a lower priority in your son's or daughter's life. Your part is to play second fiddle, and that is OK. A key problem in marriages, not only in America but all over the world, is the failure of mothers to let go of their children. This may be particularly difficult if you are very close to your child. It's not easy to stand beside and encourage your child to make it his or her first priority to please his or her spouse rather than mom and dad. In many cultures and economic situations, families live with parents and grandparents. While I don't recommend this kind of living relationship, the key is letting go emotionally, which goes much deeper than physically distancing yourself.

Action: Ways to Stand Beside

- Give a special gift to your future in-law.
- Realize that the wedding is theirs. One friend told me, "I'm getting along great with my future daughter-in-law. She's in a continual battle for control with her mom. I simply give no opinion, so I'm the good guy!"
- Don't interfere. Whatever they choose to do, when the ceremony is over, they will be married and you will be a mother-in-law.

Build Your Own Marriage

"What do we do now that our children are grown?" asked one mom. We were speaking to a group of parents who were entering the empty nest stage of family life and one big concern surfaced. Many had little in common with the other bird left in their empty nest. It was as if their marriage relationship had hibernated until their children grew up and married. Their children had been the focus of their family life, and the temptation now was to be over-involved in the lives of their married adult children.

Maybe one reason my own mother-in-law, Lillian, has always related to me in such a healthy way is that she focused on building her own marriage, not on being overinvolved in ours. When your own marriage is sour, it's easy to become emotionally dependent on your adult children and their spouses. If you are single at this stage of life, it's time to build positive relationships with other adults. It's time to broaden your horizons to include people other than your offspring.

Attitude: I Choose to Do All I Can to Enrich My Marriage.

You may be a mother-in-law who still has younger children at home. It's never too early, even for you, to begin planning for enriching your marriage when the nest empties. For years we talked about taking a trip to New England the autumn after all our sons had left home, and it actually happened. The trip allowed us to set fresh goals for our marriage and enjoy being just two again.

A word to the wise: don't wait until your children grow up to build your marriage. Now is the time to build for the future. Look at the time you have right now and use it. As we did, your married children will benefit from a parental model of a healthy love relationship.

Action: Ways to Build Your Own Marriage

- Start dating your mate. Plan a date with your mate for this week.
- Plan a twenty-four-hour getaway for two.
- Read a book on marriage, such as *The Marriage Track* (Nashville: Thomas Nelson, 1992), or *60 One-Minute Marriage Builders* (Nashville: Thomas Nelson, 1993).
- Sit down with your husband over a cup of coffee or tea and talk about your hopes and dreams. Don't talk about your kids and in-laws.

Learn to Laugh Together and Cry Together

Sometimes there is a fine line between laughter and tears. Both can help blend families together, and both will happen when we are vulnerable and real with each other. We have always laughed a lot in our family; tears are more rare. One time we did cry together. It was a couple of years ago when my dad passed away.

All our sons and daughters-in-law came from different parts of the United States, even though it was a very inconvenient time. Just watching the way they swung into action to support their mom gave me strength. They let me be real. We cried together, and we reminisced and talked until the wee hours of the morning. In our sorrow, we even found laughter as we talked about Father and all his wonderful antics, like the fruitcakes he used to make and his trying to tune the piano—he always thought he could do anything! In my vulnerability, I found comfort and closeness that to this day is a precious memory.

Other times in our life, we have roared with laughter. One time on my birthday we played "Claudia Trivia" with categories like "Claudisms" and "Name That Book." "Claudisms" were my favorite sayings, like "It takes a little insanity to keep our sanity" and "You have so much potential." The "Name That Book" category included quotes from books I had written that were taken totally out of context—to make me look ridiculous, of course!

Attitude: I Will Share My Emotions, from Laughter to Tears. I Will Be Real.

When we hurt, it is OK to say so. One friend shared with me how her daughter and son-in-law expected to be remembered on their birthdays but often forgot hers. So once she simply ignored their birthdays. They were extremely hurt until they realized, "Hey, we've been doing the same thing!"

It can build relationships when you are willing to be real. When you feel like someone is overwhelmed, let him or her know you've been there before. Ask yourself what you can do to give that person a reprieve.

Action: Ways to Promote the Sharing of Life's Laughter and Tears

- Give comfort and share joy through cards and notes. When my dad passed away, the most comforting note I received was from someone who simply wrote a few lines but who was able to identify with my loss.
- Refuse to assign blame.
- When someone hits a rough spot, help him or her get back on track. Think about what you can do to help.
- Know the difference between tension and sorrow. Joking may relieve tension, but it may be inappropriate when someone is grieving a loss.
- Plan a fun family event. Ask each couple to prepare a skit or bring their favorite game or silly reading. We still read from the book *Where the Sidewalk Ends* by Shel Silverstein.
- Remember your child's anniversary.

Take a Mother-in-Law Pill Every Morning

What I need is a mother-in-law pill. One that includes a daily dose of love, acceptance, patience, and tolerance would be great.

The problem with becoming a mother-in-law is that it often happens about the same time we begin going through menopause. While this may not be the easiest transition in life, there are some things we can do to maintain our sanity and healthy in-law relationships.

We're not just getting older, we're getting better. This can be a time of new horizons if we focus on the future instead of the past. "Wait a minute" said my friend, Marge. "I just can't agree with you. What's 'better' about hot flashes and sleepless nights! I'm not sure I like this stage of life."

To be honest, few of us would choose menopause, but we can choose to manage it appropriately. It's up to us to take control of this stage of life and do what we need to do to maintain our sanity and equilibrium. We can choose our attitude.

Attitude: I Choose to Look at This Time of Life as a New Beginning—as My Second Adulthood, and I Will Do What I Can to Maintain a Healthy Body, a Proper Mental Perspective, and a Positive Relationship with My Son- or Daughter-in-Law and Other Family Members.

First, educate yourself about this new passage of life. The best book I've read on the subject is *The Silent Passage* by Gail Sheehy. She brings up many issues and decisions that only you can make. Sheehy discusses the pros and cons of hormone replacement therapy and gives the reader enough understanding and knowledge to ask her doctor intelligent and relevant questions.

Second, get a complete physical and do what you can do to live a healthy life style. I'm a great believer in exercise, and I can tell a real difference on the days I miss it. If there is ever a time to evaluate your eating habits, this is it. Whatever you do to feel better about yourself will flow over into your family relationships.

Third, remember that this too shall pass. It's not the end of the world or the end of your life. You are simply moving on to a new era.

Action: Ways to Maintain a Healthy Body and Mental Perspective During Menopause

- Eat sensibly. Begin to count grams of fat and watch your cholesterol.
- Consider joining an aerobics class or working out at a gym.
- Make an intelligent choice about hormone replacement. Ask your doctor about anything that concerns you. Don't be shy.
- Read *The Silent Passage* and other books on the subject.
- Be open with your family as to how you feel and where you are in life.

On Being a Grandmother

*I*t is the culmination of motherhood—
grandmotherhood!
If you have done your work to become a whole woman, you have changed your world, and, in some ways, you have helped change the whole world. As a whole woman, you have so much to offer the younger generations—your wisdom, your acceptance, your understanding, your love. Life will be better because you have passed on the example of your wholeness to your children and your children's children.

Ramona Warren
Loving Legacy

Grandma Hugs

The Lord is near to all who call upon Him (Ps. 145:18a).

It was "Grandma and the grandchildren week" at a cabin in Wisconsin. All six of the grandchildren, age five through thirteen, were with me and having a great time. The swimming pool was just a few feet from the back door, and they spent hours playing in the water. My job was lifeguard, encourager, and food provider.

Even though the children were busy nearly every moment, I noticed that they would find time, in ones or twos, just to be close to me for a few minutes. Then off they'd go to rejoin the group.

Grandson Rob put it best one day when he came over to the deck chair where I was sitting, put his arms around me, and said, "I need a Grandma hug!"

As I hugged him back and thanked God for him, I realized this was a picture of the relationship we have with God. He is our lifesaver, encourager, and provider. We spend our time here on earth busy with many people, but every so often we need to get away from the crowd and be alone with God. We need a God hug—the reminder and comfort of His presence in our lives.

Picture of Love

Let all that you do be done with love (1 Cor. 16:14).

The kindergarteners had these things to say about their grandmothers:

"She lets me use her pillows to make a fort." Brandon.

"We go out for pizza and she reads me stories when I sleep over." David.

"She plays games like pinball with me and makes chicken, my favorite food." Andrew.

"My grandma lives a long ways away but she likes me very much, plays Candyland with me, and takes me to church every Sunday." Zackery.

"She plays trucks with me and I help her water the garden and pick the fruit." Jeff.

"She plays trucks with me and makes good oatmeal." Kevin.

"She gives me ice cream before I go to bed." Benjamin.

The things children remember most at this age are the activities we participate in and the food we fix. When we help to supply these basic needs, we are also helping lay a foundation that can lead to trust in God, whose love and care for us is shown through the love and care of family. We are meant to be pictures of God's love.

Wise Grandma

My son, do not walk in the way with them,
Keep your foot from their path.

(Prov. 1:5)

Adrienne's grandmother, Momee, was short and roly-poly. She drove her car everywhere, sometimes causing minor accidents of which she was completely unaware. Momee carried a huge purse, bulging with all sorts of things, including mints that she sometimes distributed to her grandchildren. She was talented at decorating china, and for most of her life ran a tourist home.

After her children were grown, Momee decided she wanted a college education. And so it was that she and her daughter (Adrienne's mother) attended college at the same time. They both majored in child psychology. Momee was a popular person on campus. However, she maintained a B average in grades while her daughter received straight A's. This seemed unfair to Momee because, "I proved I knew the subject because I had successfully raised my daughter!"

Grandmothers who continue to learn throughout their lives are rich examples for grandchildren. God's Word advises us to listen and add to what we know. There are no age restrictions.

Growing Older

JANUARY 1923

$\mathcal{W}$ith the coming of another new year we are all . . . a year older. Just what does it mean to us—this growing older? Are we coming to a cheerful, beautiful old age, or are we being beaten and cowed by the years as they pass?

Bruised we must be now and then, but beaten, never, unless we lack courage.

Not long since a friend said to me, "Growing old is the saddest thing in the world." Since then I have been thinking about growing old, trying to decide if I thought her right. But I cannot agree with her. True, we lose some things that we prize as time passes and acquire a few that we would prefer to be without. But we may gain infinitely more with the years than we lose in wisdom, character, and the sweetness of life.

As to the ills of old age, it may be that those of the past were as bad but are dimmed by the distance. Though old age has gray hair and twinges of rheumatism, remember that childhood has freckles, tonsils, and the measles.

The stream of passing years is like a river with people being carried along in the current. Some are swept along, protesting, fighting all the way, trying to swim back up the stream, longing for the shores that they have past, clutching at anything to retard their progress, frightened by the onward rush of the strong current and in danger of being overwhelmed by the waters.

Moving with Faith

Others go with the current freely, trusting themselves to the buoyancy of the waters, knowing they will bear them up. And so with very little effort, they go floating safely along, gaining more courage and strength from their experience with the waves.

As New Year after New Year comes, these waves upon the river of life bear us farther along toward the ocean of Eternity, either protesting the inevitable and looking longingly back toward years that are gone or with calmness and faith facing the future serene in the knowledge that the power behind life's currents is strong and good.

And thinking of these things, I have concluded that whether it is sad to grow old depends on how we face it, whether we are looking forward with confidence or backward with regret. Still, in any case, it takes courage to live long successfully, and they are brave who grow old with smiling faces.

Laura Ingalls Wilder
Little House in the Ozarks

About the Authors

Ann Kiemel Anderson is a former school teacher, youth director, college dean of women, and author of nine previous books.

Claudia Arp is the founder of MOM's Support Groups, a family enrichment resource program, which has groups throughout the United States and in Europe. She is a co-founder and co-director, with her husband, Dave, of Marriage Alive International. The Marriage Alive Workshop is popular across the United States and in Europe.

Claudia is the author of *52 Ways to Be a Great Mother-in-law,* and co-author with Dave of *The Marriage Track* and *52 Dates for You and Your Mate.* Claudia is also co-author with Linda Dillow of *The Big Book of Family Fun.*

Elizabeth Baker is a professional counselor in private practice, working with the Center for Church Renewal in Plano, Texas. She has worked as a family counselor with the Rader Institute for Eating Disorders at DFW Medical Center and in out-patient therapy for the Minirth-Meier Clinic, as well as serving as a counseling chaplain for Marketplace Ministries.

The founder of Renewed Life Seminars and a frequent guest for Christian radio and television talk shows, Elizabeth has authored several books including *Who Am I? One Woman's Guide to Self-Acceptance.* She has a Master's degree in counseling arts from Liberty University and is a charter member of the American Association of Christian Counselors.

A widow since her midthirties, Elizabeth has four children and six grandchildren. She enjoys travel, swimming, reading, and art, as well as time with her grandchildren.

Harry Beverly is the clinical director of the Inpatient Eating Disorder Program of the Minirth-Meier Clinic in McKinney, Texas.

Sue Buchanan has recovered from breast cancer and speaks on the topic as part of the speakers' bureaus for the American Cancer Association and the Koman Foundation. She has also published articles on breast cancer in *The Institute Forum Magazine* of Nashville's Institute for Aesthetic and Reconstructive Surgery. Sue is the senior vice-president and co-owner of Dynamic Media, Inc., a public relations firm which has won awards from the New York Film Festival and the International Film Festival. She is the mother of two daughters, is married, and lives in Nashville.

Linda Dillow describes herself first as a wife and a mother, and second, as a speaker, author, and marriage seminar leader on being a creative wife. She is author of the best-selling *Creative Counterpart, Priority Planner,* and *How to Really Love Your Man.* She and her husband, Joseph, lived in Vienna, Austria, for fourteen years, training Christian leaders throughout Eastern Europe and Russia. They recently moved to the Orient to continue their work.

Best-selling author, speaker, and musician **Joyce Landorf Heatherley** has a total of more than six million books in print, most of which have been best-sellers in the Christian market, including *Irregular People*—listed in *Bookstore Journal's* top ten books for the 1980s. Her film series, *His Stubborn Love,* won the President's Award from the Christian Film Distributors of America and has been viewed by more than ten million people.

Joyce has been featured in *Today's Christian Woman, Christianity Today, Moody Monthly, Virtue,* and *Christian Writer,* and has been a guest on CBN, PTL, and TBN as well as on numerous other radio and television programs.

Previous books include *The Inheritance; The Fragrance of Beauty; Fragile Times; Mourning Song; Joseph; Silent September; I Came to Love You Late; Irregular People; Balcony People; Monday Through Saturday; Unworld People;* and *He Began with Eve.*

Dr. Robert Hemfelt is a psychologist who specializes in the treatment of chemical dependencies, codependency, and eating disorders. Before joining the Minirth-Meier Clinic, he was an addictions specialist with a Fortune 500 corporation and, before that, the supervisor of therapeutic services for the Substance Abuse Study Clinic of the Texas Research Institute of Mental Sciences.

A native of eastern Pennsylvania, **Liz Curtis Higgs** spent ten years traveling up and down the dial as a popular radio personality in five states. It was in the Bluegrass State of Kentucky that she discovered the thrill of speaking before a live audience: "An Encourager" ® was born.

Since becoming a professional speaker in 1987, Liz has presented hundreds of humorous, encouraging programs for businesses, associations, hospitals, and churches all over America. She is a member of the National Speakers Association, and earned their prestigious designation of C.S.P.—Certified Speaking Professional—in 1993.

As a member of the Fellowship of Merry Christians and the American Association for Therapeutic Humor, Liz believes in the value of laughter. She fills her presentations, her writing, and her life with a healthy dose of fun. She also enjoys singing in the choir, watching old movies, shopping for clothes, and playing Go Fish with her family.

Liz received her Bachelor of Arts in English from Bellarmine College in 1990—finally! She and her husband, Bill, a computer systems specialist, have two young children, Matthew and Lillian, and one old house in the country, east of Louisville, Kentucky.

Editor **Stephen W. Hines** has loved Laura Ingalls Wilder's books since he was a boy, and this love is evident in the careful research and arrangement of these delightful articles. Hines graduated from the University of Kansas and received his M.A. in journalism from Ball State University in Muncie, Indiana. He has worked in publishing since 1979.

Ken Jones lives in Modesto, California, where he serves as senior pastor of Neighborhood Church. He and his wife, Randee, have three sons: Marcus, a communications major at the University of California, San Diego, and Nathan and Simeon, who are still living at home.

In addition to being a busy pastor, Jones is a frequent speaker at retreats, seminars, and workshops on a variety of topics, including ministry to adult singles, family, parenting, and men's issues. He and his wife have been instrumental in developing support groups for parents of children with learning difficulties and have also been involved in home schooling.

Jones loves music, writing, reading, and golf.

Dr. Grace Ketterman is the medical director of the Crittenton Center in Kansas City, Missouri, and is the author of more than seven books, including *How to Teach Your Child About Sex* and *You Can Win Over Worry*. After having received her M.D. degree from Kansas University Medical School, she was affiliated with Menorah Medical Center, Kansas City General Hospital, and Western Missouri Mental Health Center. Undergirding Dr. Ketterman's medical career is her spiritual faith, which she describes as "practical, commonsense, and deeply committed."

Beverly LaHaye is the founder and president of Concerned Women for America, a group that represents 700,000 citizens and has more than 1,200 prayer/action chapters across the nation. Their motto: "Protecting the rights of the family through prayer and action." LaHaye represents the women of CWA on family issues at congressional hearings and at rallies and seminars throughout the country.

She is the coauthor of *The Act of Marriage* and author of *The Spirit-Controlled Woman*, *Who But a Woman*, and *The Desires of a Woman's Heart*.

Nancy LeSourd is a partner with Gammon & Grange in Washington, D.C., and provides legal counsel to tax-exempt organizations. She is a graduate of Agnes Scott College, has her M.A. in education and American history from Tufts University, and her J.D. from Georgetown University.

She and her husband, Jeff, live in the D.C. area with their son, and daughter.

Diane Lewis is founder and president of Interviewing Dynamics, Inc., a personnel consulting firm with more than five hundred client companies worldwide that has, in its twenty-two years, successfully placed thousands of people in satisfying careers. She also travels extensively to Europe, the Middle East, and Africa as president of her own international trading company. The mother of two sons, Lewis flies her own plane, conducts job seminars, and is active on the lecture circuit.

Florence Littauer has been listening to the pains and problems of men and women for more than twenty-five years and has effectively helped them to find positive healing through her speaking and writing.

Fred Littauer is a lay expert in the field of abuse and was a victim of abuse himself. He has trained pastors, counselors, and laymen in how to pray with a victim for memory retrieval.

Dr. Paul Meier is co-founder of the Minirth-Meier Clinic in Dallas, Texas, one of the largest psychiatric clinics in the world, with associated clinics in Chicago; Los Angeles; Little Rock, Arkansas; Longview, Fort Worth, Sherman, and Austin, Texas; and Washington, D.C. **Dr. Meier** received an M.S. in cardiovascular physiology at Michigan State University and an M.D. from the University of Arkansas College of Medicine. He completed the last year of his psychiatric residency at Duke University.

He also holds a degree from Dallas Theological Seminary and with Dr. Frank Minirth has coauthored over thirty books, including *Happiness Is a Choice.*

Dr. Frank Minirth is co-founder of the Minirth-Meier Clinic in Dallas, Texas, one of the largest psychiatric clinics in the world, with associated clinics in Chicago; Los Angeles; Little Rock, Arkansas; Longview, Fort Worth, Sherman, and Austin, Texas; and Washington, D.C.

Dr. Minirth is a diplomate of the American Board of Psychiatry and Neurology and received an M.D. from the University of Arkansas College of Medicine.

Lois Mowday writes, leads Bible studies, and is a frequent speaker for Christian Women's Clubs. She was formerly director of public relations for Evangelism Explosion International in Fort Lauderdale, Florida.

Mowday played herself in the film *Fire in the Sky,* produced by Mel White Productions, Pasadena, California, and distributed by Gospel Films. The film documents the death of her husband and his friends in a hot air balloon accident.

She is the author of *The Snare* (NavPress, 1988) and various articles published in *Decision Magazine, Moody Monthly,* and *Christianity Today.*

She is the mother of two daughters, Lisa and Lara, and makes her home in Colorado Springs, Colorado.

Deborah Newman, D. Phil., is a psychotherapist specializing in eating disorders with the Minirth Meier Clinic outpatient and hospital units in Richardson, Texas. She received her doctorate from Oxford Graduate School. Deborah is married to Dr. Brian Newman and is the mother of two children, Rachel and Benjamin.

Stormie Omartian, a survivor of child abuse, brings a deep understanding of recovery issues to her books. She is also an authority on health and exercise and has exercise videos that have attained "gold" status for sales. A regular contributor to *Total Health* magazine, Omartian is also a popular seminar speaker. She is the author of *Greater Health God's Way* and *Stormie*.

Currently Founder and Publisher of *Guideposts* magazine, **Ruth Stafford Peale** is the recipient of numerous national awards and honors. She and her husband, Norman Vincent Peale, live in New York, where he was pastor of the Marble Collegiate Church for 52 years.

Jan Kiemel Ream is a professional psychologist. She describes herself as mother, wife, therapist, speaker, daughter, friend.

Edith Schaeffer is the prolific author of nine books, including her most recent, *Lifelines*. Her books have sold more than one million copies in the United States alone and have been translated into twelve languages. Edith Schaeffer, along with husband, Francis Schaeffer, founded the Christian community known as *L'Abri* ("The Shelter"), which is centered in Switzerland and has branches in England, the Netherlands, and the United States.

Dr. Sharon Sneed is a registered dietitian and a practicing nutritional consultant. She has been an assistant professor at the Medical University of South Carolina and a postdoctoral fellow at the University of California at Berkeley. She has written and coauthored more than a dozen research articles and books, including *Love Hunger Weight-Loss Workbook* and *Love Hunger: Recovery from Food Addiction*.

Dr. David Stoop is a clinical psychologist in private practice in Newport Beach, California, and is clinical director for the Minirth-Meier Clinic West, a psychiatric treatment program. He is a graduate of Fuller Theological Seminary and received his Ph.D. from the University of Southern California.

Jan Stoop is a graduate of Fuller Theological Seminary and is a doctoral candidate in clinical psychology. She has worked with her husband, Dave, in his writing, and together they have led seminars and retreats across the country and in France and Australia.

Pam Vredevelt, M.S., is a licensed professional counselor at Christian Counseling Services in Portland, Oregon. Specializing in eating disorders, codependency, and sexual abuse issues, she is the author of seven books and several magazine articles.

Deanna Wallace is a freelance writer currently working on a biography for European publication. She is also a featured vocalist and workshop leader for church groups, seminars and conferences throughout the United States. She speaks on the subjects of childhood sexual abuse, adoption, and parenting.

Deanna has an unusual assortment of children. Four of her six children are adopted and come from diverse ethnic backgrounds including East Indian, Korean, African-American, and Cherokee Indian. She likes to call it a "rainbow" family. Deanna also works for Family Connections Adoptions as the Ethiopia Program Coordinator, helping orphaned Ethiopian children to find adoptive homes.

Deanna is a former fashion model and finalist in several beauty pageants. She attended Seattle Pacific University. Presently, she resides in Ceres, California.

Joanne Wallace is a very gifted and talented woman: best-selling author, media personality, internationally known seminar speaker, successful former corporation president, award winner, wife, mother, and grandmother (not listed in order of importance!). Joanne has received the prestigious award of CSP (Certified Speaking Professional) from the National Speakers Association and "1989 Award of Excellence" from the International Image Industry. She held the title of Mrs. Oregon 1969 and competed in the Mrs. America Pageant. In her earlier years, she was a fashion model, winning many awards.

In 1969, she founded the internationally known Image Improvement, Inc., now headquartered in Camp Hill, Pennsylvania. She attended Seattle Pacific University and Portland State and has teaching experience in several community colleges, including Warner Pacific and Western Baptist College in Oregon. She also was active as chairman and speaker for Christian Women's Clubs.

The author of numerous books, Joanne won the "1979 Best Writer" award for the *Image of Loveliness* from the Northwest Christian Writer's Conference. She has audio and video cassettes of her sessions that can be used as resources for group meetings. Gospel Films is distributing internationally her video series "Being Your Best for Him."

Joanne is married to Robert Lovelace. She has two children and six grandchildren.

Ramona Warren is a minister to children and the administrator of daycare and summer day camps at First Baptist Church in Elgin, Illinois. A freelance writer and editor for David C. Cook, she leads workshops and speaks at conventions throughout the United States.

Ramona is the grandmother of six grandchildren. She is also the minister to children at First Baptist Church in Elgin, Illinois. Her previous books include *Nurturing Nursery*.

Laura Ingalls Wilder (1867–1957) began writing, at age 65, a series of eight children's books about her life in the pioneer west—the *Little House* books—which we all know and love. Yet, twenty years before she even started these books, Wilder wrote articles for regional newspapers and magazines. *Little House in the Ozarks* is a collection of these articles—most of which have not been published since the early 1900s.

Other Books by the Authors

Anderson, Ann Kiemel. *And with the Gift Came Laughter.* Wheaton, IL: Tyndale, 1987.
I Gave God Time. Wheaton, IL: Tyndale, 1984.
Open Adoption: My Story of Love and Laughter. Wheaton, IL: Tyndale, 1990.

see **Jan Kiemel Ream.** *Struggling for Wholeness.*
Arp, Claudia. *52 Ways to Be a Great Mother-in-law.* Nashville: Thomas Nelson, 1993.

and **Dave Arp.** *52 Dates for You and Your Mate.* Nashville: Thomas Nelson, 1993.
The Marriage Track. Nashville: Thomas Nelson, 1992.
60 One-Minute Marriage Builders. Nashville: Thomas Nelson, 1992.
60 One-Minute Family Builders. Nashville: Thomas Nelson, 1992.
60 One-Minute Memory Makers. Nashville: Thomas Nelson, 1992.
The Ultimate Marriage Builder. Nashville: Thomas Nelson, 1992.
Building a Positive Relationship with Our Children. 5-part video series. Elgin, IL: David C. Cook
Building Positive Relationships for the Teen Years. 5-part video series. Elgin, IL: David C. Cook.
For more information on workshops by the Arps, or to obtain a guide to leading Marriage Track 4 × 4's, write the Arps at
   Marriage Alive
   P.O. Box 90303
   Knoxville, TN 37990

and **Linda Dillow.** *The Big Book of Family Fun.* Nashville: Thomas Nelson, 1992.

Baker, Elizabeth. *Who Am I?* Nashville: Thomas Nelson, 1994.

Beverly, Harry. see **Pam Vredevelt.** *The Thin Disguise.*

Buchanan, Sue. *Love, Laughter, and a High Disregard for Statistics.* Nashville: Thomas Nelson, 1994.

Dillow, Linda. *Creative Counterpart, revised.* Nashville: Thomas Nelson, 1993.
How to Really Love Your Man. Nashville: Thomas Nelson, 1994.
Priority Planner, revised. Nashville: Thomas Nelson, 1993.

see **Claudia Arp.** *The Big Book of Family Fun.*

Heatherley, Joyce Landorf. *Changepoints.* Dallas: Balcony Publishers, 1992.
For These Fragile Times. Dallas: Balcony, 1990.
Fragrance of Beauty. Dallas: Balcony, 1990.
He Began with Eve. Dallas: Balcony, 1990.
The Inheritance. Dallas: Balcony, 1990.
Irregular People. Dallas: Balcony, 1990.
Monday Through Saturday. Dallas: Balcony, 1990.
My Blue Blanket, revised. Dallas: Balcony, 1991.
Richest Lady in Town. Dallas: Balcony, 1992.
Silent September. Dallas: Balcony, 1992.
Unworld People. Dallas: Balcony, 1992.

Hemfelt, Dr. Robert.

and **Dr. Frank Minirth, Dr. Paul Meier,** and **Don Hawkins.**
Love Is a Choice. Nashville: Thomas Nelson, 1989.
——. *Love Is a Choice Workbook.* Nashville: Thomas Nelson, 1991.

and **Dr. Richard Fowler, Dr. Frank Minirth, Dr. Paul Meier.**
The Path to Serenity. Nashville: Thomas Nelson, 1991.

and **Dr. Frank Minirth, Dr. Paul Meier,** and **Dr. Sharon Sneed.** *Love Hunger: Recovery from Food Addiction.* Nashville: Thomas Nelson, 1990.
——. *Love Hunger Weight-Loss Workbook.* Nashville: Thomas Nelson, 1991.

and **Dr. Paul Warren.** *Kids Who Carry Our Pain.* Nashville: Thomas Nelson, 1990.

see **Dr. Frank Minirth.** *Passages of Marriage.*

Higgs, Liz Curtis. *One Size Fits All.* Nashville: Thomas Nelson, 1993.
Does Dinner in a Bucket Count? Nashville: Thomas Nelson, 1993.

Hines, Steve. *I Remember Laura: The Life and Times of Laura Ingalls Wilder.* Nashville: Thomas Nelson, 1994.
Little House in the Ozarks. Nashville: Thomas Nelson, 1992.

Jones, Ken. *When You're All Out of Noodles.* Nashville: Thomas Nelson, 1993.

Ketterman, Dr. Grace. *Before and After the Wedding Night.* Old Tappan, NJ: Flaming Revell, 1984.

A Circle of Love. Old Tappan, NJ: Fleming Revell, 1986.

The Complete Book of Baby and Child Care, Revised. Old Tappan, NJ: Fleming Revell, 1986.

Depression Hits Every Family. Nashville: Oliver-Nelson, 1987.

How to Teach Your Child About Sex. Old Tappan, NJ: Fleming Revell, 1971.

199 Questions Parents Ask. Old Tappan, NJ: Fleming Revell, 1985.

When You Feel Like Screaming. Wheaton, IL: Harold Shaw, 1988.

You Can Win Over Worry. Old Tappan, NJ: Fleming Revell, 1984.

You and Your Child's Problems. Old Tappan, NJ: Fleming Revell, 1983.

and **Truman E. Dollar.** *Teenage Rebellion.* Old Tappan, NJ: Fleming Revell, 1985.

LaHaye, Beverly. *The Desires of a Woman's Heart.* Wheaton, IL: Tyndale, 1993.

How to Develop Your Child's Temperament. Harvest House, 1981.

The Spirit-Controlled Woman. Harvest House, 1976.

Understanding Your Child's Behavior. Harvest House, 1988.

and **Tim LaHaye.** *The Act of Marriage: The Beauty of Married Love.* Grand Rapids, MI: Zondervan, 1989.

The Act of Marriage. New York: Bantam.

What Lovemaking Means to a Man: Practical Advice to Married Men about Sex. Grand Rapids, MI: Zondervan, 1984.

What Lovemaking Means to a Woman: Practical Advice to Married Women about Sex. Grand Rapids, MI: Zondervan, 1984.

LeSourd, Nancy. *No Longer the Hero.* Nashville: Thomas Nelson, 1992.

Lewis, Diane. *Equal to the Challenge.* Nashville: Thomas Nelson, 1988.

The Insider's Guide to Finding the Right Job. Nashville: Thomas Nelson.

Littauer, Florence. *After Every Wedding Comes a Marriage.* Harvest House, 1981.

Blow Away the Black Clouds. Harvest House, 1986.

Blow Away the Black Clouds: A Woman's Answer to Depression, large type ed. Walker & Co., 1988.

Dare to Dream. Dallas: WORD, 1991.

Hope for Hurting Women. Dallas: WORD, 1985.

How to Get Along with Difficult People. Harvest House, 1984.

It Takes So Little to Be Above Average. Harvest House, 1983.

I've Found My Keys, Now Where's My Car? Nashville: Thomas Nelson, 1994.

Out of the Cabbage Patch. Harvest House, 1984.

Personalities in Power: The Making of Great Leaders. Lafayette, LA: Huntington House, 1988.

Personality Plus. Old Tappan, NJ: Revell, 1992.

Raising the Curtain on Raising Children. (Write for information.) Dallas: WORD, 1988.

Silver Boxes. (Write for information.) Dallas: WORD, 1989.

Your Personality Tree. (Write for information.) Dallas: WORD, 1986.

and **Fred Littauer.** *Get a Life Without the Strife.* Nashville: Thomas Nelson, 1993.

and **Marita Littauer.** *Personality Puzzle: Understanding the People You Work With.* Old Tappan, NJ: Revell, 1992.

Littauer, Fred. *The Promise of Healing.* Nashville: Thomas Nelson, 1994.

Meier, Dr. Paul. *Don't Let Jerks Get the Best of You.* Nashville: Thomas Nelson, 1993.

The Third Millennium. Nashville: Thomas Nelson, 1993.

and **Dr. Frank Minirth, Dr. Richard Meier, Dr. David Congo,** and **Dr. Allen Doran.** *What They Didn't Teach You in Seminary.* Nashville: Thomas Nelson, 1993.

see **Dr. Robert Hemfelt.** *Love Hunger.*

————. *Love Hunger Weight-Loss Recovery Workbook.*

————. *Love Is a Choice.*

————. *Love Is a Choice Workbook.*

————. *The Path to Serenity.*

Minirth, Dr. Frank. *Beating the Odds: Overcoming Life's Trials.* Grand Rapids, MI: Baker, 1987.

Happy Holidays: How to Beat the Holiday Blues. Grand Rapids: Baker Books, 1990.

Taking Control: New Hope for Substance Abusers & Their Families. Grand Rapids: Baker Books, 1988.

The Healthy Christian Life. Grand Rapids: Baker Books, 1988.

You Can Manage Your Mental Health. Grand Rapids: Baker Books, 1980.

and **Betty Blaylock,** and **Cynthia Spell Humbert.** *One Step at a Time.* Nashville: Thomas Nelson, 1991.

and **Dr. Les Carter.** *The Anger Workbook.* Nashville: Thomas Nelson, 1993.

and **Dr. Richard Fowler,** and **Dr. Brian Newman.** *Steps to a New Beginning.* Nashville: Thomas Nelson, 1993.

and **Dr. Brian Newman,** and **Dr. Paul Warren.** *The Father Book.* Nashville: Thomas Nelson, 1992.

and **Paul D. Meier.** *Counseling and the Nature of Man.* Grand Rapids: Baker Books, 1989.

Happiness Is a Choice: Overcoming Depression. Grand Rapids: Baker Books, 1978.

Free to Forgive. Nashville: Thomas Nelson, 1989.

and **Dr. Paul Meier,** and **Don Hawkins.** *Worry-Free Living.* Nashville: Thomas Nelson, 1989.

and **Dr. Paul Meier, Dr. David Congo,** and **Janet Congo.** *A Walk with the Serenity Prayer.* Nashville: Thomas Nelson, 1991.

and **Mary Alice Minirth, Dr. Brian Newman, Dr. Deborah Newman, Dr. Robert Hemfelt,** and **Susan Hemfelt.** *Passages of Marriage.* Nashville: Thomas Nelson, 1989.
————. *New Love.* Nashville: Thomas Nelson, 1993.
————. *New Love Study Guide.* Nashville: Thomas Nelson, 1993.
————. *Realistic Love.* Nashville: Thomas Nelson, 1993.
————. *Realistic Love Study Guide,* Nashville: Thomas Nelson, 1993.
Renewing Love Study Guide. Nashville: Thomas Nelson, 1993.
Steadfast Love. Nashville: Thomas Nelson, 1993.
Steadfast Love Study Guide. Nashville: Thomas Nelson, 1993.
Transcendent Love. Nashville: Thomas Nelson, 1993.
Transcendent Love Study Guide. Nashville: Thomas Nelson, 1993.

see **Pam Vredevelt.** *The Thin Disguise.*

and **Dr. Paul Warren.** *Things That Go Bump in the Night.* Nashville: Thomas Nelson, 1992.

et al. *Ask the Doctor: Questions & Answers about Your Mental Health.* Grand Rapids: Baker Books, 1991.
Beating the Clock: A Guide to Maturing. Grand Rapids: Baker Books, 1986.
How to Beat Burnout. Chicago: Moody Press, 1986.
One Hundred Ways to Live a Happy and Successful Life: Overcoming Depression. Grand Rapids: Baker Books, 1986.
The Workaholic and His Family: An Inside Look. Grand Rapids: Baker Books, 1981.

Mowday, Lois. *Daughters Without Dads.* Nashville: Thomas Nelson, 1991.
The Snare. Colorado Springs: NavPress, 1988.

Newman, Dr. Deborah.

and **Pam Vredevelt, Dr. Frank Minirth, Dr. Robert Hemfelt,** and **Harry Beverly.** *The Thin Disguise.* Nashville: Thomas Nelson, 1992.

and **Dr. Richard Fowler Jerilyn Fowler,** and **Dr. Brian Newman.** *Day by Day: Love Is a Choice.* Nashville: Thomas Nelson, 1991.

see **Dr. Frank Minirth.** *Passages of Marriage.*

Omartian, Stormie. *Better Body Management.* Nashville: Sparrow, 1994.
Greater Health God's Way. Nashville: Sparrow 1984.
A Step in the Right Direction. Nashville: Thomas Nelson, 1992.
Stormie. Harvest House, 1986.

Ream, Jan Kiemel. *Struggling for Wholeness.* Nashville: Oliver-Nelson, 1986.

Schaeffer, Edith. *Christianity Is Jewish.* Wheaton, IL: Tyndale, 1977.
Dear Family. San Francisco: HarperCollins. 1989.
Forever Music: A Tribute to the Gift of Creativity. Grand Rapids, MI: Baker, 1992.
The Hidden Art of Homemaking. Wheaton, IL: Tyndale, 1985.
L'Abri, rev. ed. Bishop, Lila, ed. Crossway Books, 1992.
The Life of Prayer. Bishop, Lila ed. Crossway Books, 1992.
Lifelines: God's Frame Work for Christian Living. Crossway Books, 1982.
Mountain Songs. Grand Rapids, MI: Zondervan, 1988.
Songs from Green Pastures. Grand Rapids, MI: Zondervan, 1988.

Sneed, Dr. Sharon. *Love Hunger Action Plan.* Nashville: Thomas Nelson, 1992.

and **David Sneed.** *The Hidden Agendas: A Critical View of Alternative Medical Therapies.* Nashville: Thomas Nelson, 1992.
———. *Prime Time.* (Write for information.) Dallas: WORD, 1991.
———. *Understanding Your Family Chemistry.* Servant, 1992.

see **Dr. Robert Hemfelt.** *Love Hunger: Recovery from Food Addiction* and *Love Hunger Weight-Loss Workbook.*

and **Joe S. McIlhaney, Jr.** *PMS: What It Is & What You Can Do About It.* Grand Rapids, MI: Baker, 1988.

Stoop, Dr. David. *Forgiving Our Parents, Forgiving Ourselves: Healing Adult Children of Dysfunctional Families.* Ann Arbor: Servant, 1992.
Hope for the Perfectionist. Nashville: Thomas Nelson, 1987.
Self Talk. Tarrytown, NY: Revell, 1981.

and **Stephen Arterburn.** *The War Is Over but Children Still Have Questions.* Wheaton: Tyndale, 1991.
The Angry Man. Dallas: Word, 1991.

and **James Masteller.** *Forgiving Our Parents, Forgiving Ourselves.* Ann Arbor: Servant, 1991.

and **Jan Stoop.** *The Intimacy Factor.* Nashville: Thomas Nelson, 1993.

Stoop, Jan.

and **Betty Southard.** *The Grandmother Book.* Nashville: Thomas Nelson, 1993.

see **Dr. David Stoop,** *The Intimacy Factor.*

Vredevelt, Pam.

and **Dr. Frank Minirth, Dr. Robert Hemfelt, Dr. Deborah Newman,** and **Harry Beverly.** *The Thin Disguise.* Nashville: Thomas Nelson, 1991.

Wallace, Deana.

and **Joanne Wallace.** *Starting Over Again.* Nashville: Thomas Nelson, 1989.

Wallace, Joanne. *Being Your Best for Him.* (5-part video series.)
The Confident Woman.
Dress to Fit Your Personality.
How to Be Your Best.
The Image of Loveliness.
The Working Woman.

and **Deanna Wallace.** see *Starting Over Again.*
For more information on how to order any of these titles, please write Joanna Wallace Seminars, P.O. Box 2213, Fremont, CA 94536, or call 910-797-2785.

Warren, Ramona. *Enjoying Life with Little Ones.* Elgin, IL: David C. Cook.
Loving Legacy. Nashville: Thomas Nelson Publishers.
Nurturing Nursery. Elgin, IL: David C. Cook.
Parenting Alone. Elgin, IL: David C. Cook.
Preschool Bible Learning Centers. Shining Star.
Easter Handbook. Child's World.

Notes

Chapter 4 I Choose to Put Away My Blue Blanket
1. Sam Shoemaker, *Extraordinary Living for Ordinary Men* (Grand Rapids, MI: Zondervan, 1965), 8.
2. Keith Miller, "Short Cut Home" reprinted with permission of Keith Miller, Copyright © 1984.

Chapter 6 Why Am I Under All This Stress?
1. Dr. Doyle Carson, cited in "Mind Games and High Stakes," a special advertising section published by *Texas Monthly*, June 1992.
2. Fred Littauer, *The Promise of Healing* (Nashville: Thomas Nelson, 1994), chapter 9.

Chapter 7 The End of the Chain: The Wall of Depression
1. Dowling, *The Cinderella Complex.*
2. James Dobson, *Emotions—Can You Trust Them?* (Ventura, CA: Regal Books, 1980), 88–89.
3. David Stoop and Steve Arterburn, *Angry Man* (Dallas, TX: Word, 1991).
4. Dobson, *Emotions,* 86.
5. Neil Clark Warren, *Make Anger Your Ally* (Garden City, NY: Doubleday, 1983), 97–98.
6. *Random House Dictionary* (New York: Random House, 1991).
7. Minar, *Unrealistic Expectations,* 50–51.
8. Ellen McGrath, Gwendolyn Puryear Keita, Bonnie R. Strickland, Nancy Felipe Russo, eds., *Women and Depression* (Washington, D.C.: American Psychological Association, 1990), xxii.
9. McGrath, *Women and Depression,* 48.
10. McGrath, *Women and Depression,* xii.
11. Maggio, *The Beacon Book of Quotations by Women,* 79.
12. Florence Littauer, *Dare to Dream* (Waco, TX: Word, 1991), 317.
13. Warren, *Make Anger Your Ally,* 21.
14. Harriet Lerner, *The Dance of Anger* (New York: Harper & Row, 1985), 71.

Chapter 9 Sexuality and Shame
1. Adapted from Pamela Vredevelt and Kathryn Rodriguez, *Surviving the Secret: Healing the Hurts of Sexual Abuse,* rev. ed. (Tarrytown, NY: Gleneida Publ., 1992).
2. *Ibid.*

Chapter 11 All It Takes Is a Little Willpower
1. "Growth and Recession in the Diet Industry, 1989–1996," *Obesity and Health,* January/February 1992.
2. "Let Them Eat Cake," *Newsweek,* 17 August 1992, 57.
3. Seid, *Never Too Thin,* 105.
4. Ibid, 107.

5. Ibid, 138.
6. Nancy Roberts, *Breaking All the Rules* (New York: Viking Penguin, 1987), 34.
7. Susan Kano, *Making Peace with Food* (New York: Harper & Row, 1989), 3.
8. Sally Squires, "Which Diet Works," *Working Woman,* October 1992, 92.
9. Carol Johnson, "Fasting: The Problem Lies in the Fast Part," *On a Positive Note,* February 1990, 3.
10. Janice Kaplan, "Regardless of How Fit Women Are, We Still Want to Be Thin," *Self,* September 1989, 195.

Chapter 13 How Can I Plug In to the Power?
1. Oswald Chambers, *My Utmost for His Highest,* December 30.
2. *Ibid.,* October 23.

Chapter 14 But God Meant It for Good
1. A. W. Tozer, *The Knowledge of the Holy* (New York: Harper and Row Publishers, 1961), 10. This book is a classic on the attributes of God. For further study, InterVarsity Press publisher a Bible study guide entitled, "Recovery from Distorted Images of God," which examines from Scripture the reality of these distortions of His character: the God of impossible expectations, the emotionally distant God, the disinterested God, the abusive God, the unreliable God, and the God who abandons.
2. Wilson, *Counseling Adult Children of Alcoholics,* 95–100.
3. *Ibid.,* 101.
4. J. I. Packer, *Knowing God* (Downers Grover, IL: InterVarsity Press, 1973), 184. This book is particularly helpful to anyone desiring a study of God's attributes. J. I. Packer has a fresh, intimate knowledge of God and supports his points with numerous Scripture references.

Chapter 17 Intimacy: Building Close Relationships
1. Thomas Hughes, *Treasured Thoughts for Today, Tomorrow, and Always* (Kansas City, MO: Hallmark Editions, 1974), 21.
2. "Lifewire" newsletter, Christian Singles Alive (Salem, OR: First Church of the Nazarene, March 1988), 2.
3. Charles McCabe quoted in article by Juliet V. Allen (Salem, OR: "Statesman-Journal," Nov. 1982).
4. Dinah Maria Mulock Craik, "Friendship," *Treasured Thoughts for Today, Tomorrow, and Always* (Kansas City, MO: Hallmark Editions, 1974), 19.

Chapter 21 Pursuit of Excellence
1. Thornton Wilder, *Our Town: A Play in Three Acts* (New York: Harper and Row, 1957), from Act 3.
2. Ed Wheat, M.D., *The First Years of Forever* (Grand Rapids, MI: Zondervan, 1988), 177.
3. Stephen R. Covey, *The 7 Habits of Highly Effective People* (New York: Simon and Schuster, 1989), 98.
4. Charles R. Swindoll, *Strike the Original Match* (Portland, OR: Multnomah, 1980), 165.
5. *USA Today,* 16 December 1991, 2.

Chapter 23 The Working Wounded
1. Tournier, *The Healing of Persons,* 108.
2. Bryan E. Robinson, Ph.D., *Am I Addicted to Work?* (Deerfield Beach, FL: Health Communications, 1989), 1.
3. *Ibid.,* 2.

4. Interview with Douglas LaBier, "Healing the Wounds of Success," *Washington Post*, July 23, 1989, H1, H4.

5. "Waking Up to Workplace Depression," *USA Today*, January 7, 1991, 1–2.

6. LaBier, *Washington Post*, H4.

7. Dr. Herbert J. Freudenberger, *Burn-Out: The High Cost of High Achievement* (Garden City, NY: Anchor Press, Doubleday and Co., 1980), 16.

8. *Ibid.*, 19.

9. J. Patrick Gannon, *Soul Survivors: A New Beginning for Adults Abused as Children* (New York: Prentice Hall, 1989), 142–43.

10. Bronston T. Mayes and Daniel C. Ganster, "Exit and Voice: A Test of Hypotheses Based on Fight/Flight Responses to Job Stress," *Journal of Organizational Behavior*, 1988, vol. 9, 199–216.

11. Gannon, *Soul Survivors*, 137.

12. Freudenberger, *Burn-Out*, 49.

13. Eliza Collins, "Why Employees Act the Way They Do," *Working Woman*, December 1990, 60–61. Reprinted with permission from *Working Woman* magazine. Copyright © 1990 by WWT Partnership.

14. Janet Geringer Woititz, Ed. D., *Home Away from Home: The Art of Self-Sabotage* (Pompano Beach, FL: Health Communications, 1987), 47–49.

15. Dr. Michael Diamond and Dr. Seth Allcorn, "The Freudian Factor," *Personnel Journal*, March 1990, vol. 69, no. 3, 53.

16. *Ibid.*, 54–55.

17. Manfred F. R. Kets de Vries and Danny Miller, *The Neurotic Organization* (San Francisco, CA: Jossey-Bass Inc., 1984), 95.

18. *Ibid.*, 81.

19. *Ibid.*, 82.

20. Diamond and Allcorn, *Personnel Journal*, 54–55.

Chapter 24 Working with Your Working Mate

1. Leslie Dreyfous, "Family Finances Are Sophisticated Family Affair," *Knoxville News-Sentinel*, 9 June 1991, D–7.

2. To purchase *Manage Your Money*, write MECA Software, Inc., 327 Riverside Avenue, P.O. Box 907, Westport, CT 06881.

Chapter 25 Middle-Aged Women

1. Daniel J. Burbach and Charles M. Borduin, "Parent-Child Relations and the Etiology of Depression," *Clinical Psychology Review*, vol. 6, 1986, pp. 133–153.

2. *The Diagnostic and Statistical Manual of Mental Disorders*, 3rd ed. (American Psychiatric Association, 1980), p. 217.